ORDNANCE SURVEY MEMOIRS OF IRELAND

Volume Thirty-four

PARISHES OF COUNTY LONDONDERRY XIII
1831–8

Published 1996.
The Institute of Irish Studies,
The Queen's University of Belfast,
Belfast.
In association with
The Royal Irish Academy,
Dawson Street,
Dublin.

Grateful acknowledgement is made to the Economic and Social Research Council,
the Department of Education for Northern Ireland, Derry City Council, the Cultural Traditions
Group of the Community Relations Council, the Ulster Local History Trust Fund and the
Honourable the Irish Society for their financial assistance.

British Library Cataloguing-in-Publication Data.
A catalogue record for this book is available from the British Library.

Paperback ISBN 0 85389 556 2
Hardback ISBN 0 85389 557 0

Printed by W. & G. Baird Ltd, Antrim.

Ordnance Survey Memoirs of Ireland

VOLUME THIRTY-FOUR

Parishes of County Londonderry XIII
1831–8

Clondermot and the Waterside

Edited by Angélique Day, Patrick McWilliams, Lisa English and Nóirín Dobson

The Institute of Irish Studies
in association with
The Royal Irish Academy

This book has received support from the Cultural Traditions Programme of the Community Relations Council, which aims to encourage acceptance and understanding of cultural diversity.

CONTENTS

List of selected maps and drawings

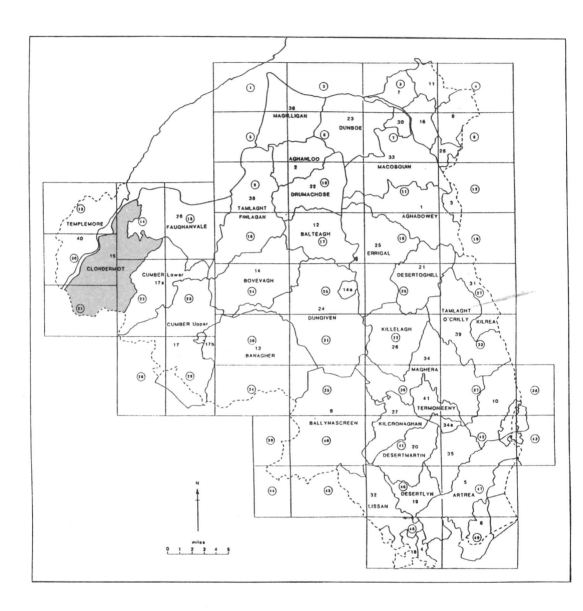

ACKNOWLEDGEMENTS

During the course of the transcription and publication project many have advised and encouraged us in this gigantic task. Thanks must first be given to the Royal Irish Academy which has made available to us the original manuscripts. We are also greatly indebted to Librarian Siobhán O'Rafferty and her staff for their continuing help in deciphering indistinct passages of manuscript.

We should like to acknowledge the following individuals for their special contributions. Dr Brian Trainor led the way with his edition of the Antrim Memoir and provided vital help on the steering committee. Dr Ann Hamlin also provided valuable support, especially during the most trying stages of the project. Professor R.H. Buchanan's unfailing encouragement has been instrumental in the development of the project to the present. Without Dr Kieran Devine the initial stages of the transcription and the computerising work would never have been completed successfully: the project owes a great deal to his constant help and advice. Dr Kay Muhr's continuing contribution to the work of the transcription project is deeply appreciated. We would like to thank the Director of the Ordnance Survey, Dublin and the keepers of the fire-proof store, among them Leonard Hines. Finally, all students of the nineteenth-century Ordnance Survey of Ireland owe a great deal to the pioneering work of Professor J.H. Andrews, and his kind help in the first days of the project is gratefully recorded.

The editors would like to thank Derry City Council, the Cultural Traditions Group of the Community Relations Council, the Ulster Local History Trust Fund and the Honourable the Irish Society for their generous support in funding the work of publishing this volume.

We would also like to mention the valuable advice and assistance received from Brian Lacey, director of the Heritage and Museum Service in Derry, and Annesley Malley of the North West Archaeological Society.

The essential task of inputting the texts from audio tapes was done by Miss Eileen Kingan, Mrs Christine Robertson, Miss Eilis Smyth, Miss Lynn Murray and, most importantly, Miss Maureen Carr.

We are grateful to the Linen Hall Library for lending us their copies of the first edition 6" Ordnance Survey Maps: also to Ms Maura Pringle of QUB Cartography Department for the index maps showing the parish boundaries. For providing financial assistance at crucial times for the maintenance of the project, we would like to take this opportunity of thanking the trustees of the Esme Mitchell trust and The Public Record Office of Northern Ireland.

Left:
Map of parishes of County Londonderry. The area described in this volume, the parish of Clondermot, has been shaded to highlight its location. The square grids represent the 1830s 6" Ordnance Survey maps. The encircled numbers relate to the map numbers as presented in the bound volumes of maps for the county. The parishes have been numbered in all cases and named in full where possible, except those in the following list: Agivey 3, Arboe 4, Ballinderry 6, Ballyaghran 7, Ballyrashane 9, Ballyscullion 10, Ballywillin 11, Bovevagh 14a, Coleraine 16, Derryloran (no Memoir) 18, Kildollagh 28, Killowen 30, Maghera 34a, Magherafelt 35.

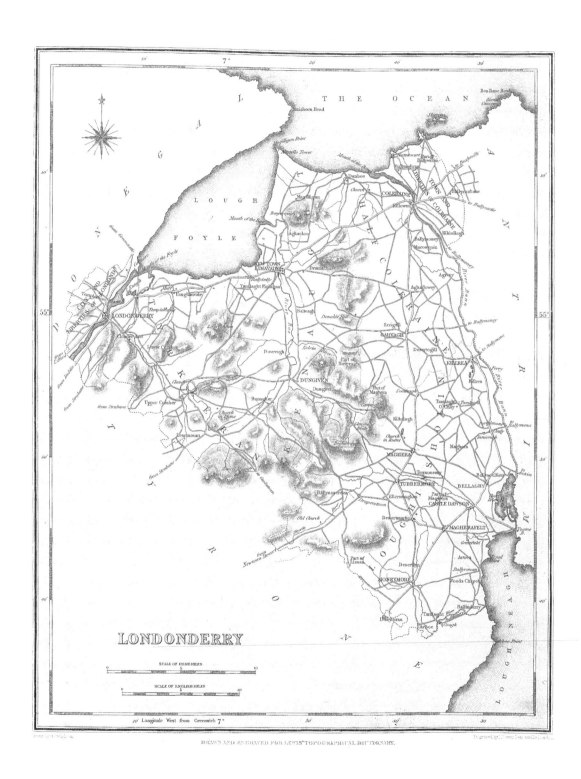

Map of County Londonderry, from Samuel Lewis' *Atlas of the counties of Ireland* (London, 1837)

INTRODUCTION AND GUIDE TO THE PUBLICATION OF
THE ORDNANCE SURVEY MEMOIRS

The following text of the Ordnance Survey Memoirs was first transcribed by a team working in the Institute of Irish Studies at The Queen's University of Belfast, on a computerised index of the material. For this publication programme the text has been further edited: spellings have been modernised in most cases, although where the original spelling was thought to be of any interest it has been retained and is indicated by angle brackets in the text. Variant spellings for townland and lesser place-names have been preserved, although parish and major place-names have been standardised and the original spelling given in angle brackets. Names of prominent people, for instance landlords, have been standardised where possible, but original spellings of names in lists of informants, emigration tables and on tombstones have been retained. We have not altered the Memoir writers' anglicisation of names and words in Irish.

Punctuation has been modernised and is the responsibility of the editors. Editorial additions are indicated by square brackets: a question mark before and after a word indicates a queried reading and tentatively inserted information respectively. Original drawings are referred to in the text, and some have been reproduced. Manuscript page references have been omitted from this series. Because of the huge variation in size of Memoirs for different counties, the following editorial policy has been adopted: where there are numerous duplicating and overlapping accounts, the most complete and finished account, normally the Memoir proper, has been presented, with additional unique information from other accounts like the Fair Sheets entered into a separate section, clearly titled and identified; where the Memoir material is less, nothing has been omitted. To achieve standard volume size, parishes have been associated on the basis of propinquity.

There are considerable differences in the volume of information recorded for different areas: counties Antrim and Londonderry are exceptionally well covered, while the other counties do not have quite the same detail. This series is the first systematic publication of the parish Memoirs, although individual parishes have been published by pioneering local history societies. The entire transcriptions of the Memoirs made in the course of the indexing project can be consulted in the Public Record Office of Northern Ireland and the library at the Queen's University of Belfast. The manuscripts of the Ordnance Survey Memoirs are in the Royal Irish Academy, Dublin.

Brief history of the Irish Ordnance Survey in the nineteenth century and the writing of the Ordnance Survey Memoirs

In 1824 a House of Commons committee recommended a townland survey of Ireland with maps at the scale of 6", to facilitate a uniform valuation for local taxation. The Duke of Wellington, then prime minister, authorised this, the first Ordnance Survey of Ireland. The survey was directed by Colonel Thomas Colby, who had under his command officers of the Royal Engineers and three companies of sappers and miners. In addition to this, civil assistants were recruited to help with sketching, drawing and engraving of maps, and eventually, in the 1830s, the writing of the Memoirs.

The Memoirs were written descriptions intended to accompany the maps, containing information which could not be fitted on to them. Colonel Colby always considered additional information to be necessary to clarify place- names and other distinctive features of each parish; this was to be written up in reports by the officers. Much information about parishes resulted from research into place-names and was used in the writing of the Memoirs. The term "Memoir" comes from the abbrevia-tion of the word "Aide-Memoire". It was also used in the 18th century to describe topographical descriptions accompanying maps.

In 1833 Colby's assistant, Lieutenant Thomas Larcom, developed the scope of the officers' reports by stipulating the headings or "Heads of Inquiry" under which information was to be reported, and including topics of social as well as economic interest. By this time civil assistants were writing some of the Memoirs under the supervision of the officers, as well as collecting information in the Fair Sheets.

The first "Memoirs" are officers' reports covering Antrim in 1830, and work continued on the Antrim parishes right through the decade, with special activity in 1838 and 1839. Counties Down and Tyrone were written up from 1833 to 1837, with both officers and civil assistants working on Memoirs. In Londonderry and Fermanagh research and writing started in 1834. Armagh was worked on in 1835, 1837 and 1838. Much labour was expended in the Londonderry parishes. The plans to publish the Memoirs commenced with the parish of Templemore, containing the city and liberties of Derry, which came out in 1837 after a great deal of expense and effort.

Between 1839 and 1840 the Memoir scheme collapsed. Sir Robert Peel's government could not countenance the expenditure of money and time on such an exercise; despite a parliamentary commission favouring the continuation of the writing of the Memoirs, the scheme was halted before the southern half of the country was covered. The manuscripts remained unpublished and most were removed to the Royal Irish Academy, Dublin from the Ordnance Survey, Phoenix Park. Other records of the Ordnance Survey, including some material from the Memoir scheme, have recently been transferred to the National Archives, Bishop Street, Dublin.

The Memoirs are a uniquely detailed source for the history of the northern half of Ireland immediately before the Great Famine. They document the landscape and situation, buildings and antiquities, land-holdings and population, employment and livelihood of the parishes. They act as a nineteenth-century Domesday book and are essential to the understanding of the cultural heritage of our communities. It is planned to produce a volume of evaluative essays to put the material in its full context, with information on other sources and on the writers of the Memoirs.

Definition of descriptive terms

Memoir (sometimes Statistical Memoir): an account of a parish written according to the prescribed form outlined in the instructions known as "Heads of Inquiry", and normally divided into three sections: Natural Features and History; Modern and Ancient Topography; Social and Productive Economy.

Fair Sheets: "information gathered for the Memoirs", an original title describing paragraphs of information following no particular order, often with marginal headings, signed and dated by the civil assistant responsible.

Statistical Remarks/Accounts: both titles are employed by the Engineer officers in their descriptions of the parish with marginal headings, often similar in layout to the Memoir.

Office Copies: these are copies of early drafts, generally officers' accounts and must have been made for office purposes.

Ordnance Survey Memoirs for County Londonderry

This volume, the thirteenth for the county and the thirty-fourth in the series, contains the Memoir for the parish of Clondermot on the east bank of the Foyle, opposite the historic core of Derry city (Templemore parish). This area covers the settlements of Waterside, New Buildings and Drumahoe, as well as the picturesque valley of the Faughan river and the hillier countryside above the River Foyle as far north as Enagh Lough.

The numerous duplicate and overlapping accounts and many working papers indicate that preparations for the publication of this Memoir had reached an advanced stage by 1838: there is even a section entitled Printers' Copy. Frequent references occur in the Clondermot papers to the Templemore Memoir, published in 1837 after a tremendous team effort by the Memoir writers in the north west. Many of the same authors are responsible for the drafts of the Clondermot Memoir, with George Petrie, John O'Donovan and Thomas Larcom himself playing an active role in supervising and correcting work.

The chronology of Irish history and clan genealogy, together with the detailed etymologies of townlands, are typical of the Petrie and O'Donovan contributions. Where printed authorities quoted by them are clear, the titles have been given in full, otherwise the citation is left as written. The other writers, C.W. Ligar, J.B. Williams, G. Downes and J. Bleakly, the writer of the Fair Sheets, are familiar figures among the Memoir team and their descriptions, often jointly written, date from 1832 through to 1838. Doubtless the critical reception of the Templemore volume, plus the expense of effort on other Memoirs for different parishes in Londonderry and Antrim, forestalled the publication of Clondermot at the time.

The influence of renowned geological writer and statistician, Captain J.E. Portlock, is obvious in the detailed Productive Economy tables, which exist also for the neighbouring parishes of Faughanvale, Cumber, Errigal, Banagher and, further afield, Magherafelt, and which, though not formally dated, were probably produced in 1838. Besides these tables, which describe the ownership, soil, cultivation and labour of the land, as well as the stock and implements, Portlock wrote notes on the compilation of these statistics and included some observations on local standards of living.

The race tables for Clondermot, which are unique among the Memoirs, were probably instigated by Larcom, who was also to work on the collection of census material in the 1840s. They also owe much to Portlock, whose rigour in collecting statistics is documented in the Larcom papers and in the working papers associated with the Productive Economy tables. These race tables are demographic statistics which attempt to analyse the population of each townland in the parish by religion and race, in other words, cultural origin. As such, they are an interesting exercise in anthropological-sociological categorisation, typical of the early Victorian Statistical Movement which influenced Thomas Larcom's work, evident from the list of books he kept at his headquarters in Phoenix Park.

The Clondermot Memoir provides a good picture of the economic life of an area in the hinterland of Derry, an important and ancient port and city. In many respects it provides both a reflection of the more developed urban area of Templemore, as well as demonstrating the contrasts of a more rural parish.

A variety of local manufacturing industries were in operation: 2 tanneries, a brewery at the Faughan bridge and a distillery in the Waterside, besides a spade mill, plough manufactory and an important bleach green at Ardmore, where a large number of people were employed, mostly bleaching the coarser grades of linen. Domestic linen manufacturing was under threat, chiefly hand-spinning which was made so unprofitable by mill-spun thread, but weaving was still important in local households.

Many farmers were employing innovatory stock and cultivation techniques, and there was enough patronage to support a tree nursery at Knockbrack, as well as a local branch of the agricultural improvement society, the North West Society.

Proximity to a port facilitated a trade in eggs and butter to Scotland and England; this provided important additional household income and was very often in female hands. However, the problem of transporting produce across the River Foyle and the need for a toll-free bridge is commented on. Details of usage of the contemporary single bridge show, over a two-day period in June, the immense volume of pedestrian and wheeled traffic; and the amount of money raised by the tolls indicate what a burden they were to small producers.

The London guilds, representing the Grocers' and Goldsmiths' Companies, figure as important landlords and contribute to the dispensary and schools in the neighbourhood, as did the Irish Society. The parish had a wide range of educational institutions which are described in considerable detail. There are also organisations for remedying poverty, the local Poor Shop and Loan Fund being initiated and administered by local landlord families (particularly the female members) with the support of the Irish Society, as well as more self-help local arrangements like money clubs.

There are some interesting observations of everyday life among the people. Although there are not as many accounts of traditional beliefs as in the adjacent parishes of Cumber and Banagher, mention is made of witches or cunning women, and a description of the evolution of a station to a well connected with a local benefactor, Colonel Mitchelburne, indicates that many pagan beliefs lingered on discreetly in this district. Prominence is given to the famous story of "Half-hanged MacNaghten", who seduced a Miss Knox of Prehen with tragic consequences, and even details of her poetic preferences are listed. There are also useful comments on migration and emigration in a district so near to one of the principal points of departure for the New World and Australia.

The number of gentlemen's seats indicate the importance of Derry as a regional cultural and economic capital.

This area was not remarkable for prehistoric antiquities but the castle of Enagh Lough, once an O'Cathan stronghold, and other fortifications in the area, as well as early ecclesiastical sites, are well recorded and show how important control of this district was in the past.

The papers on which the editors worked were transcribed recently by former team member Nóirín Dobson, and to her much of the credit for this volume belongs. However, we must salute the work of the late Mabel R. Colhoun, Fred Timmins and others of the North West Archaeological Society who worked on the Clondermot Memoir papers under Brian Lacey's direction during the 1960s.

Drawings in the Memoir papers are listed below and are cross-referenced in the text. The manuscript material is to be found in Boxes 34 and 35 of the Royal Irish Academy's collection of Ordnance Survey Memoirs, and section references are given beside the parish below in their printed order.

Box 34   I: 24[a] and 42, 31, 4, 44, 48, 10, 29 and 21, 7, 12, 68D, 43, 9[b], 65, 64, 19, 40, 26 with 29 and 1, 3 and 36, 37, 52, 57, 68H, 50, 51, 66, 68F, 68G, 2, 11, 60, 9[d], 8 and 68B, 5, 9[c], 16, 17, 23, 24[b], 33, 35, Box 35 I 2 and 1, Box 34 I 47, 28A

Duplicate drafts (not reproduced)

Box 34   I: 1, 6, 9[a], 13-15, 18, 20-22, 25, 27-8, 30, 32, 34, 36, 38-9, 41-2, 45-6, 49, 53-6, 58-9, 61-3, 67, 68A-C, 68E, 68I-M, Box 35 I 3-6

Drawings

(Sections 26, 29, 31 and 68, copies at 11, 15, 16, 24, 28):

Ground plan of Enagh church, showing position of north side.

Ground plan of giant's grave in Glenderowen, showing position of hole made by treasure seekers, with dimensions and scale.

Rough plans of 3 tablets: marble tablet on southern gable of old Presbyterian meeting house, with inscription; freestone table near former, with inscription; slate tablet in east gable, with inscription.

Rough plan of oblong tablet in east gable of meeting house in Altnagelvin townland, with inscription.

Plan of 2 wheels of spade mill in Ardkill, with dimensions.

Parish of Clondermot, County Londonderry

Printer's Copy of Memoir with notes and corrections by George Downes, November 1835

NATURAL STATE

Name

[Insert note: Sheets 13, 14, 20, 21, 22 county map].

, The name of this parish is now generally but erroneously written Glendermot, apparently from a supposition that it has been derived from a glen so called. It is written Clondermot by Sir William Petty, owing probably to its supposed derivation from *cluain* "a retired lawn" [crossed out: fertile valley]; but in the great inquisition of 1609 it is more accurately given as Clandermot, a name obviously identical with that of a tribe which was very powerful in the neighbourhood of Derry during the 11th, 12th and 13th centuries, and whose territory appears to have been then very extensive, although, from the increasing power of the Tirconnellians on the one side, and of the O'Cathans or O'Kanes on the other, it became subsequently circumscribed within the limits of the parish.

This view of the origin of the name is strongly supported by the facts, that most of the proper names of the Irish part of the parishioners, such as O'Carolan, McGettigan etc., differ only in orthography from those originally borne by the chiefs of the clan, and that the usage of giving the names of the families to their territories was general in Ireland.

"The custom of our ancestors" says O'Flaherty, "was not to take names and creations from places and countries, as it is with other nations, but to give the name of the family to the seignory by them occupied (*Ogygia vindicata*). Some historical notices of the clan Dermot will be found [further on].

Locality

This parish is situated in the north western part of the barony of Tirkeeran. It is bounded on the north by the River Foyle, Lough Foyle and Faughanvale, on the east by Lower Cumber, on the west by the River Foyle and on the south by Donaghedy in the county of Tyrone.

, Its extreme length along the Foyle, which separates it from Templemore, is nearly 9 miles and its extreme breadth is above 5. It contains (including 173 acres of water) 21,514 acres 2 roods 14 perches, of which 4,410 acres 3 roods 21 perches are uncultivated; and it is divided into 77 townlands.

In the *Parliamentary boundary report* of 1832 this parish is considered identical with the east (correctly south east) liberties of Derry. This designation, however, is applicable only to a part of the parish (see parish of Templemore, Municipality), and the liberties, as a baronial division, are recognised only on the west of the Foyle.

NATURAL FEATURES

Hills

In the western portion of the parish commences a series of short elevated ridges, the first of which separates the River Foyle from the deep valley of Glendermot. From its highest point at Warbleshinny, 726 feet above the sea, this ridge, under the name of the hill of Clondermot, stretches north eastward to the Faughan and forms on one side the bold and moderately steep slope of the Glendermot valley. On the opposite side of that valley rise the Brown mountain and Nod's Top, which are separated by a narrower glen from the more elevated and massive ridge of Slieve Kirk, the summit of which, 1,224 feet above the sea, is the highest ground of the parish. Beyond Slieve Kirk other glens and other ridges fill up the intervening space between it and the lofty mountain range, of which Sawel, 11 miles beyond the parish, is the point of highest elevation, 2,239 feet above the sea. The sides also of Slieve Kirk are fissured by the glens of Lisdillon and Knockbrack.

This system of hills is separated by the Faughan from another similar in arrangement, though of less elevation, of which Avish is the highest point within the parish. In the opposite direction also, towards west into Tyrone, the hill of Clondermot, though falling abruptly on the south west at Warbleshinny, is continued in hills of lesser elevation; and in like manner, Tirkeeveny and Solus may be considered the prolongation of other portions of the system.

Lakes

About 3 miles from Derry, and between the Foyle and the [crossed out: Derry and Belfast] mail coach roads, are 2 small lakes called eastern and western Lough Enagh, which are 200 feet asunder and connected by an inconsiderable stream, [crossed out: and never known to have been frozen over]. The eastern lake occupies 46 acres and the western 25. In each the bottom, which is chiefly of gravel, slopes gradually to the centre,

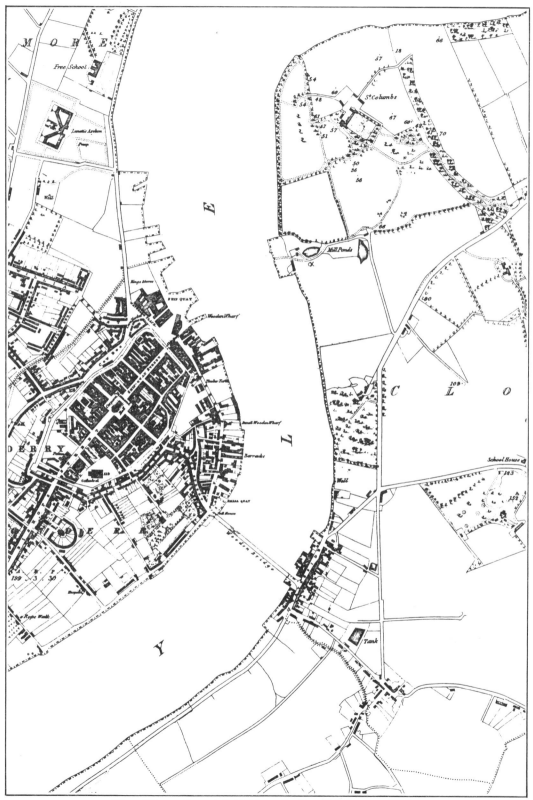

Map of Derry city and district from the first 6" O.S. maps, 1830s

where it is about 33 feet deep. Both lakes are supplied solely by water which, percolating through the accumulation of surrounding gravel, issues in springs into the hollows which they occupy. During the summer there is no discharge, evaporation balancing the supply of water, but in the winter the lakes rise and the superabundant water is discharged by a very short and rapid course into the Faughan.

A corn mill, now in ruins, was formerly worked by this stream. It has been replaced by the mill of Templemoyle erected by the Grocers' Company near Muff, and in consequence allowed to go to decay.

The eastern lake contains 2 wooded islets, called Rough Island and Green Island, each of which is about 150 feet in diameter. The former, called locally the Orchard, is said to have been the garden of a castle belonging to the O'Cathans [crossed out: or O'Kanes], which stood on the latter and of which slight vestiges still exist, consisting of plum and apple trees.

The ruins of the church of Enagh, which stand on an eminence between the lakes, add much to their interest; and the varied surface of the neighbouring [crossed out: environing] ground, with the beauty of the distant prospects, open an enviable field for the improvements of the landscape gardener.

Rivers: Faughan

The Foyle, which as already mentioned forms the western boundary of the parish, has been described in the parish of Templemore.

The Faughan rises in the mountain Sawel, in Banagher, at an elevation of 1,050 feet above the sea and about 20 miles from Lough Foyle, into which it flows after a course of about 24 miles through various parishes, in the several descriptions of which it will be specially alluded to. [Insert marginal query: Shall the Faughan be described here or in the barony?]. On approaching the lough it passes between the present parish and Faughanvale. In the upper part of its course its falls are considerable and its velocity great, affording facilities for the application of water power, of which only a very partial advantage has as yet been taken.

Being the only outlet for the waters of an extensive mountain district, it is subject to great and sudden overflows which, however, as speedily subside after the rain which caused them has ceased to fall. Until the autumnal equinox they are rare and unimportant. [Crossed out: The damage,

often in less than 6 hours, occasioned by these inundations varies considerably in different parishes. They begin, generally, at the end of August and continue until March or April; until October or November, however, they are rare and insignificant]. [Insert marginal note: Add the falls from Faughanvale unless given in the barony].

The direction of the Faughan for 3 miles after it enters the parish is from south east to north west. It then turns at right angles towards the north east and preserves this course until it flows into the lough. It averages about 100 feet [insert marginal query: consult map] in width above the bridge on the Belfast mail coach road, 1 and a quarter miles above its mouth, from which point to the lough it gradually expands. It is within the tideway, by which it is affected for 3 and a quarter miles in high spring tides, and it is navigable for boats and lighters up to the bridge on the mail coach road, a distance of 1 and three-quarter miles. It has no falls nor rapids during its progress through this parish, but 4 artificial overflows have been constructed, 1 at Ardmore, 2 at Drumahoe and 1 at Ardlough. The inundations cause considerable loss to the landholders where they occur while the crops are standing, but contribute to enrich the soil by leaving behind them deposits of fine sand.

The bed of the river consists of gravel and rolled pebbles. In the upper part of the parish its banks are in many places richly wooded and of a bold precipitous character; on approaching the lough they become tame, sinking gradually into a broad flat level which is again bounded by secondary retired banks of gravel and sand.

Other Rivers

The Glendermot, Lisdillon and Knockbrack streams are tributaries to the Faughan. The first rises in the county of Tyrone, the other two in the mountain range called Slieve Kirk, at the height of about 900 feet above the sea. The Glendermot stream is almost level; the others are very rapid, falling about 800 feet in a course of about 2 miles. They are all employed as mill-races, the supply of water being ample for 9 months of the year.

The parish abounds in springs of a good quality; that of Bogagh is mineral.

Bogs

In the northern part of the parish the bog is nearly exhausted, but in the southern there is still a large tract [crossed out: which is particularly valuable to the bleachers]. Its height varies from 400 to upwards of 1,200 feet above the sea, capping the summit of Slieve Kirk, 1,100 above the Faughan. [Crossed out: The mountain district appears to have been overspread with bog, which filled up all the irregularities of the ground]. Its depth varies from 2 to 10 feet and the subsoil is composed of clay and gravel. A small quantity of timber, chiefly fir, occurs imbedded in the bog; the stumps are upright and all broken about 2 feet above the roots.

Woods

Knockbrack glen is lined throughout by a natural growth of birch and ash, with a little oak. In Lisdillon glen there is some stunted natural wood. Some fine trees, shoots of the first growth which was cut down about 60 years ago, are standing in the plantations of Ardmore, especially near the Ardmore Altar (see Gentlemen's Seats).

From the following passage of Sir Henry Docwra's *Narration of the services done by the army employed to Lough Foyle etc.*, it appears that about the beginning of the 17th century the river was skirted by a wood of birch in that part of the parish opposite Derry, "and O'Cane having a woode lying right over against it (on the other side of the river), wherein was plentie of old growne birch, I daylie sent workemen with a guard of souldiers to cutt it downe, and there was not a sticke of it brought home but was first well fought for."

Coast

Between the Rivers Foyle and Faughan the parish is bordered by Lough Foyle. On the fall of the tide a wide expanse of mud is left bare by the receding waters.

Climate

[Insert note by Dawson: Captain Portlock must do this for us; this I will attend to].

A storm on the 20th November 1830 blew down the spire of Glendermot church; *Londonderry Journal*, 30th November 1830.

MODERN TOPOGRAPHY

Towns: Waterside

There is no town in the parish. The village of the Waterside, which is properly a suburb of Derry, is situated on the eastern bank of the Foyle, exactly opposite that city, with which it communicates by the great wooden bridge described in the first volume of the Memoir. The houses extend partly along a mail coach road and partly along the old Dungiven road, which here ascends a steep hill

within the suburb, called the Quay Brae Head or Quay Brae Face.

The Waterside contains 120 habitations, of which about 50 are mere cabins. The lower part, however, contains several respectable trading establishments, including a distillery and a brewery [insert marginal query: do they still use it?], with 2 good inns. [Insert note: Transfer distillers and brewers to Productive Economy. Foyle brewery, James Mehan of distillery, 1836].

In 1833 there were 6 new houses built and in 1834 one; [insert marginal query: how many in 1835 and 1836?]. The shops appear to be improving; this, as well as the general prosperity of the village, is attributable to the heavy tolls of the bridge which impede the intercourse between Derry and the district on the east of the Foyle. The population is about 1,000.

There are carriages and cars for hire at the inns, where also private conveyances usually stop without entering Derry, in order to avoid the tolls of the bridge.

The tank or reservoir which supplies Derry with water is in Clooney and immediately above the Waterside; it is itself supplied from a larger one in Corrody (see parish of Templemore). [Insert note: A. White].

Village: New Buildings

The village of New Buildings is situated about 3 miles from Derry, on the coach road to Dublin. It owes its origin to the Goldsmiths' Company, who erected here their castle. [Insert marginal query: Is this certain and when?]; [insert note: See Antiquities, Christian, Military]. This and the village itself were burnt during the war of the Revolution in the reign of King James II; one of the original cottages, however, still exists, which escaped destruction from the lowness and loneliness of its situation. [Insert marginal note: Mention it in History].

This village consists of a single street containing 37 habitations, of which several are badly thatched [insert query: still?]. Among the inhabitants are a blacksmith, a miller and 4 spirit dealers; the rest are either farmers or cottiers [insert query: in Productive Economy?]. The population is about 150 [insert query].

Enagh Lough

The hamlet of Enagh Lough, adjacent to the 2 lakes of Enagh, is remarkable for its neat cottages and picturesque situation. There are some other villages which, though small, contain several comfortable cottages.

Public Buildings: Church

The places of worship are 5: a [crossed out: Protestant] church, 3 [crossed out: Dissenting] meeting houses and 2 [crossed out: Catholic] chapels. Of the meeting houses, 2 are Presbyterian and the third Covenanting. The church and the Presbyterian meeting houses are all in Altnagelvin.

The [crossed out: Protestant] church [crossed out: which is in Altnagelvin] is situated about 1 mile from Derry, on the Dungiven road. Its site is conspicuous, being on the brow of the Clondermot hill. It is a plain substantial building, and was erected in 1753 at an expense of 500 pounds; the belfry, which was added in 1789, cost 280 pounds. A wooden spire covered with copper was erected in 1794, but blown down by a storm in November 1831. The pews are numerous and commodious, and the addition of a gallery is in contemplation. [Insert marginal query: Has it been added and at what expense?]. There is accommodation for 330 persons [insert query: more if gallery be added].

[Insert note: The deputation of the Irish Society, on Saturday July 21st '38, directed a railing to be made around the monuments recently erected in the churchyard (*Derry Journal*, 24th July 1835). Whose monuments are these?].

Meeting Houses

The old Presbyterian meeting house was erected in 1696 and enlarged in 1748 by Thomas Hogg, architect. In 1833 the seatholders collected 100 pounds to provide a new roof and repair the entire. The masonry is substantial and there is accommodation for 650 persons.

[Crossed out: On the southern gable there is a marble tablet about a foot square, which is thus inscribed: M I H, 1696]. Above the entrance door [crossed out: in the middle of the southern front] there is a sundial with this inscription: "The gift of Thomas Hogg to the congregation of Glandermod, anno domino 1748, William Hair, minister." The following also occur on the outside of the building: "M I H 1696;" [crossed out: on a marble tablet] "how amiable are thy tabernacles O Lord, [Master?] John Avery [blank] 96;" [crossed out: on a freestone tablet with half of the date obliterated] "Revd William Hair, 1747;" [crossed out: on a slate tablet] and "1696."

The new Presbyterian meeting house [crossed out: which is in Altnagelvin] stands at the foot of Clondermot hill, on the Dungiven road. It is a plain substantial building and was erected nearly a century ago, as appears from the following

inscription on a tablet inserted in the eastern gable: "Revd J. Holms, 1744." It has been newly roofed and the exterior is in good repair. It has 2 galleries and can accommodate 350 persons.

The Covenanting meeting house, which is in Fincarn, stands near the Faughan bridge and the Dungiven road. It is a small rectangular building and has lately undergone thorough repair, including a new roof, ceiling and side wall. It was erected in 1786 by subscription and can accommodate 300 persons.

Chapel

The old chapel, which is in Currynierin, was erected in 1791, at an expense of 400 pounds. It can accommodate 560 persons, but is at present in bad repair [insert marginal query: still in bad repair?]. Before the erection of this place of worship [crossed out: Roman Catholic chapel] mass was celebrated in Ardmore and Fincarn glen, in situations admirably adapted for concealment during the operation of the Penal Laws.

The Ardmore Altar will be described in Gentlemen's Seats. [Crossed out: Properly speaking, the altar on which mass was celebrated is in all about 8 feet long with a projecting table of loose stones and 2 flags forming steps].

The Fincarn Altar is an accidental stone, selected by the priest as a convenient substitute for a regular altar.

The new chapel has been [crossed out: is in contemplation to be] built at the Waterside from collections, partly made in England and Scotland. It stands on an acre of ground, granted in perpetuity by the present member for the city of Derry.

Dispensary

The dispensary, a neat slated building in Altnagelvin [crossed out: was established in 1826, but no house] was erected in 1832, at an expense of 50 pounds 6s, which sum was raised by subscription. The schoolhouses [insert note: see Lower Cumber].

Gentlemen's Seats

The parish contains a number of gentlemen's seats remarkable for [insert alternative: possessed of] both natural and artificial beauty.

Prehen, the seat of Colonel Knox, is beautifully situated on the eastern side of the Foyle, about 2 miles above the bridge of Derry. The plantations, which sweep down to the water's edge, extend an entire mile, and the demesne is ornamented throughout with a great number of old and picturesque trees. The house is very substantial and commodious; in its rear is a spacious walled garden and a large orchard.

St Columb's

St Columb's, formerly Chatham, the seat of George Hill Esquire, is opposite to Derry and on the eastern side of the Foyle, of which, owing to its elevated situation, it commands extensive views. The house is itself a handsome object, as seen from several points in the city, especially from Ship Quay Street. The demesne is planted with great taste, for the display [crossed out: exertion] of which the undulations of the ground presents a considerable facility; but the most interesting feature is the ruined church of St Columb, to which the villa owes its present name, which was bestowed on it by its last occupant, the late John Rea Esquire.

Ashbrook

Ashbrook, the seat of William Hamilton Ash Esquire, is situated about 2 and a half miles from Derry, on the southern side of the Faughan. The house has a small old-fashioned front but an ample rear. The family arms are displayed in niches on each side of the front entrance. The demesne is embellished with very fine trees and the ornamental grounds about the house are tastefully arranged and kept in good order.

Ardmore

Ardmore, the seat of John Acheson Smyth Esquire, is situated 3 and a quarter miles from Derry, on the southern bank of the Faughan, which here possesses much beauty. Among the most attractive features of the demesne is a deep precipitous ravine, the bed of a rapid stream.

Near the point where this stream enters the Faughan, and in a picturesque situation within a deep wood, stands the Ardmore Altar before alluded to, which consists of a wall about 8 feet long, with a projecting table of loose stones and 2 flags forming steps; its immediate site is a green platform about 20 feet long, and it is overhung by a birch tree. The house is commodious; and between it and the river is a grassy sloping bank used as a bleach green.

Larchmount

Larchmount, the seat of Cary McClellan Esquire, which is on the southern side of the Faughan, adjoins Ardmore without even a fence of separation. The Ardmore bleach green extends also over [crossed out: encroaches on] the lawn of this

demesne. The house is small, arches in front, [crossed out: provided with] a veranda; the garden is good but unwalled.

Beech Hill

Beech Hill <Beach Hill>, the seat of Conolly Skipton Esquire, is situated 2 and three-quarter miles from Derry, on the southern bank of the Faughan. It possesses much natural beauty, highly improved by art. Close to the house is a small but deep glen, shaded by large old trees and watered by a stream. The house, which is old and square, is approached by a straight avenue formed of several rows of old lime trees, an unusual and interesting feature. The ornamental grounds are in perfect order. The garden is large, well walled and well stocked with fine fruit trees; over its gate is the following inscription: "Thomas Skipton Esquire, 11th April 1783."

Bellevue

Bellevue, the seat of the Revd John Dickson Maughan, is situated near the Waterside, on the new road from Derry to Dungiven. The house is good, but the planting is as yet young [crossed out: does not possess much beauty].

Other Seats

To the above may be added the following residences: Ardkill, Robert Stevenson Esquire; Ardnabrocky, James Brook Esquire, [crossed out: Lieutenant Carmalt]; Cah, John Alexander Esquire; Clooney, Revd Anthony G. Cary; Cock Hall, Mr Samuel Ewing; Culkeeragh, Major Richard Young; Glenkeen, Captain Reynolds; Hollymount, Charles Martin Esquire; Salem or Foyle View, Samuel Haslitt Esquire; The Belt, Mrs Thompson; the name Foyle View also occurs in residences in Faughanvale.

Communications

The coach roads from Derry to Dublin and Belfast [insert marginal note: see *Derry Sentinel*, 31st March '38, Gordon's report] branch off from the Waterside. For 2 or 3 miles they are repaired with whinstone from quarries in Drumahoe and at Newtown Hamilton. The roads in the southern part of the parish, including even the coach road, are seldom in good order. Many of the crossroads, although running direct, are frequently impassable for carriages. The coach roads are upwards of 30 feet broad; the other county roads vary from 18 feet to 30.

That part of the Dublin line of road between the Waterside and New Buildings was made about 1795. It runs for 3 miles along the shore, within a few yards of the water's edge.

The coach road to Belfast by Newtownlimavady passes for 4 miles through the parish in a north easterly direction and is kept in good repair.

The coach road to Belfast by Dungiven branches off from the former at the Waterside and lies for nearly 3 miles through the parish in a south easterly direction. Above the Waterside it ascends a steep acclivity, and at Clondermot hill, about 1 mile further, it descends a similar declivity. This road is kept dry and in very good repair.

There still exists in Clooney the track of an old road which led to the forest of Curragh Camon in Culkeeragh, and along which timber is believed to have been conveyed for the original erection of Derry.

Bridges

There are 3 stone bridges across the Faughan in this parish. 2 of them, which are situated on the roads from Derry to Newtownlimavady and to Dungiven, are in good repair; the former was erected about 40 years ago. [Crossed out: There are 2 old stone bridges across the Faughan, one in Drumahoe about] 2 miles from Derry, the other at the hamlet of Enagh Lough. The former, which is on the coast road between Derry and Dungiven, is in good repair. [Insert marginal note: Description of second bridge?]. The roadway of the third, which is at Enagh Lough, on an old hilly road leading to Muff (in Faughanvale) and which was formerly the high road between Londonderry and Newtownlimavady, has been long neglected.

The bridge itself, however, is good and substantial. It is of 6 arches and varies in breadth from 15 to 18 feet. It is so old that its date cannot be ascertained.

There is a flat wooden bridge of the simplest form across the Faughan at the Ardmore bleach green, erected at the expense of the neighbouring gentry [crossed out: who built it for their own convenience]. It measures 91 feet by 21 and is 16 feet above the water.

At the junction of the River Foyle with the lough of the same name there is an ancient ferry (see parish of Templemore).

At Knockbrack there is a ford across the Faughan, which in dry weather is about 2 feet deep but is sometimes impassable. The erection of a stone bridge here would be very useful, for a long circuit, either to the wooden bridge of Lower Cumber or to that of Ardmore, would be thus avoided; besides, as the coach road runs along the opposite bank, facility of communication is here peculiarly desirable.

General Appearance and Scenery

The scenery of the parish is varied and beautiful: from Prehen the view of Derry is particularly interesting, the picturesque city and its bridge, which spans the broad and smooth river, being seen to great advantage, backed by the Inishowen [crossed out: Ennishowen] hills, Lough Foyle and Binevenagh <Benyevenagh>, while the foreground is formed of the fine trees of the demesne.

At Clondermot hill the Foyle and the Faughan present themselves, each in its deep and well-wooded valley. The former, rolling in full maturity, is seen to lose itself in the broad expanse of its own lough, and the eye follows the latter towards its source among the highest mountains in the county which, with intermediate hills of less pretension, exhibit a succession of broken and pleasing outlines. The high road to Dungiven, as it ascends the valley of the Faughan, is enlivened by prospects which, although inferior in extent, are rendered rich and attractive from the well-wooded villas on the opposite bank, and the numerous vistas of the river in its sinuous course break upon the eye of the traveller. The deep recesses of the mountain glens are here also not devoid of interest and beauty.

SOCIAL ECONOMY

Progress of Improvement

The industry of the parish has been much promoted within the last 20 years from the fostering influence of the late North West of Ireland Society (see parish of Templemore), and its branch and ultimate successor, the Tirkeeran Farming Society, who assemble at Clarke's Hotel at the Waterside and hold general meetings annually on the first Wednesday of November.

The Tirkeeran branch became embodied as an independent society on the 6th August 1834. The management is vested in a president, 3 vice-presidents, a committee of 9, a treasurer and a secretary. The subscription is 5s, but individuals of the upper classes frequently subscribe 5 pounds. The present number of members is 84, one-third of whom belong to the gentry. Prizes varying from 2 to 5 pounds are awarded for ploughing, reclaiming land, enclosing and fine crops, to the amount of 37 pounds, for which, however, the gentry are excluded from contending. A silver cup has likewise been presented to the society by Major Scott.

Since the establishment of this society as a branch in 1821, prize money has amounted to above 800 pounds, besides several valuable private donations.

As this head [crossed out: article] opens with some account of the ancient inhabitants of this parish, it may not inappropriately close with the following brief notices relating to some of their successors in modern times.

Colonel Mitchelburne

[Blank; insert note: Mr Petrie is to fill this].

The Mitchelburne Well, an excellent spring in Gobnascale, cannot be ranked as holy, being indebted for its sanctity to the colonel himself, to whom that townland belonged. In a shed adjacent to the well his coffin was deposited for the 7 years previous to his death; and hither he used to walk every morning along the Foyle from his house in the Waterside (on the site of which Mrs Brown's now stands), in order to pray. A number of little boys were employed by the colonel to keep the pathway free from grass, and his piety led to the belief that some healing virtue resided in the water. It is accordingly the resort of a few superstitious old women, who drop pins into it and tie rags on the bushes about it. Stations have even been held here.

Death of Miss Knox

The death of Miss Mary Anne Knox of Prehen, by the hand of John MacNaughten or MacNaghten Esquire, on the 10th November 1761, naturally excited much interest at the time, which length of years has but slightly abated. According to a manuscript account of this transaction, written by a female friend of Miss Knox, this ill-fated young lady, believing that her father had consented to her union with MacNaghten, a condition which she had made indispensable, went through the marriage ceremony with him in private, but on learning that deception had been practised on her, refused to live with him. He pursued her to different places under various disguises, but in vain. However, being at length informed that she was on her way to Dublin with her parents, he overtook the carriage on the road between Lifford and Strabane, and lodged a bullet in her side, which in a few hours occasioned her death. For this crime MacNaghten and an accomplice were soon after executed.

The statement from which these particulars have been derived is annexed to a few poems

"copied from Gray's works by the lovely but unfortunate Mary Anne Knox," and preserved "as a relique of that much and justly esteemed and admir'd lady."

It is believed that MacNaghten, after having been for some time concealed from the officers of justice by different females of his acquaintance, was discovered by some person who had observed a lady bringing food to an outhouse in which he was at the time secreted. He suffered at Strabane, justly, although perhaps for an unintentional crime, as it is supposed by some that the bullet [crossed out: firelock, weapon] which occasioned the death of Miss Knox had been intended [crossed out: aimed] at her father.

In the church of Killygarvan in the county of Donegal is a tablet erected in the memory of the father of the present Colonel Knox, at the head of which is engraved: "Mariana filia obiit November 1761."

Local Government

[Insert note: Middle, like Education?, to balance Municipality in Templemore].

The jurisdiction of the Derry municipality extends over a great part of this parish, as being included in the liberties of that city (see parish of Templemore). In addition there are 2 non-stipendiary magistrates, who usually attend the petty sessions in other parishes, either at Muff in Faughanvale, [crossed out: or, under particular circumstances] at Claudy, in Upper Cumber, or at Derry.

Names [and] residences: John Acheson Smyth Esquire, Ardmore; William J. Hamilton Ash Esquire, Ashbrook.

There are no resident police. Illicit distillation was suppressed about 40 years ago through the vigilance of the Derry excise officers, by whom the parish is occasionally well searched.

The Goldsmiths' Company possessed a manor court, the right of holding which has passed to the purchasers of their estate but has not been exercised by them.

The number of resident freemen of Derry residing in this parish is 21.

Education

Physical instruction: there is no establishment for physical instruction in the parish.

Intellectual instruction: the parish is provided with 16 schools [crossed out: or 17, if that of Ardmore (see table) be considered as two]. These, with one exception (a clerical school in

Drumahoe), being intended for the lower orders, are confined to an English elementary course. The entire number may be divided into 5 public and 11 private schools.

[Insert note: Among the public schools that of Ardmore seems to claim particular notice, especially on account of its connexion with another benevolent institution which shall be described hereafter (see Poor Shop in the section Benevolence). It was established in 1819, at Beech Hill, by Miss Beresford and some other ladies, and continued after the principal founder had left the country. It was originally restricted to female pupils and a Sunday school (founded in 1815) is combined with it.

In 1826, in consequence of a memorial from the secretary of the institution, the deputation of the Irish Society recommended "that the arrears due to the late school be repaid to the managers of the Ardmore school, and that the annual donation of 5 guineas be continued." This donation has since been increased to 10 pounds annually, which is on particular occasions still further augmented.

The *Report of the deputation of the Irish society* in 1835 states: "a memorial was presented from the Roman Catholic congregation of the parish of Glendermott and the Waterside, opposite Derry, for aid to build a schoolhouse for the education of children of all denominations. We recommend that 50 pounds be quoted them for that purpose, the same to be paid when the building is roofed in"].

The sum of 50 pounds has been lately granted by the Irish Society towards the erection of a school in Rossnagalliagh. [Insert marginal note: Practical instruction].

The moral instruction of the parish is superintended by the [crossed out: Protestant curate] ministers of the different places of worship, as specified in the annexed table, compiled from the *First report of the commissioners of public instruction.*

Sunday Schools

The Sunday schools of this parish formerly constituted a part of the Londonderry School Union. The Glendermot (Clondermot) School Union was established in 1819. [Insert addition: Deputation 1826, scholars 24, Erasmus Smith's memorial], [to] which the deputation of the Irish Society in that year recommended an annual donation of 5 guineas. It subsequently merged in that of Londonderry; it was, however, since revived, and at a meeting held by the clergy and others on the 19th

April 1835, 9 schools were withdrawn from Londonderry School Union and annexed to it. The present number of these schools in Clondermot is 17, attended by 106 teachers; the number of pupils on the books is 1,125 and the average attendance 947.

Table from published report of Derry Sunday schools. [Table contains the following headings: religious persuasion, population, extent of accommodation provided in places of worship, average attendance as stated by the Commissioners of Public Instruction, periods at which divine service is performed, state of congregation, number of clergymen].

Established Church 1,237, accommodation 330, attendance 250, parish church; once on every Sunday and twice in summer, and on the principal holidays; congregation increasing; 1 clergyman, the perpetual curate; he is resident. The Dean of Derry is rector and has pastoral jurisdiction over the cure.

Presbyterians 5,402, accommodation 1,300, attendance: Presbyterian meeting house 450, Presbyterian meeting house 200, Covenanting meeting house 300; service on every Sunday in summer, none in winter; congregations: stationary, nearly stationary, stationary during the last 2 or 3 years; 1 clergyman [each].

Roman Catholics 3,676, accommodation 560, attendance 750, old Roman Catholic chapel, new Roman Catholic chapel; service once on Sundays and holidays; congregation increasing; clergymen 2, who officiate also in the chapel in the benefice of Lower Cumber.

The Seceding and Methodist congregations, having no resident ministers, attend divine worship in Derry.

Summary of Education

From the population return of 1821 it appears that not more than 80 children were then under instruction, being a small proportion of the population. In 1824 the increase seems to have been about eightfold, and in 1834, although it appears from a comparison of parliamentary tables that in the preceding 10 years the number of schools in the parish had decreased less by 6, [insert addition: the number of schools in the parish was 20 in 1824 and but 14 in 1834], the number of pupils had, however, increased by nearly one-quarter, the total in 1824 being 678, in 1834 836, taught by 16 teachers.

Indeed so strong is the general desire for education that a woman has been known to keep her children at school for some time after the death of her husband had obliged her to beg for their subsistence [insert marginal query: date?].

From comparing the school attendance alluded to with the population of the parish at each period, it will appear that the number under instruction between the ages of 5 and 15 amounts nearly to one-quarter of the total number of children between these ages.

[Insert note: Bring up Cah].

Benevolence

Establishments for instruction: on referring to the head of Education, it will be seen that there are 1 free school and 3 others partly supported by public bodies.

Establishments for the indigent: as in Templemore, what are here understood by establishments for the indigent may be subdivided into 2 classes; first, such as are intended for the working classes; second, such as are intended for paupers. The former class comprises 2 [insert alternative: 3] money clubs, which hold their meetings at the [blank]; and 2 temperance societies. Such institutions, when prudently conducted, are peculiarly laudable inasmuch as they render the working man *his own benefactor*.

The parish is also well provided with endowments for the poor, properly so called. Of these, the most beneficial is the Poor Shop, next to which is the Poor Loan Fund. To these should be added 7 bequests; 4 of these were left by Colonel Mitchelburne, but these have been suffered to lapse, as has likewise that of Alderman Tomkins which, as will subsequently appear, was intimately connected with the Mitchelburne charities.

[Insert note by Dawson: I have accidentally mislaid my list of these clubs, but I will send you one the moment I get back more to the purpose than this, for it is ground requiring caution].

Money Clubs

Within the last 2 years several money clubs have been formed at the Waterside. There are at present 3, which hold their meetings at 2 public houses. Each member pays in 2s a week for the purposes of the club, and an additional 1d ha'penny to remunerate the publican. The disbursements are conducted by a kind of lottery and members may hold a plurality of shares, the numbers of which in the 3 clubs are at present 56, 50 and 40.

The clubs assemble every Saturday night. Tickets corresponding in number with the undrawn shares are put into a hat or similar depository, and one under a candlestick. Whoever draws from the

hat the duplicate of this letter is entitled to the amount of the subscriptions. On the next night 1 ticket fewer is put into the hat, and so on, until have been all exhausted.

Should the fortunate drawer not be in present need of the money, he may dispose of it at a premium, which varies according to the period, but is generally about 5 per cent, upon which the latter exchanges places with the buyer. When a member has drawn his money his name is marked off, and he must give approved security on a stamp for his future repayments.

[Crossed out: [Within the] last 2 years 3 money clubs have been formed at the Waterside. One of them, held at the house of Mr McShane, a publican, numbers 56 members, who pay in 2s ha'penny a week, every Saturday night. It is conducted by a kind of lottery. The tickets, which entitle the holder to the loan of 3 pounds for 40 weeks, are deposited under an old candlestick, and one is drawn at each meeting. If the holder be not in immediate want of the money, he sells his ticket for a small sum to another, who must give security for repayment. The drawing is succeeded by lodgements which are made from weekly savings of 1s 7d ha'penny, whereof 1d ha'penny are spent on drink, as a remuneration to the publican for the use of the club room. The number of the members is limited to 40.

Another money club or fund, established on the 10th April 1834, is held at the Waterside, at the house of another publican, every Saturday night. This also is conducted by a kind of lottery. A ticket entitles the drawer to receive 4 pounds 12s 6d, on his giving security for the repayment by regular weekly instalments of 1s 6d. The drawing is succeeded by lodgements which are made from weekly drawings of 1s 9d, whereof 3d are spent as in the other money club.

This institution, which is spreading throughout the parish, is rapidly increasing both in numbers and capital. [Insert note: Another account gives the dates of foundation: 8th November 1834, 4th April 1835, January 1835].

A meal-man acts as joint president and treasurer, and the secretary is a carpenter. The depositors, who are either artisans or labourers, already amount to 40, and males and females are alike admissible].

The 2 temperance societies are held one near the church and the other at New Buildings.

Poor Shop

The Poor Shop is located in the vestry room of the new Presbyterian meeting house and opened at stated intervals. It was instituted in 1822 [insert query: 1824?], in connection with the Ardmore female school, through the benevolent exertions of one lady; and the objects are to sell goods to the poor on approved security, for the payment by weekly instalments of 1d in the shilling; and to employ poor women in spinning, for which they are paid the usual price, and the yarn is sold in the market. [Insert note: And the sum of 30 pounds was lent by the ladies of the London and Irish Society, on condition that thrice that sum should be lent out yearly, otherwise the money should be refunded. The accounts are sent annually to the society in London and the condition has been hitherto fulfilled].

The funds were very small at the commencement but were assisted by [insert superscript: a subscription of 50 pounds 1s and a loan of 30 pounds from] the ladies of the London and Irish Society, established in London for the relief of Irish necessity. This money was lent free of interest and with the understanding that the principal should not be reclaimed as long as it was loaned thrice in the year.

[Insert note: In 1826 also, in consequence of a memorial from the secretary, stating that the failure of the flax crop endangered that branch, the deputation of the Irish Society recommended a donation of 20 pounds to the institution].

Although the full price is charged for each article, there is still a certain degree of loss to be sustained: about 3 years ago, in particular, imposition was practised to a serious extent by means of forged letters, most of which were presented by strangers passing through the parish.

No more than 15s worth is sold at a time to any one individual, and then only on the recommendation of a respectable person [insert addition: to be paid for in weekly instalments of 6d, 1s or 1s 6d]. In the first year the sales amounted to 232 pounds 17s 4d.

The following list, which is for one year, is a pretty fair average of their return: the value of the articles was 282 pounds 12s 9d; 106 pair of blankets, 348 shirts, 278 shifts, 189 petticoats, 176 gowns, 82 waistcoats, 91 pair of trousers, 15 counterpanes, 10 cloaks, 18 beds, 11 bolsters, 91 aprons, 87 pair of shoes, 68 sheets, 56 shawls, 16 caps, [total] 1,641.

Charitable Loan

The Charitable Loan was established in 1814, chiefly through the exertions of the curate, the Revd A.G. Cary, and is supported by subscription. The main object is to lend to industrious housekeepers sums from 1 to 5 pounds, free of interest but on approved security, to be repaid by weekly instalments of 6d in the pound, but the loan sometimes consists of looms or spinning wheels.

The management is vested in a committee of 4 governors, composed of the parochial clergy of every denomination, with a few of the neighbouring gentry, who meet on the first Monday of every month in the session house of the Presbyterian meeting house. The funds at present amount to [blank], and the trustees are the Bishop and Dean of Derry, with the curate for the time being.

[Insert note: The treasurer pays the loans at the parish schoolhouse, which is the office, on the second Monday in every month, and the schoolmaster receives 18 pounds a year for acting as clerk. No person in any degree connected with the sale of malt or spirituous liquors is admissible to the benefits of the institution; the object of the loan must be stated; no second recommendation within a month is attended to; the security must be perfected in the presence of the governors in their board; and the smallest irregularity in the payment of the instalments is followed by immediate and summary process for the recovery of the principal.

The *Report of the deputation of the Irish society* in 1836 contains the following testimony in favour of this institution: "The directors of the Glendermott Charitable Loan Committee memorialized us for assistance to their funds; and finding it to be a most excellent institution (the number of families relieved last year by small loans amounted to 452 and consisted of 2,307 individuals), we recommend that 10 pounds annually be granted to this charity"].

[Insert addition: The Poor Loan Fund to which the gentry subscribe was established in 1830. The main object is to lend sums of 2 pounds free of interest, to be repaid by instalments of 1s a week. The curate is the conductor of the charity, the business of which is transacted once a month at the Poor Shop].

[Crossed out: An anecdote connected with this fund is worth recording, as it shows how an intercourse between the upper and lower classes may be cultivated to the benefit of the latter.

In 1831 a very poor man applied for 2 pounds to meet a demand so urgent that non-compliance with it would prove his ruin; however, his security not being approved, the accommodation was refused. While on his return he was met by a gentleman who, on learning the issue of his application, desired the poor man to attend him in an hour at his father's house. Here he was handed 5 pounds to pay the demand with part and dispose of the remainder to the best advantage. Adopting a suggestion of his benefactor, he accordingly bought an ass and retailed eggs and fowl in the Derry market. He has since repaid the entire sum, being now able to trade on his own capital].

Colonel Mitchelburne's Will

Foremost in the list of deceased benefactors stands Colonel John Mitchelburne. The following bequests are extant in his will, dated the 12th July 1721.

Firstly, 86 pounds "to be put to interest for the maintenance of 8 poor inhabitants of the parish of Clondermot, particularly those of the Waterside, to each 3d a week forever, the said poor to be such as have nothing but charity to support them." This distribution, amounting to 5 pounds 4s annually, *continues to be made*]; [insert marginal query: see Benevolence].

Secondly, 67 pounds, the interest of which was allowed to the schoolmaster for teaching 12 poor children of the said parish, to be of the Church of England, 4 pounds sterling per annum forever, "and also privilege to teach other scholars." This charity has, however, lapsed.

Thirdly, 25 pounds, the interest of which, amounting to 30s annually, was "to be distributed and given to 30 of the poor inhabitants of the said parish, and they to be of the Church of England, 12d to each of them." In connection with this bequest he ordered that his body should be buried in Enagh church and the distribution made on the 1st of August at his tombstone. He was, however, interred in Clondermot churchyard [insert marginal query: why?]. This charity also has lapsed.

Lastly, 140 pounds, the interest of which should afford "to 16 of the poor inhabitants of Clondermot, being of the Church of England, half a peck of meal weekly to each forever, to be given after sermon." The meal, which was ground at a neighbouring mill, was distributed every Good Friday from a heap deposited on the Colonel's tombstone, but as soon as the lease of the mill had expired, the charity was allowed to lapse on the grounds that it had formed part of the engagement of the lease. The distribution is said to have been made at the Waterside for a short time before its total cessation.

Another bequest can hardly be classed as benevolent. It runs thus: "I order for maintaining the flag in the steeple of Derry 50 pounds, for which I have already given my bond."

Notes on Bequests

The following information concerning these bequests is current in the parish.

Almost 20 pounds were collected during the curacy of the Revd W. Boyle in the parish of Clondermot, in the year in which the late Bishop Knox was appointed to the see of Derry, for the purpose of instituting proceedings against the Warren family. Until within a few years from that period the Warren family had paid regularly every charitable bequest mentioned in Colonel Mitchelburne's will, but in examining the lease of their property, they found that they had been hitherto wronging themselves, as they were liable only to the payment of a part, some of the property liable to the payment having fallen by purchase into the hands of Sir R.A. Ferguson and some into the hands of Mrs Samuel Moore, the widow of Samuel Moore Esquire.

However, on the Warren family's refusing to pay the bequest as hitherto, the sum above mentioned was [insert addition: raised with the view to prosecution and] given into the hands of the Revd W. Boyle to institute proceedings, who accordingly left Clondermot for Dublin. At Armagh he was met by Bishop Knox, who was on his way to Derry, and who, on being informed of the purport of his journey, induced him to return, with the understanding that he would attend to the affair himself. He did so, and the management was entrusted to the Board of Bequests. On an application from them, Sir R.A. Ferguson and Mr Warren expressed a readiness to pay their shares, but as Mrs Moore was at the time living in France, no arrangement was made with her. Delay was thus caused and the prosecution dropped.

Alderman Tomkins' Bequest

A bequest of 50 pounds from Alderman George Tomkins was in a manner supplementary to those of Colonel Mitchelburne, as intended for the relief of 6 poor individuals of the Church of England not receiving any from the Colonel's immediate bequests, and who were each paid 10 pounds annually from the interest of the money at 6 per cent. The fund also was derived from the Mitchelburne property, as appears from the following extract from Alderman Tomkins' will, dated 24th May 1739.

"Item 1, two-thirds of the lands and tenements in Cluny and Gobnascale in the parish of Clondermot, with the house and garden which was bequeathed to be [me?] by Colonel Mitchelburne <Mitchelbourne>, I bequeath the same to the same charitable uses as the said Colonel John Mitchelburne, by his last will appointed the same."

The amount of the bequest was raised by the curate and churchwardens, and put to interest as enjoined by the will, with Andrew Knox Esquire of Prehen. The distribution was made annually by the curate on the 1st June, and the interest was regularly paid up to that date in 1831, when Colonel Knox left the country. [Insert note: A bequest from Alderman Peter Stanley, made by his will dated [blank], did not come into operation until 1764. This bequest consisted of 20 barrels of shelling, each barrel to weigh 18 score, to be distributed annually in the month of May by the curate and churchwardens to 40 poor inhabitants of the parish].

Bequest from Messrs Miller

The most recent bequests are those of Messrs Joseph and Robert Miller, each of whom left 100 pounds to the poor Presbyterian housekeepers of the parish, as appears from the following extract from Robert Miller's will, dated 12th June 1788: "That in case I died without a lawful heir of my body, that 100 pounds should be put to interest in a sure hand and that the interest thereof should be equally divided among 12 or 24 poor housekeepers, members of the 2 Dissenting congregations of Clondermot; and my brother did by his said will recommend it to me to put 100 pounds with the said 100 pounds as ordered by him to put to interest as aforesaid, now I do hereby leave the said sum of 100 pounds so ordered to be put out at interest by my said brother, with the further sum of 100 pounds; for which said 2 sums of 100 pounds each it is my will and desire that my executors herein after mentioned shall laid (lay?) out at interest in sure hands immediately after my death and that the interest thereof shall always be annually paid to 12 or 24 poor housekeepers, members of the 2 Dissenting congregations of Clondermot, in equal shares and proportions, share and share alike." Joseph Miller's will was dated in January 1783.

Poor

There are 540 paupers who receive alms, either at the residences of the gentry or of the respectable shopkeepers of the Waterside. These amount in money to about 2 or 3 pounds a week, but there is also a distribution of alms in kind, that is in milk, meal, soup, tobacco, salt, eggs, vegetables, [insert addition: soap], fuel and old clothes. [Insert query: Potatoes; potatoes is the common gift given to a beggar in the country? [Answer] "Vegetables" includes potatoes].

A peculiar class called *decent beggars* comprises all those impoverished by misfortune such as losses in trade, diminution of business, the death of husbands or fathers etc. The males of this class sometimes follow the occupation of thatching or any other which they may have casually acquired, and sometimes employ themselves in herding, gardening or weeding about their little huts. The females spin, sew, knit, weed or nurse for farmers' families etc. This industry has acquired for them the application [insert alternative: appellation] of "decent," to distinguish them from the sturdy travelling beggar, who loves to rove through the country, feels contented with his situation, believes himself worth 10d day and would not change situation even with the farmer. When by the death of a male decent beggar his widow is reduced to a lower grade of pauperism, and obliged to "look for her meat," she is usually spoken of as "the desolate creature."

The paupers generally tenant small hovels, at a trifling rent, paid either in money or kind. They frequently receive a night's lodging for charity. They are prevented by the civic regulations from begging either in the city of Derry or the rural part of Templemore, although the poor of that parish are allowed to roam through Clondermot, where they are relieved by the parishioners, indiscriminately with their own poor and those from more distant parishes. In this instance the tolls of the bridge are beneficial, being a considerable bar to such inroads.

Most of the cottiers are in degree paupers. There are but few individuals who subsist wholly on begging. The season for going abroad for alms is before the potato harvest. Of the cottier class, there are 480 families; [insert marginal note: compare with Productive Economy].

Foundlings are frequently adopted and reared, on the payment of 10 pounds by the parish; 2 only are at present [insert addition; exclusively] supported in this way.

Establishments for Mental and Bodily Diseases

The parishioners are admissible to the lunatic asylum and infirmary of Derry, being county establishments.

The dispensary was established in 1826, although no building was erected for the purpose till 6 years after. From the following table it would appear that the parishioners suffer much from cutaneous diseases, although there is no remarkable [blank] apparent in either their persons or habitations. Since the establishment of the dispensary the smallpox has nearly vanished and scrofula become much abated. Fever also is less prevalent than formerly, in consequence of the cleanliness enforced on its appearance and the instructions given of the danger of contagion. The district is confined to the parish.

Courts

As Derry is the county town and no court is held in the parish, the information given under this head in Templemore must be considered applicable in degree to this parish. [Insert marginal query: Is the manorial court re-opened?].

Commerce

That part of the scanty commerce of the parish which belongs to the Waterside has been already adverted to in a description of that place as a village of this parish, or it may be considered as an integral part of the commerce of Templemore, the Waterside being also a suburb of Derry [insert marginal note: see Productive Economy].

[Crossed out: The principal trading establishments are a distillery and a tannery at the Waterside, and a brewery at the Faughan bridge on the Dungiven road in Drumahoe.

The tannery was established upwards of a century ago. The proprietor keeps on an average 4 or 5 men, who receive in wages from 20 to 30 pounds without diet.

There are 2 corn merchants at the Waterside who buy grain on market days at their own stores, one on his own account for the Liverpool market, the other on commission for that of Glasgow. The grain is shipped on the spot].

Population

Adopting the same wide meaning of the term population as in the first volume of this Memoir, the consideration of this head as modified by the local circumstances of the parish is [blank] fold. The earliest numerical notice on record of the families located in this parish is contained in the following extract from Pynnar under the head Gould Smiths Hall, "3,200 acres, John Freeman Esquire has this proportion, containing by estimation 3,210 acres. Upon this proportion there is a bawn of lime and stone, 16 feet high with 4 flankers. Also there is a large castle or stone house building within the wall which was 2-storeys high, and the workmen earnestly at work to finish it at all haste. There are also 6 houses of stone and 6 of timber, very strong and well built, and seated

in a very good and convenient place for the king's service.

I find planted and estated upon this land of Brittish tenants, freeholders 6, viz. 1 having 180 acres, 5 having 60 acres a piece; lessees for years 24, viz. 2 having 300 acres a piece, 2 having 120 acres a piece, 1 having 100 acres, 10 having 60 acres a piece, 1 having 50 acres, 4 having 40 acres a piece, 2 having 30 acres a piece, 1 having 46 acres, 1 having 20 acres. Total 30 families who, with their undertenants, are able to make 90 men armed and have taken the Oath of Supremacy."

Table of Population

1821, houses: inhabited 1,825, uninhabited 27, building 1; persons: families 1,926, males 4,725, females 5,236, total 9,961; occupations: number of persons chiefly employed in agriculture 1,811, number of persons employed chiefly in trades and manufactures [insert addition: or handicraft] 3,075, number of all other persons occupied and not comprised in the 2 preceding classes 378, total number of persons occupied 5,264; schools: male pupils 80, total 80 pupils.

1831, [insert addition: English estate area], houses: inhabited 1,869, uninhabited 77, building 12; persons: families 1,921, males 4,930, females 5,408, total number of persons 10,338, males 20 years of age 2,486; occupations: families chiefly employed in agriculture 1,092, families chiefly employed in trade, manufacture and handicraft 390, all other families not comprised in the 2 preceding classes 439.

1834, from the First Report of the Commissioners of Public Instruction. 1831 according to enumerator's return: Established Church 1,237, Roman Catholics 3,675, Presbyterians 5,402, other Protestant Dissenters none, total 10,315; 1834, as determined by the commissioners: members of the Established Church 1,287, Roman Catholics 3,825, Presbyterians 5,621, other Protestant Dissenters none, total 10,733. 23 persons are omitted whose religion could not be ascertained.

The average annual number of Protestant births for the years 1827, 1828 and 1829 was 39, and of marriages 9.

Habits of the People

In the lower or Enagh Lough district some of the habitations are slated and otherwise comfortable.

[Crossed out: In the upper or Warbleshinny district even those above the rank of *hovels* have an *old and dilapidated appearance*. The thatch is generally black and slimy, the walls crazy and

unplastered. Farmhouses, too, of a superior description are occasionally met with, which exhibit a painful contrast to their former state, in the
decay of the once large and ornamental window,
the neglected state of the roof, the fracture of
some little architectural ornament and the dirty
state of the walls. Some cottages have wattled
chimneys smeared with clay, and the triangular
part of the gable built of sods. There are none
actually of mud, as the parish abounds with stone.
Excepting at the Waterside, few habitations have
more than 1 storey, but a kind of loft is common
which is used to store firing and timber].

Comfort and cleanliness exist in various degrees. A mixture of meal and water is often
employed in place of soap. [Insert note by Dawson:
This requires still further modification which I
will attend to].

Food and Drink

The small tradesmen and artisans of the Waterside are very fond of tea; on stated holidays the
poorer farmers also endeavour to procure it.
Throughout the parish, however, stirabout forms
the principal dish, especially when potatoes are
scarce. In the huckster's shops at the Waterside
the demand for meal is found to be greatest from
May to September.

Temperance is said to have increased, owing
partly to the want of money, occasioned by the
declining profit [of] cottage spinning, which the
greater productive power of the mills have caused,
partly to the temperance societies.

In the mountainous districts a miserable substitute for milk is used, called "sowen shirings."
This is made from a refuse of the mill called *tail
meal*, which is soaked in water and then strained.

Fuel

In a few years fuel will be scarce. Although much
turf is cut in Lisdillon, many of the peasantry are
obliged to resort to Lower Cumber and to
Donaghedy in the county of Tyrone, a distance of
from 4 to 7 miles, and to pay 12 pounds an acre for
bog. English and Scotch coals procured from
Derry are beyond the means of the poorer classes.

Dress

There is no characteristic uniformity of costume,
but linen trousers of the coarsest description and
the Scotch lowland cap are common. Clothing,
except shoes and linen, is mostly bought from
pawnbrokers and vendors of old clothes. Many
farmers manufacture for themselves and families

frieze, linen, hosiery, stuffs etc. The garments of
the abject poor are frequently patched until every
trace of the original stuff has disappeared.

A complete dress for a female, when the materials are bought at the shop, costs about 1 pound
3s; it will last about 2 years by repeated patching
and darning.

Longevity and Marriage

The parish is not remarkable for longevity. 2 or 3
individuals, however, are said to be above 95.

Marriages are commonly contracted between
the ages of 16 and 20. In Ardmore several years
ago a male of 15 years was united to a female of
14. Indeed a girl begins at 20 to pass for an old
maid. The dowry usually given consists of linen
yarn, tea-things etc., to which one or more cows
are frequently added. Wealthy farmers, of which
class there are but few, add from 10 pounds
upwards.

Amusements

Amusements seem to be rare. Except on festival
days the females are consistently [crossed out:
almost perpetually] employed in spinning.

The Irish cry: funeral cries have fallen into
complete disuse.

Emigration

It is believed that in 1833 at least 360 individuals
of both sexes emigrated from this parish across
the Atlantic. One-half of the gross number was
Roman Catholic, the other of the Established
Church and Presbyterians in equal numbers.
Emigration has continued for a long series of
years, and is consequently at present not so extensive as in some of the more upland parishes. In
1834 it was not greater than usual, but it is always
sufficient to check materially the increase of the
population. The number of the Roman Catholic
emigrants is becoming greater. Many of those
who emigrate are valuable members of the community, such as weavers. More capital is taken
out now by each emigrant than formerly. The
emigration too is mostly from the lower and more
fertile districts [insert marginal query].

In most cases from 1 to 3 of the youngest, stoutest
and healthiest of a family, without distinction of
sex, emigrate together, and send for the older members the following season under favourable circumstances. Numbers are sometimes obliged to return
home for want of accommodation in the vessels.
The demand for berths was so great that the charge
was raised 10s; indeed some advance occurs to-

wards the end of every season. Two others had the
expenses of their passage defrayed by earlier emigrants. The majority sailed for the Canadas.

By the latest account from America, the landing stations seem to have been overstocked. Letters have arrived, some of a discouraging and
some of an encouraging tendency. The latter,
which appear to have gained most credence, have
spread the contagion of emigration. An individual speaking of it said that the country was
"rising up to follow them," that is those who had
already gone. In fact, the people, especially the
Scotch settlers, are beginning to consider America
as much "their own country" as this.

The few who furnish their entire passage-money
themselves are only the respectable farmers, or
individuals from whose families no emigration
had yet been made. [Crossed out: Those who can
afford to transport a family at once generally
consider themselves gentlemen]. Australian emigration is becoming more popular than at first,
especially with females.

Migration

From 100 to 200 individuals, male and female, go
every year to reap the harvest in England and
Scotland. A young man often takes either his wife
or a sister with him, as the Ulster women are
usually good shearers and can, with sufficient
exertion, earn as much in a day as the men. All
these are cottiers who, as soon as they have sown
a small quantity of potatoes, flax etc., cross the
channel to earn as much by harvest work as will
pay the rent of their habitation, reserving the crop
for their winter sustenance.

Benevolence: Establishments for the Indigent

[Table contains the following headings: name,
object, management, number relieved, funds from
public bodies and private individuals, annual expense of management, relief afforded, when
founded].

4 schools, object: the removal of ignorance;
managed by sundry societies; 266 pupils receiving instruction; house rent: interest of 215 pounds,
the expense of erection; salaries 85 pounds; when
founded: Altnagelvin, Ardmore, Ballyshasky,
Clooney.

3 money clubs or money funds, object: to lend
small sums from savings; [insert addition: 146
members receiving loans]; funds: 2s per week
from each member; house rent: 1d ha'penny a
week from each member is spent in drinking, to
remunerate a publican for the use of his room;

relief: a loan of a sum equal to the amount of
subscriptions to one member each week, to be
repaid by weekly instalments of 2s without interest; founded 5th April 1834.

Money Club, object: to lend small sums from
savings; rent: 3d per week from each member is
spent in drinking, to remunerate a publican for the
use of his room; founded 10th April 1834.

Temperance Society (near church), Temperance Society (New Buildings), object: to promote
sobriety.

Poor Shop, object: to sell goods to the poor at
reduced prices, payment made by weekly instalments; management: local committee of ladies;
numbers relieved: [crossed out: 2,242 sales, comprising various articles of clothing in 1 year],
1,641 articles of cloth apparel; funds: a loan of 20
pounds from London Ladies' Society, from private individuals variable, subscriptions amounting to 50 pounds 19s; relief afforded: 1,641 articles in one year; founded 1822.

Poor Loan Fund, object: small loans to the poor
without interest, to be repaid by instalments;
managed by curate of the parish; funds from
private individuals variable; founded 1830.

Bequest; object the relief of poverty; 8 poor
inhabitants of the parish relieved; funds from Colonel Mitchelburne 86 pounds, lapsed; relief afforded:
5 pounds 4s a year; founded 12th July 1721.

Bequest, object: the removal of ignorance;
educating 12 poor children of the parish; funds
from Colonel Mitchelburne 67 pounds, lapsed;
relief afforded: 4 pounds a year; founded 12th
July 1721.

Bequest, object: the relief of poverty; 30 poor
inhabitants of the parish relieved; funds from Colonel Mitchelburne 25 pounds, lapsed; relief afforded:
1 pound 10s a year; founded 12th July 1721.

Bequest, object: the relief of poverty; 16 poor
inhabitants of the parish relieved; funds from
Colonel Mitchelburne 140 pounds, lapsed; relief
afforded: half a peck of meal to each, interest on
140 pounds; founded 12th July 1721.

Bequest, object: the relief of poverty; funds
from Alderman Tomkins, lapsed; relief afforded:
3 pounds a year.

Bequest, object: the relief of poverty; 40 poor
inhabitants of the parish relieved; funds from
Alderman Stanley; relief afforded: 18 barrels of
shelling annually, each barrel to weigh 18 score;
came into operation 1704.

Bequest, object: the relief of poverty; number
relieved: 12 or 24 poor housekeepers, being members of the Dissenting congregations of
Clondermot; funds from Joseph Miller, 100

pounds capital; relief afforded: the interest of 100 pounds; date of will 12th June 1788.

Bequest, object: the relief of poverty; number relieved: 12 or 24 poor housekeepers, being members of the Dissenting congregations of Clondermot; funds from Robert Miller, 100 pounds capital; relief afforded: the interest of 100 pounds; date of will January 1783.

Bequest [insert addition: places of worship], object: the relief of poverty; management: the churchwardens and others; numbers relieved: variable.

Residences of the gentry and of shopkeepers, object: the relief of poverty; management: the gentry; numbers relieved; 540; relief afforded: sundry articles of food, from 2 to 3 pounds per week.

[Insert note by Dawson: Cannot be called indigent when contributes to money club. The truth is they scarcely belong to Benevolence, if we can find another place for them; perhaps in Habits of the People. [Elsewhere] it is said one of Colonel Mitchelburne's charities continues to be paid].

Establishments for Mental and Bodily Diseases

Dispensary; management: committee (of governors); number relieved: 1,690 annually on an average of 5 years; funds: Irish Society 5 pounds annually, Grocers' Company 5 pounds 5s, county grant variable, governors' subscriptions; expenses: house rent, interest on 50 pounds 6s, the money sunk in building the house, salaries 50 pounds [insert query: 51 pounds?]; expenses of patients: 90 pounds on an annual average of 3 years; founded 1826. [Insert query: Do the governors (i.e. subscribers of 1 pound 1s a year) elect a managing committee?].

[Insert note by Downes: Is the dispensary year from 1st April throughout? Another table gives Irish Society 5 pounds, Grocers' Company 5 pounds 5s, [insert note: confirmed by *Londonderry Sentinel*, 23rd January 1836 as annual], private individuals 41 pounds 5s 6d, county grant (say) 51 pounds 5s 6d [insert query: 51 pounds 10s 6d?].

Dispensary of Faughanvale which includes part of this parish in the district; see parish of Templemore.

Infirmary of Templemore: see parish of Templemore.

ANCIENT TOPOGRAPHY

Memoir Writing

[Insert footnote by [Downes?]: Notice on ancient matters, 10 coins found at Prehen in 1826. See Lieutenant Vicars' Statistical Reports; Colonel Mitchelburne's epitaph].

Draft Memoir by C.W. Ligar and J.B. Williams

NATURAL FEATURES

Hills

The principal hills rise to the following elevations above the sea: Slieve Kirk, 1,224, Nod's Top, 986, Brown mountain, 973, Tirkeeveny, 503, Clondermot hill, 726 and Avish, 541 feet above the sea. The first 4 terminate the northern face of a chain which extends beyond the parish in a south easterly direction to Sawel, the highest point. This chain is bounded by the Faughan and Clondermot stream, the former of which, on reaching the mountains, then turns abruptly to the north east. At this bend the Clondermot stream empties itself and forms with the lower part of the Faughan nearly a straight line.

On the northern face of the hills mentioned above are 2 valleys or gorges of some importance called Lisdillon glen and Knockbrack glen.

A long ridge, 1 and a half miles broad, the highest part of which is called Clondermot hill, is separated from the surrounding mountain district by the deep glen of Clondermot and the broad valley of the Foyle. The west side of the former is formed by the precipitous descent of the ridge above mentioned, which on the west falls gradually to the Foyle. A great part of the ridge varies in height from 200 to 300 feet, but its greatest elevation is on the southern extremity. From this it falls precipitously to the south, to the foot of another ridge similar in character but of less importance which extends into the county of Tyrone. Of this, the highest point at the southern extremity of the parish is 496 feet.

The remainder of the parish is separated by the Faughan river from the part already described. It consists of a ridge almost parallel to that of Clondermot, and partaking of the same character, being precipitous towards the south and east. The most important part of it is Avish, which rises no more than 541 feet above the sea.

Lakes

Between the Foyle and the Derry and Belfast mail coach road, and 3 miles from the former, are 2 small lakes called eastern and western Lough Enagh, 200 feet asunder and connected by a small stream. The eastern occupies 46 and the western 25 acres. The bottom in both, which is principally of gravel, slopes gradually to the centre, where it attains the depth of about 32 feet. They formerly derived a supply of water from 2 small streams, which have been turned in another direction [insert alternative: course] since the mill they fed has been disused. Their only other supply at present is their own spring and the scanty superabundant surplus water which flows into the Faughan.

The eastern lough contains 2 wooded islets called Rough Island and Green Island, each about 150 feet in diameter. The latter was the site of an ancient castle of the O'Kane's, of which some vestiges remain. The former, which is locally called the Orchard, is said to have been the garden belonging to the castle and still contains some apple and plum trees.

The ruins of Enagh church, which stands upon some rising ground between the 2 lakes, add considerably to their interest [insert marginal query: transfer to General Appearance?]; and the varied surface of the ground in the immediate neighbourhood of the lakes, together with fine distant prospects, renders it very capable of being easily beautified and fitted for a gentleman's park or demesne. The neighbouring Faughan being considerably lower, it is likely that these lakes could be easily drained.

Rivers: Faughan

There are 2 important rivers, the Foyle and the Faughan. The former has been mentioned already (see parish of Templemore) [insert marginal note: parish boundary?].

The Faughan takes its rise near Sawel mountain in Banagher, 20 miles from the sea. Its direction for 3 miles after it enters the parish is from south east to north west. It then turns at right angles towards the north east and preserves this course until it falls into the sea [insert alternative: lough]. It averages about 100 feet in width above the bridge on the Belfast mail coach road, 14 miles above its mouth, from which to Lough Foyle it expands gradually, and at its mouth it suddenly merges in an estuary 2,000 feet wide. It is very shallow and is navigable only so far as the bridge above mentioned, and there only for small shell boats. It is not obstructed by any bar or deposit at its mouth. It has no rapids or falls in passing through this parish, but 4 artificial overflows have been constructed, 1 at Ardmore, 2 at Drumahoe and the third at Ardlough. The supply of water is abundant and the river, being very rapid, affords much greater power than is made available.

This river is the only outlet for the waters of the long line of mountainous country through which it passes, and is consequently, in rainy weather, subject to sudden and great floods. These com-

mence towards the latter end of August and continue until March or April. However, they are here insignificant until October or November. They cause considerable damage while their crops are on the ground, but afterwards benefit and enrich the soil by depositing fine sand. They subside very rapidly, often in less than 6 hours. [Insert marginal query: Does the damming assist in causing this overflow?].

The bed of the river consists of gravel and rolled pebbles. In the upper part of the parish the banks of the Faughan are peculiarly beautiful, being in many places richly wooded and of a bold precipitous character. Nearer the sea they become rather tamer, sinking into a broad level district of a rich nature but not much ornamented with planting.

Streams

The Clondermot, Lisdillon and Knockbracken streams are tributaries to the Faughan. The first takes its rise in the county Tyrone, the other 2 in the mountain range called Slieve Kirk, at the height of about 900 feet above the sea. Glendermot stream is almost level. The other 2, on the northern [insert note: face of Slieve Kirk] range, are very rapid, falling almost 800 feet in a course of about 2 miles. The streams are useful for mills, the supply of water being ample during 9 months of the year.

Good springs are abundant.

Bogs

In the northern portion of the parish the bog is nearly exhausted, but in the southern there is a vast tract which is particularly valuable to the bleaching establishments. The height of the bog varies from 400 to 1,200 feet above the sea and from 300 to 1,100 above the Faughan. A very small quantity of timber, chiefly fir, has been found imbedded in the bog. The stumps were upright and all broken about 2 feet above the roots. The bog appears to have overspread the mountain, filling up the irregularities of the ground. Its depth therefore varies from 2 to 10 feet but the general average is about 5. The interior is composed of blue marl, clay and gravel.

[Crossed out: As the bog is scarce in the northern part of the parish, the poor suffer much for want of a comfortable firing]. [Insert note: Transfer to Habits of the People].

Woods

Knockbrack glen is lined throughout with a natural growth of birch, ash and a little oak. In Lisdillon glen there is some stunted natural woods, and some fine trees, shoots of the first growth which was cut down almost 60 years ago, are standing in the plantations of Ardmore, particularly [insert alternative: especially] near the Ardmore Altar.

[Insert note: This is a Roman Catholic altar and was used before the chapel in Currynierin was built in 1791. It is situated on a retired and picturesque bank of the Faughan, and commanding beautiful views from amongst the trees with which it is surrounded, both of the river and of the opposite country].

Coast

The parish borders Lough Foyle between the mouth of the Foyle and the Faughan. The coast here possesses no interest; on the contrary, when the tide is out a large tract of mud is left exposed.

MODERN TOPOGRAPHY

Towns: Waterside

A suburb of Londonderry called the Waterside and a small village called New Buildings are situated in the parish, but there is no town of importance in it.

The Waterside is immediately adjoining the bridge of Londonderry on the eastern side of the river, extending along 2 mail coach roads which then work towards the north and south along its banks and also up a steep bank on the old road to Dungiven called Brae Face. The whole suburb consists of 120 houses, of which 50 are wretched cabins, and mostly [insert alternative: chiefly] situated on the steep bank above mentioned.

In the other parts there is a great proportion of very respectable houses and 2 good inns; see Table of Occupations [insert marginal note: introduce table].

The arrangements with respect to lighting, paving and watching, and other municipal regulations, are the same as in the city of Londonderry. The shops appear to be improving. In 1833 there were 6 new houses built and 1 has been built in 1834. It is under the same regulations as the city.

On Wednesdays and Saturdays, which are the market days of the city, 2 merchants purchase corn at their own stores at the Waterside from persons who thus avoid the toll of the bridge. Carriages and cars are kept for hire at the 2 inns; here also many persons coming from the east side of the Foyle leave their conveyances and horses during the time they transact business in the city.

The Waterside owes its increase to the heavy tolls of the bridge.

The reservoir which supplies the city of Londonderry with water is in the townland of Corrody. The water is led through pipes to a second and smaller reservoir in Clooney, immediately above the Waterside, from whence it is conveyed in pipes across the bridge to the town. The cost of conveying the supply, which was 1,000 pounds, was met by a loan from government not yet repaid.

Hamlet: New Buildings

New Buildings is a hamlet or village situated near the Foyle, about 3 miles from Londonderry and on the high road from that city to Strabane. This village owes its origin to the incorporation of the Goldsmiths' Company and the erection of their bawn and castle. Both were burned during the revolution of 1688. One of the original cottages still remains, which escaped destruction from its concealment and the lowness of its situation. Many of the houses are badly thatched, and on the whole the hamlet presents a poor appearance. The inhabitants are principally farmers and cottiers. Among them are 1 blacksmith, 1 miller and 4 spirit dealers. The entire population is 75.

Occupations

Table of occupations at the Waterside: public houses 9, spirit dealers and grocers (in conjunction) 6, grocers 4, haberdashers 2, inns 2, lodging houses 2, timber yards 2, distillery 1, coach wheelwright 1, blacksmith 1, baker 1, leather store 1, glueworks 1, shoemaker 1, tailor 1, fruit and cake shop 1, public stabling establishment 1.

Public Buildings: Meeting House

The old Presbyterian meeting house of the Revd William Monteith, situated in the townland of Altnagelvin, was erected in 1696, and enlarged and repaired in 1748. On its southern gable, on a marble tablet about 1 foot square, is the following inscription [drawing]: "MIH, 1696."

Near to this, on a freestone tablet, a little larger and which has been much injured by the weather, is the following inscription [drawing]: "How amiable are thy tabernacles O Lord MS John Avery, 1696." The 2 figures in the left hand bottom corner have been obliterated.

In the east gable, on a slate tablet, is the following inscription: "Revd William Hairs, 1747."

Above the entrance door in the middle of the southern front is the inscription under a sundial: "The gift of Thomas Hogg to the congregation of Glandermot anno domini 1748, William Hair, minister.". This Thomas Hogg was the architect who repaired and enlarged the building.

On the northern gable is also a large inscription on freestone, of the date of the erection of the building. [Insert marginal query: Why not give this inscription?].

In 1833 the seatholders collected 100 pounds for the purposes of putting on a new roof and repairing the interior of the building, which is now in very good order. The masonry appears very substantial. It accommodates 650 people.

Covenanting Meeting House

The Covenanting meeting house is situated near the Faughan bridge, on the road from London-derry to Dungiven, in the townland of Fincarn. It is a small rectangular building capable of accom-modating 300 people. It is now undergoing a thorough repair; a new roof, a new ceiling and a new side wall are built. It was erected in the year 1786 by subscription.

Roman Catholic Chapel

The Roman Catholic chapel, which stands in the townland of [crossed out: Currynierin] is now in bad repair. It was erected in 1791 at the estimated cost of 400 pounds. It will accommodate 560 persons.

Dispensary

During the prevalence of fever in 1817 a dispensary was established. On the abatement of the malady it was discontinued for a few months, and re-estab-lished on a permanent footing, the grand jury grant-ing a sum equal to the amount of private subscrip-tion. In 1831 the house which is now used was built at a cost of about 60 pounds, which sum was raised by the subscription being increased for that year.

The following is a statement [insert alternative: report] for the year 1834 up to the 1st April: patients remaining under care April 1st 1833, 94; recommended since that period 1,558; of the above number were cured 1,333, relieved 158, incurable 9, died 18, remaining under care 134, total number 1,652; number visited by express order at their own houses 129.

The following are the diseases, the most preva-lent being placed first: dyspepsia, cutaneous <cutanious> diseases and pulmonic complaints.

Charitable Institutions: Poor Shop

In 1831 Miss Smyth opened a Poor Shop the object of which is to distribute to indigent persons clothes and bedding, the cost being repaid by weekly instalments of 1d in the shilling. On every Tuesday the shop is opened from 11 to 2 o'clock for receiving payment and to 4 o'clock for giving out clothes. Miss Smyth has lately commenced a system of lending religious books through the parish.

Schools

The schoolhouse which is now called the Glendermot national school was built in 1829 by local subscription and cost 68 pounds. The aver-age attendance is 60 boys and girls, indiscrimi-nately mixed. The addition of 1 room to the present house, to be set apart for the accommoda-tion of the girls, is now in contemplation. In 1832 it became subject to [crossed out: it came under the direction of] the National Board, from which it receives 15 pounds per annum, and books and other school requisites at half price. The hours of attendance are from 10 to 3 o'clock winter and summer. The house stands at the mearing of Ballyshasky and Currynierin, adjoining the Ro-man Catholic chapel.

List of Gentlemen's Seats

1. Prehen, Colonel Knox; 2. St Columb's, G. Hill Esquire; 3. Ashbrook, W. Ash Esquire; 4. Ardmore, J.A. Smyth Esquire; 5. Larchmount, C. McClellan Esquire; 6. Beech Hill, C. Skipton Esquire; 7. Cah, [Blank] Alexander Esquire; 8. Clooney, Revd William Cary; 9. Salem or Foyle View, Mr Hazlitt; 10. Bellevue, Revd Mr Maughan; 11. The Bell, Mrs Thompson; 12. Hollymount, C. Martin Esquire; 13. Ardkill, Mrs Stephenson; 14. Cockhall, Mr Ewing; 15. Culkeeragh, Major Young; 16. Glenkeen, Cap-tain Reynolds; 17. Artnabracky, Mr William Hatrick; [insert marginal query: who lives at Artnabracky?].

Gentlemen's Seats

Prehen is beautifully situated on the eastern side of the Foyle, above the bridge [crossed out: with its old house and demesne]. The plantations, which extend to the water's edge, occupy 1 mile [insert marginal query] of the bank of the river. [Crossed out: The oldest fruit trees in the parish are to be found here and at Beech Hill]. The extensive demesne is ornamented with a number of picturesque trees. The house is very substantial and commodious, and in its rear are a good extensive walled garden and a large orchard.

St Columb's is nearly opposite Derry, on the east bank of the Foyle. Its former name was Chatham but its late proprietor changed it to that of St Columb's, in allusion to a very interesting ruin situated in a beautiful part of the demesne. The dwelling house is a handsome object [crossed out: and spacious, and presents a pleasing view], as seen from several parts of the city of Derry, especially from Shipquay Street. The demesne is extensive and planted with great taste, judicious advantage being taken of the varied lie of the ground. The ornamental grounds are in very good order. [Crossed out: The garden is good and large].

Ashbrook is situated on the southern bank of the Faughan, 2 and a half miles from Londonderry. The house presents a small old-fashioned front but has sufficient [insert alternative: adequate] accommodation in the rear. In niches on the front of the building at each side of the front entrance are displayed the arms of the family. The demesne is embellished with very fine trees and the ornamental grounds about the house are tastefully arranged and kept in good order. [Crossed out: The garden is not very good; it is enclosed by a low wall not well adapted for espalier fruit trees].

Ardmore is situated 3 miles from Derry, on the southern bank of the Faughan, which is low and on a part where the river presents a beautiful appearance. The house is commodious and commands a good prospect but a bleach green encroaches upon the demesne. One of its great ornaments is a deep precipitous ravine, the bed of it a rapid stream. Near to the place in which it empties itself into the Faughan is an interesting ruin in a picturesque situation, known by the name of the Ardmore Altar [insert marginal query: transfer].

Larchmount, the residence of C. McClellan Esquire, is situated close to Ardmore, the demesne of the 2 places having no fence of separation. The house is small, provided in front with a veranda. The garden is good but not walled [insert alternative: unwalled]. There the bleach green encroaches on the grounds.

Beech Hill: this residence, which is also on the southern bank of the Faughan, presents much natural beauty, highly improved by art. A stream runs through a small but deep glen close to the house, shaded by large old trees. This house, which is old and square, is approached by a straight avenue formed by several rows of old lime trees which render it peculiar in this country and very interesting. The ornamental grounds are in the most perfect order. The garden [crossed out: at some distance from the house] is large,

well walled and well furnished with fine fruit trees. Over the gate into the garden is this inscription: "Thomas Skipton Esquire, April 11th 1783."

Bellevue, the residence of the Revd W. Maughan, is near to the Waterside, on the Dungiven road. The house is good but the planting, which is but young, does not possess much beauty.

Bleach Greens, Manufactories and Mills

There is 1 bleach green in Ardmore, a plough manufactory in Lisnagelvin and a spade manufactory in Ardkill. In the latter the machinery is driven by 2 separate wheels turned by the same fall of water; one is for the bellows, the other for the hammer and anvil. The diameter of the larger is 14 feet.

There are 5 corn mills, 1 flour mill, 2 flax mills, 3 bleaching mills and a tuck mill. With but few exceptions the mills have breast wheels.

A mill at New Buildings is worked by an undershot wheel. Another mill is near it, the wheel of which at present is undergoing repair. The wheels are at an average 13 feet in diameter and 20 inches broad.

That of Mr Smyth's corn mill in the townland of Altnagelvin is upwards of 18 feet in diameter. It is remarkable for the excellence of its construction. It is a breast wheel and turned by Glendermot stream, and is dry in summer. The pit or main wheel, which is inside the mill, is 8 feet in diameter. The internal wheels are of metal and are all new. The flakes of the kilns for drying the corn are of sheet iron. This mill works 2 hoppers at a time, hence it is called "double-geared," and it is the only instance of the kind in the parish. The machinery is of the best description.

In the Drumahoe flax mill the revolution of the fly axle is 150 times in a minute.

There is a good brewery at the Faughan bridge, built in 1801, and a distillery and a tannery [crossed out: in the highest part of the village] at the Waterside. The distillery at the Waterside was repaired for the malt distillery in 1834 and distils 4,000 gallons per month. [Insert marginal query: Produce?].

Communications

The mail coach road to Belfast through Newtownlimavady passes through the parish in a north east direction for a distance of 4 miles and is kept in very good repair.

The road from Londonderry to Belfast through Dungiven branches from the Waterside and passes through the parish in a south east direction, and is

3 and half miles in length. Immediately on leaving the Waterside there is a steep ascent, and a steep descent at about a mile from it called the Clondermot hill. The road is kept dry and in very good repair.

[Crossed out: The mail coach roads from Londonderry to Dublin and Belfast branch off from the Waterside and pass through the parish. The former is repaired with limestone from the quarry in Prehen which, however, is of much too soft a nature for the quantity of traffic and soon grinds down.

The roads in the southern part of the parish, including the mail coach road, are seldom in good order. This may be partly attributed to the effect of not sufficiently deepening the ditches on each side, which cause the rain water to lodge on the surface of the road. Many of the crossroads though in the most direct lines are frequently impassable for carriages.

The present line of the mail coach road between Waterside and New Buildings was made about the year 1795. It runs along the shore for 3 miles, not many yards distance from the water's edge.

There is still to be seen in the townland of Clooney an old road remarkable for a tradition which will be mentioned further on.

There is a flat wooden bridge of the simplest form across the River Faughan at the bleach green of Ardmore, which also accommodates the neighbouring gentry who built it for their own convenience. It is 91 feet in length by 21 in width and is 16 feet above the surface of the water.

The coach road from Londonderry to Dungiven crosses the Faughan by an old stone bridge which is still in very good repair.

At Knockbrack there is a ford across the Faughan which is about 2 feet deep in dry weather but it is not passable at all seasons. A stone bridge equal in size to the wooden one at Ardmore would be useful if erected here.

There is apparently no impediment from litigated or other disputes. The parishioners frequently cross at the ford to save themselves the trouble of either going round by the wooden bridge of Lower Cumber or that of Ardmore. The coach road being at the opposite bank renders facility of communication particularly necessary.

A ferry at Culmore forms the principal communication between the northern part of the parish and Inishowen.

The mail coach roads are upwards of 30 feet broad; the other country roads vary from 18 to 30 feet].

General Appearance

[Crossed out: The parish, which is in general well cultivated, is very varied in surface and cheerful in appearance [insert alternative: aspect]. It possesses within itself fine bold objects of nature and, being surrounded with them, is rendered most abundant in everything that can please the eye. From Clondermot hill the 2 large rivers, the Foyle and the Faughan, with their deep and well-wooded valleys, present themselves. The former, which rolls on as it were in maturity [crossed out: in full growth], is seen to lose itself in the broad expanse of Lough Foyle. The latter can be traced to its source amongst the highest mountains in the county. These, with intermediate hills of lesser elevation, offer a succession of outlines of the most pleasing character. The road to Dungiven, which passes up the valley of the Faughan, is enlivened by interesting prospects, though not so extensive, yet rendered as pleasing by nearer views of the well-planted seats on the opposite bank.

The views of Londonderry are particularly fine from Prehen; there this picturesque city, rising out of the water, and the bridge, stretching across the broad smooth river, are seen to great advantage, being backed by the Inishowen mountains, Lough Foyle and Binevenagh, and having for a foreground the fine trees of the demesne].

Presbyterian Meeting House

The Revd Mr Carson's meeting house is in the townland of Altnagelvin and on the same side of the road as the church, at the foot of the hill. It is a plain but substantial building and was erected in 1744, as is shown by a tablet in the east gable, "Rev. I. Holms, 1744." It has been newly roofed and the exterior is in good repair. With the assistance of 2 galleries it accommodates 350 persons, but the seats are out of repair.

Public Buildings

There are 5 places of worship in the parish, the parish church, 3 Presbyterian meeting houses and the Roman Catholic chapel.

The parish church is 1 mile from Londonderry, on the road between that place and Dungiven, at the steep slope on the coast side of Clondermot hill, and from its very elevated position is a conspicuous object in the landscape. It is a plain but substantial building, erected in the year 1753 at a cost of 500 pounds and will accommodate 330 persons. The tower was added in 1789 and cost

280 pounds. A spire of wood covered with copper was put up in 1794 but was blown down by a storm in November 1831. The inside of the church is well supplied with commodious pews, and it is in contemplation to build a gallery.

Draft Memoir by J. Stokes, with corrections by G. Downes

MODERN TOPOGRAPHY AND SOCIAL ECONOMY

Towns

New Buildings is a hamlet or village situated near the Foyle, about 3 miles from Londonderry and on the high road from that city to Strabane. It consists merely of a single street of 37 thatched houses. [Crossed out: It is on a picturesque situation for a town and is not far from the edge of the Foyle, whose glittering expanse, however, is seldom interrupted by a sail].

This village owes its origin to the incorporation of the Goldsmiths' Company and the erection of their bawn or castle. Both were burnt at or about the period of the wars of James II. One house still remains, which escaped destruction from its concealment and the loneliness of its situation. Many of the present houses have old green and mossy thatch, and some are provided with chimneys of open wickerwork. Among the inhabitants are a blacksmith, a miller and 4 spirit dealers; the remainder are cottiers and agriculturists. There appears to be a new house building. There are, however, 2 ruined ones. The population is 75.

Barracks is another and a smaller hamlet, in the townland of Prehen. It is merely a cluster of insignificant cabins. (Clachans are very frequent in the neighbourhood of Fincairn glen).

Public Buildings

There are 5 different houses of worship in the parish, the Protestant church, 3 [Dissenting?] meeting houses and the Roman Catholic chapel. Of the meeting houses, 2 are Presbyterian and 1 Covenanting.

The church, which stands in the townland of Altnagelvin, was erected at a cost of 500 pounds. The steeple was built in 1789 at a cost of 280 pounds. A spire of wood covered with [copper?] was put up in 1794 but was blown down by a [storm?] in November 1831. It is a plain ugly building and is too small for the congregation.

The old Presbyterian meeting house, the Revd Mr Monteith's, was erected in 1696 and enlarged and repaired in 1748. It is situated in the townland of Altnagelvin. Upon the wall is a sundial, the gift of the original builder.

The Roman Catholic chapel, which stands at the mearing of Ballyshasky and Currynierin, was erected in 1791 at the estimated cost of 400 pounds.

The reservoir which supplies the city with water is in the townland of Corrody, and runs through pipes to a second and smaller one in Clooney immediately above the Waterside, from whence it is conveyed in pipes across the bridge to the inhabitants. The cost of conveying the supply, which was 16,000 pounds, was met by a loan from government not yet repaid.

Presbyterians

In 1744 there was a schism in the Presbyterian congregation. Mr Hare the pastor could not, consistently with the rules of the Kirk of Scotland, comply with some new regulations which the elders had attempted to force on him. In consequence of this non-compliance, the elders divided

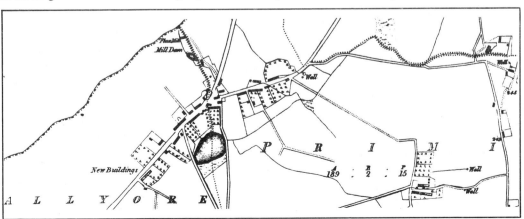

Map of New Buildings from the first 6" O.S. maps, 1830s

and raised a fund sufficient for the erection of a new house of worship. They also formed a second congregation and called the Revd John Holmes to the pastoral charge.

Mr Monteith, the present minister of the old Presbyterian congregation, receives annually 80 pounds stipend and 100 pounds regium donum. In consequence of the latter emolument, he is also styled a first-rate minister. The former arises chiefly from seat rents, which are thus classed: first class of seats for gentlemen 1 pound 10s; second for farmers 1 pound; third class for artisans and cottiers 15s. There are other emoluments also, such as fees arising from marriages, christenings. The clergy of all denominations frequently receive payment in fowl, butter, corn and the labour of men or horses.

[Crossed out: This minister is unpopular. He is what is called a first-rate minister, or one of the class entitled to 100 pounds of regium donum, and he is also entitled the senior pastor of the Presbyterian congregation of Clondermot, Mr Carson being the junior pastor. No difference exists between the 2 congregations further than a few trifling regulations which formed the subject of contention in 1744].

Mr Carson, minister of the Presbyterian congregation, receives annually 70 pounds stipend and 80 pounds of regium donum or royal bounty. He enjoys other perquisites as regulated by the elders, who not only rule the income but govern the clergyman also.

Mr Sweeny, minister of the Covenanting congregation, receives the same amount of stipend but no regium donum. Ministers of this class are in consequence more liberally dealt with by the hearers, who contribute in many cases to make them comfortable.

The Seceding or Methodist congregation pay donations to the city clergymen. There are no resident pastors of the Seceding or Methodist congregation.

Roman Catholics

A new Roman Catholic chapel at Waterside is in contemplation. Subscriptions towards its erection are collecting by the priest in England and Scotland. Before the erection of the chapel in Ballyshasky the Roman Catholic congregation attended divine service in the townland of Ardmore and in Fincairn glen, in situations admirably adapted for concealment during the time of the Penal Laws.

The Ardmore Altar, as it is called, which is adjacent to Mr Smyth's house, stands in the depths of a thick wood, on a green platform about 20 feet in length and on the brink of a fearful precipice overhanging the Faughan. The altar, on which mass was celebrated, is a wall about 8 feet long with a projecting table of loose stones and 2 flags forming steps; above it is a birch tree.

The Fincairn Altar is an accidental stone which the priest elected as being well adapted for his purpose.

SOCIAL ECONOMY

Income of the Clergy

The income of the parish priest is properly at the discretion of the laity, but the following are the parochial rules. Every head of a family pays annually in the following proportion: gentlemen 1 pound, farmers 10s, artisans 5s, cottiers and servants 2s 6d. In addition to the above, they receive fees for marriages, christenings, funeral services etc. The several remunerations are thus regulated: marriage of a gentleman, farmer or grazier 1 pound 10s; marriage of a tradesman, cottier or servant 16s; christenings for the rich 10s; christenings for the poor 2s 6d; station, office etc. 5s; funeral service 5s.

The above are cheerfully paid, the stipends reluctantly and in many cases not paid at all, especially by the lower classes. The richer farmers give seed-oats to the clergy, a barrel or half-barrel annually, the poorer, butter, yarn, eggs, fowl etc.

Habits of the People: Houses

The houses of the lower, or Lough Enagh, part of the parish are not unusually wretched. Some of them indeed are slated and otherwise comfortable. The houses of the upper, or Warbleshinny, part, although they cannot all be termed hovels, have a crazy and old appearance. The thatch is generally black and slimy, and the walls rickety and unplastered, as if many years had elapsed since their erection. Farmhouses are occasionally seen showing traces of better days and exhibiting a painful contrast in the dilapidation of the once large and ornamental window, the neglected state of the roof, the total ruin of any little architectural ornament and the dirty unwhitewashed state of the walls. Such circumstances appear to evince increasing poverty in these particular instances.

Houses are sometimes to be seen with wattled chimneys encased with clay and the triangular part of the gable end built of turf sods. There are no houses actually of mud, the parish being in general hilly and abounding with stone. More than 1 storey is unusual, except in the village of Waterside. A kind of loft is frequent and is used as a receptacle for firing and timber.

Comfort

[Crossed out: For the degree of comfort enjoyed by the parishioners not much can be said, as it exists in all the grades from the luxurious bed of down to the primitive shakedown of straw. However, even beggars will endeavour to be luxurious on tea and a pipe of tobacco <tobbaco>, and can be comfortable in their own way. It may be said that part of that quality consists in the capacity of being pleased].

Comfort exists in various gradations and cleanliness is not unattended to. A mixture of meal and water is frequently employed in place of soap, and in some cases with much effect.

Food

The small tradesmen and artisans of Waterside hold stirabout in some contempt and are much more addicted to tea drinking than the rest of the parishioners. A disregard of economy seems in many instances to increase with poverty. Throughout the parish, however, stirabout forms the principal dish most parts of the year. It is chiefly eaten in seasons when potatoes are not plentiful. It is found in the huckster's shops of Waterside that the chief run upon meal is from the 1st of May to the 1st of September. When at meal-times there happens to be a short allowance of milk, the addition of a new-laid egg the head of the family and those who labour always enjoy the best, the women and the useless hands being allotted the simple dry potatoes which, however, they endeavour to render palatable by crisping [crossed out: roasting and carbonizing] it in the ashes.

The poorer farmers generally endeavour to drink tea on stated holidays, such as Christmas Day and Easter Sunday. Temperance has increased in the parish. The habit of whiskey drinking has been diminished partly by the want of money, which arises in a great measure from the decline of the linen trade, and partly by 2 temperance societies, one in the neighbourhood of the church, the other near New Buildings.

Begging

The beggars who attend at the helping days of Waterside are universally in the habit of spending their alms at the neighbouring grocer's shops on tea, sugar, snuff, tobacco, spirits and soap. In the mountainous parts of the parish they use a miserable substitute for milk, namely a liquid called "sowen shirings," which is made from a refuse meal called "tail-meal" which is soaked in water and strained through a sieve. When a female beggar goes out to look for alms, if the first person she meets be tall, or in any other way a pleasing sample of humanity, she will consider it a favourable omen and say "Good luck to your foot."

Fuel and Dress

In a few years turf will be very scarce indeed. Although a considerable portion is still cut in Lisdillon, a large number of the parishioners are at present obliged to resort to the parishes of Donaghedy (in the county Tyrone) and Cumber, a distance of from 4 to 7 miles, and pay at the rate of 12 pounds an acre for bog. English and Scotch coal also are used, which are procured from Londonderry.

The poorer class purchase the principal part of their apparel from pawnbrokers and vendors of old clothes, with the exception of shoes and linen. In many cases the farmers manufacture the clothing of themselves and families, such as frieze, linen, hosiery and stuffs. The clothes of the abject poor are frequently so patched that every trace of the original stuff has been obliterated.

Linen trousers of the coarsest kind, with the Scotch lowland cap, are frequently to be seen upon the men. The complete equipment of a female, including every article of dress, will cost about 1 pound 3s and continue decent for only 1 year. By repeated patching and darning, however, its duration may be extended to 2. This suit is supposed to have been bought at the shops. Being cheap the stuffs are bad, and here the utility of the Altnagelvin Poor Shop becomes apparent.

Longevity and Marriage

The longevity of Clondermot is much inferior to that of Faughanvale. 2 or 3 only are said to be above 95 and allowance must be made for the usual uncertainties of such a statement.

No remarkable instances of early marriages have been found, except in Ardmore where several years ago a male aged only 15 was united to a female [crossed out: Miss Magill] aged only 14 years. Marriages are commonly contracted in this parish between the ages of 16 and 20, and if the female happens to pass the latter she is counted an old maid and perhaps allowed to remain so for life.

Poor

It may be nearly said that every cottier is more or less a pauper. There are but few individuals who subsist wholly on begging. The season at which almost all go abroad for alms is before the coming in of the potato crop. Of the cottier class, there are 480 families. [Crossed out: Many travelling beggars from distant parishes come into Clondermot to avail themselves of the periodical distribution of alms. These, as they pass through, frequently endeavour to commit a forgery on the Poor Shop]. The neighbourhood of Lough Enagh is the richest and that of Warbleshinny is the poorest in the parish.

[Crossed out: Widow Welsh of Warbleshinny, said to be the granddaughter of a Mr Carroll of Sligo, is supported by the charity of a cottier who is nearly as worthy of charity as herself. She is unable to walk and is an object of commiseration to the inhabitants].

Money Club

At McShane's in Waterside there is a money club of an older date than that held at McCann's. It may therefore be considered as a parochial society for mutual assistance. There are 40 members, which is the limit. Someone of the 40 draws 3 pounds every Saturday night for 40 weeks. The drawing then ceases and the lodgements begin, which consist in each case of a weekly saving of 1s 7d ha'penny, 1d ha'penny of which are drunk as a remuneration for the use of the clubroom. If the person who wins the money ticket is not in want of the cash, he sells it for a small sum to another, who gives security for repayment. It is obtained by a sort of lottery and the tickets are shaken under the bottom of an old candlestick. Some alteration of the rules is very desirable.

Religion

The Protestants, Presbyterians (including Dissenters of other denominations) and Roman Catholics are to one another as the numbers 1, 5 and 9, but the Protestant congregation is increasing. There are 5 congregations provided with houses of worship and 2 unprovided. The former have the church, the chapel and 3 meeting houses. The latter, the Seceding and Methodist congregations, are obliged to attend divine service in the city, as their number is too small for the creation of a fund to erect houses of worship in their own parish. They sometimes attend service in the open air and frequently hold prayer meetings in private houses.

[In a different hand] This parish is one of the five which are attached to the deanery of Derry and is served by a curate who receives 100 pounds a year late Irish currency, of which 75 pounds is paid by the dean and 26 pounds 6d as an augmentation by the Board of First Fruits. There is a glebe house attached to the cure, distant about an English mile from the church. The house was purchased by a grant from the Board of First Fruits about 4 years

ago. There is a glebe of 20 acres profitable, which produces 30 pounds, the average value being 1 pound 10s an acre, subject to a rent of 20 pounds a year payable to the bishop. There are also [blank] of glebe belonging to the deanery.

The amount of tithes is computed at 926 pounds 16s 1d; the articles titheable are corn, hay and potatoes. However, the parish being under composition, the amount annually received varies according to the facility of recovering debts and the prices of titheable produce, but always falls, as is observed, considerably short of the sum stated above. The separation of this parish from the deanery, on the next avoidance, is recommended by His Majesty's Commissioners, when the perpetual curate shall become ipso facto rector and the perpetual curacy be abolished.

Draft Memoir by J. Stokes, with corrections by G. Downes

SOCIAL ECONOMY

Education

[Insert note by Downes: Some of the schoolmasters have a strong desire for assistance from the National Board of Education, although they do not openly express it]. As usual the number of children and the proportion of males and females at different seasons of the year fluctuate exceedingly. The desire for education is strong, but it is uncertain whether increased morality has been the consequence. So strong is that desire that a female beggar kept her children at school for a short time after the death of her husband.

Poor: Bequests

By the will of Colonel Mitchelburne (whose tomb is in a discreditable state of dilapidation) the sum of 86 pounds was allotted to be raised and given to the corporation of Londonderry, at 6 per cent interest. This was to be distributed at the rate of 3d a week to 8 poor persons in the townland of Clooney, who had nothing else but charity to support them. The interest, amounting to 5 pounds 4s, continues to be paid annually. He also bequeathed 4 pounds annually forever to a schoolmaster, for teaching any number of children of the Church of England establishment. This was to be paid from the interest of 67 pounds which was placed in the hands of the corporation; it has, however, lapsed; and he further directed that 1s annually should be given off his tombstone to 30 poor persons, to be paid from the interest of 25 pounds; this also has lapsed.

Lastly he bequeathed 146 pounds to 16 poor people of the Church of England, each to receive from the interest half a peck of meal during his life by weekly distribution. The meal was ground at a neighbouring mill, but as soon as the lease expired the charity was allowed to lapse, on the plea that it had formed part of the engagement of the lease.

Notwithstanding the liberality of these bequests, his own private desire that he should be buried at the church of Enagh was not complied with.

The interest of Colonel Mitchelburne's legacies continued to be paid by the trustee up to the year 1802, when he discovered that other parts of the same property were liable to it, which were then in the possession of Mrs Sam Moore and Sir Robert Ferguson Bart. He therefore refused to pay any longer, unless jointly with them. The parish raised a sum to defray the minister's expenses, who had been deputed to journey to Dublin and institute proceedings. On the road he met the late bishop, who desired him to return to his parish and stated that he would have the matter investigated. Nothing further was, however, done until Mr C. Beresford was elected churchwarden, when upon his memorialing the Board of Charitable Bequests the solicitor wrote to Sir Robert Ferguson and Mrs Moore. Mrs Moore died and Sir Robert immediately declared that he was ready to pay his share. However, the matter was a second time dropped and the bequest is considered to have lapsed.

On every Good Friday the meal was distributed in the open air in the yard of the old church of Clondermot, from a heap deposited on the tomb of Colonel Mitchelburne. A short time before the distribution ceased it is said to have been given out in Waterside. Alderman Tomkins also left 50 pounds to be distributed among the poor.

Poor Shops

However, although the older endowments have with one exception ceased, several have sprung up in their place. Of these, the most beneficial is the poor shop of Altnagelvin, which is held in the vestry room of the Presbyterian meeting house at stated intervals.

It was instituted in 1822. The funds were very small at the commencement but were assisted by the ladies of the London and Irish Society, and attended by a subscription of 50 pounds 19s. In the first year goods were sold at reduced prices, to the

amount of 232 pounds 17s 4d. The regulations are good and the accounts kept in a business-like manner. Not more than 15s worth is given at a time and this on the recommendation of a respectable farmer. It is repaid in small weekly instalments.

However, there are not wanting individuals among the parishioners who impose on these ladies by forged letters of recommendation. These are frequently strangers passing through the parish, but very frequently too such delinquents are found among the parishioners, and they avail themselves of the natural reluctance of the sex to institute legal proceedings.

This institution owes its origin entirely to the benevolence of one individual, who will be gratified to learn that her exertions appeared to have been received with gratitude.

The institution of poor shops, especially that of Clondermot, has given to the lower orders an advantage which is in fact equal to a temporary increase in income. The poorest individuals are found to pay the most punctually. The higher orders, to avoid the annoyance of beggars coming to their doors, contribute largely to the poor by sending money to their respective ministers, by whom it is put into the poor box on Sundays and sent equally to the Waterside and Clondermot. Here it is distributed on Mondays and Thursdays by a certain number of inhabitants in rotation. There are generally more than 100 in attendance, who receive either 2 or 3 ha'pence each.

The following are some of the individuals who contribute: Sir Robert Ferguson, George Hill Esquire, Captain Plunkett, Lieutenant Adams, C.H. Ash Esquire, Pitt Skipton Esquire, J.A. Smythe Esquire, J. Smythe, farmer, Cary McClellan Esquire, Revd Mr Cary, parish curate, Revd Mr Carson, Presbyterian pastor, Revd Mr Monteith, Presbyterian pastor, Revd Mr Sweeny, Covenanting pastor, Revd Mr Carron, parish priest, Captain Lindsay, Patrick Mehan, Mrs Maughan, [blank] Boyle Esquire, [blank] Babington Esquire, [blank] Blacker Esquire, [blank] Bond Esquire.

Poor Loan Fund

There is also a poor loan fund subscribed to by the gentry, which lends to each applicant 2 pounds free of interest and on approved security, to be repaid by instalments of 1s a week.

The fund was established in 1830 and is subscribed to by the landholders of the parish. It is conducted by the curate and the meetings take place once a month at the Poor Shop in Altnagelvin.

This Poor Shop is in fact the vestry room of the adjoining meeting house. The loans sometimes consist of spinning wheels and looms, the prices of which are repaid in the same manner.

Much money is expended in alms by the families on the southern bank of the Faughan. From these, and in particular from that of J.A. Smythe Esquire, the paupers derive their principal support.

Paupers

There are 540 paupers who receive alms, partly in kind and partly in money. That given in kind consists of milk, meat and soups, tobacco, salt, soap, eggs and vegetables and old clothes. A number of these paupers are called *decent beggars*, which class comprises all those who have been reduced to that state by invisible causes, such as lapses in trade, diminution of business, the death of husbands or fathers etc. Nearly all the female beggars have become so by their husbands' deaths. In every cottier family, if the father die before the mother and before the children have reached a mature age, all must beg, as all had previously depended wholly on the labour of the deceased. The fevers which have at times visited the parish have thus greatly contributed to increase the number of paupers. Saving is a thing unthought of.

The male paupers are those who had been comfortable cottiers, artisans or weavers. Those who are of the class called *decent* generally follow the occupation of thatching or any other which they may casually acquire. Those who are beggars by misfortune do not, like the others, after receiving their alms on the helping days of the week, beg at large through the parish, but employ themselves about their little huts, the females in spinning, sewing, knitting, weeding and nursing for farmers' families, the males in herding, gardening, cleaning and weeding. By their anxiety for employment and their industry when employed they secure the sympathy of the farmers, and earn the appellation of "decent," to distinguish them from the sturdy travelling beggar.

The prostitutes of the parish are included among the beggars of the latter description.

The mendicants in general possess small hovels, for which they pay a trifling rent, either in money or in kind, and into which they retreat at night. Very frequently, however, they receive lodging for charity. They are prevented by the city regulations from begging in the parish of Templemore or city of Londonderry, although the poor of that parish and city are not only at liberty to come into the parish of Clondermot but are served by the parishioners indiscriminately with their own poor, as well as beggars from more distant parishes. The tolls of the bridge, however, act as a considerable check to this intercourse.

State of the Poor

To illustrate the state of the poor and to explain the various causes of pauperism, it will be useful to detail the various steps through which the youngest son of a farmer descends until he leaves his offspring in the lowest grade of beggars.

Being the youngest son, he is not an object of the exertions generally made for the sake of the older. Thus he is provided for in the cheapest mode, namely by being furnished with a little stock, with which he proceeds to rent a small patch of ground from some farmer. Here he employs himself in the usual cottier employment of labouring for superior farmers, while his wife works at her spinning wheel. Employment soon becomes scarce: the farmers, for want of capital, hire fewer labourers; he thus becomes idle and his resources fail.

Presently he is ejected for non-payment of rent, for the small farmer is unavoidably merciless in this respect. He then takes another cabin, begs and follows the occupation of a thatcher. If his wife dies about this time he marries again! If not, she spins, sells fowl and begs, while he, if possible, emigrates to reap the harvest in England or Scotland. However, his means of support become more and more contracted.

About this time the father either dies by an accident or a fever, or becomes infirm from hard work, upon which the whole family descend from the rank of decent beggars, among whom, however, more real distress exists than among any other class, to follow more systematically the practice of "looking for their meat." The widow is called the "desolate creature" and the children grow up to become male and female beggars. What now occurs is difficult to be ascertained, but generally speaking, a beggar, though he *is* a beggar, has been often the cause of multiplying pauperism a hundredfold by his increased propensity for marriage.

Remarkable Events and Traditions

"Rooks" is a common name for Presbyterians from their being habitually dressed in black.

Phelimy Ruadh is well known in this parish, but they say "he did not come into these parts."

There is a tradition about a bargain between the first of the Skiptons and O'Cathan, which is precisely the same as one that exists near Kilrea.

Funeral cries were formerly practised among the Warbleshinny Catholics but they are now extinct.

Foundlings are frequently adopted and brought up on the payment of 10 pounds by the parish. The number is diminishing and 2 only are at present supported exclusively by the parish.

Emigration

It is confidently believed that at least 350 persons of both sexes emigrated across the Atlantic in 1833 from the parish. One-half of the gross number were Catholics, the other Protestants and Presbyterians in equal numbers. Emigration has continued for a long series of years and consequently is at present not so much as in some of the more upland parishes. For 1834 it is not more than usual. It is always sufficient to prevent in a great degree the increase of the population. The number of Catholic emigrants is increasing.

The favourite season for emigration to America is from March to June. This arrangement is preferred because it allows an opportunity of disposing of property in the preceding winter months and also because it secures an arrival early in the year, which tends very much to success in procuring employment and in making the preparations necessary for settlers.

In most cases from 1 to 3 of the youngest, stoutest and healthiest of the family, no matter of which sex, go in one year and send for the older members the following season, if they have succeeded.

In 1836 numbers were obliged to return home for want of accommodation. Two-thirds had the expense of their passage defrayed by individuals who had gone before them. The majority took their passage for the Canadas. The demand for berths was so great that they raised the charge by 10s for each individual. Some advance occurs towards the end of every season.

It is worthy of remark that the emigration of Clondermot is chiefly from the lower and most fertile part. Very little occurs on the Ponsonby estate, in comparison to what occurs elsewhere. The feeling which has induced the parishioners to emigrate is not that of political irritation but principally a wish to better their condition, combined with the absence of encouragement on the part of their landlords. Affection also induces many to follow their departed relations. To these causes may be added the decrease in capital, for although there is more existing in the parish than there was 15 years ago, that is probably less than there was 4 years ago.

Remarks on Emigration

There is not a single individual among the lower orders of the parish who has not a relation on the other side of the Atlantic, and there are very few who would not go if they had the means. Those who emigrate are always among the most valuable members of the community. A great number of weavers are annually deserting the country. More capital is carried off by each emigrant now than formerly, but it is difficult to ascertain the precise amount.

The latest accounts from America are not very encouraging. The landing places there seem to have been overstocked. Letters have arrived which intimate that as soon as the writers have earned their passage-money they will return home, and in which they entreat their relations not to venture over at least for the present. Other letters are, however, of a contrary tendency and contain in addition strong encouragement for future settlers.

[Crossed out: Some such letters have occurred, but whether generally or only partially has not been ascertained. If the parishioners went out independently and uninfluenced by letters, the emigration would never have arisen to such a great height as to excite the astonishment of individuals who do not understand its cause. That cause has naturally a multiplying tendency. It is the hope of an improvement in condition combined with a sympathy for relations].

Those who had gone before offer to pay for those who come after them and who again play the same part towards others; and the inclination thus excited is only checked by the want of money to lay in sea-store, by the consideration of the time which had elapsed before any improvement took place in the condition of those who went before and by the necessity of devising what should be done on gaining the American shore.

Notes on Productive Economy by J. Stokes and Another

PRODUCTIVE ECONOMY

Commercial

The most thriving branch of productive economy is the export of butter and eggs. Of the latter, 25 ton are sent weekly to the Liverpool and Greenock markets. These, however, are not all laid in this parish; see parish of Templemore. No fewer than 40 men and women earn a good livelihood collecting eggs and selling them at market prices.

Hand-spinning is universal, but weavers were formerly more numerous than they are at present. A spinner can scarcely earn with all her industry more than 1s a week, a weaver scarcely more than 4s 6d. The finest webs are what are called thirteen hundred linens. They are made from this denomination down to seven hundred, which are of a coarse quality and generally used by the poor or for wrapping bales of goods. These numbers are apparently expressions of the quantity of threads in a given space.

Tow is sold for 3d ha'penny a pound. The profit of weaving 103 yards of seven hundred and eight hundred linen is 13s in 3 weeks, or 4s 4d a week. Of the same web they can weave 7 yards a day but of a twelve hundred or thirteen hundred only 3.

There is a warping machine in the townland of Clooney, in that of Altnagelvin, and several others elsewhere. Their number is increasing. W. McCarter's tanyard is situated on the top of Waterside hill. He has a wheel for grinding bark, which is extensively imported. In Altnagelvin corn mill 500 tons of corn and barley have been ground in the last 12 months for the distillery in William Street, Londonderry. A spinning mill near Ardkill is in contemplation, the expense of erecting which has been estimated at 40,000 pounds. This will give a strong impulse to the productive economy.

Bleach Green

In the townland of Ardmore is the bleach green of McClelland and Company. The linens chiefly belong to the proprietors and are purchased at the different markets in Tyrone and Londonderry. At Fintona and Omagh seven-eighths wide at from 6d to 12d per yard; at Strabane and Newtownstewart (a little finer) from 8d to 15d; at Derry 1s to 1s 2d; Coleraine and Ballymoney 1s 2d to 3s 6d.

Formerly great quantities of yard-wide linens were got from Armagh, Belfast, Lisburn and Banbridge; five-fourths coarse sheeting from Cootehill, coarse seven-eighths from Ballina and Sligo; but for the last 2 years, owing to the falling-off in the trade, scarcely any have [been] purchased at these places.

About 500,000 yards of linen are annually bleached at this green. In addition to this, during the year 1830, 200,000 square yards of calico, varying in breadth from 30 to 60 inches, have been bleached for a manufacturing company at Glasgow. The proprietors of the green are paid 1d per yard and pay the carriage to and from Glasgow.

The number of persons employed is 48 men and 12 boys. The daily wages of the men is 9d; boys under 16 are paid from 7s to 14s a month.

There are 2 beetling machines, 4 wash mills and 5 soaping machines; for driving these there are 4 water wheels averaging 5 horsepower. The business of the green at present compared with the 2 preceding years is considerably on [manuscript torn]; has been seldom worked to the [full?] [remainder illegible].

Spade Mill

The Ardkill spade mill had been working since 1813. Up to 1821 it was the only spade manufactory within 35 miles round. It produces annually 500 dozen of spades, which are sold at from 1s 4d to 1s 12d a dozen. There are 8 men employed and the spades are made to order.

The Union duty on spades (a measure of the Act of Union intended to protect Irish manufacture from English competition) should have expired in 1820 but was allowed to stand until 1822. The amount was 10 per cent nominally upon invoice, but in the way in which it was levied it operated as a duty of 12 and a half per cent. An act was passed for its gradual reduction by taking off 2 per cent in the first 2 years, 2 and a half in the next 2, and in another 2 to abolish it altogether. Immediately after the passing of this act it was repealed and the duty was abolished from a certain day. This operated as a full reduction of 10 per cent on profits, which were still further reduced by an influx of English spades upon the Irish market.

However, there is in almost every parish a variation in the form of the spades. Different soils require different forms: for instance mountain soils require the long, good soils the broad spade, and these pass into each other by imperceptible gradations. An Irish spademaker has perhaps 20 different patterns of spades and knows the different places in which he can find vent for them. These local necessities will hinder the manufacture from becoming extinct and will probably at last restore it to its former prosperity.

In the plough manufactory of Lisnagelvin belonging to J. Lindsay there are annually manufactured 35 carts, 30 ploughs, wooden and iron, 10 winnowing machines and 8 pair of angled harrows.

Memoir on Habits of the People by Captain J.E. Portlock

SOCIAL ECONOMY

General Remarks

In considering a subject of such great importance, inasmuch as it exhibits the results and brings home to the understanding the workings of the whole social system, it is necessary to bear in mind that all parts of that system mutually act and react upon each other. It is in this manner that a moral, frugal and intelligent gentry produce by example, frequent inspection and occasional intercourse an effect on the poorer neighbours and tenants calculated to elevate their character and improve their condition; whilst the contemplation of reckless extravagance and dissipation in the higher will as assuredly produce corrupt and idle habits in the lower classes of society.

Of the advantages flowing from the more favourable state of these relations, the inhabitants of a large portion of this parish are partakers in a high degree, as there are many highly respectable gentlemen resident amongst them; and if over some of these the frugal and business-like habits of commercial life have exercised an influence the effect has assuredly been a beneficial one. It may be added that the renewed occupation of Prehen is likely soon to extend still further these advantages.

Houses

The external appearance of the habitations of the peasantry is in general simple and humble. In the eastern portion of the parish, particularly in the vicinity of Enagh lough, there are several neat and comfortable cottages, and there are many others combined occasionally with more substantial farmhouses in the lower parts of the vale of Glendermot and in the many little rural villages which are scattered through the parish. Some have even been recently erected near the summit of Warbleshinny which, though small, are neat, whitewashed and well thatched.

The ruins of a house abandoned in consequence of the union of two small in one larger farm, the sinking of a roof partly from the defective materials of which it was originally constructed and partly from the weight of the sods or scraws which underlie the thatch, and the mouldering state of some of the roofs due in part to the thin and meagre straw of mountain corn, or to its partial destruction in the rude operation of threshing on the roadside or on the dirty outhouse floor, an evil consequent on the want of barns or to its use in eking out a scanty supply of fodder for the cows, are blots on the landscape which an improved system of agriculture would speedily obliterate.

In internal accommodation there is yet ample room for improvement, for though in the houses of the small farmers the rooms are separated, in those of the poor cottier one contains everything, the bed of the young couple being planted perhaps close to the fireside and supported by the rudest framework, whilst those required by the family as it increases are crammed together in some other corner, being separated by what may be called wooden curtains, a state of things inconsistent with proper delicacy or cleanliness.

The mud floor is also a serious evil but if its abandonment does not precede, it will in all probability follow, the growing taste for good clothes which is spreading amongst the rural belles, finery and filth being mutually inconvenient. With all these drawbacks the inside of a cottage in this parish is not devoid of comfort, and poor indeed must it be if not provided with the simple luxury of a dresser stocked with articles of plain but useful earthenware.

Food

In foods the small farmers are well supplied, adding to the universal potato, butter and herrings and occasionally, though rarely, bacon. The cottier, from the inadequacy of his little patch of ground to supply potatoes for the whole year, is obliged to make up the deficiency by purchasing meal and sanctioned by (here the mill-tail mixture which, however, I must enquire into). A better management of even that little ground and the introduction of useful vegetables, instead of a handful of corn, might avoid much of this distressing inconvenience.

Physical Appearance

In personal appearance and manner the union of northern steadiness with the cheerfulness of the Irish has produced a mixture far from unpleasing, and those who witness the females coming into market at Derry must feel that they exhibit far more delicacy of person than of rustic coarseness. If the spinning factories have lessened the profits of home spinning they have increased those of the farmer, and amusement still combines with ancient habit to keep the wheel in motion whose hum adds to the harmony which a cheerful fire contributes to spread over the simple inhabitants of a rude but often happy habitation.

Extracts from Draft Memoir on Social
Economy by G. Downes, J. Stokes and
Others

SOCIAL ECONOMY

Legends and Superstitions

The superstitions of the parish are not, however,
confined to legends. If business fails, recourse is
had to some preternatural observances. The first
step is to search about the hob for crickets, to
which, if found, the evil is attributed. The harm-
less insects are then usually scalded to death, after
which the hob and fire are removed to the other
end of the room, at whatever expense or inconvenience. Should this prove insufficient, one of
the room doors is altered. Application to a cunning woman is the last resort.

When the marriage bed seems likely to prove
unfruitful, application is similarly made to a cunning woman, without consideration of the expense or the distance of her abode. The first
preliminary is a tender of gold or silver, this being
indispensable for eliciting the magic spell. After
some further formalities, the applicants are gravely
advised to remove their bed to another part of the
house, to repeat so many prayers, to use meagre
diet, to avoid groomsmen and bridesmaids etc.
These imposters are well rewarded.

So prone indeed are the people to superstition
that they believe themselves honoured, not only
by the residence of cunning women among them,
but even of *reputed witches*.

In the neighbourhood of the parish church it is
the general opinion that the high wind which in
1831 blew down the spire was caused by the
illness and death of Bell Miller, an old woman of
Ardlough, for, say they, "the moment she expired, the wind ceased to blow." She was believed
to have the power of transforming herself into any
shape, and her neighbours would sooner forfeit a
sum of money than incur her displeasure, being
persuaded that she had similar power over themselves and their cattle.

It is believed that if a mare have foaled in a
roofed house, the foal when led to drink will
always advance so far into the water as to expose
his conductor to imminent danger and also lie
down if not well watched. To prevent such mis-
haps, the owners of brood mares always keep
them in the open air about the time of foaling, at
night as well as by day.

On first hearing the cuckoo in the early part of
May, the peasant immediately examines under

the right foot, where he is sure to find a hair, either
on the ground or attached to his person. The
colour of this hair decides that of his fate for the
current year. If it be white he anticipates success
in all his undertakings; if black, the reverse; if it
point towards the ground his death is certain; if
towards one of the cardinal points, he is sure of
spending a part of the year in that quarter.

The above and probably other degrading superstitions, which appear to be equally prevalent
among all religious persuasions, occasion the
expenditure of considerable sums on that which
yields no return. There is an absurd tradition at
variance with historical fact about a bargain concluded between the first of the Skiptons and an
O'Cathan; it is precisely the same as one that
exists near Kilrea respecting the O'Cathans and
the Cannings.

[Insert query by Downes: Whether any
scapulars or St John's are sold has not been
ascertained with certainty].

So much for the superstitions of Clondermot.
As may well be supposed there are probably
many still kept in secrecy. When the parishioners
complain of rents being high they ought also to
wish that superstitions were low.

Traditions concerning Monuments

Probably the rock in the Fincairn glen called the
Bell Crag is connected in its name with the witch
Bell Miller. The Scoto-Irish settlers of that neighbourhood do not seem to know anything at all about
it. Equally unable are they to explain the origin of
the name Janet lough, which is applied to a spring
at the head of the glen, and most probably refers to
some other witch. The Nob's Hole was probably the
scene of some enchanted catastrophe.

In the month of May 1834, say the parishioners,
a dame came from foreign parts to see the grave in
Glenderowen. On enquiring at the place it was
found that a man dressed like a sailor had actually
come, who gave his name as Lynch. The people did
not appear to think that the circumstance required
any scrutiny whatever, but may he not have been a
treasure dreamer like themselves? A visit of the
same kind, it seems, took place at Rosnagalliagh,
and they will tell how a foreigner once came and
silently contemplated the ruins of that church.

The tradition has there [been] handed down
from father to son that the departed souls of the
nuns of Rosnagalliagh are prayed for at Rome in
some kind of psalter adapted to the subject. This
is perhaps true, for may not the poor nuns, notwithstanding their Sentry hill, have been inhu-

manly slaughtered in one of the many military expeditions that have ravaged this country? Their tragical fate may have thus excited commiseration and produced the service alluded to, and perhaps the visit. The ruin of the building and the dismantling of the church may have taken place at the same time.

Ownership of Parish

At the Plantation of Ulster a portion of this parish became property of the Grocers' Company, but the greater part was included in the proportion of the Goldsmiths which was sold in 1730 to the Earl of Shelburne for 14,000 pounds. The proportion is now the property of Lady Ponsonby. One townland, Lisdillon, and one-half quarter were given as a native freehold to Bryan O'Kane, but forfeited in 1641. There were also 6 Crown freeholds made, all of which have subsequently passed, by purchase, from the families of the original lessees.

[Crossed out: "The attention and capital of a landlord should be bestowed upon those permanent improvements which, in their execution, withdraw too large a portion of the tenant's capital from the cultivation of his land, and which, from their extent, benefit more than 1 farm, and from their expense will not make a sufficient return within the ordinary endurance of a tenant's occupation. This is the landlord's proper line of duty and well suited to his station and position in society," Loch's *Account of the improvements of the Marquis of Stafford*. Nothing [insert alternative: but little] of this, however, is to be seen in Clondermot. To describe the feelings entertained by the majority of the inhabitants towards their landlords would be to incur the suspicion of exaggeration].

The parish has been much improved within the last 20 years, partly by the increase of agricultural knowledge introduced by the North West Society, partly also by the necessity for incessant industry to meet the increase of rent [crossed out: which occurs on the drawing of every new lease. It is highly probable, however, that no further increase will be demanded].

Legend of Killsill

A subdenomination of the townland of Clooney is called Killsill. In this place a cock has been never known to crow since the departure of St Columbkille from his favourite residence. This singular tradition, it is said, was handed down through succeeding generations from the parish of the saint's departure until a few years ago, when a gentleman who

rented the townland heard of it; and to try its merits caused 2 cocks to be brought to Killsill, under the impression that they would infallibly decide the matter, as it is well known that 2 strange cocks when brought together immediately crow and fight. The experiment was tried but they neither crew nor fought. The parishioners further aver that the crowing of a cock has not been heard in Killsill since the experiment, no more than before, and relate the following puerile legend to explain the circumstance.

It was with St Columbkille a season of persecution; his grief was great, not only from this but from the necessity he was under of leaving a place that had been to him a paradise. His grief was equalled only by that manifested by the people of the districts on the announcement of the departure of their saint. They had learned that he would leave them at cock-crow in the morning, and immediately began to tie up all the beaks of the chanticleers in the neighbourhood.

The saint well knew the time appointed for his departure, but the weakness of the people led them to believe that they had taken effective measure to prevent it. However, to the great astonishment, not only of the people but also of the saint, they found their hopes frustrated by the neglect of one woman, an inhabitant of the aforesaid Killsill, who, either through neglect or in contempt of the experiment, had not adopted the precaution, insomuch that her cock crew at the usual hour. Upon this the saint grieved at the disappointment of the people, and at his own departure pronounced the malediction: "As long as time shall be time a cock shall not crow in this place."

Traditions relative to Lough Enagh

Queries by Lieutenant Larcom, dated 6th September 1832.

Is there any ruins of the castle of the O'Cathans near it (ruin at Lough Enagh <Enach>) or is there a tradition of any such having existed? Is there any recollection in the country of this church, St Columb's, having been taken down by Nicholas Boston?

Query no.1, 27th February 1833. The name of Enach was given to the lough from a circumstance connected with the building of the ruin or abbey, as it was called by the inhabitants. The saint who built it intended to have done so in *Templemoyle*? The building was supernaturally prevented and at length a bird, taking up a book, flew and deposited it between the loughs, whence it was called Enach. This saint or "holy man" was not St Columba. His name is forgotten. Enquiry was made for Carragin. A place called Tarragull exists 1 and a half miles from Enach.

In the bog near the ruin a great many agricultural implements have been found. Also querns and a greasy substance buried and wrapped <wrapt> up in bark, said by the country people to have been originally butter.

The builder of the ruin is sometimes called a clergyman, and the foundations represent a long room with a side aisle. It has a Gothic window and was destroyed by Cromwell. The churchyard wall appears to be of ancient masonry.

On the island in the lough next the Newtown road, and which is closest, there existed the castle of the O'Cathans or, as it is now pronounced, the O'Ke-ans. The farmhouses on the borders of the lakes were built from it.

O'Cahan ruled over the county Londonderry and part of the county Tyrone. He had 7 sons and 1 daughter. Each son had a castle of his own, one near Newtown, another at Brackfield, a third somewhere else in the county and the rest in the county Tyrone. For his daughter he in particular built the castle at Enach. She being very ugly, or "not eyesweet" as the country people said, was found difficult to be married by her father. A young man that he wished to do so declared that he would suffer death first and accordingly he was hanged by O'Cathan at Newtownlimavady.

O'Cathan granted to one of his following, called Mullan, a tract of mountainous country called the Ballymullans to this day. The quantity was equal to 7 townlands. The greater is at present under Mr Beresford.

The narrator was a very old man called Jack McDiarmid, who lives near the blacksmith's shop at the loch. His house is the second on the right-hand side of the Newtown road going from that shop towards Derry. The first house is very close to the blacksmith's shop. He, Diarmid, is a Catholic and a simple, benevolent-looking man.

Diarmid, a man in a public house, Mrs Carolan, who lives close to the ruin, and another man all concurred in saying that a castle stood upon the island.

A man, a peasant named Mullan, lives near Garvagh of ancient descent. His ancestors were crusaders, and a tomb of his name exists in the churchyard of Errigal <Aragal> with a crescent on it.

Query no.2. There is no recollection of Nicholas Boston among the country people. There is, however, a tradition that a long time ago an English bishop pulled down a ruin in Inishowen to build a palace, and that Mr Gore of that country knew all about it.

Sir Cahir O'Doherty ruled Inishowen. He was not contemporary with O'Cathan. He built the castles at Elagh, at Birt and at Buncrana, at present inhabited by Mr Todd.

Draft of Memoir Sections, with corrections by George Downes

MODERN TOPOGRAPHY

Bleach Greens, Manufactories and Mills

There is 1 bleach green in Ardmore. There is a plough manufactory in Lisnagelvin and a spade manufactory in Ardkill. In the latter the machinery is driven by 2 separate wheels turned by the same fall of water. One is for the bellows, the other for the hammer and anvil. The diameter of the larger is 14 feet. The erection of a spinning mill in this townland is contemplated. There are 5 corn mills, 1 flour mill, 2 flax mills, 1 bleaching mill and 1 tuck mill.

With few exceptions the mills have breast wheels. A mill at New Buildings is worked by an undershot wheel. The wheels are at an average 13 feet in diameter and 20 inches broad. That of Mr Smyth's corn mill in Altnagelvin is upwards of 18 feet in diameter. It is remarkable for the excellence of its construction. It is a breast wheel and turned by Glendermot stream, which is dry in summer. The pit or main wheel, which is within the mill, is 8 feet in diameter. The internal wheels are all new and of metal. The flakes of the kilns are of sheet iron. This mill works 2 hoppers at a time. It is hence called "double-geared," and it is the only instance of the kind in the parish.

The common and poor mills are all of wood, and the corn kilns generally of stone and sticks. In the Drumahoe flax mill the fly axle revolves 150 times in a minute.

There is a distillery at the Waterside and a good brewery at the Faughan bridge.

Communications

The mail coach roads from Londonderry to Dublin and Belfast branch off from the Waterside. The former is repaired with limestone from the quarry in Prehen, which is, however, of much too soft a nature. The roads in the southern parts of the parish, including even the mail coach roads, are seldom in good order.

[Crossed out: The old road led to the forest of Curragh Camon in Culkeeragh and is believed to have been the trace of the road which conveyed the timber to the first erection of Londonderry].

Culmore in the county Derry: this ferry can hardly be said to be the principal communication with Donegal while there is a bridge at the city.

PRODUCTIVE ECONOMY

Manures

[Crossed out: The usual manure is stable dung mixed with bog, clay and lime]. Lime is sold at the rate of 1s 4d the barrel of roache <roche> lime, or 8d the barrel of slaked lime. One barrel of lime is equal to 2 bushels statute measure. But little lime is bought or sold except for building, and none is used in manure except by superior farmers. No quarries are at present worked, although the parish contains limestone of middling quality. It is chiefly procured from the parish of Lifford in the county Donegal.

Implements of Husbandry

Messrs McClintock and Kirkpatrick have each a threshing machine. Mr Smyth is constructing a third.

The common wheel or slide car appears to be rare except near Warbleshinny, and perhaps in the neighbourhood of Fincairn glen. There are not many oxen used in agriculture.

Crops

The usual rotation of crops is potatoes, corn, flax, corn, then 3 or more years of pasture. In many cases the tenant cannot afford to let his ground lie sufficiently long in pasture, and it consequently becomes exhausted. In the potato crop the quantity of seed is to that of the return, on an average, as 1 to 10.

The middling classes of the parish are beginning to cultivate onions to a much greater extent than heretofore. The smaller farmers particularly have found this root so useful in the absence of other and more substantial relishes that they endeavour at all times to be furnished with a supply. The seeding and weeding of this crop are the principal expenses. One acre of onions producing 8 tons is in value 64 pounds, expense of sowing and weeding 21 pounds.

Grazing and Cattle

None of the farms are devoted exclusively to grazing. The pastures are generally laid down with rye grass and clover. Irrigation is very little practised but drainage fully. It is performed by cutting a drain 2 feet wide piped underneath and covered with stones and earth. Much land exists from Warbleshinny westwards which could be converted into sheep-walks. The fences are universally bad and incapable of keeping out cattle, except on the farms of those gentlemen whose names have been already given.

The wages of labour are from 6d to 1s a day.

The parish contains 4,500 head of black cattle and 3,600 sheep. The breed is a mixture of Scotch, English and Irish breed. The poorest people have a purely Irish breed.

Uses of Bogs

The bogs are grazed in autumn but the grazing is very bad. The turf is principally sold in Londonderry at 2s 6d a load, but it is of an inferior quality to the Dunemanna turf. There is no free right of grazing.

Turf-cutting is restricted on the same principle, but not exactly in the same mode, as in the parish of Faughanvale. Very little turf, if any, is converted into charcoal. The bog wood is variously used, the oak for roofing cabins, the fir for laths when split and for torches, as also for the axle trees of mills.

Drainage and Planting

No effort appears to have been made by landlords either to drain or otherwise improve any bog. Some have been made by tenants, who have reclaimed the mountain turf by the usual process of paring, burning, potato-planting etc.

It is uncertain whether the planting has been profitable except at Prehen; it is at all events ornamental. The nursery at Knockbrack contains oak, beech, alder, sycamore, larch, Scotch fir, birch, elms, common ash, mountain ash; all without exception are sold at 12s 6d a thousand. It is in an exposed situation and has very little shelter. The consequence is that the young plants are very hardy and the plantations produced from them seldom fail.

4 individuals of the higher rank in the county are the chief customers, Messrs Lyle, H.B. Beresford, J.C. Beresford and Hunter. The others are in general farmers. The numbers of purchasers of the latter class is decreasing, but the demand is on the whole stationary.

Coast and Fishing

The small line of coast which this parish possesses on the shore of Lough Foyle can afford but a very trifling supply of seawrack.

The Faughan is a good fishing river. The right of the salmon fishery which it nurses is farmed by the Irish Society to [blank] Little Esquire. Keepers are placed on the river itself after the salmon has descended into the lough. The Faughan also contains much trout.

General Remarks

In the townland of Lisdillon the cultivation is carried to the height of 750 feet above the sea. The aspect of the parish is various and the soil also. It is best in the neighbourhood of Lough Enagh, along the banks of the Faughan. Towards Warbleshinny it is rocky.

Although the introduction of the sheep-walks on the mountainous part of the parish is not impossible, yet it would require a greater expenditure of capital than a similar attempt in Faughanvale. The land is well adapted for plantations of oak. The parish in general is not easily accessible, but the communications will be probably improved by the county surveyor (transcription ends).

Draft Memoir on Productive Economy by George Downes, J. Stokes and Others

PRODUCTIVE ECONOMY

Turbary

About two-thirds of the southern part of the parish are under cultivation. A great portion of the remaining part is turbary, which is very valuable to the inhabitants and especially to the bleachers. Large quantities of turf are sent daily to Londonderry on sale, from the neighbourhood of Slieve Kirk. [Insert marginal query: Is this still bleachers?].

Cultivation and Farms

Cultivation is every year making rapid advances towards the summits of the hills in this part of the parish. [Insert marginal query: What part?].

The size of farms varies from 5 to 30 acres. Those held on old leases let at from 8s to 10s an acre; those held on modern average from 30s to [blank].

Crops

The general produce of the land consists of potatoes, oats, barley, flax, turnips and wheat, except in the southern portion of the parish where the latter is seldom met with, and never but in the neighbourhood of a gentlemen's seat, the land being there much too light for this crop.

Potatoes average from 1,440 to 1,500 stones the Irish acre and sell at from 2d to 3d a stone.

Oats produce from 168 to 180 stones the acre and average 9d ha'penny per stone.

Wheat yields about 180 stones the Irish acre and sells at usually from 27s 6d to 30s a barrel of 20 stones.

Flax, when cleaned and ready for market, averages 4 and a half to 5 and a half cwt the acre and sells at from 55s to 62s 6d a cwt.

Barley yields about 168 stones the acre, but some lands of a better description produce from 190 to 200 stones. It sells at from 1s to 1s 1d a stone.

Turnips are also found very valuable for stall feeding, a practice becoming very general in the neighbourhood.

Soil and Manures

Sir William Petty remarks that the "soyle is for the most part mountainous, having no improvements thereon." At present nearly the whole of the parish is under tillage and cultivation is making rapid strides, even towards the summit of many of the hills.

The manures are generally those of the stable or farmyard, or a compost of animal manure, bog earth and lime. Towards the northern point of the parish, where easy access is obtained to the shell banks in Lough Foyle, shell manure is in common use, but lime is generally employed by those who can afford it; it is procured from a quarry in Prehen in the southern portion of the parish and from the adjoining parish of Cumber, and sells at 6d per barrel.

Quarry and Distillery

The slate quarry in Gorticross was opened in 1821. The slates have no defect but their deformity [crossed out: are ugly]. It is not at present worked, but slates are procured from Donegal. The slates, which were always sold at the quarry, brought from 1 pound to 1 pound 8s a thousand.

The distillery at the Waterside distils 57,000 proof gallons of spirits in the season.

Landlords and Tenants

There are 7 non-resident landlords. In most cases, however, the agents are resident, especially those of the larger properties. They are generally, perhaps universally, paid 1s in the pound as receiver's fees. There are not more than 4 or 5 farms above 100 acres and none above 150 (exclusive of mountain). More than one-half of the arable land is in holdings of from 25 to 50 acres.

Leases are generally granted for 21 years, or 31 years, or 31 years and 3 lives. The holdings are generally direct from the landlords, but some small farms are held from middlemen. Many farmers occupy land as an advisable investment of small capital, but generally with a view to support rather than to speculation. Some land is let in conacre, which is always preferred by the poorest class.

Size of Fields

The general size of the fields and enclosures is 3 acres. On the western bank of the Faughan, from Altnagelvin upwards, they are in general very well shaped, being all rectangular with the fences running perpendicularly down the slope of the hill. In that part of the parish which looks towards the Foyle an exactly contrary arrangement seems to have taken place. [Crossed out: On the other side the longest side of the field was in most cases perpendicular to the hill slope, particularly near Prehen, [where] it ran horizontally].

Near Disertowen in the valley of Warbleshinny they are crooked, triangular, obtuse-angled etc. It is a general practice with the poorer parishioners to have more than one crop in one field. Whenever they have manured more than enough for 1 field but not enough for 2, the second is divided, part being brought under crop and part being left in a lea state. They collect as much manure as they can, and put out all without any regard to the proportion of enclosures. These sub-fields, which chiefly occur in the poorest parts of the parish, are separated merely by little furrows.

On the western side of Warbleshinny mountain, towards the bottom and especially in the direction of New Buildings, the fences are completely nominal, being merely low earthen divisions. Higher up the enclosures diminish in size, but the fences improve. There are but few hedges throughout the parish.

Taxes

The only local imposts are tithe, church cess and county cess. The former cess is collected for repairing all houses of worship of whatever denomination. In a farm in Altnagelvin of 10 acres the tithe and cess amounted to 1 pound 12s 2d annually.

The expenditure was as follows: putting in corn, 5 acres, 3 pounds 15s; putting in hay, 1 acre, 1 pound 16s 2d; putting in potatoes, 1 acre, 1 pound 13s 6d; total 7 pounds 4s 8d; rent 15 pounds 4s, tithe 18s, cess 14s 6d, total 24 pounds 1s 2d. In this instance, and most probably in all, the excess of income above expenditure is devoted to the purchase of cattle.

Superior Farmers

The farm buildings of the upper classes are in general good; none are erected nor kept in repair by any non-resident landlord. The following are the names of those parishioners who, in various degrees, possess superior knowledge, and whose exertions have acted as examples: [blank] Alexander Esquire, Mr Alexander, [blank] Ash Esquire, Mr Bond, Mr Burnside, Mr Cary, Lieutenant Carmalt, Mr Carson, Mr Coghran, Mr Ewing, Mr Hannah, Mr Hattrick, Mr Hazlitt, Mr Henderson, G. Hill Esquire, [blank] Kirkpatrick Esquire, Mr Lithgow, Mr McCarter, Mr McClelland, Mr McClintock Esquire, Mr McCutchen, Mr Maughan, Mr Miller, Mr Mills, Mr Morton, Mr Reynolds, Mr Semple, Mr Skipton Esquire, J.A. Smythe Esquire, [blank] Stephenson Esquire, Mr Tait, Mr Teadlie, Mr Thompson, Mr White.

Model Farms and Methods

Lieutenant Carmalt's farm in Ardnabrocky contains 50 acres Cunningham measure; 38 are under tillage and the sixth lot system is practised. The annual rent is 92 pounds, the local taxes 12 pounds. The stock consists of 13 head of black cattle and 3 horses. The horses are fed during the winter on cut straw and potatoes with boiled turnips, evening and morning. Lieutenant Carmalt sinks a cistern in the cowhouse and stable which conveys the urine to the dunghill. One cistern is capable of manuring 2 acres of potatoes or turnips, and he esteems it superior to any other manure. He finds also that soap boiler's lye poured on a compost of clay, and kept constantly turned, makes excellent manure, particularly for flax.

He has also found by experience that the best method of cultivating the potato crop is as follows: to make ridges 10 feet wide, manuring them well and, having kibbed the potatoes across the ridge, earth the leaves with a broad hoe as soon as they have made their appearance. Fresh clay is to be put between the intervals before the leaves begin to close in the evening. The size of his hoe is 10 inches by 6, its weight 3 lbs. Lieutenant Carmalt manufactures all the wooden parts of his own implements of husbandry. He uses a barn steelyard.

Mr Burnside's farm in Carrakeel contains 88 acres Cunningham measure, of which 40 are under tillage, and the fifth lot system is practised. The annual rent is 80 pounds, the local taxes 20 pounds. The stock consists of 3 horses, 10 cows and 102 sheep; the last are kept in an allotted sheep-walk. He uses horse manure and his rotation of crops is potatoes, wheat, oats, barley, clover laid down with grass seeds, pasture. The Grocers' Company have expended a considerable sum in ditching, fencing etc. on his farm. The enclosures are laid out in a neat and systematic manner.

Mr McClelland spreads on his ground carpenter's chips and shavings, which have the effect of removing rushes from the surface. He feeds his cows, horses and pigs with flax seed.

Mr Morton of Hollymount introduced the practice of cutting corn with a scythe. This displeased the rural legislators of the day, who immediately destroyed his crop.

Mr A. Miller's farm in Lisaghmore contains 49 acres. The annual rent is 25 pounds 4s. He introduced the use of salt as a manure.

Mr Hannah's farm in Brickkilns is well fenced and the rotation of his crops good. The only deficiency is in his implements of husbandry.

The cheese made in this parish is all for domestic consumption. It is superior in quality to that of Faughanvale.

Freeholders

The native freeholders in Clondermot appear to have been: Tullyally, Manus O'Cahan, Lord De Blacquiere; Gortgranagh, Lisglas, [blank] Wray Esquire; Ballyshasky, Ardmore, Glenkeen, Lord De Blacquiere; Lisdillon forfeited by Bryan O'C[ahan] in 1641, Lord Londonderry; Ardkill, Knockbrack, Lord De Blacquiere; Goshendon (in Cumber, forfeited in 1641 by Gilleglass McRory O'Cathan), Lord De Blacquiere. [Insert marginal note: These 3 townlands appear from Sampson's map to be in Cumber].

Church townlands: Clonie, Lisachory, Templelowe, Stradreagh, Cah, Ballyoan, Carn, Killfinan, Lisneal, Ardlough, Ardnabrocky, Enagh, Chatham, Crumpkill, Clondermot [insert marginal note: bishop's lands].

Crown freeholds: Culkeeragh, [blank] Young Esquire; Gobnaskeal, Sir J. Strong, Baronet; Tamnymore, [blank] Lecky Esquire; Prehen, [blank] Knox Esquire; Lisamore, Right Honourable Ponsonby; Gortinure, [blank] Ash Esquire;

Gortin, Killymallaght, [blank] Warren Esquire.

Society's townlands: Gransha, Rosnagalliagh.

Working Papers

SOCIAL ECONOMY

Remarkable Events

The parish has not given birth to any remarkable person, neither has it been the scene of any remarkable circumstance since the cessation of the "wars of Ireland."

The late meeting of the Synod of Ulster in Londonderry, although it did not occur in Clondermot, may be noticed in passing as it there excited such interest among the Presbyterians that in the townlands where they formed the mass of the population it was found that all the males had left their homes to attend the synod.

PRODUCTIVE ECONOMY

Londonderry Bridge

[Table contains the following headings: number of foot passengers, carriages, private cars, drays and wheel cars that crossed the bridge of Londonderry on the second and third days of June 1834, with the number of horsemen].

Monday the 2nd June, from 7 a.m. to 9 p.m.: 983 foot passengers, 49 carriages, 31 post cars, 147 drays, 13 wheel cars, 113 horsemen, 82 private cars.

Tuesday the 3rd of June, from 9 a.m. to 10 p.m.: 1,004 foot passengers, 51 carriages, 23 post cars, 123 drays, 7 wheel cars, 76 horsemen, 89 private cars.

Total for 2 days: 1,987 foot passengers, 100 carriages, 54 post cars, 270 drays, 20 wheel cars, 189 horsemen, 171 private cars.

On fairs and market days there is at least 3 times the above number.

Toll-Gate

The toll-gate is annually put up to auction by the corporation and the highest and fairest bidder will then receive it on approved security, the bridge therefore becoming the private property of the purchaser. He may stipulate at pleasure with the county and city gentlemen for a certain sum, according to the extent of their business on trespass on the bridge for the current year. The proprietor must take an annual sum from all government establishments.

The bridge is crazy and old, and seems to

require perpetual repairings. The heavy weight of the pipes and gas-lamps on the southern side will be probably in the end injurious by producing an unequal pressure. An instance has been known of a farmer who seriously damaged the fabric by loading his cart too heavily.

The tolls of this bridge are fully equivalent to a tax of 1,000 [pounds?] a year on each of the parishes of Templemore, Faughanvale, Clonder-mot and Cumber. The tolls of the bridge are equivalent to a tax of from 10 to 30 and 50 per cent on all purchases of small articles in the city by the poor of Clondermot. They cannot afford to purchase much at a time and are accordingly debarred by the heavy percentage of the toll, which acts in the following manner.

In buying a whitefish from the city, value 6d, the toll of 1d must be paid, which is equivalent to a duty of 16 and a half per cent; in buying a lb. of beef, value 5d, the toll is 20 per cent; in buying 10d worth of mutton the toll is 10 per cent; 9d worth of pork, 11 per cent; vegetables, 2d worth, 50 per cent; grocery, 6d worth, 16 and a half per cent; fuel, 3d worth, 30 per cent.

The above purchases are as much as the poorer orders can afford to make at one time.

However, herrings are sold at the Waterside. Other kinds of fish can only be had in the city, as the fishermen all live on that side of the Foyle and bring up their fish to be sold there.

As long as the capital of the county of Londonderry is besieged by a toll-gatherer, the advantages of a free communication will be diminished and the communication itself decreased. The city is nearly as it was when it only had the ferryboat.

There are other obstructions to improvement as well as this wooden bridge, i.e. some of the parochial landlords.

Schedule of Tolls

Painted on a board at the bridge: payable at the bridge of Derry in British currency, on the 5th January 1826.

Coaches with 6 horses: for every coach, Berlin chariot, calash, chaise or chair, drawn by 6 or more horses or other beasts of burthen, the sum of 3s; if drawn by any lesser number of horses or beasts of burthen than 6 and more than 2, the sum of 2s 6d; if drawn by 2 horses or other beasts of burthen, the sum of 1s.

Wagons <waggons> with 4 or more horses: for every wagon, waincart, dray car or other carriage with 4 wheels, drawn by 4 or more horses or other beasts of burthen, the sum of 1s. By less than 4 horses: if drawn by less than 4 horses or other beasts of burthen, the sum of 10d. Wagons with 2 horses: if drawn by 2 horses or other beasts of burthen, the sum of 6d ha'penny.

Gig or jaunting car with 1 horse: for every carriage with 2 wheels, commonly called a chaise, chair gig or jaunting car, drawn by 1 horse or other beast of burthen, the sum of 6d; if drawn by 2 or more horses or beasts of burthen, the sum of 10d.

For every sedan chair the sum of 4d.

Wagons with 1 horse: for every wagon, waincart, dray car or other carriage drawn by 1 horse or other beast of burthen, the sum of 4d.

Sledges without wheels: for every sledge, slide or other carriage without wheels, drawn in any manner, the sum of 9d.

For all carriages whatever, drawn in any other manner than aforesaid, the sum of 6d, together with the sum of 1d ha'penny for each animal employed in drawing the same.

Single horse: for every horse, gelding, mare, mule or ass, the sum of 1d ha'penny.

Droves of cattle: for every drove of oxen, cows, heifers or meat cattle, the sum of 3s 4d per score and so in proportion for any greater or less number.

For every calf, hog, pig, sheep or lamb, the sum of 1d.

Foot-passengers: for any passenger passing over said bridge, except such persons as drive or shall be driven in such coach, Berlin chaise, chair, calash, gig or jaunting car, a ha'penny and every horse and man 2d ha'penny.

For every single horse 1d ha'penny.

For every person carrying or conveying any kish, basket, sack, load or package of any kind, the weight of which shall amount to 30 lbs, the sum of 1d.

This last clause was strictly imposed, in consequence of a practice resorted to by the peasantry to evade the charge for cart-loads. They unloaded at the Waterside and carried the load down in moderate parcels on the human back.

The tolls were altered in 1826. Up to 1833 the charge for foot-passengers was 1d. Many individuals among the parishioners compound annually with the toll-gatherer for a certain sum, in order to obtain the privilege of walking through the gate without stopping.

Notes and Working Papers by J.B. Williams

Miscellaneous Notes

Londonderry Post Office, income: quarter ending 5th April 1834, 1,058 pounds 19s 3d; 5th July

1834, 1,036 pounds 14s 3d ha'penny; 5th October 1834, 904 pounds 11s 11d; 5th January 1835, 1,047 pounds 11s 8d; total for year ending 5th January 1835, 4,047 pounds 17s 1d ha'penny.

Parish of Clondermot: the right has passed to the purchasers of the Goldsmiths' estate, but they do not hold a manor court. It is considered to encourage litigation and on this account is not held; and as the estate is partly in the liberties of Londonderry it has the advantage of the mayor's court which, together with the quarter sessions, is thought sufficient.

The proprietor of this glasshouse is gone to Swan's river. His father, from whom I am to procure the necessary information, lives out of town, and I have written to him and am promised an answer immediately.

The registry of freeholders and the series of grand jury warrants were given to me without cost.

A regulation made by the Ballast Office Committee differs from a by-law: it is made for the conducting of the internal business of the office, under power given by act of parliament. The repeal of the by-laws does not affect the office regulations. I have given in a former paper the date of the new table of the rates of pilotage.

I did not procure the limits of the mayor's jurisdiction from any one authority, as there is no regular list of them in any of the public offices. I got it first from Mr Clerk, had the information corroborated by a great number of countrymen who were there in his office on road business, and lastly checked this information by application to the process servers, who do not serve any notices without the limits of the mayor's jurisdiction.

The telescope of the theodolite was on a level with the base of the tower; this I discovered by means of the spirit level attached to it.

Clondermot: contents of 71 townlands within the liberties 19,098 acres 2 roods 9 perches, also of 6 townlands without the liberties 2,409 acres 3 roods 12 perches, [total] 21,508 acres 1 rood 21 perches; 19,098 acres 2 roods 9 perches [plus] 12,615 acres 2 roods 8 perches [equals] 31,714 acres 17 perches, mayor's portion.

11th April 1835,

Sir,

On enquiry I find that Mr Robert Miller left only 100 pounds for a charitable purpose. I suppose the mistake must have taken place from his brother, Mr J. Miller, having left a similar sum to the poor of the parish. I am your obedient servant Anthony Cary; [to] J.B. Williams Esquire.

Report of Deputation of the Irish Society, 1836

SOCIAL ECONOMY

Glendermot Churchyard

In the course of our survey of the Goldsmiths' proportion we visited the burial place formerly attached to the parish church of Glendermot. This spot, in consequence of a new church having been erected in another part of the parish, has become wholly neglected. The ruins of the old church have disappeared and the ground is overgrown with weeds. In this cemetery are buried the remains of the gallant Colonel Mitchelburne, who commanded the garrison during the siege of Londonderry, and to whose skill and bravery, in conjunction with that of the Revd George Walker, is mainly to be attributed the failure of the siege. He led the defenders in several sorties against the besiegers and, with his own hand, captured 2 of the enemy's standards. [Insert footnote: These were French, which are now hanging over the altar in the cathedral in Londonderry, with an inscription of which the following is a copy (see *Ordnance memoir* vol.1 p.105)].

Colonel Mitchelburne's Will

Distinguished as Colonel Mitchelburne deservedly was as a patriot and as a soldier, he was equally estimable in private life for his benevolence and philanthropy. By his will he bequeathed 20 pounds a year to the poor of Clondermot, the payment of which he charged on his real estates, but which sum, for want of due attention, has been unpaid for many years; and as, from the information we obtained, we are of opinion that the payment of this charitable legacy can be enforced, we recommend that application should be made to the parties holding the lands charged with this annuity, to pay their arrears; and, unless they forthwith come to a satisfactory arrangement, such proceedings as the society's solicitor may deem necessary should be instituted to cause the benevolent intentions of the testator to be carried into effect.

It was with feelings of deep concern and regret that we observed the stone which covers the grave of this gallant soldier and excellent man broken into fragments, so that the inscription is nearly obliterated; and considering that a testimonial of the gratitude of posterity should mark the burial place and perpetuate the merits of so distinguished an individual, we recommend that a neat monument be erected over his remains by your honourable society; and having mentioned to your surveyor, Mr Tite, our intention to make this recommendation, he has kindly furnished us with a design, which we submit in the appendix for your approval, on which should be engraved the present inscription which is as follows.

"Here lieth the body of Colonel John Mitchelburn, grandson to Sir Richard Mitchelburn, of Broadhurst and Stanmore in the county of Sussex, a valiant soldier, faithful, pious and charitable, expecting the resurrection of the just. He was governor and commander-in-chief at the late memorable siege of Londonderry in 1689, in defence of the Protestant interest, in the first year of the reign of King William of blessed memory. He had many thanks from the king for that eminent service and deceased the first day of October in the year of Our Lord 1721, in the seventy-sixth year of his age." And we further recommend that on some part of the monument be inscribed under what circumstances and by whom it was erected, and that the ancient inscription be restored.

Glendermot Schoolmaster

We visited a school in Glendermot churchyard which is well attended. The dean gives a subscription of 40s a year to this school, and we recommend that the society allow 5 pounds per annum to the schoolmaster, provided that, in addition to his scholastic duties, he shall look to the preservation of the monument about to be erected to the memory of Colonel Mitchelburne.

Culkeeragh School

A memorial was presented from Miss Young of Culkeeragh <Cool Kerreagh>, county of Derry, by Major Young, her father, stating that the schoolhouse at Culkeeragh had been closed for 2 years for want of funds for its support; that numerous applications had been made by the parents of the poor children in the neighbourhood to have their children educated, and therefore praying for assistance to reopen the school. We recommend that 10 pounds per annum be granted in aid of so excellent an undertaking.

Gransha School

Mr Samuel McClintock presented a memorial with plan and specification drawn by Mr Stewart Gordon, the county surveyor, for a schoolhouse at Gransha <Grandsagh>, which is to be open to all without regard to their religious persuasions, free of all charges; the expense of creating which, it

was stated, would be 126 pounds 15s, and requesting the society's assistance in the undertaking. We recommend that a donation of 50 pounds be granted in aid of the building, when the same is completed, and 10 pounds per annum towards maintaining the school.

Memorial to Irish Society, 1826

Memorial to Irish Society

Schulte's report, 1826. To the deputation of the Honourable the Irish Society,

Gentlemen,

When the deputation in 1819 visited this county, a school was established at Beech Hill by Miss Beresford and some of your memorialists, for the use of which the deputation gave a grant of 5 guineas a year. On Miss Beresford's leaving the neighbourhood your memorialists continued the Sunday and female day schools, the object of the former being to make the children practically acquainted with the leading truths of the Gospel without interfering with the popular tenets of any denomination of Christians, while that of the latter is to instruct the female children in reading, writing, arithmetic and such kinds of work as may be suited to their situation in life.

In order to contribute in some small degree to relieve the pecuniary wants of the neighbouring poor, your memorialists established in 1824 a poor shop, where blankets and such articles of clothing are sold and paid for by weekly instalments of 1d in the shilling. From the same establishment several poor women are supplied with spinning, for which they are paid the usual price, and the yarn is sold in the market; but, from the very low state of the funds, your memorialists fear they shall be obliged to give up this branch of the establishment, though the general failure of the flax crop would render it peculiarly necessary to provide employment this year for the female poor.

The school is now called the Ardmore school, and consists of a school for males, a separate school for females and a Sunday school. Upwards of 200 children are educated at these schools. The only funds for the support of all these departments are the annual subscriptions of your memorialists, amounting to about 14 pounds, the payment of 1d a week from the pupils and the small profits of the work done in the female school, of which a great part is given to the elder girls as a remuneration for their labours. Out of these funds are defrayed many expenses incidental to this establishment, besides

18 pounds a year to the mistress of the female school, who is also provided with a house and fuel. Mr Smyth give 5 pounds a year to the master and has built the schoolhouse at his own expense. The managers of these establishments would be most happy in having an opportunity of showing their beneficial effects to the deputation.

Your memorialists humbly request that you will order the grant of 5 guineas a year made to Miss Beresford's school to be transferred to the Ardmore school, and that you will take the other branches of the establishment under your consideration; and they beg to refer you to your agent, Mr Beresford, for any further information on the subject. Signed, by order of the managers of the Ardmore school, in the parish of Glendermot and liberties of Londonderry, Esther Smyth, secretary, Ardmore, 20th September 1826.

Having taken the subject of this memorial into consideration, and consulted with the general agents thereon, who assured us that the affairs of the establishment were most usefully conducted, we recommend that the arrears due to the late school be paid to the managers of the Ardmore school and that the annual donation of 5 guineas be continued; and having further considered the privations which the failure of the flax crop may occasion, we also recommend a donation of 20 pounds to be paid to the managers of the Poor Shop connected with the above establishment, in aid of the funds for its support.

Schools

The Roman Catholic Sunday school formerly held in Lisdillon schoolhouse has fell into a decline; the revival of it again is uncertain.

A female day school has been established at the Catholic chapel of Clondermot, on the 1st March 1836. The number of scholars in attendance is 75; Miss Marryann Walch teaches.

Gortnessey: there is no day school here at present; the master is gone to America.

Report on Schools

List of Schools

List of schools visited in December 1835 and January 1836.

1. Presbyterian school, Derry, superintendent Mr McClure; Mr White, schoolmaster, reports one-fifth less in attendance on the 10th December than what was on 10th June; supposed because the school being composed of the poor class of children are unable to attend in winter, being thinly clad, want of shoes etc.

2. Mr Stantan, Protestant, Belagrey, reports one-fourth less of day scholars, but has formed a night school of grown-up boys from 10 years old to 20; this is called a night school or writing school; those writing schools commence at 5 o'clock p.m. and continues to 10 o'clock; cause of decrease in day scholars: small children, having to come perhaps better than 1 mile through fields etc., are not fit to attend, besides thin clothing.

3. Mr Dinsmore, schoolmaster, Prehen, reports one-fourth less in attendance since 10th July; cause small children and others of the lower class for want of proper clothing. Mr Dinsmore has a night school that makes up in a great measure for the decrease of day scholars.

4. Mr Michal, schoolmaster, Kilmalagh, reports one-fifth less in attendance comparing 10th July with 10th December; cause small children unable to cross fields and those of the poorer classes for want of suitable winter clothing. Mr M. has a writing school also; these night schools is a common practice with all country schoolmasters. Farmers' servants and small farmers' sons generally attend these schools, and are chiefly indebted to them for their information, both in writing and arithmetic.

5. Mr McAlister, schoolmaster at Glendermot church, reports one-fourth less in attendance comparing 10th December with that of July; cause small children unfit and those of the poor class for want of clothing. Mr McAlister has no night school this winter.

6. Mr McGuinness, schoolmaster in Dileey Hall, Catholic, where most of the children of Molenan go, reports one-third less in attendance comparing 10th December with that of July; cause small children are unfit to cross fields and many of them but badly clad. He is going to commence a night school also; expects to have 20 scholars.

7. [Crossed out: The greatest numbers that attend Sunday school is from the 10th March to the 1st August, when they begin to fall off; and by the 1st November they have decreased one-third; cause of decrease the harvest; many of the day scholars quit about this time and seldom rejoin before the spring of the year. All the class leaders I have spoken to tell me the same story of the decrease of Sunday schools].

8. Mr Gill, schoolmaster at Catholic chapel, Glendermot, reports one-third less comparing 10th June with that of December; cause small children not able to come through fields and some for want of close [clothes?] fitting for the winter. Mr Gill has a writing school or night school. The

regular charge for the night school is 2s for 24 nights; the master finds candles <candels> and ink. Some of these schools is held every night, others is only 2 nights in the week. Some of the masters have 2 or 3 night schools; these are held 2 nights and in different townlands where the masters and scholars have appointed.

9. Mr Bond, master, Salem school, reports one-fifth less in number comparing 10th June with that of December. This is always the case in winter. Mr Bond says the children begin to fall off in August and towards November the small classes are unfit to attend; but at this season of the year the night schools commence, which make up in a great measure the loss of the day scholars. Mr Baird has a night school 20 in number and about to commence the second.

10. T. McNamee, schoolmaster, Waterside, has experienced no decrease in number comparing 10th June with that of December; cause the greatest number of children in attendance belong to the same street and have only to come a short distance, and that along the pavements. Mr McNamee has 2 night schools; one of these is in the town and the other is 3 miles in the country, where he attends 2 nights in the week, namely Thursday and Saturday.

11. Miss Steel, Waterside, has experienced a decrease of one-half. This she says was in consequence of a part of the children come from the country, chiefly females, and never remain in the winter. She has a few from about the doors but has no night's school.

12. Bellview school: Mrs Simpson reports a decrease of one-sixth comparing 10th June with that of December. This is owing to the winter cold; all her small classes are broke up, and some of the larger children for want of suitable clothing are not able to attend; Mrs Simpson has no nights or evening school.

13. Mr Moore near the playhouse, city, reports one-sixth less in number comparing June with December. This he says is owing to families leaving town and a few boys he had from the country during the summer.

14. Mr McCloskey, schoolmaster, racecourse, reports rather an increase comparing June with December. This he considers is owing to entering in to the new house and the lowering of the charge by the quarter. Mr McCloskey keeps a night school; consists of 20 boys from 12 to 20 years of age.

15. Mrs [Carney or Camey], Streetstown, reports a decrease of one-third comparing June with December. This decrease is owing to the small children not being able to attend and some of a larger size for want of clothing suitable for the season. Mrs [Carney?] dreads the continuation of the decline of her school, on account of the new house and Mr McCloskey's low charge.

16. Mr McAlwane, schoolmaster, Culmore, reports one-third of decrease comparing June with December. This he considers is owing to the winter; small children are not fit to cross fields and many of them are not clothed for the winter. Mr McAlwane has no night school as yet, but expects one in a few days.

Brief Notes by J. Bleakly, September 1832

SOCIAL ECONOMY

Mitchelburne's Property

Gobnascale was the property of Colonel Mitchelburne. Mrs Brown's house is built on the spot where Mitchelburne's house formerly stood at Waterside, and Mitchelburne's well is in this townland, an excellent spring. Colonel Mitchelburne used to take a walk every morning from his house to this well along the side of the River Foyle, in order to pray, and his coffin was deposited in a shed at this well 7 years previous to his death.

Superstitions of the People

The superstitious people tie rags on the bushes and throw pins into the well, and say as Colonel Mitchelburne was so pious a character, there must be some healing virtue in the water. Stations are performed at this well by superstitious Roman Catholics.

Some years ago about 20 pounds was collected in this parish, in order to take law proceedings against the Warren family and to recover, if possible, the bequests of Colonel Mitchelburne to the poor of this parish.

Colonel Mitchelburne used to employ a number of little boys (who had no work to do) to pick up the grass on the walk leading to this well. Information obtained from Mrs Brown and son at Waterside.

Grocers' Company

[Crossed out: On the Grocers' property each tenant holding 20 acres are allowed to keep 1 cottier, a tenant holding 40 acres 2 cottiers, and so in proportion, which is a great injury to the poor. Information obtained from Revd Mr McCarren, P.P. of Clondermot].

Note on Parish Name

Origin of Name

The original ecclesiastical name of this parish, properly written Clan-dermot, is not its original ecclesiastical appellation but rather a territorial one adopted popularly since the eleventh or twelfth century, when the Clan Dermot, a powerful tribe of the Kinel-Owen, crossed the Foyle and located themselves in this district. This custom of the Irish, in giving the names of tribes or families to the territories which they occupied, has been already shown in the observations of the name of the barony. The original name of the parish is not preserved by tradition and has not been discovered in historical records.

Draft Memoir by George Petrie, with insertions by J. Stokes and Others

Pagan Antiquities

Sepulchral: the progress of cultivation has spared but few remains of pagan times in Clondermot, but the names of several townlands indicate their former existence. There are remains of a sepulchral monument of the class popularly called giant's graves [insert addition: usually called druidic] in Edenreaghbeg. It consists of 9 large stones forming a square enclosure of 4 feet. When perfect it stood 9 feet high, but many of the stones have been broken and it is much obscured by a ditch which passes directly over it.

Giant's Grave in Glenderowen

[Insert addition by Stokes: This is a remarkable monument of that kind in the valley of Warbleshinny which, when perfect, must have been one of the most curious in the county. Although called by the neighbouring peasantry a "giant's grave," it is probable that it was also an altar. The stones at present stand 4 feet from the ground and are perfectly perpendicular. Stones similar to it formerly extended along the dotted line k j h g. The interior stones were ranged in a similar manner, and a stone, thin and tabular like the rest, lay at the top, covering the space b m n d and resting on the edges of the side stones.

The farmer who occupied the land broke all these but one and destroyed the covering one because it seems *it cumbered the earth*. A treasure seeker next dreamed of gold and made a considerable excavation. Previous, however, to his attempts there had been found some links of chains and a few other antiquarian relics. The stones, or rather, slabs are all very nearly equal in height except the 2 smaller ones which seem to have been broken. Many loose stones and fragments of stones are around the ground.

[Ground plan, scale 4 feet to an inch, showing extant stone slabs and dotted outline of original arrangement of stones, annotated with key and dimensions, and showing "hole made by treasure seekers"].

Giant's Grave in Edenreagh

A ditch passes directly over this monument enveloping the stones in its material. They are 9 in number, forming a small enclosure of 4 feet every way. Many of the stones have been broken and otherwise defaced, and the monument is completely obscured by rubbish. When perfect it stood 9 feet high.

Standing Stone

There was formerly a standing stone at Mr Morton's farm in Lissaghmore called the Hanging Stone. It was destroyed by his predecessor.

Forts and Coves

There are 7 earthen forts of the usual form at present in Clondermot. A cove exists stopped up and there is also another said to be in Fincairn. That at New Buildings is a third.

Miscellaneous Discoveries

Many coins, stone hatchets, wooden swords have been found by the parishioners, with cannon-balls fired at the siege of Derry. In the bottom of a small bog near Kittylane the foundations of an ancient edifice were discovered several years ago].

Coves

Subterranean stone galleries, here properly called coves, are sometimes discovered. There is one in Glenderowen, another in Fincairn and a third at New Buildings, but they do not present any peculiar features worthy of notice.

Military Remains

Of this class, there still remain about 7 earthen forts or raths of the usual form and presenting nothing remarkable. Stone hatchets, *wooden swords* and other antique remains indicating a very early in-habitation of the parish are sometimes found, and some years ago the foundations of a house were discovered at the bottom of a bog near Kittybane. [Insert marginal query: Was this house a barrack?].

Christian and Ecclesiastical Antiquities

The number of ecclesiastical ruins in this parish indicates a considerable amount of piety, if not of population, in its inhabitants at a remote period. The ruins of the old parish church, of which the foundations only remain, are situated in the townland of Clondermot. Neither its original name nor that of its patron saint has been discovered in any historical document, but as a sacred well in the adjacent townland of Rossnagalliagh bears the name of St Cogal or Comgal, the celebrated contemporary and friend of St Columbkille, and founder of several churches in the county, it may perhaps be assumed that this church also owes its origin to that eminent man. [Insert addition: We may believe it to be one of Columbkill's founda-tions, as the glebe belonging to it, which is situ-ated in and gives name to the adjoining townland, was called anciently Columbkilla, though now corrupted into Clumkill and Crumkill].

The church, having been in a ruinous state after the Plantation, was re-edified by the Company of Goldsmiths and was used for worship till about 20 [insert alternative: 70] years ago.

The graveyard contains a great number of monu-ments of the last century, of which the most remark-able is that of the celebrated Colonel Mitchelburne, which is thus inscribed: "Here lyith the body of Colonel Michelburn, grandson to Doctor Richard Michelburn of Broadhurst and Stanmer in the county of Sussex, a valliant soldier, faithful, pious and charitable, expecting the resurrection of the just. He was governor and commander in chief in the late memorable siege of Londonderry in 1689, in defense of the Protestant interest, in the first year of the reign of King William of blessed memory. He had thanks from the king for that eminent service, and deceased the first day of October in the year of Our Lord 1721, and in the seventy-sixth year of his age." [Insert marginal note: Copy this inscription in the order of the lines etc., as in the drawing].

Logan Family

[Insert addition: The arms of Logan, of which name there are several families in this parish, are sculptured on their tombstone with the motto, as blunderingly carved: "Pro rege and (et) patria;" the date is 1740.

This family, which is probably of Anglo-Nor-man origin, were located in Scotland and, as it would appear, in the north of Ireland, as early as the 13th century. Walter Logan was a witness to the charter of Richard de le-Glen at Berwick, 11th November 1292, Rot. Scot., and the roll of the 21st Edward I 1292-3 recites that the Bishop of St Andrews and Glasgow, John Comyn James, Seneschal of Scotland, and Brian FitzAlan: "nuper custodes jusdem regni Scotiae concesserint Waltero Logan custodiam terrarum et haec dum Heris de Wyston defuncti etc. (m. 5 November, castr. 4th January)."

In the writ: "De protectione hominibus Regis Angliae in Scotiam profecturis et moraturis, Rot. Scot."

William FitzWarrin, who dwells in the afore-said parts [blank], has letters of the king of attor-ney in Ireland under the names of Robert Logan and John de Berkway until etc., 26th Edw. I (1297) mem.1., Westminster.

Walter and John de Logan were summoned as barons to the Irish parliament in 1310; and among the powerful nobles who opposed Edward Bruce on his landing near Carrickfergus in 1315 Barbour, in his poem of The Bruce, enumerates the Logans: "Bot the lordes of that countre, Maundivill, Bisat and *Logane*, their men assemblyt wirilkane etc."

In 1316, according to Pemridge's annals, "on the Monday before All Souls Day many of the Scots were slain in Ulster by John Logan, Hugh, Lord Bisset, namely about 100 with double arms and 200 with single arms. The slain in all amounted to 300, besides the foot" and in the same year "on the eve of St Nicholas, Lord Alan Stewart, who was taken prisoner in Ulster by John Logan and Lord John Sandale, was carried to Dublin Cas-tle."

Notwithstanding, however, the evidences of loyalty furnished by John Logan on these occa-sions, it appears from Friar Clynn's annals that he was shortly after implicated, with the Mandivilles <Maundivilles>, as a principal in the murder of their lord, the young Earl of Ulster, William de Burgo. The words of the annalist may be trans-lated as follows.

"6th July, 1333. In the octave of Trinity, William de Burgo, Earl of Ulster and Lord of Connaught, was treacherously slain near Knockfergus by his own esquires (in whom he confided). The authors of this crime were John de Logan, Robert, son of Lord Richard Mandiville, Robert, son of Martin Mandiville, who, however, obtained from this (act but) a short and temporary solatium [insert alternative: comfort"].

Indeed a heavy measure of retribution soon fell upon the murderers and their abettors. As stated in the *Annals of the four masters*, "the English men who perpetrated the slaughter were put to death in various manners by the people of the King of England, some being hanged, some slain and others torn limb from limb in revenge of his death." According to other authorities, 300 of them were killed in one day by the country people; and in all pardons granted about that time, this clause was inserted "excepting the death of William, late Earl of Ulster" (*Lodge's Peerage*).

It is probable that the Logans, as well as the Mandivilles, never recovered from the effects of this severity; yet they were not wholly extinguished in Ireland, as appears from the writ: "Quod magnatis Hiberniae; subscripte ad regem accodant in scolia cum equis et armis AD 1335," in which among the armigers, after the names of John de Savage and John de Mandeville, the name of Radulph Logan follows (Rot. Scot. 9th Edw. 3.m, 36.d. in Ten. Lond.); and in 1394 a safe conduct was given for Robert Logan and John de Ramorgny out of Scotland "versus terram nostram Hiberniae" (ib. 18 Richard II m.2. Westm. 2 Feb.).

The name does not subsequently appear in connection with Irish history, but the Antrim Inquisition and other authorities show that the Logan arms were not extinct in their ancient locality in the 17th century, and are probably still to be found there.

John Logan, who had been in Derry during the siege by the army of James II, died at Carrickfergus in 1742, aged 100 years. (McSkimmin's *History and antiquities of Carrickfergus*, second edition)].

Watson Family

Another tombstone preserves the arms of the English family of Watson, who are still numerous in the parish. These arms are the same as those borne by the family of Lord Londes (see annexed woodcut). The inscription is as follows: "Here lyeth the body of Richard Watson Junior, who departed this life June, 13th day, 1729 aged 23 years." [Insert note: These 2 inscriptions to follow that to Colonel Murray, putting the Logan monument first].

Enagh Church

"There were anciently," says Archbishop King, "in this parish 3 chapels, Annagh, Cloney and Ivy chapels, that are all now demolished. Annagh was formerly a parish in itself," but as Bishop Downham states "by the great office or inquisition which was made at Londonderry (in 1609) is found to be part of Clondermott." [Insert marginal note: Yet Annagh as a barony appears to be nearly identical with Tirkeeran]. Of these chapels, the ruins of Annagh, or as it is now usually written Enagh, and Clooney still remain but of the third there is no vestige, and even its site is unknown.

The church of Enagh is beautifully situated on a bank of the eastern lake of that name. It is much dilapidated, but enough remains to shew its original form and the style of its architecture, in both of which it is very similar to most of the other ancient churches of the county. Its form was originally an oblong of 91 feet by 23, but a side chapel of about 23 feet square was subsequently added to its south side. The stonework, which is polygonal is large and good, but that in the side chapel is superior to the earlier portion. The entrance doorway is destroyed and of the windows, the eastern one only remains. The window, which is 9 feet high and 2 feet 9 inches wide, is as usual of the lancet form, with deep moulding, and its material is of red sandstone. (Insert cut of window here): [plan of church, indicating north side; [insert note: this side uppermost in wood cut].

The church and cemetery are filled with inscribed gravestones of the 17th and 18th centuries, chiefly belonging to the families of the Scottish settlers. The oldest inscribed tomb is that of Cornet Heard, who died in 1655, aged 74, and Captain Stephen Heard, who died in 1695. The latter was one of the persons attainted by King James' government in 1689.

A woodcut of the arms sculptured on this tombstone is annexed. They are not the same as those borne by a family of this name now existing in the county of Cork, who came originally from Wiltshire. The inscription may be deciphered as follows: "Heare lyith the body of Cornet Stephen Heard, who depearted this lyf the 14th day of December in the year of his eag 74 anno 1657. He beareth Ermin (the chief) charged (with a) crescent between 2 lyons' heads errased azure armed and langued of the third in chief, and on a helm wreath of his cullers a lyon's head errased as the foresaid borien by the name of Heard.

Here lyeth the body of Captaine Stephen Heard, who departed this lyf the 14th day of January anno domni 1695.

Here lyith the body of John Wardene, who departed this life May ye 6 1775, aged 78 years."

The name of Heard is not now existing in the parish or county. Another tombstone preserves the arms of one of the many families of the name of Smyth as represented on the accompanying woodcut. This family, which settled in Derry at the Plantation, is supposed to be of Scottish origin and is still numerous in the parish. The inscription is as follows: "Here lyeth the body of James Smyth, who departed this life [blank] ninth 1724, aged 73 years." The motto, which is much obliterated appears, to have been "Pro rege et patria."

The foundation of the church of Enagh, which was originally monastic and is still popularly called the abbey, is ascribed by Colgan to St Columbkille. This supposition is, however, unsupported by any evidence and is obviously erroneous, as there is the evidence of tradition supported by history to prove that its erection should be attributed to St Cainneach, the patron saint of Kianachta, Aghaboe and Kilkenny, who died in the year 598 (ann 4. mag.). The Irish calendars [insert addition: martyrologies] record the names of St Moclan and Columba-creg as being worshipped here, the former on the 4th January and the latter on the 22nd September.

This Columba, who was a contemporary of the great St Columbkille, is spoken of by Adamnan, who calls him a venerable clergyman "venerandum clericum" (L.1. c.2.). [Insert addition: Of the history of St Moclan, nothing is known. St Columba-creg, who was archinneach or proepositus of the church of Enagh, was the disciple and friend of the great St Columbkille].

Clooney Church

The church of Cluain-i, or Clooney as it is now called, is situated in the townland of that name, on the east bank of the Foyle immediately opposite Derry, and is at present enclosed within the demesne of George Hill Esquire, by whom its ruins are carefully preserved as a feature of ornament and interest in his grounds. Its foundation is attributed to St Columbkille. It is of mean architecture and small size, being but 35 feet long and 25 feet wide, and the gable walls only now remain. According to an account given by O'Donnell, in his *Life of St Columb*, it was reduced to a dilapidated state by Nicholas Boston, or properly Weston, Bishop of Derry from 1466 to 1484, for the purpose of using its materials in the erection of a palace at Bunseantuinne in its immediate neighbourhood. This demolition, O'Donnell adds, had been prophesied by its founder in a poem written in his native language, but God punishing the sacrilegious attempt of the bishop on account of the merits of the saint, the project was abandoned.

The martyrologies commemorate St Cobhran, the son of Enan and nephew of St Columbkille by his sister Minchotha, as being worshipped in this church on the 19th July, and also St Milla or Millan on the 19th of March. It may be here remarked that Colgan, in his notices of the saints venerated here and at Enagh, speaks always of them as the one place, under the name of Cluain-i-Enagh or Cluain-an-Enach, but that this is an error will appear evident from the following notice in the *Annals of the four masters*, as well as from the facts already given.

"AD 1197, Rotsel Pyton [insert addition: Peyton] set out upon a predatory excursion (from his newly erected castle on the Bann) and, coming to the harbour of Derry, he plundered (the churches of) Cluain-i, Enach and Dearbruach, but he and his party were overtaken by Flahertach O'Maoldoraidh, Lord of Tyrone and Tirconnell, and some of the northern Hy Niall [insert addition: Kiall]. A battle ensued on the shore of Ua Congbhala (Faughanvale), in which the English and the son of Ardgall McLoughlin were dreadfully slaughtered through the miracles of the saints Columbkille, Caineach and Brecain."

There can be no doubt, therefore, that the churches of Cluain-i and Enagh were those of which the saints Columbkille and Cainneach were the founders and patrons; but, as already stated, of St Brecain's church of Dearg-bruach there are no remains and its situation is now unknown.

It may, however, be conjectured with tolerable certainty to be the ruin which existed in King's time, called Ivy chapel [insert addition: or perhaps the neighbouring townland of Donnybrewer in Faughanvale is but a corruption of its name; many names of places in the county have become equally distorted]; and its situation on the east bank of the Foyle, in the townland now called Gransha, or the Grange as it is written in the Down Survey, is ascertained from the inquisition taken at Derry in 1609, according to which "the grange of Dirge-broc, consisting of one-half quarter of land situated in O'Kane's side of the Foyle, and then in the occupation of Thomas Reade, was found to be part of the possession of the abbey of Derry." This identity of the present Gransha with the ancient grange of Dearge-bruach is fully corroborated by the etymology of the name (see Townlands).

Ruin in Rosnagalliagh

There are also some vestiges of a small religious house in the townland of Rosnagalliagh or "the wood of the ruins," from which the name was derived. The great inquisition of 1609 found that this was a parcel of the possessions of the nunnery of Derry [insert addition: situated on the southern side of the city of Derry, in the island of Derry]. The ruins are those of the chapel of the convent and consist merely of 2 parallel walls 15 feet long and 15 feet asunder. It was formerly surrounded by a graveyard of nearly 3 acres, now, however, almost wholly broken up and cultivated to within a few yards of the church. It contained no inscribed or squared tombstones, the locality of each grave being merely marked by a small stone or rounded water pebbles. There have been no interments in it since the commencement of the last century.

[Insert addition by Stokes: The old ruin of Rosnagalliagh is immediately at the side of the high road and presents nothing more than a part of 2 parallel walls very close to one another, and the interior filled up with brambles and holly. These 2 fragments of walls are 5 feet from the ground. They appear to be composed of stones, not large but well fitted. The present ruin is but a trace of a once larger one. It is 15 feet long and 15 wide.

This was not the convent itself but only the church, according to the relations of the inhabitants. It was once surrounded by a churchyard of nearly 3 acres now, however, almost wholly broken up. It is cultivated to within a few yards of the church. Although it contained graves it had neither gravestones or tombs. The locality of each grave was merely marked by the insertion of a small stone or water pebbles.

The neighbouring farmer relates that he destroyed an ancient paved road which entered the eastern part of the churchyard and seemed to come from Warbleshinny glen.

The nunnery itself stood between the remains of the church and the bank of the Foyle. No traces of it, however, are anywhere visible.

There are no crosses known in the neighbourhood. Burying by the poorer orders continued in the churchyard up to the period when a Mr Brown got possession of the farm in which it was in. This was a short time after the troubles of James II. He, Brown, was one of the first individuals who settled in the neighbourhood on the re-establishment of peace.

Within a short distance of the old church there is a solid stone 5 feet in height, width, length and depth. This is believed to have been used as an altar or table on which religious ceremonies were performed. There is also a hill, on the summit of which is a hawthorn bush, and by it a large flat stone. This is called Sentry hill and is believed to

have been occupied as such by the inmates of the abbey.

Not far from the churchyard there is a holy well dedicated to St Cogle, the water of which is believed to have been the source of many miraculous cures. There is another in the townland of Magheracannon, to whom dedicated unknown. The water is believed to be miraculous, and pilgrims coming to receive the benefit leave old rags of linen, silk and calico sticking on the branches and trunk of the large old hawthorn bush that still overhangs the well. By the long continuation of this practice, thousands of these marks of reverence have been collected].

Within a short distance of the chapel there is a remarkable stone of a square form, which is popularly believed to have been an altar or table on which religious ceremonies were performed. It is 5 feet in height, length and depth, and probably was used as a temporary resting place for bodies previously to interment.

Holy Wells

There are 2 springs in the parish which are considered sacred and supposed to possess miraculous healing powers. One is situated near the church of Rossnagalliagh, near the ruins of the church, and is dedicated to St Cogal or Comgal, the founder of the church of Camus near the Bann. The other is in the townland of Maghera Cannoin or "the field of the canons." An ancient hawthorn bush which impends over it is hung with some thousand bits of rags, the votive offerings of the pilgrims who have come to seek benefit from its supposed sanative virtues. This is a custom still preserved in the East [insert marginal query: where?], as shown by Dr O'Conor in his interesting essay on the pagan origin of well worship; see Columbanus's letters.

Military: Castle

The castle of Enagh, which was one of O'Cahan's chief fortresses, and which for a time gave name to the barony, was romantically situated on the small island, now called Rough Island, in the eastern lake, and occupied nearly the whole of its extent. But little more than the foundations now remain, the stones having been carried away to build houses in the neighbouring village. The date of its erection has not been ascertained, but it is not likely to have been earlier than the close of the 15th century [insert addition: and is traditionally said to have been the residence of Manus Gallda, the anglified O'Kane].

Whatever strength this castle might have derived from its peculiar situation before artillery was used in the country, it was but of little consequence afterwards. The *Annals of the four masters* at the year 1555 record that it was demolished by [insert addition: the son of] O'Donnell (Calbach), by means of a piece of ordnance called *gonna cam* or "the crooked gun," which he had brought with him from Scotland. This was probably the first piece of artillery seen in the north of Ireland. O'Donnell was attended on this occasion by a number of troops which he had obtained from MacCalin (Campbell) Gillaspuig Donn, under the command of the master Archbold.

The castle must have been re-edified speedily, as it is marked as a fortress on the maps made at the close of the 16th century. It was taken by Sir Henry Docwra shortly after his settlement at Derry, as thus stated by himself.

"About the 20th of June (1600) I brought the Derrey cannon I had to Ainagh, a castle of O'Caine's, standing in a lough not much above a myle from the Derrey, but the river betweene, with which I beate upon it the first day a good distance of, and did little good, but at night wee drove the battery within 80 paces and the next morning wee founde the ward was runne out of it."

Docwra immediately placed a company of 100 foot under Captain Sydney at Enagh, and at the close of the war it was garrisoned by the companies of Captain Lewis Orrell and Captain Ellis Floyd, consisting of 100 men each. The garrison was shortly after withdrawn as unnecessary and, according to tradition, the place was last held by Manus Gallda or "the anglified O'Kane." (See genealogy of the O'Kane's in the general county history).

[Insert note: In 183[blank] the antique ornament represented in the annexed woodcut was found in this island. Its material is Celtic bronze and its style of workmanship, though good, indicates an early antiquity. The design is 3 serpents intertwined, but of one of the serpents only a part remains. The use of this curious ornament must be left to antiquarian conjecture; possibly it may have been a fibula].

Castle, Bawn and Village

The castle, bawn and village of the Goldsmiths' Company, in whose proportion the greater part of the parish was comprised, were situated near the village of New Buildings, in the townland of Ballyore and adjacent to the Foyle. They were thus described by Pynnar in 1618-19.

"Upon this proportion there is a bawn of lime and stone, 100 feet square, 16 feet high with 4 flankers. Also there is a large castle or stone house in building

within the wall, which was 2 storeys high, and the workmen earnestly at work to finish it with all haste. There are also 6 houses of stone and 6 of timber, very strong and well built, and seated in a very good and convenient place for the king's service."

[Insert note: The architectural character of the castle and adjacent buildings, as well as the names of their original occupants, are preserved in a rude drawing of "the buildings belonging to the Company of Goldsmiths, 2 miles from Londonderry" in Sir T. Phillips' *Briefe survey of the present estate of the plantation of the countyes of London Derry*, in the Lambeth library, from which the annexed reduced copy has been made. The localities of the other houses are marked in his *Plot of the lands belonging to the company of Goldsmiths*, namely in Promata (Primity) 4 and in Prehen, Lisaghmore, Tamnymore and Gobnascale 1 each. These townlands, it will be observed, all lie along the east bank of the Foyle and adjacent to Derry].

According to popular tradition the castle and adjacent houses were destroyed by fire during the civil wars of 1641, only one of the stone houses having escaped the flames. This house, which is said to have been the blacksmith's, still exists. It is built of coarse irregularly-sloped stones and roofed with Glenwood oak, which is still perfectly sound.

[Crossed out: According to tradition there was a second castle in the townland of Primity (properly Tromata), immediately opposite to and at the distance of about 100 perches from the former. Considerable ruins of this castle remained till the year 1799, when they were totally destroyed by the farmer on whose lands they were situated, for the sake of the ground which they occupied].

Battery

In the townland of Lisaghmore may still be seen the remains of an entrenched battery thrown up during the siege of Derry. It is known by the name of French hill, and its situation is marked on Nevil's map of the siege. It is most probable that this was Brigadier Wancot's, which was at the Prehen side of the Foyle.

Castles and Houses

[Insert addition by Stokes: A large castle formerly existed in Ballyore, immediately adjoining the village of New Buildings and on its western side. It is believed to have been burned with the rest of the village by a ravaging army. The parishioners recollect a large tract of ground which was a waste under rubbish, stones and mortar until subjected to cultivation. These were the demolished ruins of the castle. There were discovered a number of underground apartments, kitchens, cellars and vaults of a very large size. So late as 1833 there has been one of the large cellars discovered supposed to have been a liquor store. The flags raised from the floor are at present standing against the back wall of a house in the village.

This discovery has had the effect of fully convincing the occupiers of the soil that the relations handed down to them by their forefathers had been founded on truth. It was made by a man who was preparing a vegetable garden on the site of the ruins.

Not many yards off there is still one of the houses which had escaped the conflagration. The dense quantity of smoke arising from the castle and other buildings when on fire so completely overshadowing the little cottage is believed to have been the sole cause by which it escaped a similar fate. It is also believed to have been the house where the blacksmith who worked for the castle lived and had his forge.

It is built of coarse irregular stones, roofed with Glenwood oak, perfectly sound although in use for 200 years. There stand several uprights of the same timber in the walls with which the couples are so securely connected that the wall bears none of the weight. The greater part of them, however, have been removed and the roof will soon be made to rest wholly on the wall. The rafters and wattles have continued unchanged, but the windows have been altered in shape.

Castle and Fortification

In the townland of Primity, immediately opposite and at the distance of about 100 perches, there stands another of these extensive castles. A great portion of this building remained completely mantled over with ivy and in such a state of preservation that it would have borne out its venerable appearance for centuries to come had it not been taken down by a Mr McClosky, who obtained possession of the farm on which it stood and, believing that the space of ground occupied by it would greatly augment the size of his field, he pulled it down in the year 1799. But the recollections of the size, extent and appearance of the ruin is still in the minds of the present residents.

Within the last 10 years a search was made for a limestone quarry in the field in which it had stood. On penetrating the ground to the depth of 10 feet, the workmen found a cellar, the floor of which was well laid with flags and surrounded by walls about 7 feet high, and in good preservation. Neither the

flagging or wall have since been removed but have been filled up on a level with the surface and is now bearing a good crop of oats. There has also been discovered a cove supposed to lead from one to the other of these castles. It is now stopped up.

In the townland of Lissaghmore there are some entrenchments said to have been cast up by an English squadron in the wars of 1641. An old ruined barracks stands near. The place is known by the name of French hill. It is believed to have [been] chosen as a place of encampment, to strengthen which strong fortifications were drawn up on the rising grounds of the townland].

Seal of Goldsmiths' Company (for illustration). At the Plantations of the county by the London companies in 1611, the quarter part of the parish of Clondermot fell to the lot of the Goldsmiths' Company (see Townlands) and has remained in their possession.

HISTORY

People or Present State

Of the history of this and the other parishes of Tirkeeran <Tir Kerin>, anterior to the 11th century, a sketch has been already given in the notice of the barony; and the Irish annals do not furnish materials for a more minute detail. The Orgallian tribe of Hy MacCarthen, by whom they were occupied in the 4th century, having retained possession but a few centuries before they were subdued and dispossessed by the increasing power of the Kinel-Owen, by whom the O'Colgans and O'Connells were placed over the territory as chiefs, had consequently no hereditary bards or antiquaries interested subsequently in preserving their genealogical history; and it may be here remarked that, generally speaking, it is only of those families which retained power till the period in which the annals were compiled that the early history was carefully collected and preserved.

Of this class were the Clan Dermott, another family of the Kinel-Owen, who succeeded the O'Colgans and O'Connells, and appear from the annals to have been one of the most powerful tribes in the neighbourhood of Derry during the 11th, 12th and 13th centuries, after which they were in turn overpowered by their kindred tribe of O'Cathan or O'Kane.

In the *Books of Lecan* and *McFirbis* the origin of the Clan Dermott is set down among "the men of Moy-Ithe, an ancient territory lying along the west shore of the Foyle." These were otherwise called the Clan Connor, as being the descendants of 12 sons of Conor, the son of Fergal, King of

Ireland, who was killed in the battle of Allen in 718, according to the *Four masters*, or 722 according to Tighernach and O'Flaherty. From Dermott, one of these 12 sons of Connor, they derived their peculiar appellation of Clan Dermott, after they had split into the several families of O'Caireallain, O'Kennedy, O'Murry, O'Corran and O'Corraighte or Corry, and of all these the O'Caireallains were the chiefs. The connection of these families is thus given in the *Book of McFirbis*.

Genealogical Tree of Clan Dermott

[Insert note: This branch to be printed in small capitals].

Fergal, the son of Maolduin, King of Ireland 10 years, father of Conor, father of Dermott, a quo Clan Dermott. Dermott, father of Baigheall and Maolpadraig. Baigheall, father of Cairreallan and Cinnidigh; Maolpadraig, father of Corran (the priest) and Mothla. Caireallan, a quo Maolduin; Cinnidigh, a quo Maolphadruig and Dubhagan; Corran, a quo Fogartach, Maolfabhail and [?] Maolbriget; Mothla, a quo O'Corry; this line is not preserved. Maolduin, father of Aongus; Maolphadraig, father of Muireagan; Dubhagan, father of Cearnach; Fogartach, father of [?] Curaille and [?] Murcheadal; [?] Maolbriget, father of Dubhgiolla. Aongus, father of Ruadugh; Muireagan, father of Maolmathill; Cearnach, father of Faghertach and Muchadh; Cercaille, father of Maolfabhaill and Maolruany; [?] Murcheadal, father of Cathal no Conn; [?] Dubhgiollin, father of Ainbhidh and [?] Maolbridhe, the priest. Ruadugh, father of Aodh; Maolmathill, father of Gilla Phadrugh, Cuchogaidh, Fogartach and Cu-brathach; Faghartach, father of Muireagan, [?] Muircheada and Giolla Duill; Muchadh, father of Giolla Cuanastan; Maolfabhaill, father of Murchadh, Maolduin and Naoindenach; Maolruany, father of Aodh and Giolla-mo-dronn no mo-lugha, [?] Malgare, Fearghal and [?] Murmadhat; Cathall no Conn, father of Teig; Ainbhidh, father of [?] Culum; Maolbridhe the priest, father of Maolpadruig the priest. Aodh, father of Maolruany; Muireagan, father of Giollabrach; Maunbeach, father of Giolla-da-bhog; Giolla Duill, father of Giolla Martin; Maolruany, father of Aodh; Aodh, father of Maolruany O'Cairellan.

The O'Cathans, by whom the Clan Dermott were overpowered, were also of the Clan Connor, being, with these families derived from them, the descendants of Drugan, a brother of Dermott, the progenitor of the Clan Dermott.

11th and 12th Century Chronology

The following notices of the O'Caireallains and Clan Dermott occur in the *Annals of the four masters*.

1090, Mulroney O'Caireallain, Lord of Clan Dermott, and Gillchrist O'Luine (Loony), Lord of Kinel Moen, were slain on the same day by Donall, the grandson of Loghlin, King of Ireland.

1135, Rory O'Cananain, Lord of Kinel Connell, a warlike tower of defence, a man of charity and humanity, was slain by the men of Moy-Ithe, i.e. by Mulrony O'Caireallain and the Clan Dermott. The Kinel Connell afterwards cut off the Kinel Eogan with great slaughter.

1137, Connor O'Caireallain was killed by the inhabitants of Fermanagh.

1138, Mulrony O'Caireallain, lamp of the north of Ireland for personal form, wisdom and prowess, was slain by the Kinel Moen.

1177, O'Muldony and the Kinel Connell [insert addition: Tirconallians] were defeated by Conor O'Caireallain in a battle in which O'Searraigh (Skerry) and many other distinguished men of Kinel Enda were slain. The daughter of Roderick O'Conor, King of Ireland and wife of Flaherty O'Muldony (Lord of Tirconnel), was killed by the sons of O'Caireallain.

John de Courcy and the knights made an incursion into Dalriada and into Dun-da-leith-glass (Downpatrick), where they slew Donnell the son [insert addition: grandson] of Cathasach (Casey), Lord of Dalriada, and plundered and destroyed the town. They erected a castle there, from which they twice defeated the Ulidians, and once the inhabitants of Tirone and Oriel, and slew Conor O'Caireallain, a chief of the Clan Dermott, and Giolla MacLiag O'Donnelly, chief of Ferdroma. They, moreover, wounded Donnell O'Flaherty to such a degree by arrows that he died of his wounds in the church of St Paul at Armagh, after having received the body and blood of Christ, and the sacraments of penance and extreme unction. They also slew many other chieftains besides these already enumerated.

Niall O'Gormley, Lord of Moy-Ithe and Kinel Enda, was slain by Donagh O'Caireallain and the Clan Dermott in the middle of Derry Columbkille. They first burned the house in which he was, and Niall, endeavouring to make his escape, was killed in the doorway of the house.

[Insert addition: These events are related with somewhat greater detail in the *Annals of Innisfallen* as follows: "A valiant knight of the English, viz. John de Courcy, together with 22 knights and 300 of the English, came from Dublin to Downpatrick without the knowledge of the Irish and built a [crossed out: ditch] or wall there from sea to sea, and made a strong fort of stones and clay, and destroyed the town and all Ulster, but he was defeated and the greatest part of his men were slain and himself taken by Rughry MacDon-sleibhe, and he gave him his liberty again, upon which the English took courage and made a bloody slaughter of the Irish, who left behind them in the field the crozier (of) Tighnin and of Ronan. Rughruidhe Paor was a powerful knight in that engagement.

The English of Dublin came together to the assistance of John de Courcy. A great hosting by Maolseachlinn O'Neill to Cineal Eogan, together with Rughruidhe, son of Donsleibhe, with the Ultonians and Giolla an Coimhdhe O'Carnan, the comorba of Patrick, with the nobility of the north and the clergy, to take Downpatrick from John de Courcy, and a stout battle was fought between them; and the Cineal Eogan were defeated with the Ultonians and 500 of them were slain, the comorba of Patrick was taken prisoner with his clergy, the crozier of Comhgall and the organ and the crozier of Daciarog and other relicks, but the English gave liberty to the comorba of Patrick and to the Bishop of Down (who is called the Bishop of Ulster) to go off free, and they gave the cannons of Patrick and the bells back again after killing the clergy, and the Englishmen have the Bachull's crozier as yet [insert marginal query].

There were slain there Donell O'Flaherty, the chieftain of the sept of Hamill, and Conor O'Ciorallan, the chief of the tribe of Dermot, Giolla MacLiag O'Dongan, the chieftain of the men of Droma, Giolla Coimdhe Ma[c] Tumulty, chieftain of the family of Cartan, and the chieftain of the clan Fogarty].

1179, Donagh O'Caireallain and the Clan Dermott made peace with the Kinel Moen and O'Gormly, i.e. Auliffe, the son of Meanman, brother-in-law to Donagh O'Caireallain. This peace was solemnly concluded between them in the church of Ardstraw before the relics of that church, and also of those of Domhnach More (Donaghmore) and Ernaidhe (Urney). O'Gormly (Auliffe) came the next day to the house of Donagh O'Caireallain to demand further pledges, but was killed in the midst of a multitude in the doorway of the house, in the presence of his own sister, the wife of Donagh. 3 of his adherents were also killed, viz. Kineth, the son of O'Bracain, the son of Gilchrecst McCormaic, and the son of Riodan, the foster brother of Donagh O'Caireallain.

1180, Donagh O'Caireallain was killed by the people of Tirconnell, in revenge of his treacherous conduct towards O'Gormly. His death was the effect of the miracles of the saints whose guarantee he had violated.

Randal O'Caireallain was killed by the Kinel Moen in the middle of Derry Columbkille.

1197, Magrath O'Laverty, tanist of Tirone, and Mulrony O'Caireallain, chief of Clan Dermott, were slain.

13th Century Chronology

1200, Egnechan O'Donnell, Lord of Tirconnell, dispatched the ships of Tirconnell (13 in number) by sea and the remainder of its forces by land. The latter encamped at Gaoth-an-Chairrgin (Carrigins). The Clan Dermott on the other hand came to Port-Rois (Rosses bay on the Foyle) to meet the ships. As soon as the crews of the 13 ships perceived this, they attacked and defeated the Clan Dermott.

MacLoughlin (Conor Beg, son of Murlogh) came to their assistance, his horse was wounded under him and he himself thrown. He was afterwards slain by the Kinel Connell, in revenge of the contempt with which he had sometime before treated the comorba and shrine of St Columbkille. Murrogh O'Criochan, Lord of Hy Fiachrach, was killed for the same reason. The people of Egnechan following up the rout made a dreadful slaughter of the Tironians and Clan Dermott.

1205, Randall, the son of Dermott, Lord of Clan Dermott, died.

1206, Egneachan O'Donnell made a predatory incursion into Hy Forannan and Clan Dermott; his army seized upon many cows and killed many people, but were overtaken by the Hy Dermott, the O'Forannans and the O'Gormlys, and a battle ensued in which many were slain and drowned. The Kinell Connell finally carried off the booty but with much difficulty.

1215, Aoengus O'Caireallain, chief of Clan Dermott, was slain by his own relations. During this and the preceding centuries the O'Caireallains were at the summit of their prosperity and power, as sufficiently appears, not only from the preceding notices, but also from the remarkable fact that no less than 3 of them held the bishoprick of Tirone or Derry in immediate succession from 1185 to 1293; see Bishops of Derry. Henceforward, however, their names as chiefs of a tribe or country wholly disappears from history, their little territory having become a portion of the extensive lordship of O'Cahan. Yet still they did not for some centuries after, or probably till the general ruin of the native Irish consequent upon the rebellion of 1641, become wholly plebeian; and though no longer distinguished as warriors, their name occasionally received some historic lustre from distinguished ecclesiastics.

[Insert addition: Same year Teige McEtigen, chief of Clann Dermott, died.

1230, Florence O'Carolan, Bishop of Tirone (Ardstraw), a noble select senior, died in the eighty-sixth year of his age.

1250, Maurice Fitzgerald, joined by Cathal O'Reilly, Cuconnaught O'Reilly and all the other chiefs of Hy Briuin, marched with a great army into Tirone and remained for 3 nights at Tulach Og, where they suffered much from toil and underwent great hardship, without obtaining either submission or hostages by their expedition. On their return into Tirconnell, Maurice Fitzgerald made O'Ceannannain, lord of that country, prisoner under protection of Bishop O'Carolan, (i.e. his safety was guaranteed by Bishop O'Carolan, O'Conor Autogr). O'Ceannannain, upon afterwards attempting to escape, was slain by Fitzgerald's people].

15th Century Chronology

In 1430 Donal or Donagh O'Caireallain was constituted a sub-guardian of the see of Derry by Archbishop Swain during the suspension of the bishop for various crimes, and at the same time the rural deanery of Moy-Ithe was conferred upon him during pleasure.

Later Chronology

[Insert note: In 1537 a grant of English liberty was made to Cormack Kerrulan, chaplain, (patent rolls 27-28, Henry VIII)].

And in 1542 Hugh O'Caireallain was confirmed in the see of Clogher by King Henry VIII at the same time when Con O'Neill, whom he accompanied to England, was received into favour, renounced the name and title of O'Neill, and was created Earl of Tyrone (Ware's *Annals*).

Previously to the Plantation of Ulster, a branch of the O'Caireallains possessed the Bishop of Derry's erenachy in the parish of Clonleigh or Lifford, consisting of 2 quarters of land, a gift most probably conferred by the bishops of the family in the 12th or 13th century. (See inquisition taken at Lifford in 1609, in which the names of Morice O'Kirolan and Cole or Charles O'Kirolan appear as jurors).

This tribe is still numerous in that vicinity, as are their original stock in their ancient locality of Clondermot and Cumber. Their name, however, appears under a variety of orthographical forms, as Carlin, Curlan, Curland, Carrlan, Kerrlan, Gartland, and in the English Carleton, as in the instance of the distinguished author of the *Traits and stories of the Irish peasantry*, [crossed out: who has given the noblest evidence of illustrious descent in the productions of a vigorous mind, and if to the first of Irish story-tellers, would be added the first of Irish melodists [insert alternative: bards].

That he is of the family of O'Caireallain, he himself confesses; and if it were equally certain that the minstrel O'Cairreallain were of the same race, which is by no means sure, they could boast of having, even in their legend state, produced the first of the modern Irish story-tellers and the best of the Irish bards.

[Insert note: And under one of the above orthographical disguises, that of Curling, the name appears among the signatories of the Protestant gentlemen defenders of Derry who, having survived the calamities of the siege, sent a loyal address to Their Majesties on its termination, viz. the governor, the celebrated George Walker (see Walker's [true?] account of the siege of London Derry)].

As already stated, the period has not been exactly ascertained when the O'Caireallains or Clan Dermott was dispossessed of this and perhaps some other parishes of Tirkeeran by the O'Cathans: but it appears to have been at the close of the 13th or commencement of the 14th century, as the O'Caireallains are not noticed in the Irish annals as chiefs after that time.

It was most probably to secure their possession of the barony of Tirkieran that the O'Cathans erected the castle of Annagh in this parish, which appears to have been, till after the Plantation of Derry by Sir Henry Docwra, their chief residence, and probably was the first castle erected by them in the English style.

A portion of the parish remained in the possession of this powerful clan till the confiscations immediately preceding the plantations by the City of London in 1611; but as early as 1602 the castle of Annagh with the lands etc. lying between the Rivers Faughan and Ban Gibbons, now the Glendermot river, on the one side and the Foyle on the other, were obtained by the Crown by grant from Sir Donnogh O'Cathan, for the purpose, obviously, of strengthening the British plantation at Derry under Sir H. Docwra at that time.

The documents connected with this grant are preserved in the Rolls Office in Dublin, and as they have not been hitherto published and are very important to the history of that period, they are here copied in full.

Will of Donnagh O'Cane

"Knowe all men by these presents that I, Donnogh O'Cane of Lamevadde in the countye of Colrane, in the province of Ulster, in the realme of Ireland, chiefe of my septe and famylie, in consideration of the gratious favor and clemencye shewed to me, the above-named Donnogh O'Cane, by my most gratious and dread soveraigne Lady Elizabeth, by the grace of God, Queen of England, Ffrance and Ireland, Defender of the Fayth, in pardoninge me for my late unnaturall and wicked rebellion comytted againste Her Highnes, her crowne and dignytie, and sufferinge mee to possesse all my land and goodes which in justice Her Majestie might have ceased and taken to her selfe, to be disposed at Her Highnes will and pleasure and for divers other good causes and consyderations, mee thereunto specially moveinge have given and granted and for mee, myne heires and assignes, do by these presents give and grante to my above-named soveraigne Lady Queene Elizabeth, and to her heires and successors, all that my castle and mansyon house called Aynough in the countye aforesaid, together with all lande, tennements, pastures, meadowes, woodes, heaths, loughs, waters, fyshings, realtyes, services and all other proffitts and comodities whatsoever to the said castell or mansyon house belonginge or any wayes apperteyninge to, or with the same used, occupied or enjoyed.

And also all othere landes, tennements, pastures, meadowes, woods, heaths, loughs, waters, fishinggs, realtyes, services, proffitts and comodities whatsoever to mee at any tyme before the date of these presents belonginge or apperteyninge, sett lyeinge and beinge betweene the Ryver of Ffaghan and Lough Foyle, so farr as to one other ryver called Bangybbon which runneth into the said ryver of Ffoghan and from thence betweene the same ryver of Bangibbon and Lough Foyle so far as any of my lands and possessions do reache or extende themselves; and also all the whole ryver of Ffoghan and Bangibbon, together with the fyshinge of them or either of them, as also all my right, tythe or interest whatever in the ryver of Lough Foyle or the fyshinge thereof from the Ffoghan's mouth so far as lyeth uppon any parte of my aforesaid contrey, to have and to hould the above-named castle or mansyon house of Aynough and the above recyted lands, tennements, pastures, meadowes, woods, heaths, loughs, waters, fyshings, realties, services and all other the premises whatsoever to my said soveraigne

Lady Queen Elizabeth and to hir heires and successors for ever.

And I, the above-named Donnogh O'Cane, for the better strengtheninge and ratification of this my gift and grant, do further by thes presents surrender remyse, release and quyte clayme for mee, myne heires and assignes all myne estate, right, tythe, clayme and interest which I, myne heires or assignes at any tyme from the beginninge of the world untyll the daie of the date of their presents have hadd or by any meanes myght have had in or to the above-named castell of Aynough, or any of the before recited premyses; and doe alsoe by these presents bynde my selfe and myne heires for ever hereafter to warrant and defende against all men the said castell or mansyon house of Aynough and all the above given and granted premyses.

And do also by thes presents constytute, ordeyne and make my well-beloved in Christ, Darby Newman of Derry, gentleman, my true and lawfull attorney for mee, and in my name and stead to deliver and give to Sir Henry Docwra Knight, governor and commander of Her Majesty's forces at Lough Foyle, livery and seasyne of the said castell or mansyon house of Aynough, and all and singular the above-named premyses to the use and behoofe of our said soveraigne ladie Queen Elizabeth and of hir heires and successors.

In witness whereof I have hereunto sett my hand and seal the 28th daie of September Anno Dom. 1602. [Signature] O'Cane, his mark." Sealed and delivered to Captaine Derby Newman, to the use of our soveraigne lady the Queene, in the presence of Robert Cartwright, John Killyen, James Markhame, Derby Newman, Gorey W. O'Cane (pendit sigillum).

Endorsements: mind that the 25th day of September 1602 livery and seasin etc. was by Derby Newman, gent., taken and delivered to Sir Henry Docwra Knight, governor of Lough Foyle, for and to the use of our soveraigne lady the Queene, that now is, as well as of the castle or mansion house of Anough with all the lands thereabouts belonging and given to the Queene's Majestie, that now is, in the presence of John Sydney, Basill Brooke, George Blundell, A. Vowghtoy, John Wraye, (John Sydney).

[Insert marginal note: Cobran, delibatus in plena suae p[er] manus Johanus Da. [?] milit. de esse xi die February 1604. [Insert note: The following document is connected with this by indented slips of parchment].

Wee whose names are hereunder written, being impanelled upon a jury to inquire what lands, tenements, hereditaments were made over to our late soveraigne Queene Elizabeth by one Donnogh O'Cane of Lemavaddy in the county of Colrane, do fynde by the evidence of one deede which hereunto we have caused to be annexed and inseparably fastened, beareing date the eighteenth day of September anno 1602, that all the landes, castles, tenements and hereditaments, with all realties, services and other commodities thereunto belonginge, and in the same expressed, were by the said Donnogh O'Cane, of his own free and voluntary accord, without compulsion, threatening or force, conveighed and made over unto our said late soveraigne lady in manner and forme as is therein mentioned; divers of the witnesses whose names are thereunto opposed having before us viva voce testified as much upon their oaths and that the said deed is truly without all fraude, collusion and deceipt, the very free acte and deede of the said Donnogh O'Cane.

And furthere wee do also fynde by testimony of divers of the witnesses upon their oaths that were present at the same, that lyverie and seisine was openly, quietly and peacably given and taken, as well of the said mansion house or castle of Ainough, as of all other the lands, tenements and hereditaments in the said deed mentioned, in manner and forme as by the indorsement thereupon made doth appear.

And further we do fynde by the evidence of one dede or writt bearing date at Dublin the xviith day of May in the fower and fortith yeare of the reigne of our soveraigne lady the Queene, subscribed and examined by one Richard Colman, haveing annexed unto yt the seale of our said late soveraigne lady Queene Elizabeth in greene wax, which deede or writt hath been openly shewed and reade before us, that the said mansion house or castle of Ainogh, with all the lands, tenements and hereditaments in the said deeds of conveighance to our late said queene, mentioned were given in custodie to hold, use, occupie and enjoye, to Sir Henry Docwra Knight, governor of Her Majesty's fforces at Lough Foyle dureing pleasure, and that by a generall acknowledgement of the whole contrey and to many of our own perticuler knowledges also the said Sir Henry Docwra, for the space of one whole yeare at least, did hould, use, occupie and enjoy the same by virtue of the said custodie.

In witness of all which wee, the said jurors, have hereunto putt our handes and seales, at the city of Derry, on the one and twentith day of Januarie, in the second year of the reigne of our soveraigne lord King James over England, France and Ireland, and over Scotland the eight and thirtith. Humphroy [?] Vaile, Charles Harrison's marke, George Corivin's marke, Henry Sadler, Anthony [blank].

Endorsements: By virtue of the king's majesty's commission, directed unto us Henry Harte and William Illinge Esquires, or to either or any of us, to enquire by such meanes as to us or either of us shold seem fittest what landes, castles, tenements or hereditaments have been made over to our late soveraigne lady Queene Elizabeth by one Donnogh O'Cane of Lamevaddy in the county of Colrane, in the province of Ulster, and to certifie what we ffynde concerninge the same into His Majesty's courte of exchequer at Dublin, which commission beareth date the xxiiiith day of December in the second year of his highness raigne over England, France and Ireland and over Scotland the 24th, as by the same yt selfe doth and may at all tymes more plainly and more at large appeare, I the said Henry Harte (the other committee being absent out of the country and so not able to attend or execute that business) do hereby certify and make knowen unto all men to whom it appertaineth that I have caused a jury of 12 honest men, dwellers and inhabitants of the city of Derry and country neare about adjoininge, to be empanelled and sworen to make dilligent enquiry of the premises and their true verdicte to give what they fynde concerninge the same, which jury of 12 men have thereupon returned their answere in manner and forme, as on the other side of this present writinge is mentioned.

In confirmation whereof they have thereunto putt their hands and seales, and I as a witness before whome the same was done have also hereunto subscribed my name this present [day] 21st January 1604. [Signed] Henry Harte.

17th and 18th Century Chronology

It appears from Sir Henry Docwra's "Narrations" that some time in the year 1604 he let or disposed of his interest in these and the other lands of the Derry to Sir George Pawlet, whom he appointed Vice-Provost of Londonderry, and in whose possession they probably remained till his death in 1608. At the plantation of the county by the City of London the greater portion of these lands, together with others in the parish and some in Faughanvale, amounting in all to 44 and three-fifth townlands, fell to the Goldsmiths' Company, by whom they were let to their agent or farmer, John Freeman Esquire, at the annual rent of 331 pounds, as stated from rent roll of 1628 in Sir T. Phillips' manuscripts.

From the following notices in the *Concise view of the Irish society* it appears that the Goldsmiths' proportion was, early in the seventeenth century, let on lease to W. Warren and ultimately sold in 1729 to Henry, Earl of Shelburne: "3rd November (1715), the wardens of the Goldsmiths' Company attended the society and produced the counterparts of the lease from that company to W. Warren, of the manor of Goldsmiths' Hall.

31st October (1729), the master and wardens of the Goldsmiths' Company represented to the society that they had agreed to sell their manor of Goldsmiths' Hall to the Right Honourable Henry, Earl of Shelburne, for 14,100 pounds, but being advised that they could not make a proper conveyance without the concurrence of the society, they requested the society to join with them in making a title to the said earl, which they consented to do, upon being indemnified."

Derivation of Townland Names by John O'Donovan

NATURAL STATE

Summary of Townlands

1. Altnagelvin: appears to be a pretty high place.
2. Ardkill: proper Ardchoill or "coille," a long woody range of mountains.
3. Ardlough: though no lough appears now, the neighbouring marsh must have been one.
4. Ard-na-Brocky appears to be an ard.
5. Ard More: there is an ard on the map.
6. Ballyoan: must be Ballyowen, for if named from the ruin it should be Bailenahavan.
7. Ballyore: likely so called from the stones or from the family of Gould.
8. Ballyshasky: this shews some shesk.
9. Bogach: not a particle of bog appears on it.
10. Bolies: from cows in some sense.
11. Cah: Cluain Catha or Cluain Cátha, i.e. "cluain chaff."
12. Carn: means "a heap" of anything, as well as "a small hill" or ardan.
13. Carnafarn: proper Ceathramh-na-fearna; some mountainy places appear.
14. Carrakeel: Ceathramha Coille; it is not from "caol," it being broader than the other quarters.
15. Clamparnowe: *ata se clamparach go leor, agus mise leis a charadh.*
16. Clochore: a good deal of bog appears on this; I think it is *Clochra*.
16. Clondermott: "the children of poor Darby [Darly?], a discovery."

17. Cloony: Cluain.
18. Corroddy: appears to be *high* land; Con Rhody "Rhody's tiring [crossed out: place] hill."
19. Craigtown: appears craggy; Baile-na-Craige.
20. Creeve Donnell: a boggy mountainy-looking place.
21. Cromkill: the Kerry name for Columkill.
22. Cuilkeeragh: this is a cuil.
23. Curryfree: Curragh Fraoigh appears to be a heathy place.
24. Currynierin: no curragh appears here.
25. Disert Owen.
26. Drumahoe: is a rising ground on the immediate bank of the Faughan; could it be *Drom-na-habhan*?
27. Druim Conan: appears a druim.
28. Dun Hugh: no forth [fort].
29. and 30. Edenreagh: appears to be a large piece of uncultivatable land and will bear the name Riach.
31. Eanagh: must have retained its name from the carn given.
32. Evish: on the map Avish; shews nothing.
33. Fincharn.
34. Glendoire Owen: there appears to be a glen and doire here.
35. Glenkeen: this does make a glen or cluain with the Faughan.
36. Gobnascale: this townland terminates in a point to the south.
37. Gortgranagh.
38. Gorticah: "the battle or the chaff field."
39. Gorticross.
40. Gortin: "small field" or "Finn's field."
41. Gortinure: there are 2 forts on this.
42. Gortnessy: some small streams appear on this.
43. Gortfree: proper Gort Fraigh; fraoch appears on it.
44. Gransha: must be from grain.
45. Kilfinan: no ruin or church appears.
46. Killymallaght.
47. Killybane: this must be Ceide Ban; a ceide appears on it.
48. Knock Brack: appears to be a long mountain [insert alternative: hilly] range.
49. Lisdillon: is a very extensive heathy range without a lios.
50. Lios Glas: no lios, but a heathy mountain.
51. Lioscarrole: a fort appears on the north side.
52. Liosnagelvin: Liosgilligan; no fort.
53. Lios Neill: no fort.
54. Liossaghmore: Leithsheirrech Mor; is a large ploughland.

55. Liosahawly: *Leithshesrech Amhlaoidh*; a very small ploughland.

56. Machaire Cannon: *Na Ceanannach*.

57. and 58. Managh More and Beg: *Muinech*; they have no appearance of hills.

59. Maydown: *Magh Duin*; no fort.

60. Prehen: and he who came to scoff, remained to pray.

61. Primity: *Priomh Uite*.

62. Ross-na-gCailiach: *Ros-na-ccailleach liath*; the ruins of an abbey appear on this, as does the ross.

63. and 64. Stradreagh: *Srath Riabhach*; very near the lakes Enagh.

65. Taghirina: nothing appears on this; *Teachfhir Udhna, Aitfhir Udhna*.

66. Tamnymore: there is a large piece of bog here.

67. Templetown: has the ruin of a church.

68. Tirbracken: Breacan must have been a man's name.

69. Tirkieveny: *Tir-mhic-Uibhne*.

70. and 71. Tully Upper and Lower: are rising grounds.

72. and 73. Tullyally: *Tullaidhe Aille*; are sloping grounds.

74. Warbeshinny: has nothing remarkable.

Brickkilns: a townland not in your list.

Dromagore: Drom-an-Ghabhair, not in your list.

Derivation of Townland Names

1. Altnagelvin: called Altcongalluan one balliboe of land in the Charter of Londonderry, Altnagelvin on Sampson's map and Altnagalvin in some modern tythe books. The etymology seems to be *Alt-na-ngealbhan* i.e. "the height or hill of the sparrows." *Alt* is derived from the Latin altitudo in *Cormac's Glossary*, which establishes its meaning to be "a height," though it cannot be easily granted that the word found its way into Ireland through the medium of the first Latin missionaries, as countless very ancient names of places in Ireland begin with it. [Insert addition: It is evidently cognate with the Latin altus, Gaulic alt, Welsh alht and the Cornish als or alz; see ard infra in Ardkill].

The word is now obsolete in the south of Ireland, but it is well understood in the county of Fermanagh, where its meaning is most strikingly illustrated by the *alt* of Tuath Ratha, a remarkable wall of limestone rocks overhanging the plain called the *Faoi Alt*, on the north west margin of Lough Erne. In this county of Derry the meaning of alt is but indistinctly understood, some taking it to mean "a woody glen," others "the sloping side of a woody glen."

Gealbhan is now the only word for the common housesparrow but it seems to have been originally of a more generic signification, as *gealbhan buidhe* is the common name for a yellowhammer. *Gealbhan* [? gobrainn] is the name of another species. [Insert note: Altclongalwin, Sir T. Phillips' map, (Goldsmiths' proportion); Altcongaluan, charter James I; Altcolgallan, Cromwell; Altcongaluan, Charles II. Altus, Latin; alt, Gallic; als or alz, Cornish, query tal, tall, by transposition; Galvan, C. and Armoric, Golmis, Greek].

2. Ardkill: is called in the Charter of Derry by the correct name of Ardkilly being one balliboe of land [insert note: in the small proportion of Brackmoy (Brackfield)]. [Insert marginal query: Is there an old church or [building?] on this hill?]. The meaning is unquestionably *Ard Coille*, i.e. "hill of the wood" or "wood hill." In *Cormac's Glossary* the Irish word ard is derived from the Latin arduus, but as it is found in the names of so many places in Ireland it is more probable that it is an aboriginal pagan Irish word, traceable to a common origin with the Latin arduus than derived from it; see remarks on *Cormac's Glossary* in *Dublin Penny journal* vol.II].

Coill, derived from *coll* "hazel," is now the common word to express a wood of any kind of trees, but it is probable that it originally meant a wood of hazel only, as did *daire*, derived from *dair* "oak," "a wood of oak." Both words are formed from the names of the 2 most common trees in Ireland and now used to express "wood" in general.

[Insert addition: As the words which form this compound enter very largely into Irish topographical names, it will not be improper to treat of them once for all in this place. The word *ard*, or as it is sometimes written *art* in ancient manuscripts, signifies literally "high, lofty" and, figuratively, "loud, noble, eminent, excellent, proud," and is evidently cognate with the Cornish ard, the Welsh garth (hence gartha, "a promontory"), the Latin arduus and the old Persic ard and art "high;" hence in Persian arta "a hero," and the ancient Irish proper name *Art*, i.e. uasal Cormac, and probably the name Arthur, i.e. "nobleman." [Insert note: In the ancient glossary of Cormac it is stated that *ard* is the same as the Latin arduus, and that *art* has 3 meanings: 1, noble, 2, God, 3, a stone]."

Used topographically it has sometimes an adjective and sometimes a substantive signification, as *tulach ard* "high hill," *ard mor* "great height." The learned Mr Armstrong, in his *Gaelic dictionary*, supposes this word to be "derived from the Celtic primitive ar, signifying 'rock or mountain,' also 'high';" hence he adds "many words in other tongues signifying elevation, as Bisc[ayan] arre 'a rock,' Malay arrang, Arab and AEthiop hhar 'hill,' Armoric ar 'elevated,' Malabar arra 'mountain' and are 'elephant,' Hebrew ar 'a rock or mountain'."

It would appear certain from the extent of these cognates, and more might be added, that some simple aboriginal word existed, of which all these, in the Indo-European as well as Semitic languages, are but modifications; but whether the Celtic ar, in the sense of "rock, mountain," as Mr Armstrong states, be that root may be doubted, as he gives no authority for his assertion (the existence of the word in that sense), and no such word has been hitherto found in any dialect of the Celtic, excepting the Irish preposition ar "upon," in which the sense (idea) of "high" is indicated; and in this sense of "height" it may possibly be the root, not only of the various words given, but also of the Greek word *aixo archos*, and perhaps also the Irish *alt* and the Latin altus, as the liquids l and r are frequently interchanged in the Indo-European languages, and as the Irish in many parts of Ireland change r into l at the present day. Nor is it improbable that the Irish word *aer* "the sky," (air), which has such direct cognates in the Greek, Latin and other languages, had originally the same signification, as the Irish of the present day rarely understand it in the sense of "atmosphere" but "sky, welkin."

The word *coill* or *caill*, genitive *coille*, plural *coillte*, is another word of extreme antiquity common to all the Celtic languages and having an evident affinity with the Greek hule and the Latin sylva, the c of the Celtic being reduced by the Greeks to the aspirate for which the Latin frequently substituted the sibilant. Connell, in his manuscript Irish Dictionary (British Museum), states that this word is derived from *coll* "hazel," and that it was originally applied to a hazel wood only; and this conjecture may possibly be well founded as it is certain that the word *doire* (daire) has been likewise used by the Irish to express "a wood" generally, though originally, as explained by Adamnan, it signified "an oakwood," being derived from the Irish dair, Welsh darw, Greek dros, Latin quercus, Persian derucht, and hence probably the English word tree, Teutonic der, Armoric dar and andar "a forest," Sanscrit druh and drus, Turkish dervent "a hill covered with trees."

On the Down Survey the name Coolistrane is written on the space occupied by this townland, and on Sampson's map this and the adjacent townland of Knockbrack are placed within the adjoining parish of Lower Cumber. It appears from Sir Thomas Phillips' map that this townland was included in the freehold of Captain Manus O'Cahan].

[Insert note: Marked Coolistrane in the Down Survey; native freehold, Captain Manus O'Chahan (forfeited), Sir T. Phillip's map; Lieutenant-Colonel Tristiam Beresford, Protestant, Ardkill, Book of Survey and Distribution].

3. Ardlough: in the Down Survey called Arlogh a part of Balliowen. The name signifies *Ard Loch* "the high lake" and must have been derived from a lough now dried up. [Insert note: I know a place called *Cnoc-an-locha* "a hill overhanging a lake"]. [Insert addition: "The height or hill of the lough" as, though there is no lake or pool in the townland at present, there is a marsh adjacent which is evidently the site of one]. *Loch* is translated stagnum by Adamnan, Abbot of Iona, and lacus by most other writers. The word is often applied by the peasantry to a very small body of water, though the Irish language affords other words to express its diminutive as *lochan, loichin* "a small lough" and *log* "a pool."

[Insert addition: The word *loch* "a lake" is used by the Irish to signify "an arm of the sea," and frequently "a very small pool of water," and there is no other word to express "a lake" generally. This is another of those primeval topographical words existing nearly in all the languages of the old world as in the following examples: Greek lakkos, Latin lacus, German lach "a pool," Welsh llych, Armoric lagen, Bisc[ayan] and French lac, English lake, Saxon and Spanish lago, Dal[matian] lakna, Cop[tic] phalakkos; also Hebrew lahh "moisture," Chaldean lachah "a marsh," Norwegian logus "marsh" and Persian lacca "a sea" (Armstrong).

It seems probable that this word originally meant water, simply as the old Latin word lix, contracted from liquis, has that meaning, or rather, perhaps, "standing water," for it will be shown in another place in this volume (parish name Lower Cumber) that there existed another Celtic word *bir*, which was equally common to the nations of the old world and applied to this element in a more extensive manner. Thus the word is always translated stagnum by Adamnan and other writers, and it has perhaps been never applied to running water.

From the Down Survey and other ancient authorities it appears that this townland was a subdivision of the dean's lands called Ballyowen; see Ballyowen].

[Insert note: Ardlough, dean's land, not marked on Sir T. Phillips' map; claimed by Captain George Hart, Arlogh, part of the same townland, i.e. Ballyowen, Book of Survey and Distribution; Lieutenant Thomas Skipton, Protestant, Ardmore, Book of Survey and Distribution].

4. Ardnabrocky: appears in the Down Survey as Alfnabracky a part of Balliowen, but alf is certainly a mistake, for alt, which is nearly synonymous with ard "a height," -nabracky, the latter part of the name, is unquestionably an anglicizing of *Na Brocaighe* "of the badger warren." *Brocach*, derived from *broc* "a badger" [insert addition: a word common to all the Celtic dialects], and anciently signifying "a badger warren" only, is now used by the peasantry, even when speaking English, to denote "fox dens" or the "lustra of any wild beasts," and sometimes "the dens or lurking places of robbers." [Insert addition: The word *brocach* is not found in any Irish written authority, the correct word according to *Cormac's Glossary* being *broiceannach* and broclach and broclann according to modern dictionaries]. This word frequently enters into names of mountain townlands but it is to be distinguished from *breacach* which signifies "spotted, brindled, mottled variegated land."

[Insert note: Byrhush Welsh, broch Cornish, broch Armoric, broich; claimed by Captain George Hart, Alfnabracky and Lisnagilligan, part of Ballyowen, Book of Survey and Distribution].

5. Ardmore: is called in King Charles' charter Tardmore being one balliboe of land. The meaning is certainly *Ard Mor*, or with the article *An T-ard Mor*, i.e. "the great height or rising ground." Nouns of the masculine gender beginning with vowels will take t prefixed to the nominative singular, and hence the tard of the charter for ard. In Sampson's copy of the charter this is erroneously printed Fardmore. (See original copy of the charter in the Four Courts).

[Insert addition: The adjective mor, which is common to all the Celtic dialects, as Welsh mawr, Cornish and Armoric maur, is cognate with the German mehr, and mor literally means "big or great," and figuratively "noble, mighty," and hence probable it is cognate with the Hindost[an] mor "a king," Syrian mar "a lord," Persian mir "a lord," Tartar mir "a prince," Turkish and Arabic e-mir "a prince."

In the charters this townland is called one balliboe of land, and it appears from Sir Thomas Phillips' map that it was one of the townlands included in the townlands of Captain Manus O'Cahan].

[Insert note: Tardmore, Charters of Derry; Lieutenant Thomas Skipton, Protestant, Ardmore, Book of Survey and Distribution].

Derivation of Townland Names

6. Ballyoan: called in the inquisition of 1603 the 2 quarters of Ballyowne and in the one of 1609 the 2 quarters of Ballyowen [insert addition: and in Bishop Downham's Visitation Book, 1622]. In the Down Survey Balliowen is represented as a general name for the north eastern portion of the parish, comprising the denominations Carickbrede, Listrely, Carnetowne, Lisneale, Kilfury, Arlogh, Alfnabracky and Lisnagillagan. [Insert addition: And of these subdenominations, Carrickbrede to the east and Listrely to the west occupy the situation of the present townland of Ballyoan].

This name may signify either *Baile Eoghain*, i.e. "the townland of Owen or Eugene," or *Baile Abhann*, i.e. "rivertown," but as this townland lies along the River Faughan it is more than probable that the latter is the true meaning.

It appears from the inquisition taken at Derry in 1609 that the Dean of Derry was seized in his demesne as of fee of and in the 2 quarters of land called Ballyowen lying on O'Chane's side, and also of and in 2 other quarters of land neere adjoyninge called Templemore and Clonskey, and thother called Coolecranagh which the jurors found to have beene in the possession of the 2 former Deans of Derry. The said lands were then in the possession of William McItegart, who was the last Dean of Derry by the pope's authority etc. (quote verbatim and at full length).

[Insert addition: From the preceding notices it is clear that the 8 townlands of the Down Survey, included under the general name of Ballyowen, constituted originally 2 quarters or the half of an ancient Irish ballybetagh. After the plantations by the Londoners the lands of Ballyowen became a part of the temporalities of the deanery and, according to Bishop Downham's Visitation Book, were let by William Webb, the first Protestant dean, for 3 lives, to John Baker Esquire for the yearly rent of 12 pounds. At the period of the Down Survey the lands of Balliowen were claimed by Captain George Hart, English Protestant, of course as lessee under the dean.

The Ballyoan of the Ordnance map is divided into Carricke-brede and Listrely on Down Survey map].

[Insert note: Claimed by Captain George Hart, Carrickbreade part of Ballyowen, Listrely part of the same, Carntowne part of Ballyowen, Lisneale part of the same, Arlagh part of the same, Killfury part of the same, Alfnabracky and Lisnagilligan part of Ballyowen; Book of Survey and Distribution.

The present townland of Ballyowen is in the Down Survey divided into 2 townlands, Listrely to the west and Caricke-brede. Observation: the tract of land lying between Clooney and

Altnagelvin, and the rivers of Foyle and Faughan, and Gransha and Templetown, is on Sir T. Phillips' map of the Grocers' proportion called "the Deane of Derry, his land;" between this piece of ground and Enagh on the same map is marked the name Ardgaire, which does not resemble any modern name which would agree in situation; (query Stradreagh? q.v.)].

7. Ballyore: called in the charter Ballyore one balliboe of land. It seems to signify *Baile Oir* "town of gold," but why it should receive such an appellation it is now vain to inquire. Many places in Ireland are called from gold and silver, perhaps sometimes from the existence of mines of these precious metals, sometimes in a figurative sense from the value of the land, and not unfrequently in an ironical sense from its poverty. The adjective *odhar*, [insert addition: cognate with the Greek *ochgos* and the English ochra] (ore) "dun-coloured," is found in the names of some mountain townlands and known to be given from the colour and appearance of the land. [Insert note: I think there is a townland in the county of Limerick of the same name, called after the occupiers *Muintir Oir*, Goolds].

The lands included under the denomination of Ballyoir are not named on Sir Thomas Phillip's map, but their situation is marked under the general appellation "the Dean of Derry his land:" "And further the said jurors doe, upon their oathes, say and present, that the said Dean of Derry is alsoe seised in his demesne, as of fee in right of his said deanery of Derry, of and in the 2 quarters of land called Ballyowen, lying on O'Chane's side, within the countie of the cittie of Derry aforesaid; and alsoe, of and in two other quarters of land neare adjoyninge, thone called Templemore and Clonekey, and thother called Coolecronagh, which the said jurors finde to have bene in the possession of the 2 former Deans of Derry.

And whereas the said landes are now in the possession of Wilton McItegart, who was the last Dean of Derry by the pope's authoritie, the said jurors doe finde uppon their oathes that the said lands do not belonge unto him, the said Wilton, as his inheritance, but that he continues the possession which he had formerly gotten in right of the said deanery; and further, the said jurors doe, uppon their oathes, say that the Lord Archbusshop of Armagh and his predecessors, in right of the said archbusshopricke of Armagh, have, tyme out of mynde, received and levied yerely out of the four balliboes of land of Clonie, and out of the fishinge thereinto belonginge, twoe markes per annum; and that the said land and fishinge were

untill fiftie yeares sithence or thereabouts enjoyed by the sept of Neale Portclony as inheritors or dowsaghes of the said landes. But the said jurors doe further present and say uppon their oathes that for the space of fiftie yeres nowe last past, the said landes and fishinge have bene, and yet are, in the possession of the said Lord Busshopp of Derry for the tyme beinge, but for what right or title the said jurors knowe not." Inquisition taken at Derry 1st September 1609.

[Insert note: Ballyoyre, Charters of Derry, James I and Charles II; Balle Oyer, Sir T. Phillip's map (Goldsmiths' Company); Ballioyre, Charter of Derry (Cromwell); C.S. (Goldsmiths) Ballioer, Book of Survey and Distribution].

8. Ballyshasky: this does not appear in the Charter of Derry, in the inquisition, nor in the Down Survey [insert addition: but it appears on Sir Thomas Phillips' map, written very correctly Balle Shaskin, and on Sampson's map and other modern authorities Ballyshasky], and is probably a subdivision of some adjoining townland. The etymology is understood in the country to be *Baile Seascaigh* "moor town or marsh town or sedge town;" *seisc* is the Irish word for "sedge," and *seisceann* or *seascann* for the place in which it grows. In *Cormac's Glossary* it is made synonymous with cuirrech "a moor." "*Cuirrech imurra doradh seiri seisceand.*"

It appears from Irish elegies repeated by the natives of the parish of Dungiven that a branch of the O'Kanes had their residence here. In enumerating the ancient relatives of Manus O'Kane of Garvagh, who died some 60 years ago, the tuire goes on: *Bhi do ghaol le leim a mhadaidh, le heanach na riogh 'sle baile sheascaigh*; "Thou wert related to (the chief of) Limavady, to lordly Enagh and to Ballyshasky etc."

[Insert note: Neither Ballyshasky nor the adjoining townland Currynierin occurs in the old authorities; but in connection with the neighbouring townlands we find mention made in the Charter of Derry of: Family, James I and Charles II, Famyllye, Cromwell, being one balliboe of land; Mr Henry Wray mortgaged to Charles Davenport, English Protestant, Ffamilly, Book of Survey and Distribution; Killamrisreogh, James I and Cromwell, Killanirisreogh, Charles II, being one balliboe of land; Maghiereneskeagh, James I, Maghereanskeagh, Cromwell, Maghierenesteagh, Charles II, being one balliboe of land (not so much in connection as the preceding), which cannot be identified with modern names; Ballyvadigan, Charter of Derry, not in name book, see Glenderowen; Belud, Sir Thomas Phillips' map (Grocers' Company), see Lisnagelvin; "Capten Manus O'Cahan, his freehold Balle Shaskin," Sir T. Phillips' map (Grocers' Company)].

9. Bogagh: this does not appear in any of the old authorities and must be a subdivision of some larger denomination, [insert addition: but it is found on Sir Thomas Phillips' map in the slightly varied orthography of Bogan, and on Sampson's map and other modern authorities it is written Bogagh]. *Bogach*, derived from the adjective *bog* "soft," [insert addition: cognate with the Cornish and Armoric boucg and with the bogo of the Algonkine language of North America] is always used to signify "a bog," to which it bears the strongest affinity in sound and sense.

[Insert note: Bogan, Sir Thomas Phillips' map (Goldsmiths' Company); C.S. (Goldsmiths) Boygagh, Book of Survey and Distribution].

10. Bolies is also a modern subdivision. It is an Irish word made plural according to the English mode, which is very frequently done in the north of Ireland, as Drummans, Pullans, Tullans, Derrins, Mullans etc. *Buailidh*, derived from *bo* or *buaibh* "cow," is understood throughout Ireland to mean "a milking place," but in this county it is generally applied to temporary sheds erected by families in the mountains, where they retired with their cattle during the summer season to make butter, a custom which generally prevailed in this county not many years ago. The Irish plural is *buailte* according to Duald McFirbis and Connall Mageoghegan, who translated it "derie places" in 1627. For an account of Irish boolies and boolying, see Spenser, *View of the state of Ireland*, edition 1809.

[Insert addition: Boolies: this name is not found in connexion with the locality in any ancient authority, and the townland is a modern subdivision of the ancient balliboe of Prehen. The word means "milking places," being an anglicised plural of the Irish *buailidh*, cognate with the Greek *boaulion* and the Latin bouile. The correct Irish plural is *buailte*, but in most parts of Ireland where the English language has taken root it has become the custom to form the plural of Irish topographical words according to the English instead of the Irish mode, as Knockans, Tullans etc. The word *buailidh* is of the most remote antiquity in Ireland, being found in the oldest manuscripts extant, and from this the Irish formed the word *buailidheacht* and the Anglo-Irish boolying to express the nomadic pastoral existence so prevalent in the reign of Elizabeth and not yet quite extinct, which Spenser considered as a remarkable evidence of their Scythian origin.

(Ireneus): "I will begin then to count their customs in the same order that I counted their nations, and first with the Scythian or Scottish manners. Of the which there is one [in] use amongst them, to keepe their cattle and to live themselves the most part of the year in boolies, pasturing upon the mountaine and waste wilde places, and removing still to fresh land as they have depastured the former. The which appeareth plaine to be the manner of the Scythians, as you may read in Olaus Magnus and Johannus Bohemus, and yet is used amongst all the Tartarians, and the people about the Caspian Sea, which are naturally Scythians, to live in heards as they call them, being the very same that the Irish boolies are, driving their cattle continually with them and feeding onely on their milk and white meats" etc; see Spenser's *View of the state of Ireland*, Dublin 1809].

Derivation of Townland Names

11. Cah: called Chay one balliboe, one of the 8 balliboes of Annaght, in an inquisition taken at Ballykelly in the 14th year of the reign of James I; Cagh in the Charter of Derry; the 2 townes of Key in the Down Survey, and the quarter of Clonkey [insert addition: Clonekey] in the inquisition of 1609. The local pronunciation is Caw. The etymology is uncertain but it may be conjectured that as clon was anciently prefixed that it might be *Cluain Catha* or "the lawn of the battle," as the same name occurs in the *Annals of the four masters* at the year 1236. [Insert note: Not marked on Sir Thomas Phillips' map, see Gransha townland; Mrs Humberstow and Deane Wentworth's widow, English Protestants; the 2 townes of Key, Book of Survey and Distribution].

[Insert addition: It appears from the authorities above quoted that this townland was originally one of the 16 balliboes which constituted the ancient ballybetagh of Annaght; and on Sir Thomas Phillips' map it is included in the deanery lands; and according to Downham's Visitation Book (1622) was let to John Wray Esquire as lessee in trust to the use of the wife and sister of Dean Webb (the first Protestant dean) for the term of 21 years].

12. Carn: called Carne in the charter and Carne towne, part of Balliowen, in the Down Survey. The word *carn* frequently enters into the names of countless places in Ireland and signifies "a heap of earth or stones" [insert addition: "a conical heap of stones, artificially formed"]. It is translated tumulus by Colgan [insert addition: as "carn, lamha, tumulus manuus," *Triadis Thaumaturgae*], and it is traceable to a common origin with the Welsh carn and the Hebrew keren. It is sometimes used, especially

in the Highlands of Scotland, to signify "a sepul-chral pile of stones," in which sense it is synony-mous with the Irish *leacht*, an honorary sepulchral monument erected on the spot where some person met a sudden death. *Carn* is the only common word in the Irish language to denote a heap or pile of earth, stones, potatoes, snow or any other substance, and it does not appear it was originally a sacred word or that it ever signified a pagan altar, as asserted by some modern antiquaries.

[Insert addition: The great carns of the British Isles have been referred to a druidical origin con-nected with sun worship by Toland, who has col-lected all the evidences attainable to support this theory, which has been very extensively adapted by succeeding antiquaries. There is, however, in these evidences, though ingeniously urged, nothing con-clusive, and they are opposed to the whole stream of Irish history, both written and traditional, which assign to them an origin exclusively sepulchral; and that such was their primary, if not sole, use will be abundantly proved in the course of this work.

On Sir Thomas Phillips' map the locality of this townland is included in the lands of the deanery and in the Down Survey it is marked as 1 of the 8 townes or balliboes of Ballyowen; see Ballyowen].

[Insert note: Carn in Dungiven parish; claimed by Captain George Hart, Carntowne, part of Ballyowen, Book of Survey and Distribution].

13. Carnafarn: called in the charter by the more correct name of Carrowneferny being one balliboe of land. It is unquestionably an anglicised abbrevia-tion of the Irish *Ceathramhadh-na-fearna*, i.e. "quar-ter of the alder trees." Ceathramhadh is translated quarterium and carnucata by O'Flaherty in his *Ogygia* and in the Ulster inquisitions. It originally meant the fourth part of a ballybetagh or the one hundred and twentieth part of a triochadh cead or barony. [Insert addition: This word when taken adjectively is the ordinal formed from the numeral *ceathair* by adding *amhadh*, which is equivalent and probably cognate with the English termination th, as in four, fourth, but when taken substantively it signifies "a quarter or fourth part"].

Fearn, now generally fearnog [insert addition: cognate with the Welsh and Cornish guernen and the Armoric guern], is the ancient word for the alder tree, which is a native plant of Ireland and has given names to countless places throughout the kingdom.

[Insert note: Carrowneferny, Charter of Derry, James I and Charles II; Carowneferne, Sir T. Phillips' map (Goldsmiths' Company); Carrowneferry, Char-ter of Derry, Cromwell; C.S. (Goldsmiths), Carnefeaine, Book of Survey and Distribution].

Carrakeel: called in the charter by the more correct name of Carrowkilly being one balliboe of land. The etymology is unquestionably *Ceathramhadh Coille*, i.e. "wood quarter;" see Carnafarn and Ardkill supra. [Insert addition: This name is written Carrowkilly in all the Char-ters of Derry, Carunikeele [insert alternative: Carumkeele] on Sir Thomas Phillips' map and Carrakill on Sampson's map. This townland is marked on Sir Thomas Phillips' map as belong-ing to the Grocers' Company].

[Insert note: Carrowkilly, Charters of Derry; Carumkeele, Sir Thomas Phillips' map (Grocers' Company); query: can this be the Cornellkrunaght of inquisition 14th, James I?; (Grocers) Kerrumkill, Book of Survey and Distribution; Carrowvesragh, charter; see Gortree].

14. Clampernoe: this, which is a very small subdivision, does not appear in any of the ancient authorities. [Insert addition: Written Clampernow on Sampson's map]. The name means *Clampar Nuadh* "new dispute or contention." Sir William Petty has marked several spots in this county as "controversies," as being claimed by (disputed between) different persons, but as the name of this subdivision is Irish, it seems to have been given from a dispute between some Irish families before the Down Survey was taken [insert alternative: made]. [Insert addition: The townland is included under Tullagh Otragh (Upper Tully), on Sir Thomas Phillips' map, of which it is obviously a modern subdivision].

15. Cloghore: does not occur in the ancient authorities. The name may signify *Cloch Oir* "golden stone" or *Cloch Odhar* "dun or brownish stone," but more probably the latter. The town of Clogher in Tyrone was anciently called *Cloch Oir* according to Cathal Maguire, deacon of Clogher, from a stone ornamented with gold on which the pagan Irish offered sacrifice to the god Kermon Kelstach; but though this may be historical fact with regard to Clogher in Tyrone, it is not at all probable that the various other places of that name in Ireland have derived it from a golden stone similar to that men-tioned by Maguire, and it seems beyond dispute that *clochar* means simply "a stony place," as it is now understood by the natives of the county of Donegal where that name frequently occurs; but the name of the present townland is not Clogher but Cloghore, and it must have been given from the yellow (oir) of gold or brownish (odhar) colour of the stones.

[Insert note: Cloghore is included in the townland of Drumconan on Sir Thomas Phillips' map (Goldsmiths' Company); C.S. (Goldsmiths) Cloghorie, Book of Survey and Distribution].

16. Clondermot: for the etymology of this, see name of the parish. In the Down Survey this townland is called Ballynamaddy, which seems to be the same with the Ballyvaddigan of the charter. The Ballynamaddy of the Down Survey *certainly* is the Ballyvaddigan of the charter. [Insert addition: As a townland name it does not occur in the charters, but it appears on Sir Thomas Phillips' map as the Dean of Derry his lands, and includes under this name the modern townland of Glenderowen. In the charters this townland is designated by the name of Ballintemple or "the townland of the church"].

[Insert note: Sir Thomas Phillips' map (Gold-smiths' Company); Ballintample, being one balliboe of land, Charter of Derry, James I; Ballentemple, charter Cromwell, Ballintemple, charter Charles II (mentioned in the charter in connection with Gortenure, Tawnamore and Cromehill). [Insert marginal query: How dispose of both the Ballintemple and Ballyvadigan of charter? [Answer] On the Down Survey map the townland of Clondermot appears as 2 townlands, viz. Mountayns, north, and Ballinamaddy containing the church, south; Mounalane, Ballynamaddy, Book of Survey and Distribution; Ballivaddygan, James I, Ballivadigan, Cromwell, Ballivaddigan, Charles II, being one balliboe of land, Charters of Derry].

[Insert addition: O'Reilly's opinion that Clon cannot be derived from cluain is very strange. How are Clontarf, Clonmacnoise, Clonmel, Clonard, Clonfertmullan etc. written in the original Irish? If but this question were proposed to him he would have immediately changed his opinion, as he must have several times seen each and every one of them spelled cluain in the original Irish; and Clonfertmulloe is not only spelled Cluain Feart Molua but also explained (translated) "Latibulum mirabile sancti Molua." He might have said that the syllable clan in Clanrickard, Clancolman, Clankeine, Clanconway cannot be derived from cluain, as he had met them several times *Clan Riocaird*, Clan Cholmain etc. in old manuscripts].

17. Clooney: called in the inquisition of 1609 Cloonie four balliboes of land, in the charter Cloney and in the Down Survey Foure townes of Clune, and by the *Four masters* in their annals of the year 1197 *Cluain-i*; and Cluain, simply, by Manus O'Donnell in the *Life of Columbkille*. [Insert note: Clooney in Kilcronaghan, part barony Loughinshole; James Downham, English Protestant, ffoure townes of Clun, Book of Survey and Distribution; Clone, Sir T. Phillips' map (Grocers' Company); "Clowney contayninge four balliboes or townes called Lisdreenagh, Ballingtemple, Ballymully and Rossedony, which four balliboes or

townes doe containe 1 quarter, and to them there is belongonge 1 poole called Bunshanetin, and the fishinge thereof," inquisition 14th James I.

Bunseantuinne is mentioned by O'Donnell in his *Life of Columbkille*, written in 1520, as the spot in which Bishop Weston commenced the erection of a place which was never completed (see Antiquities of Clooney). The four balliboes above alluded to are now included under the general name of Clooney on the Ordnance map; "the four balliboes of land of Clonie," inquisition, 1st September 1609].

The Irish word *cluain*, which is most generally anglicised clon and sometimes cloon and cloyne, enters into the names of countless places in Ireland and signifies "a retired lawn or low rich flat between hills, free from woods and rocks, generally near a river" [insert addition: "a small plain surrounded by woods or bogs, a level spot fit for pasture"].

It is translated latibulum by the writers of the lives of St Fintan of Clonenagh and Molua of Clonfert; secessus and sometimes pratum by Colgan, and always pratum by O'Sullevan. Lhwyd, in his comparative etymology, and O'Brien, in his dictionary, state that cluain is visibly of the same root [insert addition: as the Latin planum and] with the Anglo-Saxon lawn, and that one Celtic dialect often drops an initial letter while another retains it.

The latter part of the name has 2 significations: it is sometimes an adjective and means "low," and sometimes a substantive signifying "an island," hence *i Cholaim Chille* or "Columbkille's island," the Irish name of the celebrated Iona. But whether *Cluain-i* means the "low clon" or the "insular or peninsular clon" let the locality determine. [Insert addition: But neither of these meanings is topographically applicable to the locality of this townland, nor can any probable conjecture be offered, unless it be that its church was in some way dependent on that of Hy or Iona, as St Columb was the founder and patron of both, and as cells to monastic churches sometimes took the name of the parent establishment].

The ancient Irish, be it remarked, gave the name of *i-inis* to places that were not entirely surrounded by water, and in the Highlands of Scotland inis is very frequently applied to places only half surrounded by water, as Craiginish, Deirginish and Treiginish in Argyllshire.

18. Corrody: does not occur in any of the ancient authorities. The name is synonymous with Currudda in the parish of Dungiven, but the etymology is obscure. In Dungiven it is pronounced *Cor Roda* by the Irish but its meaning is not understood. In the counties of Cavan, Fermanagh, Monaghan and Tyrone the word *cor* is applied to a particular kind

of hills with which the surface of these counties is covered. *Roda*, in the south ruide, is a kind of boggy substance deposited by water.

19. Craigtown: does not appear in any of the ancient authorities and seems a modern subdivision, as the name is compounded of the Scotch *craig* and the English *town*; the Irish would have made it Ballynacregg. It has received the name of Craigtown or "rock town" from its craggy or rocky surface. [Insert note: Cregan, Sir T. Phillips' map (Goldsmiths' Company); (Goldsmiths) Craige one towne land, Book of Survey and Distribution (mentioned in connection with Drumenegard which adjoins Craigtown].

20. Creevedonnell: does not appear in any of the ancient authorities. *Craobh Domhnaill* signifies "Donnell's bush or tree." *Craobh* now means "a branch, a triumphal branch," but it was anciently used to denote a large tree, as *Craobh Daithin*, a large ash tree which fell in the county of Westmeath in 665; *Craobh Mughna*, an aged oak which stood on the south of Moy-aloe at the present Ballymoon in the county Kildare; and *Craobh Uisnigh*, a large ash in Westmeath. It is probable that this townland derived its name from a whitethorn planted on it to commemorate the death of a chief named Donnell, but no historical passage or tradition has been discovered to prove or corroborate it.

[Insert note: Creivdonell, Sir Thomas Phillips' map (Goldsmiths' Company); C.S. (Goldsmiths) Crevidonnell, Book of Survey and Distribution].

21. Cromkill: called in the charter Cromchill being one balliboe of land; gleab of Clumkill; and in Sampson's map Crumpkill. The true meaning is *Crom Choill* "bent, drooping or stooped wood." Crom does not mean crooked but "stooped, bent or drooping." There are also several townlands in Ulster called *Creamh Choill*, which means "wood abounding in wild garlick," which might have been anglicised to Cromkill, though the usual anglicising of it is Cranfield.

[Insert note: Gleab of Clumkill, Down Survey; Crumuhill, Sir Thomas Phillips' map (Goldsmiths' Company); Clumkill, Book of Survey and Distribution; C.S. (Goldsmiths) Lissaghmore Begg and quarter of Cromkill, Book of Survey and Distribution].

22. Culkeeragh: does not occur in the ancient authorities. *Cuil Caorach* means "the angle or corner of the sheep." For the meaning of *cuil*, see townlands of Templemore nomine Culmore. *Caora* is the common word for "a sheep" in every part of Ireland. It is thus inflected: nominative singular caora; genitive na caorach; nominative plural na caoire; genitive na gcaorach. It enters into the

names of very many places. [Insert marginal note: The local position of Cuilkeeragh amply bears out the name cuil, viz. a piece of land bounded by the Foyle on the north and west and by the Faughan on the north east, east and south east. But this name more particularly belonged to [blank].

[Insert query: Can the Cowell-an-Kerreve of inquisition 14th James I be this townland; see Enagh townland; Coolkerah, Sir Thomas Phillips' map (Grocers' Company); one quarter of land called Koolekeragh, inquisition of Derry, 1st September 1609; (Mr Bassill, Aull Gon., Protestant), ffoure townes of Killkeroth, Book of Survey and Distribution].

23. Curryfree: called in the charter Coolerefry one balliboe of land. The modern name signifies *Currach Fraoigh* "heathy moor." The Coolerefry of the charter is probably a mistake. In *Cormac's Glossary* it is stated that the word *cuirrech* has 2 significations, viz. "a level plain or racecourse" and "a moor or sheskin." "*Cuirrech .i. curra .i. reidhe, cuirrech imorra do radh fri seiscend .i. corra rechait ann*, i.e. cuirrech, i.e. 'a racecourse,' i.e. 'a plain.' A moor is also called a cuirrech because it is resorted to by corra or cranes."

In another place cuirrech "a plain or racecourse" is derived from curribus or chariots, which shows that the author knew that there were chariot races held on some places in Ireland called cuirrech, such for example as the celebrated Curragh of Kildare. The most usual meaning, however, of curragh in Ireland and the Highlands of Scotland is "a shrubby moor," and such will all the places in Ireland called Curragh be found to be, with the exception of the Curragh of Kildare, and perhaps a few others, which has certainly derived its name from its being a racecourse from a very remote period. *Fraoch*, genitive *fraoigh*, is the Irish word for "heath," which is not unfrequently found growing in curraghs.

[Insert note: Cowlerefrie, Charter of Derry, James I; Coolnafree, Sir T. Phillips' map (Goldsmiths' Company); Coolereffry, Charter of Derry, Cromwell; Coolerefrie, Charter of Derry, Charles II; on Sir T. Phillips' map (Goldsmiths' Company) this townland is divided into two, viz. Coolnafree lying to the south west and Gorltawey to the north east adjoining Creevedonnell; C.S. (Goldsmiths), Curryfry, Gortilavy, Book of Survey and Distribution; Gorltawey, Sir T. Phillips' map, now Curryfree townland q.v].

24. Currynierin: this does not appear in any of the ancient authorities and must be a subdivision of [blank]. The meaning is certainly *Currach-an-iarainn* "moor of the iron," the subsoil being chiefly of iron ore. *Iarann*, the Irish word for "iron," looks

to the same source with the Latin ferrum, the Welsh haiarn, the Danish iern and the English iron. That iron was used at a very remote period in Ireland there is sufficient evidence to prove: Dr O'Brien goes so far as to state that Erin, one of the most ancient names of the island, was derived from it.

[Insert marginal note: *Goin Iarain, Ciol-an-iarain*]. Names of men were formed from iarann at a very early period, as *Iarnan*, which is translated Ferreolus by Adamnan; and one of the most remarkable mountains in Ireland is called *Sliabh-an-iarainn*, from an ancient iron mine.

Though bronze weapons are frequently found in Ireland they are never referred to in any Irish documents, which shows that the time in which they were used is beyond the historical period. Swords and other weapons of iron are mentioned in many of the old Irish poems, descriptions of battles etc., and an iron slaughtering knife has been found in the county of Meath with the bones of the Irish elk.

[Insert note: See Ballyshasky townland; Lieutenant Thomas Skipton, Protestant, Carnerin, Book of Survey and Distribution].

Derivation of Townland Names

25. Disertowen: called incorrectly Disartcowan one balliboe of land in the charter, and Desertowen or Lissatone in most modern authorities. The etymology is obviously *Diseart Eoghain*, i.e. "Owen's or Eugene's desert or wilderness." *Diseart* was borrowed from the Latin at the introduction of Christianity into Ireland. In *Cormac's Glossary* it is derived from the Latin desertus. "*Disert .i. desertus locus .i. loch fasaigh*, i.e. disert, i.e. desertus locus, a wilderness." Many places in Ireland now well cultivated were anciently wildernesses and took their name from hermits who retired into them during the early ages of Christianity, as Dysart Enos in the Queen's County, from its having been the retreat of St Enos or Aongus, the festilogist; Disert Chuimin, now Kilcummin in the King's County; Disert Dermot, now Castle Dermot.

Eoghan, now generally anglicised Owen, sometimes Eugene, and among the peasantry in this county corrupted to Oyne and Oynee, is a name that certainly existed in Ireland before the introduction of Christianity, as appears from the oldest lives of St Patrick. It is thus derived in *Cormac's Glossary* "*Eoghan, .i. eugen, .i., greigis. Eu din, Graece bonus, bona, bonum latine dicitur; gen imorru don ni is genesis .i. generatio: Eogen din bona generatio.* Eoghan, i.e. the Greek Eugen. Eu in Greek is bonus, bona, bonum in Latin and gen

is from genesis, i.e. generatio. Eogen then means bona generatio or "the goodly born or good offspring." Ainsworth explains Eugene as "nobly descended." It is, however, very much to be doubted that the Irish Eoghan is derived from the Greek, as the ancient Irish language contains 2 words from which it may be derived as *eo* "good, worthy" and *gein* "an offspring."

[Insert note: Disart Cowan, Charter of Derry, James I; Disarcowan, Charter of Derry, Cromwell; Disartcowan, Charter of Derry, Charles II; this townland is called Lisnatoy on Sir Thomas Phillips' map (Goldsmiths' Company); C.S. (Goldsmiths) Dessartdowan, Book of Survey and Distribution.

Drumagore (omitted in list): west of Disertowen; Dromnegor, Charter of Derry, James I; Drimnagor, Sir Thomas Phillips' map (Goldsmiths' Company); Dromnegoy, Charter of Derry, Cromwell and Charles II (being one balliboe of land); C.S. (Goldsmiths) Drumenegor and towne land, Book of Survey and Distribution].

26. Drumahoe: is probably the townland called Dromagtagh in the charter. Its meaning is obscure. [Insert note: Dromnecheionagh, (James I) Charter of Derry; 2 Dromhoghs, Sir T. Phillips' map (Goldsmiths' Company); Dromnehewnagh, (Cromwell and Charles II), Charter of Derry; C.S. (Goldsmiths) Drumnenaches, Book of Survey and Distribution].

27. Drumconan: called in the charter the balliboe of Drumcoran, and Drumcoran by Sampson. The name signifies *Druim Chonain* "Conan's ridge." *Druim*, which enters into the names of countless places in Ireland, signifies "a low ridge." It has been translated dorsum by Adamnan, Fordun and Usher; collis and tumulus by Colgan and O'Sullevan. *Conan*, diminutive of Con, was anciently common in Ireland as the proper name of a man.

[Insert note: Dromcoran, Charter of Derry (omnes); Drumcurran, Sir Thomas Phillips' map (Goldsmiths' Company); C.S. (Goldsmiths) Drum Kerane, Book of Survey and Distribution].

28. Dunhugh: called in the charter Doonehugh being one balliboe of land. The etymology is *Dun Aodha*, i.e. "Aodh's fort." The Irish word *dun* is explained "a hill" by some modern topographical writers, but it does not appear from any record in the Irish language that it ever bore that meaning. It is translated munitio by Adamnan; arx in an old *Life of St Bridget* quoted by Usher (Primord.); castrum by St Eleranus sapiens; and arx by Colgan. O'Flaherty observes: "There are an hundred places in Ireland called dun, which implies, no more with us than with the Gauls, Britons and Saxons "a fortress erected on a rising ground or eminence."

Charles O'Conor of Belanagare, who made Irish history his particular study, finds that forts on low ground were also called duns. In exposing MacPherson's historical forgeries he says, "nor doth don (generally a prepositive particle) signify 'a hill,' though dun in the Gaelic generally signified 'any fortified hill' and not seldom 'a fortress on low ground:' instances are innumerable."

Some (and among these may be enumerated Jocelyn and Usher) think that dun signifies simply "a hill," but though it bears that meaning in the Welsh, no Irish authority can be found in which *dun* appears to denote anything but "a fort or fortress;" and as Adamnan, who was born in 624, translates it by the Latin munitio, we can safely assume that it had no other meaning in his time; but as the ancient Irish fortresses were generally situated on hills and insulated rocks, the word has been taken by modern antiquaries to signify "a fortified hill." This word is derived from the verb *dun* "shut up, enclose or fortify," which shows that the idea of hill is secondary.

Aodh, the second part of the compound, is certainly a man's name anciently and still very common in Ireland. It signifies "fire" and has been so interpreted by Cormac, Bishop of Cashel, by the author of the *Life of St Aidus*, and by his commentator John Colgan, *Triad. Thau.*. This name is pronounced "eeoo" by the Irish speaking peasantry in this county, "ee" in Connaught and "ai" in Munster (like "ai" in air), and always anglicized Hugh. It was Latinized Aidus, Odo, Hugo and even Ignis.

[Insert note: Doonhugh, Charter of Derry; Donhugh, Sir Thomas Phillips' map (Goldsmiths' Company); C.S. (Goldsmiths) Dunhue, Book of Survey and Distribution].

Derivation of Townland Names

29. and 30. Edenreagh-beg and -more: called in the charter Treadonreough one balliboe of land; but Treadonreough is a mistake for Teadonreaugh, which is intended for the Irish *An T-eudan Riach*, t being prefixed to the nominative singular of masculine nouns beginning with vowels, when the article is expressed. *Eudan Riach* signifies "greyish hillside" [insert alternative: brow]. For the topographical signification of the Irish word eudan, see Edenballymore, townlands of Templemore. *Riach* or *riabhach*, the second part of the name, which signifies "a dark grey" (Fuscus, O'Sullivan *Historia Catholicorum*, frequently forms the latter part of the names of townlands situate on the sides of hills, or mountains which

produce coarse mountain pasture, moss or heath; but in some instances this epithet is found inapplicable to many townlands, as their appearance has been very much altered by cultivation. *Beag* and *mor*, translated parva and magna in old Latin law documents, were added to distinguish the larger and smaller subdivisions of the same townland.

[Insert note: Treadonreagh, Charter of Derry, James I and Charles II; 2 Edenreas, Sir Thomas Phillips' map (Grocers' Company); Treadowreigh, Charter of Derry, Cromwell; the Company of Grocers, London, 2 Edenreaghes, Book of Survey and Distribution].

31. Enagh: called in an inquisition taken here in 1603 one ballibetagh vel 4 quarteria de Annagh, Annagh in the one taken at Derry in 1609; Ainagh by Sir Henry Dockwra and Fynes Moryson, and *Eanach* by the *Four masters* at 1555. Colgan, speaking of the church of this place, calls it Eanach, "Ecclesia vulga Eanach dicta (juxta quam est arx nobilissimae familiae O'Cathanorum) tertio tantum miltiari versus aquilonem distat ab ipsa civitate Dorensis." It is called Anagh and Anagh [sic] in the charter, and Anagh and Aenach in the Down Survey. The name is now anglice pronounced Ai-nagh (ai like ai in ail), but always *Eanach*, pronounced Annagh, by the Irish peasantry in the mountains of Dungiven and Banagher, who retain several traditions concerning it.

Eanach, derived from *ean*, which is explained *uisce* "water" in *Cormac's Glossary*, signifies "watery land," a name which is certainly not applicable to the small townland which at present bears the name, but it appears from the inquisition of 1603, as well as from the Down Survey, that Enagh was the name of a ballybetagh containing 4 quarters of land, viz. Enagh, Lissahawley, Templetown and Stradreagh; [insert marginal note: look to this again]. The 2 lakes of Enagh and the lowlands about them must have originally received the name which was afterwards given to the entire ballybetagh, from the most prominent feature thereon. The reason that the present small townland has retained the ancient name of the large subdivision is because it contains the old church, the oldest building with which the name was identified.

[Insert note: The heirs of George Cary Esquire, English Protestant, ffoure townes of Anach, Book of Survey and Distribution; George Cary Esquire aforesaid, 1 towne of Anach, Book of Survey and Distribution; Aynough, surrender of Donnogh O'Cane 1602, Off. Cap. Rem.; Annagh, Charter of Derry, James I; Annah, Sir T. Phillips' map, Grocers' Company; Annaght, Charter of Derry (Cromwell); Annagh, Charter of Derry (Charles II).

In the grant from the king to Captain Ralph Bingley (pat. I James I) mention is made of "a chapel called the grange of Aynogh, and half-quarter of land adjoininge" in Coleraine county, immediately following the notice of the grange of Dromdrinade; see Gransha townland. "2 ruinous chapels called the grange of Dromdynad and Anogh, with half a quarter of land adjoining to each" in Coleraine county.

Grant from the king to Sir Henry Broncar, Lord President of Munster, pat. 2 James I (roll 5) part 2 facie V 5. (It appears from this grant that these granges and the other lands belonging to the abbey of Derry had been "lately granted to Sir James Fullerton in fee farm," whole rent 18d Irish per annum).

The peynote of Annaght, inquisition 14th James I: "Eight balliboes or townes lyinge in the peynote of Annaght, called Cornell Krunaght, Cantuney-loye, Cowell-an-Kerrewe, Cannenadowne, Ballnytemple, Stradereagh, Chay, Balleynygarm-agen, which 8 townes or balliboes doe contayne 2 quarters and nowe are detayned from the said bushopprick of Derry by William Webbe, dean;" inquisition 14th James I.

The following notice of the 2 quarters of Enagh occurs in Downham's Visitation Book: "2 (quarters) called Enach are let by the same Dean Webb, viz. one-quarter and a half to George Cary Esquire at the yearly rent of 10 pounds, and half a quarter to Johan Wray Esquire, a lessee in trust, to the use of the wife and sister of the saide late deane, for the term of 21 years, at the yearly rent of 3 pounds 6s 8d," see Clondermot parish; "and that the said dean is to keep here a curate, to whom belongeth a small garden plot of glebe; and the said jurors do further say and present upon their oaths that the Annagh, wherein is a chappell of ease, is within the said parish of Clandermott, and not a parish of itself, but the third part of the tithes of Annagh belonged to the bishoprick of Derry;" inquisition taken at Derry, September 1st 1609].

32. Evish: does not appear in any of the ancient authorities. It is called Avish by Sampson. The Irish pronunciation is *Eibhis* (aivish) in this county and efish in Donegal, and it is understood in both counties to signify "coarse grass or mountain pasture;" but the word is not set down in any Irish glossary or dictionary hitherto known to us, nor at all understood in the south of Ireland.

[Insert note: Avis, Sir Thomas Phillips' map (Grocers' Company), between Evish, 2 Edenreaghs (this parish) and followed in Faughanvale parish. Sir T. Phillips has the name Tullanere on his map of the Grocers' proportion (see Lisnagelvin townland).

Familly, Famyllye, being one balliboe of land occurs in the charter, evidently in Clondermot parish; see Ballyshasky townland].

33. Fincarn: called in the charter Fincharne one and a half balliboes of land. In Sampson's map and most modern authorities it is Scotticised to Fincairn. The etymology is manifestly *Fionn Charn* "white heap or cairn;" vide Carn townland. The word *fionn*, which is translated albus by Tighernach, and albus, candidus, lucidus, pulcher by Colgan and O'Flaherty, frequently enters into the names of townlands and rivers, as Finglen "the fair or white valley," Finisk "the bright water," a river in the county of Waterford or Cork.

[Insert note: Fincharne, Charters of Derry (being one balliboe of land); not on Sir T. Phillips' map; C.S. (Goldsmiths) Fflinkairne, Book of Survey and Distribution. Between this townland and Drumahoe there is a townland marked on Sir T. Phillips' map called Leagh. It is also marked on Sampson's map under the corrupted form of Leithgow; Laagh, (James I and Charles II), Laaugh, (Cromwell), being one balliboe of land, Charter of Derry; C.S. (Goldsmiths) Loughy, the same, Book of Survey and Distribution].

Derivation of Townland Names

34. Glenderowen: does not occur in any of the ancient authorities. Its etymology is *Gleann Daire Eoghain*, i.e. "the glen or valley of Oewn's oak grove:" vallis Roboreti Eugenii. The word *daire* is already explained at full length in the etymology of Londonderry, and *Eoghan* under Disertowen above. Glen, which is translated vallis by the author of the *Life of St Kevin of Glendalough* and by the annalist Tighernach, is too well understood throughout the 3 kingdoms to require any comment here.

[Insert note: Glenderowen appears to be a modern name for the Ballivaddygan of the Charter of Derry. This townland is called Lisnegarre on Sir Thomas Phillips' map (Goldsmiths' Company). [Insert query: Might not Ballyvadigan be the present Corody]? [Answer] No, see Clondermot townland; C.S. (Goldsmiths) Glendeirone, Book of Survey and Distribution].

35. Glenkeen: called Clonkem (by mistake) one balliboe of land in the charter and Clonkeine and Clonekeine in the Down Survey. Glenkeen is now, however, become the established name by a corruption which often takes place in anglicising names of places in Ireland, for we sometimes meet not only cluain but also clann anglicised to glen. For the signification of Clonkeen we have

the very ancient authority of St Evin, who wrote in the seventh century; speaking of Clonkeen in Louth, he introduces a nice little bit of a conversation between St Patrick and an angel who was sent to direct him about the erection of Armagh.

"Inde retro se convertens, regressus est sanctissimus ad populas ferrossiorum: ubi capit matari locum ecclesiae extruendae in Druim Mor justa quam in loco inferiori et amano sita est ecclesia postea cluain chaoin appellatae. Patricis enim, metas extruendae ecclesiae et fixae sedis in praedicto loco ponenti apparuit angelus admonens quod non sit ille locus in quo placuit domino ipsum fixam ponere sedem, sed alius versus septentrionem Macha vulgo nuncupatus. Et cum vir sanctus delectatus istarium partium amonitate replicaret locum illum inferiorem, Cluain Chaoin indigitans esse valde amanum et erigendae ecclesiae peridoneum; respondit angelus ita esse et ecclesiam foce in eo erigendam quoe proinde Cluain Chaoin id est secessus amanus sine delectabiles vocaretur" (*Triad. Thau.*).

The word cluain is explained above under Clooney. *Caoin*, when applied to land, signifies "tranquilly beautiful," but its acceptation is very much varied throughout the provinces: in Munster it is always "mild or tranquil," in Ulster "light or slender," and in south Leinster it is applied to the edge of a sharp weapon, and seems to be synonymous, and to look to the same origin, with the English word keen.

[Insert note: Clonkein, Charter of Derry, James I; Clonekem, Charter of Derry, Cromwell; Clonkem, Charter of Derry, Charles II; Lieutenant Thomas Skipton, Protestant, Clomkeene, Book of Survey and Distribution].

36. Gobnascale: called in the charter Gobnieskeald, Gobeneskale one balliboe of land, Gortnastall in the Down Survey and Gobnaskeal by Sampson and in most modern writings. The etymology seems to be *Gob-na-scaile* "beak or point of the shade" or "shaded point." *Gob*, which literally means "a bird's beak," is sometimes employed topographically to denote a point of land. The Gortnastall of the Down Survey is a corruption of Gortnascall, which seems the correct name as there is no remarkable gob or point of land here.

[Insert note: Gobneskeale, Charter of Derry, James I and Cromwell (in the great proportion of Lissghass); Gobneskall, Sir T. Phillips' map (Goldsmiths); one-third part of the balliboe of Gobneskrale, Charter of Derry, Charles II. Alibi: Gobneskeale aforesaid, Charter of Derry, James I and Cromwell; Gobneskale, Charter of Londonderry, Charles II (two-thirds part of the balliboe

of); in the small proportion of Monaghbegg; C.S., Mr William Warren, Protestant, mortgaged to Mr Tristiam Thorneton, Gobbinskeale, Book of Survey and Distribution].

37. Gortgranagh: called in the charter Gortnegroncha one balliboe of land. *Gort Granach* means "grainfield or cornfield." For the meaning of gort, see Templemore townlands. It might also mean *Gort-na ccrandcha* "field of the trees."

[Insert note: Gortnegroncha, Charter of Derry, James I and Charles II; Gortegroncha, Charter of Derry, Cromwell; Mr Henry Wray, mortgaged to Charles Davenport, English Protestant, Gortigranoch, Book of Survey and Distribution].

38. Gortica: called in the charter Gortchaw one balliboe of land, Gortica by Sampson and Gortecaw in some modern writings. Gortica seems to signify *Gort-a-chatha* "field of the battle;" see Cah supra.

[Insert note: Gortecha, Charters of Derry; Gortskah, Sir T. Phillips' map (Goldsmiths' Company); C.S. (Goldsmiths) Gortica, Book of Survey and Distribution].

39. Gorticross: called in the charter Gortanegrosse one balliboe of land. The etymology is unquestionably *Gort-na-gcross* "field of the crosses." [Insert note: Gortonegrosse, Charter of Derry, James I; Gortcross, Sir T. Phillips' map (Grocers' Company); Gortenegross, Charter of Derry, Cromwell; Gortanegrosse, Charter of Derry, Charles II; Gortinecrosse (with Tawnaghmore), 2 quarters, sometime possessed by O'Dowrie. Pat. 1 James I, roll 2, dorso art. LXXXVIII, being a grant from the king to Captain Ralph Bingley. Gortnecrosse 1 quarter, Tawnaghmore 1 quarter, in possession of O'Dowry. Grant from the king to Sir Henry Broncar, Knight, Lord President of Munster, pat. 2 James I (roll 5) p.2, art. V, (Grocers) Gortnigross, Book of Survey and Distribution].

40. Gortin: called Gortin one balliboe of land in the charter. Gortin is a diminutive of gort. In the south of Ireland it is always pronounced "gurteen," but in the north the accent is generally placed on the first syllable and the second very obscurely sounded. [Insert note: CFV, Gortin, [blank] Warren Esquire (coloured in red), Sampson's map. C.S. Mr William Warren, Protestant, mortgaged to Mr Tristiam Thorneton, Gortowne, Book of Survey and Distribution].

41. Gortinure: called in the charter Gortenure one balliboe of land. The meaning is indisputably *Gort-an-iubhair*, i.e. "gort or field of the yew." *Iubhar* (anciently eo) is the Irish word for "yew," which is certainly a native plant of Ireland, as it is found fossil in many bogs throughout the king-

dom and found growing in its wild state on many rocks in this and the county of Fermanagh. Irish poets frequently refer to the yew in their poems, and in *Cormac's Glossary*, a work of the tenth century, the following derivation of the word is given, which shows that the author considered it an original Irish word.

"*Iubhar, .i. eobhar: eo, .i. semper: iars an ni nat scar a bharr fris do ghres*; 'Iubhar i.e. Eobharr: eo, i.e. semper: because it never loses its top';" q.d. ever-green; see *Eocaill* in the parish of Lower Cumber. See also Armstrong's *Gaelic dictionary*, where he shows that the yew was a native plant of the Highlands of Scotland and that it frequently enters into the names of places there, as Gleniur, Duniur.

[Insert note: Gortenure, Charter of Derry, James I and Charles II and Sir Thomas Phillips' map (Goldsmiths' Company); Gortenore, Charter of Derry, Cromwell; John Lynn, Protestant, Gortinure, Book of Survey and Distribution].

42. Gortnessy: called in the charter Gortenasse one balliboe of land. The name of every place in Ireland beginning or terminating with "ass, ess, nass, ness" is known to be derived from *eas* "a waterfall;" thus Carrickiness, a castle belonging to O'Sullevan Beare, is translated torrent irupes by Philip O'Sullevan; Ballyness in Donegal is called from a small cataract. Ballysadare *Baile Easa Dara* is also well known to have derived its name from a waterfall on the river.

Colgan defines *eas* thus: "Eas Hibernis idem denotat ac catharacta sive locus scopulosus in flumine ubi aequa e scopulo vel petra desilientes cum impetu in subjectum gurgitem sive alveum de volvuntur." The Ness on the Burntollet river in this county and Assaroe on the Erne at Ballyshannon will correspond with this description, but there are several "asses" in Ireland not on rivers at all, as Eas Feenan (in the parish of Raymunterdoney in the county of Donegal), which consists of 3 small scattered spouts gushing from a rock on the sea-shore. It is probable that this townland has derived its name from a similar small trickling of water, as there is no considerable river or stream flowing through it.

[Insert note: Gortenass, Charters of Derry; 2 Gortnasses, Sir Thomas Phillips' map (Grocers' Company); the Company of Grocers, London, 2 Gortnasses, Book of Survey and Distribution].

43. Gortree: called in the charter Gortrie [insert alternative: Gorterie] one balliboe of land. The etymology is either *Gort-a-righ* "the king's gort," or *Gort-an-fhraoigh* "gort of the heath," but which cannot now be ascertained as the Irish pronuncia-

tion could not be procured.

[Insert note: On Sir Thomas Phillips' map (Grocers' Company) between Gorticross and the blank space evidently designed for Carneshrah and Gortlaugh, names which occur on Sir T. Phillips' map of the Goldsmiths' proportion, and which we have identified with Gortree, we find the name Tawnylltey, which cannot be identified with any modern name: Tawnaltoge (James I and Cromwell), Tawnaloge (Charles II), being one balliboe of land, Charter of Derry; Company of Grocers, London, Tawnially, Book of Survey and Distribution.

Gorterie being one balliboe of land, Charters of Derry. This name does not occur on Sir T. Phillips' map, but in its place the name Tawnylltey is marked]. [Insert note: No, on a comparison of the map of the Goldsmiths' and Grocers' proportion it will be seen that the place of Gortree is occupied by Carneshrah and Gortlough on Sir T. Phillips' map (Goldsmiths' Company), see Gorticross.

C.S. (Goldsmiths) Gorterrick, Book of Survey and Distribution; Coroweshragh being one balliboe of land, Charters of Derry (immediately preceding the mention of Gorterie one balliboe of land); C.S. (Goldsmiths) Carnistra, Book of Survey and Distribution].

44. Gransha: appears in the inquisitions as onehalf quarter of land called the grange of Dirgebroe and in the Down Survey Grange, Protestants' land. It is called *Dearg-bhruach* by the *Four masters* and Colgan; see Enagh church. O'Reilly writes that *grainseach*, derived from *grainne* "grain," was the name of the granary or place for the storage of corn where the farmers brought their tythes for the use of the clergy. This grainseach or grange seems to have been of the monastery, and a certain quantity of land lying immediately around it, as being the farm cultivated by the erenach for the use of the monastery, took the same name; hence it is that the granges are generally extraparochial and pay no tithes. *Grainseach* is yet used in Kerry to signify "a haggard." *Dearg-bhruach*, the ancient addition to the name of this grange, signifies "red brink or margin," so called from a reddish bank on the margin of the lough.

[Insert note: In the grant from the king to Captain Ralph Bingley (patent I, James I) mention is made of "a ruinous chapel called the grange of Dromdrinade and half a quarter adjoining" in Coleraine county, immediately after which comes the grange of Aynogh; see Enagh townland.

In a grant from Sir Ralph Bingley to Captain Edmund Leigh mention is made of "the manor of the grange adjoining the river of Lough Foyle, parcell of the lands belonging to the abbey of Derry, the river of Denide and the lands of Cuyll."

On Sir Thomas Phillips' map (Grocers' Company), under the name Grange, are included the 2 townes of Key of the Down Survey map. (Goldsmiths) Graingach, Book of Survey and Distribution.

"The one-half quarter of land called the Grange of Dirgebroe in Ochanes side, now in the possession of Patrick Read," inquisition 1st September 1609.

"And further the said jurors upon their oathes saye and present that the late abbot of the late-dissolved abbey of Collumkill of Derry, both before and at the making of the said statute of dissolution, was seised in his demesne as of fee in right of his house of and in the graunge of Bundiened, with 2 balliboes of land thereunto belonginge, and of and in the 2 parts of the tithes of fishing in 2 pooles in the river of Loughfoile adjoininge or lyinge within the said countie of Tirone; and that the said graunge lands and tithes of fishinge lately came to His Majesty's hands by the said statute of dissolution of monasteries and the tithes of fishinge in such other pooles within the said river of Loughfoile, as doe lye within the countie of Tirone, doe belong to the bushopricke of Derry," inquisition, Dungannon, 23rd August 7th year of James I].

Derivation of Townland Names

45. Kilfinnan: called in the Down Survey Kilfury part of Balliowen, but it is probable that fury is one of those blunders or mistakes frequently committed by the draftsmen employed by Sir William Petty to draw fair copies of that survey. The etymology is probably *Coill Fionnain* "Finnan's wood." *Fionnan*, a diminutive of *fionn*, is synonymous with albin or candide and was very common as the name of men, especially of saints in Ireland.

[Insert note: Claimed by Captain George Hart, Killfury, part of the same (Ballyowen), Book of Survey and Distribution].

46. Killymallaght: does not occur in the ancient authorities. The name signifies *Coill-na-mallacht* "wood of the curses." *Mallacht*, an Irish word borrowed from the Latin maledictio, forms the latter part of many places in Ireland, and traditions exist that such places were so called from their having received the curses of saints for some dreadful crimes committed in them. According to his oldest lives, St Patrick cursed many rivers in Ireland, and many fords etc. where battles were fought have also received the epithet of

namallacht, from the curses pronounced by the widows and orphans of the slain. Several Irish chieftains likewise received the same soubriquet from their having been cursed by the clergy for their violations of the ecclesiastical law.

[Insert note: The name Killamrisreagh occurs in the charter, see Ballyshasky townland; also Killamrisneglogh, James I and Charles II, Killamrisneghkagh, Cromwell (a different name); mentioned in connection with Ardmore, Lismacarrol, Glenkeen; Lieutenant Thomas Skipton, Protestant, Killamoreesreogh, Killamoreesneclogh, Book of Survey and Distribution.

Dromgortfeighnan, Charter of Derry, James I and Charles II; Dromgorteham (m in original), Sir Thomas Phillips' map; Dromegortfeighnan, Cromwell (identified beyond doubt with the Killymallaght of the Ordnance map); Edward Ffreeman, Protestant, Killimallach, Book of Survey and Distribution].

[Insert addition in a different hand: The following extract from the Pedigree of Count Antonio O'Reilly will throw some light upon what is here asserted: "The dumb Prior O'Reilly was fostered by the O'Sherridens of the island. It is said that he was a great bestower and that he was 3 days bestowing money and horses, at the end of which time he was struck dumb. Other people say that he was called Dumb Prior because he plundered and robbed Druim Leathan; for the comharb came to him and said that the plunder of that church of St Maodhog was never a source or omen of good to any person yet, and requested him to restore it, but he would not. After that the comharb went to the chapel of St Maodhog to put it in order and he went down to *Mullach-na-mallacht* (the height of maledictions) and pronounced the curse of Maodhog on the prior, upon which he was then struck dumb;" O'Reilly Pedigree].

47. Kittybane: called in the charter by the more correct name of Kedibaine one balliboe of land. Sampson calls it Cattybane, which is certainly a corruption. The name signifies *Ceide Ban* "white hill." The Irish word *ceide* has 2 meanings, viz. "*a hillock* level at the top," and "a holm or flat *near the sea-shore*." The word is always used in the latter sense in the county of Donegal and in the former in this county.

[Insert note: Kedybane, Charter of Derry (James I and Cromwell); Kedebayne, Charter of Derry (Charles II); Kedebane, Sir Thomas Phillips' map (Goldsmiths' Company); C.S. (Goldsmiths) Kittibane, Book of Survey and Distribution. Sanscrit citi, cita, monceau (Picte)].

48. Knockbrack: does not occur in any of the ancient authorities. It signifies "speckled or spotted hill." *Cnoc* is stated by several topographical writers to be a particular kind of *round hill*, but it will be found upon examining all the places in Ireland called Knock that the word means simply "a hill," and that it is as generic in its signification as the English word hill. The following words are used to express the various kinds of hill in Ireland: alt, ard, binne, ceide, cnoc, cruach, druim, leacain, muine, mullach and tulach, of which alt, ard, cnoc, muine, tulach and druim are now nearly synonymous, but their meanings still vary in some districts. Throughout the province of Ulster, in Meath and the north of Connaught the word *cnoc* is pronounced as if written croc, and every word written "cn" is pronounced like "cr," as *cnamh* "a bone," *cnodh* "a nut" etc.

[Insert note: Lieutenant-Colonel Tristiam Beresford, Protestant, Knockbrack, Book of Survey and Distribution].

Derivation of Townland Names

[Insert note: Leagh, Sir T. Phillips' map; see Fincarn townland].

49. Lisdillon: called in the charter Liseadeolan one balliboe of land, and Lisdealan and Lisdealane in the Down Survey. There is another townland in this county terminating with dillon, viz. Artedillon in the parish of Dunboe, from which it may be inferred that a family of the name Dillon once existed in this county. This must be granted, but they were not the Norman Dillons, for they were located in the counties of Westmeath and Roscommon, but the Irish *O'Diabhalmhuine* (pronounced Doulwin), which MacFirbis places in Keenaght of Glengemhin. Liseadoolan then means *Lios-ui-Diabhalmhuine*, i.e. "O'Diallon's fort."

There are 5 words in the Irish language to express the old pagan forts of Ireland, viz. *lios, rath, caiseal, cathair* and *dun*; of these, lios and rath are perfectly synonymous and signify "a rude earthen fort" or what is vulgarly called "a Danish fort," but the latter is not now understood in Ulster. *Caiseal* and *cathair* denote "a circular stone fort without cement," but the latter is not understood in Ulster, it being confined to Connaught and Munster.

[Insert note; Lissdeolan, Charter of Derry, James I; Lissdalan, Charter of Derry, Cromwell; Lisdcolan (c evidently for e), Charter of Derry, Charles II; Lisdalane (forfeited by Bryan O'Chan) in Clandermot, Sir W. Petty's survey (apud Sampson); "Lisdealan with halfe of Shean," Down Survey; Lisdelane, half of Shane, forfeited by Brian O'Chan, let to Sir John Rowley," Book of Survey and Distribution. Shian occurs in the charter, identified with that of Book of Survey].

50. Lisglass: called in the charter Lisghase [insert query: Lisglase?] one balliboe of land. The name signifies *Lios Glas* "green fort," so called from an old earthen fort with a ditch which is yet to be seen in the townland. It is to be remarked here that the ancient names of forts are generally forgotten and others formed from their modern appearance substituted in their place, as *lios dubh* "black fort," *lios ban* "white fort," *lios draoighneach* "blackthorn fort" (from blackthorn bushes growing on it), *lios durach* "oak fort" etc.

[Insert note: The great proportion of Lissghass, James I, Lissaghasse, Cromwell, Lisghasse, Charles II (Charters of Derry); Lissghass, Charter of Derry, James I and Cromwell, Lisghase, Charter of Derry, Charles II; the great proportion of Lissghasse, Charter of Derry, James I); Lisghasse, Charter of Derry, Cromwell and Charles II. Mr Henry Wray mortgaged to Charles Davenport, English Protestant, Lissglass, Book of Survey and Distribution. Immediately after Lissglass in this book follows the name Letteraine between Lisglass and Gortigranoch, all referred by a brace to the same person's name].

51. Lismacarrol: called in the charter Lismuckiriell-beg [insert query: -ik?] and Lismuckerill-more, from which it appears that this townland was anciently-subdivided. The etymology is obviously *Lios-mhic-Cairill*, i.e. "the fort of the sons of Caireall." *Caireall* and its diminutive *Caireallan* were very common as proper names of men in ancient times in Ireland, but different from *Cearbhall* and *Cearbhallan*, though they are sometimes similarly anglicised.

[Insert note: LissmcKerrillmore, James I, Lissmckirrillmore, Cromwell, LismcKerimore, Charles II (Charter of Derry); LismcKerrillbeg, James I, LissmcKirillbegg, Cromwell, Lismickirielbegg being one balliboe of land, Charles II (Charters of Derry); 2 Lismakrills, Sir Thomas Phillips' map (Goldsmiths' Company); C.S. (Goldsmiths) Lissmakerulles, Book of Survey and Distribution].

52. Lisnagelvin (north of Ardnabrocky): called in the charter Laghmagilligan [insert query: Lis?] one balliboe of land, and in the Down Survey Lissnagilligan, part of Balliowen. The correct name seems to be Lismagilligan or "Magilligan's fort," as will appear from the agreement of the Down Survey with the charter. The names must have received considerable corruption in this parish, as it lies so close to Derry and has been upwards of 200 years occupied by Scotch and English settlers.

[Insert note: Laghtmagillegan being one balliboe of land, Charter of Derry, James I; Laghmagillegan, Charter of Derry, Cromwell and Charles II; Taughmalaughlin, Sir Thomas Phillips, map (Grocers' Company); Company of Grocers, London, Tamalaughlin, Book of Survey and Distribution. [Insert marginal note: see Evish townland]. [Insert query: Can this be Lisnagelvin]? On Sir T. Phillips' map the name occurs between Avish, 2 Edenreaghs, Gortnefry, Monaghbeg and Gorticrioss. Immediately between this, Taughmclaughlin and Gortnefry, Sir T. Phillips places the name Belud (on same map). Bealad being one balliboe of land, Charters of Derry (identified by situation); Company of Grocers, Bellett, Book of Survey and Distribution; claimed by Captain George Hart, Alfnabracky and Lisnagilligan, part of Ballyowen, Book of Survey and Distribution].

[Insert note: Lisnatoy, Sir T. Phillips' map; now Desertowen q.v.].

53. Lisneal, or more correctly Lisneill: called in the charter Lisneale one balliboe of land [insert note: not the Lisneal in Clondermot. The Lisneale of the charter (in the small proportion of Carnemoyagh) was situated either in the parish of Faughanvale or Tamlaght Finlagan, as will appear as a comparison with Sir T. Phillips' map of the Fishmongers' lands, and in the Down Survey Lissneale part of Balliowen]. The name certainly signifies *Lios Neill* or "Niall's fort." *Niall*, which is Latinised Nigellus by St Bernard, was anciently and is still very common as the proper name of a man.

[Insert note: Claimed by Captain George Hart, Lisneale, part of the same (i.e. Ballyowen), Book of Survey and Distribution].

[Insert note: Lisnegarre, Sir Thomas Phillips' map; now Glenderowen townland q.v.].

54. Lissaghmore: called in the charter Lehessagmore [insert query: Lehessaghmore?] one balliboe of land, and incorrectly Lisamore by Sampson. The etymology is certainly *Leith-sheisreach Mor* "the large half-ploughland." *Seisreach*, which is generally anglicised sessiagh and translated "ploughland," was, according to Keating, the twelfth part of a ballybetagh and contained 120 acres of the *large Irish measure*; see county history, triochadh ceud.

[Insert note: Lehessaghmore, Charter of Derry, James II and Cromwell; Lehessagmore, Charter of Derry, Charles II; Lesamore or Lessamor, Sir T. Phillips' map (Goldsmiths' Company); Sir T. Phillips (same map) gives the name Lesamore also to a large townland lying between Tamnymore and Prehen [insert footnote: ditto on Sampson's

map; this space is on the Ordnance map occupied by the townlands of Bolies, Brickkilns and Corrody, which names are not to be found in the old authorities], and including the mountain of Slievenamanfin. It is connected with the former Lesamore at its north west extremity. C.S. (Goldsmiths) Lissaghmorebegg and one-quarter of Cromkill, Book of Survey and Distribution; Mr John Elwin, Protestant, Lessaghmore, Book of Survey and Distribution. This name has not been found in any of the ancient authorities.

Lissnebeare (C.S.) forfeited by Shane O'Cahan, Irish Papist, is mentioned in the Book of Survey and Distribution as in the parish of Clondermot, immediately following Lisdelane. There is another Lismabeare mentioned in same book as in Faughanvale parish, which we have identified with Whitehall in that parish q.v.].

55. Lissahawley: called by Sampson Lisachory, but probably by mistake. The name seems to signify *Leth-sheisreach Amhlaoibh* "Awley's half-ploughland." *Amhlaoibh* was a man's name which seems to have been borrowed by the Irish from the Danish Amlaff, Olaf or Olave, as it never occurs in the Irish Annals previous to the year 851, but they had the name *Amhalghaidh*, which is also anglicised Awley in Terawley.

Derivation of Townland Names

56. Magheracanon: called in the charter Magheriekenan one balliboe of land. The etymology is *Machaire-na-gcananach* "the canons' plain." *Machaire*, anciently magh, is always translated campus or planities by the old Irish Latin writers from the time of Admanan to Dr O'Conor. It is probable that this townland belonged to the canons of Derry, as did Rosnagalliagh to the nuns of Derry.

[Insert note: Magheriekenan, Charter of Derry, James I and Cromwell; Magheryekenan, Charter of Derry, Charles II; Maghere Kenan, Sir Thomas Phillips' map (Goldsmiths' Company); C.S. (Goldsmiths) Machrikennan, Book of Survey and Distribution. This townland is omitted on Sampson's map. The name Maghiereneskeagh occurs in the charter; see Ballyshasky townland].

57 and 58. Managhbeg and Managhmore (or Managh the smaller and larger): called in the charter Monagh begg and more two balliboes of land, Monagh etc. by Sampson and Managh etc. in some modern authorities. The name seems to be an anglicising of *Muineach* which means "a place full of moneys or hills." In the north of Ireland the word *muine* is understood to mean "a hill" (Latin mons) and is nearly synonymous with *druim*, as *Muine*

Mor, now the town of Moneymore, so called from the hill over the town. This word is very well understood in Ulster and enters into the names of many townlands, as do all its derivatives, as *muineach* "hilly" and *Muineachan* (now Monaghan), "a place full of moneys or hills;" and still in Munster it has a radically different signification, namely "a brake or place abounding in shrubs and briars," but in this sense it is as different a word from muine (mons) "a hill," as the English bier is from beer or bear (barley) from bear (a brute).

[Insert note: The small proportion of Monaghbegg, Charters of Derry, Monaghbegg being one balliboe of land, Charters of Derry; i Moneyr (.i. Monaghbegg), Sir Thomas Phillips' map (Grocers' Company); Monaghmore, Charter of Derry, James I; Monaghin, charter Cromwell and Charles II, being one balliboe of land and half of one balliboe of land; Money (.i. Monaghmore), Sir Thomas Phillips' map (Grocers' Company); the small proportion of Monagh-begg, James I, Monaghbegg, Cromwell, Monnaghbegg, Charles II, Charters of Derry; (Grocers) Monaghmore, Monnaghbegg, Book of Survey and Distribution].

59. Maydown: called in the charter by the more correct name of Moydoumy. The meaning is *Magh duine*, i.e. "the plain of the fort." A similar name occurs in the *Annals of the four masters* at the year 942; it is synonymous with Moyra.

[Insert note: Moydowny, Charter of Derry, James I and Charles II; Moydowney, Charter of Derry, Cromwell; Medoon, Sir Thomas Phillips' map (Grocers' Company). [Insert query: Can this be the Canenadowne of the inquisition 14 James I; see Enagh townland]; one-quarter of land called Medowne, inquisition Derry, 1st September 1609; (Grocers) Maydowne, Book of Survey and Distribution].

Derivation of Townland Names

60. Prehen: called in the printed copies of the charter Prehum and Brehime one balliboe of land. The inhabitants of the mountains of this county who speak Irish do not believe that this is an Irish name, and to account for its etymology they tell a grave [crossed out: ridiculous] story that a Cromwellian adventurer, who got this townland as debenture lands, on seeing its barren appearance sold it for *one* hen, on which he *preyed* at his next dinner "unde Prey-hen dicitur;" Dinseanchus.

[Insert note: Prehum, Charter of Derry; Prehan, Sir Thomas Phillips' map (Goldsmiths' Company); Mr John Elwin, Protestant, Prehane, Book of Survey and Distribution].

61. Primity *Priomh-shaoi an Phriomh Thighe*: does not occur in any of the old authorities. It is called Tromaty by Sampson. Primity is one of those names of places of which it would require a Ferceirtne or a Vallancey to give the etymology; perhaps *Druim-a-tighe* "ridge of the house."

[Insert note: Dromagtagh being one balliboe of land, Charter of Derry, James I and Charles II; Dromaghtagh, Charter of Derry, Cromwell; Tromata, Sir T. Phillips' map (Goldsmiths' Company); C.S. (Goldsmiths) Primitte, Book of Survey and Distribution].

62. Rossnagalliagh: called in the inquisition of 1609 Rossnegalliah a half quarter of land. The etymology is certainly *Ros-na-gcailleach* "the wood of the nuns," as we learn from the inquisition of 1609 that it belonged to the nunnery of Derry; see Ballynagalliagh in Templemore.

The Irish word *ros* (sometimes written ras) frequently enters into the names of places in Ireland and generally signifies "a point of land running into the sea or a lake," as *Na Rasa*, now the Rosses in the county of Donegal; *Ros Beag* and *Ros Mor*, 2 points running into Lough Erne. In this sense Colgan translates it promontorium; but *ros* certainly has another meaning perfectly distinct from this: when it appears in the name of a place which has no connection with water it signifies "a wood," and in this sense it has been translated nemus by O'Sullevan (*Hist. Cathol.*) and boscus by Sir James Ware.

This word is explained in *Cormac's Glossary* thus: "*ros, treidhe for dingair .i. ros fidhbhuidhe; ros lin, acos ros uisce. Sain din a chuir ar ro hainmnighedh cach de: ros fidhbhuidhe cedamus .i. roi-os; ros lin dana .i. ro ass: ros uisce dna .i. ro fhos ar ni bi acht for marbh uisce.*" "Ros: 3 things so called, viz. wood, flax seed and water, each so called for different reasons: first ros, when it signifies 'wood,' is compounded of roi-os; ros, 'flax seed,' of roi-ass (great growth); and ros 'water,' of ro-fhos 'very stagnant,' for it is never applied to any but dead (stagnant) water."

Though we have the authority of Cormac here that ros signifies "stagnant water" (*marbh uisce*) the word is always understood on the northern coast of Ireland to mean not water but "a point of land running into water." Tighe, in his *Statistical account of the county of Kilkenny*, says that ross means "a sacred place," but this must be rejected as deriving no support from authority or topographical appearance [insert alternative: evidence].

[Insert note: Rosnegalliagh, Sir Thomas Phillips' map (Goldsmiths' Company); (Goldsmiths) Rossneghalloch, Book of Survey and Distribution.

"And further the said jurors do upon their oaths say and present that there was a nunnery on the south side of the said city in the island of Derry, with a small garden or plot of ground called Garnegalliagh and a quarter of land called Ballygalliagh, to the said nunnery belonging; and that the half-quarter of land called Rossenegalliogh, lying in O'Chane's side, is parcel of the possessions of the said nunnery; and that the said nunnery, with the said garden and lands, came lately to the Crown by the said act or statute of dissolution of monasteries;" inquisition, Derry, 1st September 1609].

Derivation of Townland Names

Shian is mentioned in the charter in connection with Lisdillon, Ardmore, Glenkeen; no modern name resembling it; see Lisdillon. Lieutenant Thomas Skipton, Protestant, Machaniske (not identified), Ardmore, Clonkeene, the half towne of Sheane, Book of Survey and Distribution.

63. and 64. Stradreagh beg and more (or the small and large): called Stradereagh one balliboe of land, and in the Down Survey one of the 6 towns of Anach. The meaning of the name is *Srath Riach*, i.e. "grey strath or holme." The Irish word srath, which is often Scotticised to strath and corrupted to strad, stra, straw etc., signifies "a holme or level flat on the banks of a river or lake." It is the same word with the Cornish and Scotch strath. Colgan, in his translation of Evin's *Life of St Patrick*, renders this word pratum, as he conceived that all these irriguous flats might be called meadows, but Dr O'Conor always renders it paludosus campus, which is perhaps more correct. These straths or holmes are generally overflown in winter, but in summer they are very fertile and present a rich and vivid appearance, and many of them are meadows. For the meaning of reagh, see Edenreagh supra.

[Insert note: Stradereagh, one of the 8 balliboes in the precinct of Annaght, inquisition 14th James I. This name does not occur on Sir Thomas Phillips' map, on which this townland is called Ardgaire. On the Down Survey a part of the townland of Anach church-towne (Templetown) is called Arigara a controversie. The name Stradregh does not occur on the Down Survey map, but the present townland of Stradreaghmore is marked as "one of the six townes of Anach" and the townland of Stradregh-beg is represented as swampy and nearly all painted, as the lough is. Ariger (controversye), Book of Survey and Distribution; (Grocers) Stradreagh, Book of Survey and Distribution].

Derivation of Townland Names

65. Tagharina: does not occur in the ancient authorities. Its etymology is not evident. Tagh, the first part of the compound, must be from *teach*, which frequently enters into names of places, as Taughboyne or "St Baithen's house" in Donegal; it is always translated domus by Colgan and derived from the Latin tectum by Cormac: "*tech*, ab eo quod est tec-tum." Arina, pronounced areena, is obscure: perhaps *na rioghna* "of the queen?"

[Insert note: Taughrena, Sir Thomas Phillips' map (Goldsmiths' Company); C.S. (Goldsmiths) Tachrina, Book of Survey and Distribution. *Tochair Enna* would mean "Enna's causeway"].

66. Tamnymore: called in the charter Tawnamore one balliboe of land. The Irish word *tamhnach*, which enters into the names of countless places in the north of Ireland, is not given in any Irish dictionary nor understood in any part of Munster. It is colloquially used in the north as a common noun substantive to express "a field or flat between hills." Thus Saintfield, the name of a village in the county of Down, is a translation of the Irish *Tamhnach-na-naomh*, from which it may be inferred that *tamhnach* was understood to mean "field" when the name was translated. It has been anglicised tawnagh, tawny, tavenagh and tamny.

[Insert note: Tawnamore; Tawnaghmore (with Gortenecrosse), 2 quarters sometime possessed by O'Dowrie, patent rolls I James I (roll 2) art. LXXXVIII, being a grant from the king to Captain Ralph Bingley (see Gorticross); Tawnymore, Sir Thomas Phillips' map (Goldsmiths' Company); Lieutenant Thomas Skipton, Protestant, Tawnimore, Book of Survey and Distribution].

67. Templetown: called Ballnytemple in an inquisition taken at Ballykelly in the 14th year of the reign of James I, Templequarter in the one of 1609, Ballintemple in the charter and Aenach Churchtowne in the Down Survey. Templetown is a translation of *Baile-an-teampaill*, i.e. "the town of the church," so called from the old church of Enagh.

[Insert note: The Ballintemple of the charters is not this Templetown, but the townland of the church of Clondermot, i.e. Clondermot townland q.v.; Ba[lly] Temple, Sir Thomas Phillips' map (Grocers' Company); Ballnytemple, one of the 8 balliboes in the precinct of Annaght, inquisition 14th, James I; the heirs of George Cary Esquire, English Protestant, Anach Churchtowne, Book of Survey and Distribution].

68. Tirbracken: called in the charter Dragbracken; the meaning is *Tir Bhreacain* "Brecan's land," and it is probable that this townland belonged to Enagh church, of which St Brecan was the patron; vide Enagh church, infra. The Irish word *tir* now generally signifies "a country or territory," but it appears from the number of small townlands into which the word enters that it anciently meant "land" in general, like the Latin terra from which Cormac derives it: "*tir .i. a terra .i. o'n talmhain.*" *Breacan* was anciently the name of a man signifying "speckled or freckled."

[Insert note: Donaghbrackan, Charter of Derry, James I; Daghbracken, Charter of Derry, Cromwell; Draghbrackon, Charter of Derry, Charles II; Taghbrackan, Sir Thomas Phillips' map (Grocers' Company); the Company of Grocers, London, Tebracon, Book of Survey and Distribution].

69. Tirkeeveny: called by Sampson Tiravney, but by mistake. The name signifies *Tir-mhic-aibhne* "the land of the son of Avney or Evenew." Aveny was and is very common as the proper name of a man among the family of the O'Kanes. Tir-avney, the name given by Sampson, means "Avney's land," but it is probable that he has intentionally omitted the ic (a usual contraction for vic) to render the signification of the name obvious.

[Insert note: Tiffikene, Sir Thomas Phillips' map (Goldsmiths' Company). This is a mistake in Sir Thomas Phillips' map, q[uery?] Tirfekeone; C.S. (Goldsmiths) Tirhavenny, Book of Survey and Distribution.

Tullanere, Sir Thomas Phillips' map: see Avish townland].

70. and 71. Tully Upper and Lower: called in the charter Tully Yeightra and Tully Yowtra two balliboes of land. The "yeightra" and "yowtra" is an attempt at expressing the Irish words *iochtrach* and *uachtrach*, which mean "lower and upper." Tully is an anglicising of tulaigh or tulach, which means "a gentle hill, a gently rising ground." This word looks to the same parent language with the English hill and the Latin collis; for if the Irish "t" and the Latin "c" be aspirated they will both become sibilants (nearly "h" as in the English hill).

Lhwyd, in his comparative etymology, shows that many words beginning with h in English are to be found in other languages beginning with c and t. This word is translated collis by Colgan (*Triad. Thau.*) and derived by Cormac thus: "*tulach quasi tuluach .i. uacht inte acos i na tul .i. nocht: ar is tul cach nocht,*" i.e. tulach, quasi tuluach: from its being cold and exposed; for tul means exposed or naked." This derivation is curious [crossed out: ingenious] but visionary.

[Insert note: Tully-yeightra being one balliboe of land, Charter of Derry, James I and Charles II; Tullagh-etragh, Sir Thomas Phillips' map (Goldsmiths' Company); Tullyeightra, Charter of Derry, Cromwell; Tullyowtra being one balliboe of land, James I and Cromwell, Charters of Derry; Tullagh Otragh, Sir Thomas Phillips' map (Goldsmiths' Company); Tully-yowtra, Charter of Derry, Charles II; C.S. (Goldsmiths), Lower Tullyes, Upper Tullyes, Book of Survey and Distribution].

72. and 73. Tullyally Upper and Lower: called in the charter Tullealenowtra one balliboe of land and Tullyalenyeghtra one balliboe of land. The etymology seems to be *Tulach Aille* "sloping hill," collis acclivis.

[Insert note: Tullyalenowtra, Charter of Derry, James I and Cromwell; Tullealenowtra, Charter of Derry, Charles II; Tullyalynyeightra, Charter of Derry, James I; Tullyalimeytra, charter, Cromwell; Tullyalinyeightra, Charter of Derry, Charles II; Lieutenant-Colonel Tristiam Beresford, English Protestant, Tullyallies, 2 towne lands, Book of Survey and Distribution].

74. Warbleshinny: called in the charter Urbleshaney one balliboe of land. The meaning is unquestionably *Earball Sionnaigh* "fox's tail," a very imaginative name not unfrequently given to townlands in the north of Ireland, from some fancied resemblance to a fox's tail. *Earball*, which literally means "a tail," is used topographically to signify "a narrow stripe of land, the tail of a mountain." In the county of Donegal and throughout Connaught this word is incorrectly pronounced ruball and in Munster and Leinster *eirioball*.

[Insert note: Urbleshan [insert note: obscure], Charter of Derry, James I; Urbulsheney, Sir Thomas Phillips' map (Goldsmiths' Company); Urbleshanie, Charter of Derry, Cromwell; Urbleshany, Charter of Derry, Charles II; C.S. (Goldsmiths) Worblesheming, Book of Survey and Distribution].

The fishing of the Ffaghan [insert query: thus in original?], inquisition, Derry, 1st September 1609.

Notes on Townland Names by John O'Donovan

Natural State

Townland Names

1. Ballyowen, Ballyoan: O'Reilly's says this cannot signify "riverstown," but gives no reason. If it

be derived from *Baile Abhan*, the best spelling is either Ballyoan or Ballyone.

2. Cah, Cagh, Key: *Cath* "a tribe;" *ce* "earth" or "land," a man's name, might have been originally added.

3. Carrickabredia, Carrickbread [and] Carricebrede (Down Survey): this is most probably compounded of *carraig* "a rock" and *bradaidhe* "a thief." If there be in this townland a rock with a cave that might serve as a lurking place for a thief, this must be the derivation. Many caves and grottos in Ireland have got names from robbers, as *Poll-a-Ropaire* "the robber's cave," Tory hill, in the county of Kilkenny. If this be the derivation, Carrickabredy is the best spelling.

4. Enagh, Anagh: it appears from Down Survey that Anach was a general name for a considerable portion of this parish, comprehending the townlands Enach, Lisahawley, Templetown, Stradreagh. It is derived from the Irish word *Eanach* "marshy land." Enagh therefore is the nearest spelling to the original. However, names of places derived from this word are generally now spelled Armagh. Vide Lanigan's *Ecclesiastical history* vol.II.

5. Gransha: Grange, Down Survey, query?

6. Clohore, Clochore, Cloghore: *Clochoir* "golden stone." Cloghore preferable (multis rationibus).

7. Craigtown, Craigetown: is the first syllable of this name long or short; if short it should certainly be spelled Cragtown.

8. Crumpkill: Gleabe of Clumkill, Down Survey, query?

9. Currynearin: I think that the English dipthong 'ie' is the best symbol of *ia*; if so, Currynierin, sed quaere?

10. Disertowne, Lissatone, Desertowen, Desertoan: Disertowen is more supported by authority than Lissatone. It is for consideration whether names of places derived from *disert* (i.e. loc fas) "a desert, retirement or hermitage" should be spelled alike. At present the spelling is either Dysart, Disert, Desert, Dizert or Desart, of which Disert is the most conformable to the Irish spelling. In the parish of Ballynascreen it is spelled Dysert.

11. Drumagore, Drumagor: *Druim Gabhar* "hill of the goats." *Gabhar* is pronounced gower. The quantity of 'o' in gor is too short to represent the dipthongal sound of *abha* in gabhar. Drumagower would be the most consistent English spelling, but as there is no authority to support it Drumagore must be adopted.

12. Glenkeen, Clonkeine [and] Clonkeine, Down Survey: *Glenn Caoin* "delightful valley;" *Cluain*

Cain "planities amana;" *Cluain Caan* "the plain of Cian" (a man's name, now Kean). Let it be enquired whether there be a valley in this townland, so as to make "glen" applicable; if there be no valley Clonkeine, the name on Down Survey, is the best.

13. Fincarn: *Finn Carn* "white heap." This should be spelled Fincarn in English. To spell carn "a heap" cairn is foreign to Irish orthography, nor is there any English analogy to favour it. It is engraved Fincarn on sheet 37. Let it be enquired whether the latter syllable of this word be pronounced carn, the 'a' pronounced as in the word father or cairn, the 'ai' being pronounced as in the word gain?

14. Gobnascale: Gortnastall (Down Survey), i.e. "field of the stallion."

15. Gorton, Gortin: *Goirtin* "a little garden or cultivated place." Names of places derived from this word are generally spelled Gurteen, which is the Irish pronunciation.

16. Lisdillon, Lisdeolan, Lisdealane: O'Reilly derives this word from Lios Diolmhain, i.e. "the faithful fortress," but diolmhain is the Irish of the family name Dillon, and the meaning is more probably *Lios Diolmhain* "the fort of Dillon." If this be the proper derivation, Lisdillon is the best English spelling.

17. Rossbagalliagh, Rossmagalliagh, Rossnagallagh: *Ros-na-gcailleach*, i.e. "grove of the nuns." Rossnagalliagh is the best English spelling.

18. Tamnamore, Tamnymore, Tamneymore, Tawnamore: *Tamhnach Mor* "the large burial place." It is my opinion that, where custom favours the pronunciation of 'ni' in this word, Tamny is the best English spelling, and that all names of places derived from this word should be similarly spelled Tamny, except where custom favours Tawny.

Report on Clondermot Charitable Loan

Letter to Lieutenant Larcom

November 3rd 1835,
  Mr Larcom,
  I am making way in information. The enclosed is useful. I have also made out the mode [of] inquiry etc. of the Clondermot Charitable Loan. I see that further enquiries are needed as regards that of Templemore. Date of Clondermot 1814. In haste, ever yours, [signed] J. Portlock.

Printed Loan Forms

No. [blank], to the Governors of the Charitable Loan, Glendermott. I (1) of (2,3) do recommend (4) of (5,6), having (7) in family, he being head of said family, as a proper person to be entrusted with a loan of [blank] pounds to (8), and being, as I believe, honest, sober and industrious, and not in any degree concerned in the sale of malt or spiritous liquors; and I hereby propose becoming joint security with [blank] for the repayment of the said sum. Dated [blank] day of [blank] 18[blank], (9).

Terms of repayment: 6d in each pound per week, payable on Thursdays at the schoolhouse, Glendermott, between the hours of 1 and 3 o'clock. The smallest irregularity in the payment of the instalments will be followed in all cases by the immediate summary process for the recovery of the principal.

Directions for filling recommendations: 1, name of the security recommending; 2, residence of same; 3, occupation of same; 4, name of person soliciting loan, if female, she must say if maid, wife or widow; 5, residence of same; 6, occupation of same; 7, number in family, including applicant; 8, purpose for which the loan is requested, which should be fully and fairly declared; 9, signature of security recommending.

NB You are desired to observe, that unless the above directions are complied with in every particular, this application will be rejected. No second recommendation within a month from any individual will be attended to; and should this application be granted, the security must be perfected in presence of the governors in their board.

Loan Records

No.18, 2 pounds, 12th October 1835, pay the bearer, James Toner, 2 pounds, secured to the Charitable Loan [signed] A.G. Cary, registrar. To Cary McClellan Esquire, treasurer, Ardmore. Hempton, printer, Derry.

No.18, James Toner, sum lent 2 pounds, weekly repayment 1s; date 12th October 1835. First repayment due between 12 and 3 o'clock on 31st of October 1835.

No.18, total sum lent 2 pounds. We, jointly and severally, promise to pay unto Cary McClellan Esquire, or order, 14 days after date, the sum of 2 pounds sterling, value received in cash from the governors of the Charitable Musical Society. Dated this 12th day of October 1835, witness [signed] Samuel McAlister, applicant [signed] James Toner, recommender [signed] John Thompson.

Charitable Loan Committee

The committee for managing the Glendermott Charity Loan meets the first Monday in every month, in order to take the claims of the poor into consideration. The treasurer pays the loans every second Monday in each month. He keeps a yearly clerk and pays him 10 pounds a year. The session house belonging to the Presbyterian meeting house is the committee room and the parish schoolhouse is their office, and the master is clerk to the committee. His name is McAlister.

Notes on Charitable Loan

Glendermott Charitable Loan, established April 1814, permitted by charter from government and conducted by a committee composed of the clergymen of the parish of every denomination, together with a few of the neighbouring gentlemen. The trustees are the Lord Bishop of Derry, the Dean of Derry and the curate of the parish, for the time being.

They lend out to industrious housekeepers from 1 to 5 pounds on approved security, free of any charge whatsoever, to be repaid at the rate of 6d in the pound each week, so that 40 weeks pays up the whole sum, whether it be 1 pound or 5.

This establishment was set on foot chiefly through the means of the Revd A.G. Carey, by advancing a sum of money as capital and soliciting others to follow his example.

Documents concerning Tirkeeran Farming Society, 1835

SOCIAL AND PRODUCTIVE ECONOMY

Tirkeeran Farming Society

[Crossed out: Ardlough, September 30 1835.
Sir,
Agreeably to your desire, I send herewith a copy of the regulations of Tirkeeran Farming Society, with a scale of premiums proposed and the objects for which those premiums are usually awarded.

This society continued to be a branch of the North West of Ireland Farming Society from its foundation in 1821 until in 1834 the parent society having ceased to exist, it started on an independent footing. It at present consists of 84 members, 29 of whom belong to the higher classes and are not entitled to compete for money premiums, the original regulations confining all money premiums to persons deriving their chief support from agriculture.

Since its commencement in 1821 it has distributed among the farmers of this half-barony in money premiums (besides many valuable donations from private individuals) above 800 pounds. 5s paid annually in advance constitutes a member, but there are many gentlemen who subscribe 5 pounds. The beneficial effects of this society are already very observable in this neighbourhood. I am, Sir, James Patchell Esquire].

Printed Minutes of Meeting

Tirkeeran Farming Society. At a general meeting of the Tirkeeran branch, North West of Ireland Society, held at Clark's Hotel, Waterside, on Wednesday the 6th of August 1834, convened for the purpose of forming an independent society and making such alterations in the existing rules and regulations as should appear to be necessary, James Henderson Esquire in the chair, the following resolutions were carried unanimously.

1st. That, inasmuch as the North West of Ireland Society has withdrawn its annual grant, and this branch is now fully able to continue its operations from its own resources, we deem the dependence of this branch on the parent society no longer requisite.

2nd. That the Tirkeeran branch of the North West of Ireland Society shall in future be denominated the Tirkeeran Farming Society.

3rd. That all members of the Tirkeeran branch North West of Ireland Society shall be considered members of this society.

4th. That individuals wishing to become members in future shall be proposed and admitted at general meeting or meeting of committee, and, having paid the sum of 5s into the hands of the treasurer, shall be entitled (if deriving their principal support from agriculture) to compete for the society's premiums, 6 months after payment, and not sooner, except for ploughing premiums.

5th. That subscriptions shall be payable on the 1st October and that no member in arrears shall be entitled to compete.

6th. That members subscribing not less than 1 pound annually shall be eligible to the office of president or vice-president.

7th. That there shall be one general meeting in each year for the arrangement of premiums etc., to be held on the first Wednesday of November.

8th. That 9 members, chosen by ballot at such general meeting, shall constitute a general committee. The secretary and treasurer being ex-officio members of committee.

9th. That in all disputed cases the decision of the general committee shall be final.

10th. That no member shall be entitled to receive any premium until 14 days after judges'

decision, during which time appeals may be lodged with the secretary.

11th. That in the event of any judge not attending, the judges who attend shall be empowered to appoint an umpire.

12th. That with the above alterations and amendments, the existing rules of the Tirkeeran branch shall continue and be in force to regulate the proceedings of this society.

Signed by order, James Patchell, secretary.

NB To such members as were absent from the above, it may not be improper to state that the meeting passed the foregoing resolutions knowing that for some time past their operations had been considerably impeded by an unnecessary and merely nominal dependence on a body that was evidently just expiring, and believing that, from the munificent donation of Sir R. Bateson and Captain Jones, the patronage of the Fishmongers' and Grocers' Companies, and the increased subscriptions of many gentlemen connected with the society, their funds would be quite sufficient to give the necessary efficiency to their future exertions. Hempton, printer, Derry.

Officers of Society

President Leslie Alexander Esquire; vice-presidents Sir R.A. Ferguson, Baronet, M.P., Cary McClellan and Arthur Sampson Esquires. Committee: Mr John Cowan, Mr John Tedlie, Mr John Lithgow, Mr Robert Fairly, Mr William Cathers, Mr John Wills, Mr Ross B. Smith, Mr Alexander Noble, Mr William Stevenson. Treasurer Mr William Semple; secretary Mr James Patchell.

List of Members

Alexander, John Esquire; Alexander, Leslie Esquire; Ash, W. Hamilton Esquire.

Baird, Mr Thomas; Baird, Mr Samuel; Bateson, Sir Robert, Baronet, M.P.; Beresford, H. Barre Esquire; Brown, John Esquire, Cumber; Brown, Mr William; Brownlow, Revd Francis.

Caldwell, Mr John (g); Canning, Mr James; Canning, Mr William Junior; Carmalt, Thomas Esquire, R.N.; Cathers, Mr William; Clarke, Mr Samuel; Cobley, Mr Thomas (g); Cochran, Mr Edward Junior (g); Cochran, Mr James; Cowan, Mr Alexander (g); Cowan, Mr John; Cowan, Mr Oliver; Craig, Mr James; Craig, Mr John; Craig, Mr Richard (g); Crawford, Mr William (g).

Derry, Lord Bishop of; Derry, the Very Revd the Dean of; Duddy, Mr Peter (g); Dunlop, Mr James (g).

Ewing, Mr Samuel.

Fairly, Mr Robert; Ferguson, Sir R.A., Baronet, M.P.; Ferguson, Mr Samuel; Fishmongers, Worshipful Company of; Grocers, Worshipful Company of.

Hatrick, Mr Ezekiel; Hay, Mr Robert (g); Hayden, Revd John; Henderson, James Esquire; Houston, Mr James (g).

Jones, T. Esquire, M.P.; Lamrock, Mr William (g); Lithgow, Mr Edward; Lithgow, Mr John, Lisnagelvin; Lindsay, Mr John; Lyle, Hugh Esquire.

McCain, Mr James; McClellan, Cary Esquire; McClintock, Samuel Esquire; McCutcheon, Mr Joseph; Moncrieff, Mr Robert (g); Moore, Andrew Esquire; Morrison, Mr Alexander (f); Mullins, Mr Thomas; Noble, Mr Alexander.

Orr, Mr Joseph (g).

Paine, Mr Samuel (g); Parkhill, Mr John (g); Patchell, Mr James; Patton, Mr James.

Quigley, Mr Robert.

Ross, Mr Francis A.; Ross, Mr James.

Scott, Thomas Esquire, Wilsborough; Semple, Mr William; Skipton, Pitt Esquire; Smith, J.A. Esquire; Smith, James Esquire; Smith, Mr Ross T. Esquire; Smith, W. Lynn Esquire; Stevenson, Mr Jacob; Stevenson, Robert Esquire; Stevenson, Mr William; Swan, Mr Hugh (f).

Tait, Mr Christie; Tedlie, Mr John; Tedlie, Mr Thomas; Thompson, Mr Henry.

West, James Esquire, M.D.; White, Thomas Esquire; Wills, Mr John; Wilson, Mr William.

(g) Nominated by Charles Warner Esquire on the part of the Grocers' Company; (f) nominated by A. Sampson Esquire on the part of the Fishmongers' Company.

Premiums and Regulations of Society

At a general meeting held at the Tirkeeran Inn, Waterside, on Wednesday the 5th November 1834, Sir Robert Alexander Ferguson Baronet, M.P., in the chair; present 39 members.

A president, 3 vice-presidents and committee for the ensuing year having been elected as above, the Very Revd the Dean of Derry, Mr James Ross, Mr Francis Alexander Ross, Mr Henry Thompson and John Brown Esquire were proposed and admitted members of this institution, and the annual scale of premiums was considerably enlarged by very handsome subscriptions of 5 pounds each, from city and county representatives.

Resolved: that the sum of 50 pounds be distributed in premiums to this society for the year 1835 as follows, viz. ploughing: 1st premium 2 pounds, 2nd 1 pound 15s, 3rd 1 pound 10s, 4th 1 pound 5s, 5th 1 pound, 6th 15s, 7th 12s 6d, 8th 10s, 9th 7s 6d, 10th 5s; total 10 pounds.

To ploughmen, being servants either of gentlemen or farmers: 1st premium 1 pound, 2nd 17s 6d, 3rd 12s 6d, 4th 10s; total 3 pounds.

Regulations: to plough half a rood of ground in 2 and a half hours, the cattle to be managed in reins, the furrow to be 7 and a half inches in breadth by 4 and a half inches in depth, the ridges to be equally divided with the allowance of 2 furrows in each lot. No assistance to be given to ploughmen. No borrowed articles to be used. Ploughs to be entered at 10 o'clock, match to commence at 11 o'clock.

Resolved: that the silver cup presented to the society by Thomas Scott of Wilsborough, Esquire, and now held by Mr James Craig, be open to all subscribers in the branch on a deposit of 5s with the secretary, on or before the morning of the match, said deposits to be applied as the committee for the time being may direct.

Cup to be awarded with the first premiums, the winner to be subject to challenge for 2 years. The cup, as well as the money premiums, to be open to one plough from the agricultural seminary (if held by one of the pupils) without any deposits. Match to be held on the third Monday of February.

Resolved: that Messrs John Tedlie, John Wills and John Craig be appointed to select a field and lay it off in lots of half a rood each. This and all premium land to be surveyed by the Cunningham perch.

Resolved: that Mr William Macky, Galliagh, Mr Hugh Clarke, Mulkeeragh, and Mr James McCrea, Maghareagh, be appointed judges, and that the secretary be instructed to write to them requesting their compliance with this resolution.

Clover with grasses: 1st premium 1 pound 15s, 2nd 1 pound 10, 3rd 1 pound 5s, 4th 1 pound, 5th 15s, 6th 10s, 7th 5s; total 7 pounds.

Regulations: not less than 1 acre to compete; to be shown on the second Monday of June. Judges, Messrs John Lindsay, Ezekiel Hatrick and John Craig.

Vetches: 1st premium 1 pound 5s, 2nd 1 pound, 3rd 15s; total 3 pounds.

Regulations: half an acre may compete for any of the premiums and a rood for the third; not to be sown on land manured the previous year. To be shown on the third Monday of July. Judges, Messrs Alexander Noble, Joseph McCutcheon and William Brown.

Reclaiming land: 1st premium 2 pounds, 2nd 1 pound 10s, 3rd 1 pound 5s, 4th 1 pound, 5th 15s, 6th 10s; total 7 pounds.

Regulations: not less than 1 acre of that which is usually termed wasteland to compete; to be shown on the second Monday of December next and on the last Monday of September; judges, Messrs Edward Lithgow, James Craig and Francis Ross.

Enclosures: 1st premium 2 pounds, 2nd 1 pound 10s, 3rd 1 pound 5s, 4th 1 pound, 5th 15s, 6th 10s; total 7 pounds.

Regulations: not less than 40 Irish perches to compete. Enclosures commenced in 1834 may be shown; to be shown on the second Monday of October. Judges, Messrs John Tedlie, William Stevenson and Samuel Ewing.

Iron field gates: 1st premium 2 pounds, 2nd 1 pound; total 3 pounds.

Regulations: 2 gates at present not in claimant's possession to compete. Piers to be built after this date and neither to be lime dashed nor plastered: to be shown on the second Monday of October. Judges, Messrs John Craig, Christie Tait and Joseph McCutcheon.

Turnips: 1st premium 2 pounds, 2nd 1 pound 15s, 3rd 1 pound 10s, 4th 1 pound 5s, 5th 1 pound, 6th 15s, 7th 12s 6d, 8th 10s, 9th 7s 6d, 10th 5s; total 10 pounds.

Regulations: half an acre may compete for any of the premiums and a rood for the 5 last. Not to be shown on land manured the previous year; to be shown on the fourth Monday of October. Judges, Messrs John Wills, Edward Lithgow and James Ross.

Premium Winners in 1834

Resolved: that the following list of successful candidates in 1834 be printed in the proceedings.

Successful candidates in 1834. [Table contains the following headings: name, residence, number of premiums in ploughing, clover with grasses, vetches, reclaiming land, fences, gates, turnips, amount won].

Mr Thomas Baird, Kilfennan: ploughing 6, vetches 1, reclaiming land 1, gates 1, turnips 2; 6 pounds 2s 6d.

Mr Christie Tait, Kilfennan: clover with grasses 3, vetches 2, turnips 3; 3 pounds 2s 6d.

Mr Robert Fairly, Muff: clover with grasses 2, turnips 1; 2 pounds 12s 6d.

Mr William Brown, Tamnamore: ploughing 4, fences 3; 2 pounds 5s.

Mr John Wills, Gortnessy: ploughing 1; 2 pounds.

Mr Alexander Noble, Tamnamore: ploughing 2; 1 pound 15s.

Mr Joseph McCutcheon, Lisneal: fences 1; 1 pound 12s 6d.

Mr James Patchell, Ardlough: clover with grasses 4, vetches 3; 1 pound 10s.

Mr Samuel McClintock, Granshaw: ploughing 3; 1 pound 10s.

Mr Samuel Clarke, Waterside: clover with grasses 1; 1 pound 10s.

Mr John Tedlie, Ballyowen: fences 2; 1 pound 7s 6d.

Mr Alexander Cowan, Clonmacane: reclaiming land 2; 1 pound 7s 6d.

Mr Robert Hay, Gortnessy: ploughing 5; 1 pound.

Mr William Wilson, Ardlough: turnips 4; 18s.

Mr Oliver Cowan, Derryarkin: turnips 5; 15s.

Mr Samuel Paine, Gortnessy: ploughing 7; 12s 6d.

Mr John Lindsay, Artnabrocky: turnips 6; 12s.

Mr John Cowan, Greenan: clover with grasses 5; 10s.

Mr Samuel Ferguson, Fincairn: ploughing 8; 10s.

Mr William Crawford, Gortnessy: ploughing 9; 7s 6d.

Mr James Dunlop, Tirbraikin: ploughing 10; 5s.

To the ploughman of Thomas Scott Esquire 1 pound.

To the ploughman of J.A. Smith Esquire 17s 6d.

To the ploughman of Samuel McClintock Esquire 12s 6d.

To the ploughman of Mr John Lithgow, Lisnagelvin 10s.

Withheld for want of merit 1 pound 15s.

Total 37 pounds.

Proceedings of Society

Resolved: that all claimants for premiums shall give notice to the secretary 3 days at least before the day of show, and in reclaiming land the notice must be repeated for the second view. No notice will be attended to if not in writing.

Resolved: that a printed copy of the foregoing proceedings be forwarded to each member, and to such landed proprietors and influential farmers residing in the half-barony of Tirkeeran as have not yet become members, but whose co-operation in so useful an undertaking the society can have little reason to doubt.

Sir Robert A. Ferguson having left the chair, and Cary McClellan Esquire having been called thereto, resolved (on the motion of Major Scott, seconded by William Hamilton Ash Esquire) that the thanks of this meeting be given to Sir Robert A. Ferguson for his very proper conduct in the chair. Signed by order, James Patchell, secretary.

The members of the society and their friends will dine together on the day of the ploughing match at Clarke's Hotel, Waterside; tickets 5s, servants' dues included. A dinner list lies at the bar, to which those who intend dining are requested to subscribe. The president, vice-presidents and committee will act as stewards. Hempton, printer, Derry.

Copy of Will

SOCIAL ECONOMY

Will of Colonel Mitchelburne

In the name of God, Amen. I, John Michelburne of Londonderry, Esquire, having taken seriously into consideration the frailty of human life and the many accidents that attend in all our actions, and being desirous to settle and dispose of what temporal estates it hath pleased God to bless me with, do make this my last will and testament, and do give and bequeath the same in manner following, viz. to my cousin Elizabeth and Mary Sims 10 pounds each, to my sister Molly 10 pounds, with 20 pounds formerly given her, to Mr Dearby Clarke of Dublin 50 pounds. I order for maintaining the flag in the steeple of Derry 50 pounds, for which I have already given my hand.

Item: for maintenance of 8 poor inhabitants of the parish of Clondermot, particularly those of the Waterside, to each 3d a week forever, the said poor to be such as have nothing but charity to support them, and to be named by my heirs and the minister and churchwardens of the saide parish for the time being; and as one of the said poor dies another to be put in his room, for which purpose I order 86 pounds sterling to be put to interest for that use.

Item: to the schoolmaster for teaching 12 poor children of the said parish, to be of the Church of England, 4 pounds sterling per annum forever and also privilege to teach other scholars, for which purpose I order 67 pounds sterling to be put to interest for that use. The said master and scholars to be named and appointed by my heirs and the minister and churchwardens of the said parish as aforesaid for the time being, and the said number to be kept complete forever.

Item: to my god-daughter Mrs Tomkins 10 pounds and 10 pounds to my god-daughter Mrs Doul.

Item: to Alderman French of Dublin 10 pounds, to Mrs Lowry 5 pounds, to Captain Thomas White 5 pounds, to William Pocoke, my servant, 5 pounds, with all my wearing apparel and linen except a suit of grey cloth lined with black which I give and bequeath to Mr Richard Lowry of the city of Londonderry. To Mary Brostor, widow, 10 pounds and to Ann Brostor, my god-daughter, 5 pounds; to Mr Robert Houghton 5 pounds, to Mr William Crow of Dublin and Jane his wife 10 pounds each; to Thomas Collins during his life 40s yearly.

I order and allow for my tombstone erecting and engraving 20 pounds, and for my funeral charges 30 pounds. To the bearers of my corps, to be 6 officers of the standing army, each a scarf and gloves; and to the mayor, sheriffs and aldermen of Derry being there present, not exceeding 10 in number, each a scarf and gloves. I also order my body to be buried in Enagh church in the said parish and on the first day of August yearly forever, I order 30s to be distributed and given to 30 of the poor inhabitants of the said parish, and they to be of the Church of England, 12d to each of them at my tombstone; and I order 25 pounds to be put to interest for that purpose.

And whereas my house, demesnes, tenements, gardens, orchards, household goods, plates, jewels etc. are by contract of marriage made over to my wife, Elizabeth Mitchelburne, during her natural life as by the said marriage contract may more fully appear, and after her decease to be restored to my heirs or executors hereafter named, I therefore charge all my said estate after her decease, with 300 pounds sterling, to be disposed of as hereafter mentioned viz. to my grandson Abraham Slatter 30 pounds. I give my god-daughter Mrs Mary Gifford, wife of Giles Gifford of the said city, merchant, 50 pounds sterling to be put to interest for the use of her and her children.

Item: I give the poor of the parish of Templemore 5 pounds.

Item: I give and bequeath to 16 of the poor inhabitants of Clondermot, being of the Church of England, half a peck of meal weekly to each forever, to be given after sermon by the direction of the minister and churchwardens of the said parish for the time being to the said poor, for which purpose I order 140 pounds sterling to be put to interest at 6 per cent to maintain the said charity.

Memorandum: that the first 8 pensioners are not to receive any of this last charity.

Item: I give and bequeath to George Tomkins of the city of Londonderry, Esquire, two-thirds of all my estate, real and personal, forever; and the other third part of all my said estate, real and personal, I give and bequeath to the said Mr Giles Gifford, merchant, forever.

And lastly, I do nominate and appoint the said George Tomkins my sole executor of this my last will and testament, hereby revoking and annulling all former wills by me heretofore made. In witness whereof I, the said John Mitchelburne, have herunto set my hand and seal this 12th day of July 1721, [signed] John Mitchelburne.

Signed, sealed and delivered as the last will and testament of the said John Mitchelburne in the presence of us, after the word "third" was interlined: Thomas Lee, George Shaw, John Darcus. Not. Pub.

Copy of Will

Will of George Tomkins

George Tomkins' will, being one of the documents appertaining to the title of the Mitchelburne <Mitchelbourn> legacy to the parish of Glendermot.

In the name of God, Amen. I, George Tomkins, of this city of Londonderry, Esquire, being in health of body and of perfect mind and memory, but considering the certainty of death and uncertainty of life, do make, publish and declare this my last will and testament, in manner and form following.

That is to say I give, leave and bequeath unto my dearly beloved wife Elizabeth Tomkins all right, tithe and interest in my dwelling house in Shipquay Street, also Silver Street numbers 91, 92, 93 in the city of Londonderry, with the brick houses and porches thereunto belonging, which I hold from and under the Honourable the Society, the governors and assistants, London, of the new Plantation in Ulster within the realm of Ireland; she paying the society the rent I am obliged to pay for the same and also one half of a house in said street, numbers 117, 118 wherein Alderman William Lecky dwells, which I hold in partnership with my brother-in-law Robert Norman of the city of Dublin, Esquire, by leave from and under the said society of London, together with one-half of the acres and perches belonging to said house, she paying one-half of said society's rent.

And also one-half of or moiety of the several small tenements or houses lying in Rosemary Lane in said city, which I likewise hold in partnership with the said Robert Norman, from the said society, she paying one-half of the said society's rent; and also a tenement at the Ferry Quay in the suburbs of the said part, whereof is now let by me to Edward Matthews, nailer, and John Carlow, glover, in said city, which I hold from the said society, she paying the said society's rent for the same; and also all my rights and interests of my lease of the city of Londonderry which I hold by lease from the corporation, she paying the corporation the rent I am

obliged to pay them for townland Ferry, together with the 2 strong boats and small yawl.

And also all my land and tenements in Rossdooney in the parish of Glendermot and liberties of Londonderry, as now left by us to Allan Strawbridge and his clan, which I hold by lease from the see of Derry, she paying the rent reserved in said lease; and also my several tenements and houses at the Waterside, in Clooney in the said parish, as now let by Alderman P. Hanley, which I also hold by lease from the said see of Derry, she paying the bishop's rent reserved in said lease. And my said wife to have, hold, receive, enjoy and possess the aforesaid gifted and bequeathed houses, acres, perches, lands, tenements and ferry, together with all the dues and part of it arising out of the same during her natural life, in case the said leases of the same shall so long continue in being and the years not expire at my said wife's decease.

My will is and I do hereby order that my said wife Elizabeth Tomkins shall, by her last will and testament, or by any other act, deed or writing duly perfected under her hand and seal (after my decease), as she shall think fit, most convenient and proper give, bequeath and dispose of the aforesaid bequeathed houses, lands and tenements between my 2 daughters Margaret Gamble, wife of William Gamble of the city of Dublin, merchant, and Anne Tomkins, or to any one of them in such manner or in such part and proportion as she my said wife shall think most proper and fit, and as she shall find each of them respectfull and dutifull unto her. And if any of my said daughters should be anywise disrespectfull and undutifull to my said wife, I desire and order and my will is that my said wife do give, leave or otherwise dispose of said houses, lands and tenements bequeathed by us as aforesaid to my said wife to the other daughter that shall be most dutifull and respectfull to my said wife, as my said wife shall think fit, except the 2 bishop's leases of Rossdooney and the tenements at the Waterside aforesaid, which I desire and order and my will is that my said wife give, leave and bequeath that said 2 bishop's leases as aforesaid to my grandson Robert Gamble at her decease.

And whereas I have received the sum of 900 pounds sterling of my said wife's jointure, which I was not to receive pursuant to my settlement with her at marriage, in the consideration thereof, and she being the best of wives, I further give leave and bequeath unto my said wife Elizabeth Tomkins, her heirs, executors, administrators and assigns forever all my plates, household furniture, towels, rings, linen and all my other goods and chattells, and also all my other estates, real or personal, in the kingdom of Ireland or elsewhere, of what nature or kind soever, she my said wife paying and discharging all my just debts and also paying and discharging the legacies hereafter bequeathed and mentioned, except my freehold lands of Maboy and Killnappy in the parish of Faughanvale and county Londonderry, which I have already settled on my son Samuel Tomkins, by deeds duly perfected between us, and my second brother Norman Alexander Tomkins Esquire, William Leckey Esquire and my second son Samuel, as by the said deeds relation being [?] threat had may most fully appear.

Item: I leave and bequeath to W. Francis Andrews all my books.

Item: to my son Samuel 1 British shilling.

Item: to the poor of the parish of Templemore 5 pounds sterling, to be paid within 3 months after my decease to the minister and churchwardens of the said parish, by them to be distributed among the said poor as they shall think fit.

Item: any two-thirds of the lands and tenements in Cluny and Gobnescale in the parish of Clondermot, with the house and garden which was bequeathed to me by Colonel Mitchelburne, I bequeath the same to the same charitable uses as the said Colonel John Mitchelburne by his last will appointed the same.

And lastly I do hereby constitute and appoint my said wife Elizabeth Tomkins my sole executor of this my last will and testament, and I do hereby revoke all the other wills by me made, and declare this my last will and testament. In witness whereof I have to this my last will set my hand and seal, the 24th May 1739, [signed] George Tomkins; witnesses William Ellis, Joseph Car, William Dent. Probate granted to Elizabeth Tomkins the executrix, of the 13th day of October 1739.

Correspondence concerning Will

Will of Robert Miller

Captain Portlock presents his compliments to the Revd Mr Cary and will feel obliged to him for the following information. Was the brother of Robert Miller who left a bequest named Joseph?

Bricks Hotel, October 5th 1835,

Dear Sir,

You will oblige me by giving an answer to the above [initialled] A.G. Cary.

[Answer] Robert and Joseph Miller were brothers, and each of them bequeathed an hundred pounds Irish money to the poor housekeepers of Glendermot, that is to say, being Presbyterian regular members of the 2 Presbyterian meeting

houses. Joseph Miller was the senior brother, grand-uncle to me, Oliver Miller.

[To] Mr Oliver Miller, 9th November 1835. Captain Portlock's compliments to Mr Miller and he will thank him for the date of the will by which the bequests of his ancestors were made.

Working Papers

Poem

The foregoing poems in manuscript were copied from Gray's works by the hand of the lovely but unfortunate Mary Ann Knox, who was shot in the coach with her father and mother November 10th 1761 by John MacNaghten Esquire, with whom she had gone through the marriage ceremony in private. He having artfully deceived her in regard to her father's sentiments of the matter, which, when she found out and that her father would not give his consent to the union (which she has expressly made one of the conditions of the contract), and that he behaved in a manner the delicacy of her virtue could not bear, she refused to fulfil her contract or live with him as a wife; on which he pursued her in various disguises to different places she had fled to in order to avoid him and at last lodged a bullet in her side [insert addition: between Lifford and Strabane], while in the coach with her father and mother, on their road to Dublin, of which she died in a few hours; and for which he and an accomplice were soon after taken and hanged [insert addition: at Lifford]. These poems are presented here by the owner of this book, as a relique of that much and justly esteemed and admired lady.

The following lines were written on seeing the *Hymn to Adversity* transcribed by her hand.

Low is the hand that traced these sacred lines,
The soul that mov'd it a fair seraph shines;
Sweet maid! The prayer transcrib'd if made thy own,
Alas was fruitless at the eternal throne.
Adversity on thee laid her fell hand,
Encircled by the furies vengefull band,
And screaming horrors funeral cries,
From murder's horrid form, were thy sad obsequies.
Say in the depth of melancholy's gloom,
Did thy soft mind presage so sad a doom?
But blest in blindness to its future fate,
Unconscious of the storm that lay in wait.
Perhaps serene that present hour you past?
And saw no cloud foretell the coming blast,
Nor dreamt of ills so direfull to destroy,

The blooming hopes of innocence and joy.
Mysterious Heavens! How deep are thy
designs,
But faith and resignation read the lines
And wisdom, mercy, goodness, through them
shines.

The author know this is bad grammar but can't
be at the trouble to study any other expression.

Poems copied by M.A. Knox: *Gray's Elegy,
Ode on the Spring, Hymn to Adversity*.

Heads of Inquiry For Tirkeeran Barony

MEMOIR WRITING

Heads of Inquiry

Barony of Tirkeeran: the following inquiries are
applicable to all the parishes, but should be an-
swered separately for each. The special inquiries
adapted to each parish will be given on separate
papers. The present numerical details are to be
given in the tables and some past ones also; but it
would be desirable to obtain general details of
fluctuation, increase and diminution, for as many
past years as possible, where, from the want of
registration or other causes, there is a failure of
numerical details.

Where any institution (scholastic, benevolent
etc.) is in operation, a history of its origins, progress,
resources, management etc. should be obtained.
Similar inquiries should also be made respecting
extinct institutions, with the causes of their failure,
prospect of restoration etc.; and respecting contemplated ones, with the nature of their prospects.
Ascertain whether existing institutions are pro-
gressing, retrograding or stationary.

In order to check and verify statements, inquiry
respecting the same object should be made both
of interested and uninterested persons; the character of each referee and the means he possesses
of acquiring information being always kept in
view. In any abstract questions, it would be well
to ascertain the feelings of the higher and lower
orders, of the clergy and laity.

In all inquiries it is important to record with
scrupulous minuteness any striking facts which
may bear on or elucidate the subject in question,
adding the names of all the parties concerned and
the place and date of the transaction.

In the tables it will be of the utmost importance
to ascertain distinctly the permanent and the fluc-
tuating sources of incomes. The Irish Society and
the London companies, for example, grant very
different sums in different years, and when the

sum granted in a year is ascertained, part of it may
be a permanent subscription, part a casual donation arising from some temporary cause.

Education: the division of the heads into Physical
(including Practical), Intellectual and Moral Instruction being always kept in view, inquiry should
be made into each, of both a historical and statistical
nature, ascertaining the wants and the tastes of the
people respecting each, and the nature of the present
and probable future supply in each branch.

Ascertain whether schools wholly gratuitous, or
those partly so, are the more successful; whether
there is not some small payment in those styled
gratuitous; whether the resident gentry interest themselves in the schools by visiting; how far and by
whom moral and religious instruction are impartial
in the schools; whether there is any adult or infant
school, or any Sunday school; and what description
of persons teach in the Sunday schools, with the
feeling of the population towards them; whether
any adults attend, whether corporal punishment is
resorted to and what others.

Whether any important change in the educational amount of the parish has attended the introduction of the national system of education; whether
any of the puerile and improper books formerly
used are still used in any; and what are the feelings
of the clergy and laity towards them; whether the
gentry employ resident tutors, or send their children
to Irish or English schools, and where.

What difference of conduct and character can be
traced in after life between the educated and the
uneducated poor. Whether education can in any
instance be assigned as the cause of crime, of which
the uneducated are incapable. Whether the temper,
character and competence of the schoolmasters are
likely to produce good intellectual and moral results
in the pupils (this last inquiry should of course be
conducted with much discretion).

Ascertain what interruptions are occasioned in
the routine of the schools by harvest labour and
vacations, and whether any families are prevented
from receiving instruction by the remoteness of
their abodes or other causes. Also whether itiner-
ant schoolmasters are frequent, whether there are
any hedge schools, any instruction in the Irish
language, and whether such instruction creates an
appetite for more extended instruction in English.

Ascertain what number of children belonging
to other parishes receive instruction in the one
under consideration, from the nearness of their
residences or superiority of the instruction.
Whether any taste for literature, the fine arts and
speculation science exists among the higher orders, and to what extent cheap literature, such as

the various penny magazines and *Chambers' Edinburgh Journal*, is read by the middle and lower classes, and whether newspapers are in extensive circulation. Whether any reading associations exist in any class.

Ascertain what proportion of the population, of each religious denomination, habitually attend the various places of worship. To what extent religious tracts are circulated throughout the parish, and by what description of individuals. To what extent and with what success the parish is visited by Scripture readers. What proportion of bibles and testaments is found in the habitations of members of the Churches of England and Scotland. What opportunities of receiving moral instruction are enjoyed by the aged and infirm, who are unable to resort to places of worship. How far Scriptural reading and family prayer are practised among the different classes of society.

Benevolence (1). Indigent Poor: ascertain the amount of resident and non-resident pauperism. How many of the former paupers are relieved by the clergy from collections at places of worship, and the amount and periods of relief; how many by the gentry and others, at their dwellings. The nature of relief, whether in money, clothing or kind. The feeling of all classes as to the expediency or necessity of poor laws.

The spirit of the people (taking their race into account) in reference to industry; whether they are disposed to industry to avoid the disgrace of pauperism; whether any apparent want of industry may not arise from a lack of employment. Ascertain whether the poor are prone to assist one another, and whether any difference of benevolent feeling is traceable in the different races.

Ascertain the names of any past or present benefactors, whose charities have been or are conspicuous. What description of persons take advantage of the savings' banks, loan societies etc. Whether temperance and teetotal societies exist, and any instances of good resulting from them.

What proportion of the annual emigration is traceable to poverty. How much the amount of pauperism is increased in harvest by the families of the agricultural labourers who migrate to Great Britain or remote parts of Ireland, in search of labour.

Ascertain whether much poverty arises from early or indiscreet marriages, from gambling, drunkenness or other dissolute habits, from heavy rents or other exactions. How far the poor cottiers are deterred from endeavouring to better their condition by the want of leases, short tenures, unproductive tenements etc.

Justice: ascertain the general character of the parish as to crime, the usual nature of the crimes committed, and the causes. Whether much crime arises from drunken and idle habits. Whether in crime any distinction arises from difference of race. Whether crime is in any instances hereditary. Whether it has been diminished by the extension of education. What is the proportion of juvenile delinquency. Whether there is a disposition in the people to screen criminals from justice.

The extent of illicit distillation, and of smuggling, whether they have increased or diminished, and whether the more heinous crimes are committed under the influence of ardent spirits. What description of punishment appears to be most disliked by the people. In the case of persons discharged from prison, whether they disliked the silent or the separation system more, and whether the discipline to which they had been subjected has produced any moral reform.

Ascertain the names (Christian name and surname) of the local magistrates and their residences, specifying whether they live in the parish or not, and whether they are stipendiary or not. The number of the constabulary force, revenue police and coastguard. The general opinion which prevails respecting these different functionaries.

Ascertain whether any particular class of crime prevails among any particular class of persons, as what trades are most given to stealing or drinking or rioting etc. What effects sex and age have in the distribution of crime. What suicides have occurred, and in what years, and from what causes. What heinous crimes, as murder, arson etc. Whether infanticide has increased since the restriction of foundling hospitals.

(2) Sick poor: ascertain the character of the parish as to healthfulness. Whether any diseases are peculiar to any particular locality or classes of persons. Whether medicines are administered by any of the resident gentry. Whether any medical men are resident, whose gratuitous assistance may diminish the number of applicants at the dispensary. What resources the parish possesses for amassing adequate subscriptions for the dispensary, the nature of the dispensary attendance, its management etc. Whether the more infirm are attended at their abodes. Whether any registry of the patients is kept, or classification of diseases.

Ascertain the number of lunatics and idiots at large, and the number in the lunatic asylum sent from the parish. The cause of lunacy in the case of each individual, such as whiskey, mercury etc., the sexes and ages. Whether any have been restored to their sound mind. Whether any have relapsed.

Ascertain the usual duration of life. What instances there are, or have been, of great longevity. Whether the pursuits of life appear to influence its duration. What the habits of the individuals have been as to temperance etc.

Ascertain whether vaccination is extensively practised; whether inoculation for the smallpox ever occurs, in place of vaccination, or in addition to it.

Whether there are any fairy men, medical old women or similar rural practitioners in the parish, or whether there is a resort from the parish to any such in the neighbourhood. Whether any charms are used in reference to refractory churns, hens etc. Whether any cures are effected, or supposed to be effected, by prescriptions in old Irish manuscripts, by washing at holy wells or other such ceremonies. What means there are for curing horses or other diseased animals.

Printed Card for Schools

SOCIAL ECONOMY

Schools

Day and evening schools, under the management of J. Logue A.M., ex-sch, T.C.D.

In the day school, in addition to the usual routine of English, French and the ancient classics, with their respective accompaniments of ancient and modern history and geography, recitation, composition etc., an extensive course of mathematics, natural history and general politics has been introduced.

In the mercantile department Mr Logue is assisted by an excellent English master, and particular attention is paid to the forming of good writers and accountants; hours of attendance 9 o'clock to 3.

The evening school affords an excellent opportunity of improvement to young gentlemen whose education has been neglected, or who are desirous of preparing for college in the most expeditious manner, as it combines all the advantages of public and private tuition; hours of attendance 4 o'clock to 8.

School Statistics

SOCIAL ECONOMY

Schools

[Table contains the following headings: name, situation and description, when established, in-come and expenditure, physical, intellectual and moral education, number of pupils subdivided by age, sex and religion, name and religion of master or mistress].

Altnagelvin, public school, a large slated house, established in 1805; income: from the Dean of Derry 2 pounds, from pupils 10 pounds, charges from 2s to 2s 6d; expenditure none; physical education: none but play; intellectual education: *Dublin Reading books,* Authorised Version, *Murray's Spelling book, Manson's Dictionary*; moral education: visited by Mr Ceary, curate, catechisms not read, visits weekly; number of pupils: males, 18 under 10 years of age; females, 14 under 10 years of age; total number of pupils 32, 12 Protestants, 16 Presbyterians, 4 Roman Catholics; master Samuel McAllister, Protestant.

Ardmore, private school; income: from Goldsmiths' Company 15 pounds per annum, from pupils 7 pounds; expenditure none; attendance from 10 to 3 o'clock; intellectual education: books from the Kildare Street Society; moral education: no regular visits by clergymen, catechism not taught; number of pupils: 40 under 10 years of age, 9 from 10 to 15, total 49, all male, 13 Protestants, 25 Presbyterians, 7 Roman Catholics, 4 other denominations; master James Hanna, Presbyterian.

Ardmore, female school; income: from benevolent individuals 14 pounds, 6 pounds from pupils; expenditure none; attendance from 10 to 3 o'clock; number of pupils: 22 under 10 years of age, 32 from 10 to 15, 3 above 15, total 57, all female, 11 Protestants, 27 Presbyterians, 16 Roman Catholics, 4 other denominations; mistress M.A. Hamilton, Independent.

Ballyshasky, public school, a small slated house, established 1829; income: from the Board of Education 15 pounds, from pupils 8 pounds; charges 1d per week, two-thirds of them goes free; physical education none; intellectual education: *Dublin Reading books*, Authorised Version and extracts; moral education: visited by Mr M. Heron and Mr White monthly, catechism read; number of pupils: males, 36 under 10 years of age, 2 from 10 to 15, total 38; females, 40 under 10 years of age, total 40; total number of pupils 78, 1 Presbyterian, 77 Roman Catholics; master John Gill, Roman Catholic.

Caws or Salem, 2-storeys, roadside, built by the Kildare Place Society, grant withdrawn, established 1826; income: nothing from public societies, 8 pounds from benevolent individuals, 8 pounds from pupils; expenditure none; physical education none; intellectual education: books used published by the Kildare Place Society; moral education: patronised by the Revd A.G. Cary, visited by J. Alexander Esquire and the Revd J.D. Maughan, new and old version of the Scriptures; number of pupils: males, 31 under 10 years of age, 12 from 10 to 15, total 43; females, 16 under 10 years of age, 8 from 10 to 15, total 24; total number of pupils 67, 11 Protestants, 44 Presbyterians, 11 Roman Catholics, 1 other denomination; master Henry Bond, Protestant.

Waterside, Clooney school, roadside, Bellview, established November 1825; income: from the London Hibernian Society 8 pounds, from the ladies' committee 7 pounds, from pupils 4 pounds; other expenses 1 pound; physical education none; intellectual education: books are provided by the society; moral education: by the Revd Mr Maughan, the children catechised by the mistress and the Scriptures read in the old way; number of pupils: 20 under 10 years of age, 16 from 10 to 15, 2 above 15, total 38, all female, 14 Protestants, 13 Presbyterians, 8 Roman Catholics, 3 other denominations; mistress Sarah Simpson, Protestant.

Glebe, parish school; as far as the master can learn, it was established in the year 1738; income: from the Dean of Derry 2 pounds per annum and 1 acre of grass and the house free, from pupils 7 pounds per annum; no expenditure out of that salary; physical education: leisure hours to play; intellectual education: all books that they may bring with them; moral education: catechism taught regularly; number of pupils: males, 7 under 10 years of age, 7 from 10 to 15, total 14; females, 6 under 10 years of age, 5 from 10 to 15, total 11; total number of pupils 25, 5 Protestants, 20 Presbyterians; master Robert Hinde, Protestant.

Gortin, private school, established in 1829, about the 1st May; income: from a benevolent individual, Mr Moor of the county Antrim, who owns the estate, 6 pounds per annum, from pupils 9 pounds per annum; no expenditure from that salary; physical education: at pleasure during their leisure hours; intellectual education: books of all kinds brought by the children; moral education: catechism taught regularly, no visits by clergy; number of pupils: males, 21 under the age of 10, 2 from 10 to 15, total 23; females, 23 under the age of 10, 3 from 10 to 15, total 26; total number of pupils 49, 40 Presbyterians, 9 other denominations; master Thomas Macklin, Covenanter.

Prehen, day school for males and females, all denominations, 2 and a half miles on the old road from Derry to Strabane, established August 1818; income: from the Hibernian Society 4 pounds, from pupils 8 pounds; expenditure on salaries: Hibernian [Society] 4 pounds; physical education none; intellectual education: Old and New Testaments, *First and second spelling books*, Hibernian Society, *Dublin Reading book*; moral education: occasionally visited by Revd Mr Carey and Mr Maughan, no catechism taught here; number of pupils: males, 24 under 10 years of age, 27 from 10 to 15, total 51; females, 45 under 10 years of age, total 45; total number of pupils 96, 8 Protestants, 40 Presbyterians, 48 Roman Catholics; master Robert Dinsmore, Presbyterian.

Carn, in an old dwelling house, established May 1830; income from pupils 7 pounds; expenditure: house 20 pounds, repairs 10s; intellectual education: pupils find their own books, Bible and Testament; moral education: no visitors, children catechised by the master, Scriptures in the old way; number of pupils: males, 7 under 10 years of age, 8 from 10 to 15, 2 over 15, total 17; females, 5 under 10 years of age, 6 from 10 to 15, 3 over 15, total 14; total number of pupils 31, 4 Protestants, 12 Presbyterians, 8 Roman Catholics, 7 other denominations; master David Harpur, Presbyterian.

Curryfree, private school, established in the year 1832, at the 1st of May; no income from any society or individual, 2 pounds per annum from pupils; no expenses for anything out of that salary; physical education: leisure hours to play; intellectual education: books of all kinds brought by the children; moral education: catechism taught regularly; number of pupils: males, 7 under 10 years of age, total 7; females, 3 under 10 years of age, total 3; total number of pupils 10, 8 Presbyterians, 2 Roman Catholics; master John Bain, Covenanter.

Drumahoe Literary and Commercial Academy, Joseph Logue A.M., private day school, established 1st August 1829; income from pupils about 130 pounds per annum; expenditure on salaries: 20 pounds to a writing master; other expenses: stationery and fuel etc. about 2 pounds per annum; no regular system of physical education has been introduced; some of the boys have attended a professor of gymnastics in town; a dancing master has attended at my house for the convenience of my own children, my boarders and such of the day scholars as chose to receive lessons; intellectual education: all the books included in the entrance course of Trinity College, Dublin and of Belfast and Glasgow colleges; histories of England, Greece and Rome, ancient and modern geography, mythology, *Euclid's Elements*, arithmetic, algebra, grammar etc.; moral education: the classical and historical books above mentioned may be considered as a system of morality; for beginners the best elementary compilations; Protestants receive religious instruction; number of pupils: males, 5 under 10 years of age, 13 from 10 to 15, 16 above 15, total 34;

females, 1 under 10 years of age, total 1; total number of pupils 35, 9 Established Church, 15 Presbyterians, 6 Roman Catholics, 5 Seceders; religion of master Protestant.

[Insert note: Captain Portlock's compliments to Mr Logue and hints that he will fill up the accompanying form, the object viz. to shew distinctly the means of education in the parish, and it would be unpleasant that a blank should be formed by the omission of the details of Mr Logue's school. 9th November 1838].

This school is regularly fixed in Drumahoe, but in winter Mr Logue accommodates his pupils by attending some in Derry and the others in the evenings in Drumahoe. In summer all go to Drumahoe [initialled J.P., addressed] to Lieutenant Larcom, Royal Engineers.

Drumahoe, public school, a small slated house, established 1835; income from pupils 12 pounds; physical education: none; intellectual education: *Dublin Reading [book]* and Authorised Version and extracts, geography etc; moral education: Revd Mr Monteith 10 times per year, Revd Mr Carson 8 times per year, Mr Radcliff occasionally; number of pupils: males, 20 under 10 years of age, total 20; females, 25 under 10 years of age, 5 from 10 to 15, total 30; total number of pupils 50, 48 Presbyterians, 1 Roman Catholic, 1 other denomination; mistress Isabella Mills, Presbyterian.

Killymallaght, a private school, established 1828, commenced 19th May; no income from public societies or benevolent individuals, 15 pounds per annum from pupils; no expenditure from that salary; physical education: leisure hours for play; intellectual education: books brought by the children, of all kinds; moral education: no visits by clergy, catechisms taught regularly, 1 verse of Scripture each day; number of pupils: males, 29 under 10 years of age, 6 from 10 to 15, total 35; females, 20 under 10 years of age, 4 from 10 to 15, 1 above 15, total 25; total number of pupils 60, 11 Protestants, 52 Presbyterians, 5 Roman Catholics, 3 other denominations; master David Mitchel, Presbyterian.

Lisdillon, private school, established 1810, about 1st October; no income but from the pupils, 8 pounds per annum; no expenditure out of that salary; no physical education, leisure hours to play; intellectual education: books of all kinds brought by the scholars; moral education: no visits by clergy, catechism taught every Saturday; number of pupils: males, 14 under 10 years of age, 3 from 10 to 15, 1 above 15, total 18; females, 17 under 10 years of age, 2 from 10 to 15, 3 above 15, total 22; total number of pupils 40, 4 Protestants, 6 Presbyterians,

28 Roman Catholics, 2 other denominations; master Thomas Donald, Roman Catholic.

Waterside, private school, established May 1832; income from pupils 30 pounds; expenditure: salaries none, to an assistant 10 pounds, to a house 5 pounds; physical education: choose their own; intellectual and moral education: the Scriptures are taught in the usual way, both Protestant and Douai Bibles; no visits from clergy, catechise the children myself as they wish themselves; number of pupils: males, 30 under 10 years of age, 20 from 10 to 15, total 50; females, 12 under 10 years of age, 7 from 10 to 15, 1 above 15, total 20; total number of pupils 70, 8 Protestants, 10 Presbyterians, 52 Roman Catholics; master James McNamee, Roman Catholic.

Waterside, private school, established November 1828; income none; expenditure: house rent 8 pounds 8s, extra expenses 18s; intellectual education: the children find their own books, both bibles read here; moral education: not visited by anyone, children catechised according to persuasion; moral education: males, 5 under 10 years of age, total 5; females, 8 under 10 years of age, 7 from 10 to 15, total 15; total number of pupils 20, 4 Protestants, 11 Presbyterians, 2 Roman Catholics, 3 other denominations; mistress Rebecca Steele, Presbyterian.

Hollymount, private classical school: Mr Stanton has kept no school since March last; has commenced farming; master Thomas Stanton [insert query: or Staunton]; religious denomination Presbyterian.

Gortnessy, daily school closed, Clondermot.

Gortnessy, 2 miles west of Muff, brick and stonework, established September 1832; income: Grocers' Company 10 pounds, pupils 3 pounds, income per annum 13 pounds, probably an increase of salary from the Grocers' Company; expenditure: fuel and candles 2 pounds 13s, cow's grass 1 pound 5s, total expenditure 3 pounds 18s; physical education none; intellectual education: Kildare Street Society books; moral education: clergymen of all denominations belonging to the parish visits occasionally, Protestant, Presbyterian and Roman Catholic catechism taught on Saturday, Protestant version of the Old and New Testaments; number of pupils: males, 34 under 10 years of age, 10 from 10 to 15, 7 above 15, total 51; females, 30 under 10 years of age, 14 from 10 to 15, total 44; total number of pupils 95, 8 Protestants, 68 Presbyterians, 10 Roman Catholics, 9 other denominations; master George Inch, Protestant.

[Covering page] Captain Portlock, Royal Engineers, Londonderry.

School Statistics

Schools in 1824

[Table contains the following headings: name of townland where held, name and religion of master or mistress, free or pay school, annual income of master or mistress, description and cost of schoolhouse, number of pupils subdivided by religion, sex and the Protestant and Roman Catholic returns, societies with which connected].

Culkeeragh, master Robert McCay, Presbyterian; pay school, income about 90 pounds; schoolhouse a good thatched cabin, cost 10 pounds; number of pupils by the Protestant return: 8 Established Church, 24 Presbyterians, 4 other denominations, 12 Roman Catholics, 27 males, 21 females; by the Roman Catholic return: 6 Established Church, 26 Presbyterians, 4 other denominations, 12 Roman Catholics, 30 males, 18 females; associations none.

Disertowen, master Thomas Donnell, Roman Catholic; pay school, income about 12 pounds; schoolhouse a rented cabin; number of pupils by the Protestant return: 1 Established Church, 25 Presbyterians, 2 other denominations, 2 Roman Catholics, 20 males, 10 females; by the Roman Catholic return: 1 Established Church, 26 Presbyterians, 1 other denomination, 2 Roman Catholics, 19 males, 11 females; associations none.

Faughan bridge, Drumahoe, mistress Isabella Mills, Presbyterian; pay school, income about 26 pounds; schoolhouse part of meeting house; number of pupils by the Protestant return: 2 Established Church, 24 Presbyterians, 5 males, 21 females; by the Roman Catholic return: 2 Established Church, 24 Presbyterians, 5 males, 21 females; associations none.

Tirkeevny, master John Mathers, Presbyterian; pay school, income about 8 pounds 10s; schoolhouse a thatched cabin; number of pupils by the Protestant return: 24 Presbyterians, 3 other denominations, 3 Roman Catholics, 12 males, 18 females; by the Roman Catholic return: 27 Presbyterians, 3 Roman Catholics, 12 males, 18 females; associations none.

Avish, master James Cuthbert, Covenanter; pay school, income about 12 pounds; schoolhouse a barn in bad repair; number of pupils by the Protestant return: 2 Established Church, 21 Presbyterians, 6 other denominations, 2 Roman Catholics, 16 males, 15 females; by the Roman Catholic return: 2 Established Church, 20 Presbyterians, 6 other denominations, 2 Roman Catholics, 15 males, 15 females; associations none.

Gortican Upper, master Michael McCloskey, Roman Catholic; pay school, income about 24 pounds; schoolhouse a private house; number of pupils by the Protestant return: 4 Established Church, 28 Presbyterians, 4 other denominations, 21 Roman Catholics, 37 males, 20 females; by the Roman Catholic return: 4 Established Church, 28 Presbyterians, 4 other denominations, 21 Roman Catholics, 37 males, 20 females; associations none.

Gorticross Upper, master Thomas Craig, Protestant; pay school, income about 17 pounds; schoolhouse a good thatched cabin, cost 5 pounds; number of pupils by the Protestant return: 3 Established Church, 45 Presbyterians, 6 other denominations, 2 Roman Catholics, 25 males, 31 females; by the Roman Catholic return: 3 Established Church, 45 Presbyterians, 6 other denominations, 2 Roman Catholics, 25 males, 31 females; associations none.

Old Quay Brae, Gobnascale, mistress Sarah Cane, Protestant; pay school, income about 5 pounds 5s; schoolhouse a small room in an old house; number of pupils by the Protestant return: 7 Established Church, 1 other denomination, 9 Roman Catholics, 3 males, 14 females; by the Roman Catholic return: 7 Established Church, 1 other denomination, 8 Roman Catholics, 4 males, 12 females; associations none.

The old church on the dean's glebe, master Robert Hindman, Protestant; pay school, income 14 pounds; schoolhouse stone and lime, cost 30 pounds; number of pupils by the Protestant return: 3 Established Church, 28 Presbyterians, 4 Roman Catholics, 18 males, 7 females; by the Roman Catholic return: 5 Established Church, 24 Presbyterians, 6 Roman Catholics, 19 males, 16 females; the parish school; the dean gives 2 pounds annually, besides house and garden, [total] 4 pounds.

The new church, Altnagelvin, master Samuel McAllister, Protestant; pay school, income 20 pounds; schoolhouse a good slated house, cost 150 pounds; number of pupils by the Protestant return: 8 Established Church, 24 Presbyterians, 1 Roman Catholic, 18 males, 17 females; by the Roman Catholic return: 8 Established Church, 25 Presbyterians, 2 Roman Catholics, 25 males, 10 females; the dean gives 2 pounds and a house rent free.

Salem, Cah, master Isaac Adair, Covenanter; pay school, income 17 pounds; schoolhouse a good slated house, cost 130 pounds; number of pupils by the Protestant return: 23 males, 23 females; by the Roman Catholic return: 9 Established Church, 36 Presbyterians, 5 other denominations, 19 Roman Catholics, 40 males, 29 females; connected with Kildare Place Society.

Waterside, Clooney, master John Curry, Roman Catholic; pay school, income 23 pounds; schoolhouse a thatched cabin, cost 12 pounds; number of pupils by the Roman Catholic return: 7 Established Church, 25 Presbyterians, 10 Roman Catholics, 26 males, 16 females; associations none.

Waterside, Gobnescale, master Robert Rogers, Covenanter; pay school, income about 16 pounds; schoolhouse a loft in a slated house; number of pupils by the Protestant return: 1 Established Church, 6 Presbyterians, 7 other denominations, 2 Roman Catholics, 10 males, 6 females; by the Roman Catholic return: 1 Established Church, 5 Presbyterians, 8 other denominations, 2 Roman Catholics, 10 males, 6 females; associations none.

Waterside, Clooney, master Robert Crampton, Covenanter; pay school, income about 12 pounds; schoolhouse: master's private house; number of pupils by the Protestant return: 2 Presbyterians, 3 other denominations, 1 Roman Catholic, 6 males; associations none.

Waterside, Clooney, mistress Miss Jane Montgomery, Protestant; pay school, income 10 pounds and a house, and about 3s a quarter from the children; schoolhouse 2 rooms built by subscription; number of pupils by the Protestant return: 13 Established Church, 17 Presbyterians, 20 Roman Catholics, 50 females; by the Roman Catholic return: 15 Established Church, 17 Presbyterians, 22 Roman Catholics, 54 females; connected with Ladies' Hibernian Female School Society and London Hibernian Society, house built by subscription.

Waterside, Clooney, master Hugh Roden, Presbyterian; pay school, income about 10 pounds; schoolhouse a kitchen fitted up for the purpose; number of pupils by the Protestant return: 4 Established Church, 8 Presbyterians, 1 other denomination, 7 Roman Catholics, 16 males, 4 females; by the Roman Catholic return: 4 Established Church, 8 Presbyterians, 1 other denomination, 7 Roman Catholics, 16 males, 4 females; associations none.

The Barracks, Prehen, master Robert Dinsmore, Covenanter; pay school, income 10 pounds by scholars, a house and 20 acres of land from Colonel Knox, the patron; schoolhouse a good house, cost 50 pounds; number of pupils by the Protestant return: 12 Established Church, 19 Presbyterians, 25 Roman Catholics, 25 males, 31 females; by the Roman Catholic return: 12 Established Church, 19 Presbyterians, 25 Roman Catholics, 25 males, 31 females; books supplied by the Kildare Place Society; Colonel Knox, the patron, built the house and gave 2 acres of land rent free.

New Buildings, Ballyon, master Allen Broderick, Protestant; pay school, income 12

pounds, of which the London Hibernian Society gives 6 pounds a year; schoolhouse stone and lime, cost 4 pounds 10s; number of pupils by the Protestant return: 15 Established Church, 19 Presbyterians, 3 other denominations, 19 Roman Catholics, 36 males, 20 females; by the Roman Catholic return: 15 Established Church, 19 Presbyterians, 3 other denominations, 19 Roman Catholics, 36 males, 20 females; connected with London Hibernian Society.

Ardmore, master Dennis McCloskey, Roman Catholic; pay school, income about 29 pounds; schoolhouse a good thatched house; number of pupils by the Protestant return: 5 Established Church, 12 Presbyterians, 25 Roman Catholics, 34 males, 8 females; by the Roman Catholic return: 5 Established Church, 12 Presbyterians, 25 Roman Catholics, 34 males, 8 females; 5 pounds of master's salary is paid by local contribution.

Lisdillon, master Hugh McCook, Roman Catholic; pay school, income about 15 pounds; schoolhouse a small thatched cabin, cost 9 pounds 10s; number of pupils by the Protestant return: 2 Established Church, 13 Presbyterians, 7 other denominations, 10 Roman Catholics, 18 males, 13 females; by the Roman Catholic return: 1 Established Church, 13 Presbyterians, 7 other denominations, 10 Roman Catholics, 18 males, 13 females; associations none.

Schools in 1834

Clooney, mistress Sarah Simpson, Protestant; free school, income 18 pounds per annum; schoolhouse slated, cost 80 pounds; number of pupils by the Protestant return: 19 Established Church, 17 Presbyterians, 10 other denominations, 2 Roman Catholics, all females; supported and under a committee of ladies; assisted by the London Ladies' Society.

Drumahoe, mistress Isabella Mills, Presbyterian; pay school; schoolhouse slated, cost 60 pounds; number of pupils by the Protestant return: 5 Established Church, 50 Presbyterians, 7 other denominations, 7 Roman Catholics, 36 males, 33 females; supported by the children.

Ardmore male, master James Hannah, Presbyterian; pay school, income 25 pounds per annum; schoolhouse thatched, cost 70 pounds; number of pupils by the Protestant return: 9 Established Church, 29 Presbyterian, 4 Roman Catholics, 42 males; supported by the Goldsmiths' Company.

Ardmore female, mistress Miss Hamilton, Independent; pay school, income 22 pounds per annum; schoolhouse under the roof with male school; number of pupils by the Protestant return:

12 Established Church, 31 Presbyterians, 3 other denominations, 14 Roman Catholics, 60 females; supported by a committee of ladies.

Ballyshaskey, master John Gill, Roman Catholic; pay school, income 20 pounds per annum; schoolhouse slated, cost 65 pounds; number of pupils by the Protestant return: 4 Established Church, 8 Presbyterians, 81 Roman Catholics, 79 males, 14 females; connected with National Board of Education.

Cah, master Henry Bond, Protestant; pay school, income 8 pounds per annum; schoolhouse slated, cost 120 pounds; number of pupils by the Protestant return: 3 Established Church, 41 Presbyterians, 2 Roman Catholics, 26 males, 20 females; associations none; supported by the children.

Altnagelvin, master Samuel McAlister, Protestant; pay school, income 10 pounds per annum; schoolhouse slated, cost 100 pounds; number of pupils by the Protestant return: 8 Established Church, 12 Presbyterians, 3 Roman Catholics, 2 males, 21 females; parish school, supported by children.

Glebes, master Robert Hindman, Protestant; pay school, income 10 pounds per annum; schoolhouse slated, cost 12 pounds; number of pupils by the Protestant return: 4 Established Church, 22 Presbyterians, 4 Roman Catholics, 22 males, 8 females; associations none; supported by the children.

Gortin, master Thomas Macklin, Covenanter; pay school, income 12 pounds per annum; schoolhouse thatched, cost 8 pounds; number of pupils by the Protestant return: 20 Presbyterians, 10 other denominations, 4 Roman Catholics, 14 males, 20 females; supported by the children.

Killymallaght, master David Mitchell, Presbyterian; pay school, income 20 pounds per annum; schoolhouse on the loft of a barn; number of pupils by the Protestant return: 40 Presbyterians, 5 Roman Catholics, 25 males, 20 females; supported by the children.

Prehen, master Robert Dinsmore, Covenanter; pay school, income 18 pounds per annum; schoolhouse slated, cost 50 pounds; number of pupils by the Protestant return: 9 Established Church, 38 Presbyterians, 5 other denominations, 45 Roman Catholics, 60 males, 37 females; supported by the children.

Lisdillon, master Thomas O'Donnel, Roman Catholic; pay school, income 6 pounds per annum; schoolhouse thatched, cost 15 pounds; number of pupils by the Protestant return: 3 Established Church, 11 Presbyterians, 18 Roman Catholics; 20 males, 12 females; supported by the children.

Waterside, mistress Rebecca Steele, Presbyterian; pay school, income 20 pounds per annum; schoolhouse slated, cost 80 pounds; number of pupils by the Protestant return: 10 Established Church, 16 Presbyterians, 3 Roman Catholics; 11 males, 18 females; supported by the children.

Waterside, master James McNamee, Roman Catholic; pay school, income 30 pounds per annum; schoolhouse: loft of a dwelling house, which is of the supposed cost 60 pounds; number of pupils by the Protestant return: 6 Established Church, 12 Presbyterians, 40 Roman Catholics; 40 males, 16 [sic] females; supported by the children.

Curryfree, master John Barr, Protestant; pay school, income 4 pounds per annum; schoolhouse: thatched hovel, cost 5 pounds; number of pupils by the Protestant return: 2 Established Church, 15 Presbyterians, 15 males, 2 females; supported by the children.

School Statistics

Table of Schools

[Table contains the following headings: name of townland in which situated, number of pupils subdivided by religion and sex, how supported].

Cah, 43 Protestants, 17 Catholics, 49 males, 11 females; this school was under the Kildare Street Society but as the present master has been but lately appointed he has got very little assistance from them. He has nothing now to depend on but the children's payments.

Altnagelvin, 32 Protestants, 1 Catholic, 28 males, 5 females; the master of this school received from 6 to 8 pounds yearly from the Kildare Street Society; he has also 2 pounds from the Dean of Derry and a small sum from the children.

Clooney, 26 Protestants, 16 Catholics, 42 females; the ladies of the London Hibernian Society give the mistress 7 pounds per year and the ladies of the parish give as much and 1s per quarter for each child; promoted by the inspector at the examinations.

The above information obtained by me, [signed] [M.M.] Waters, Captain Royal Engineers; [to] Lieutenant-Colonel Colby, Royal Engineers.

Statistical Tables

Clondermot Dispensary

[Table contains the following headings: year, number of patients, number of days open each week, average hours attendance each day, fixed and variable expenses, income, number of governors. Dispensary open 2 days each week, 5 hours attendance per day in each year].

1829: patients 1,659, gratuitous visits 189; salary of surgeon or physician 40 pounds, dispensary rent 4 pounds 4s, medicine 31 pounds 5s 4d, other expenses 2 pounds 4s 8d, total expenditure 77 pounds 14s; income: subscriptions 40 pounds 3s 6d, county grant 30 pounds, total 70 pounds 3s 6d; number of governors 25.

1830: no account of patients; salary of surgeon or physician 40 pounds, dispensary rent 4 pounds 4s, medicine 36 pounds 7s 1d, other expenses 3 pounds 11s 1d, total expenditure 84 pounds 2s 2d; income: subscriptions 50 pounds 10s, county grant 48 pounds, total 98 pounds 10s; number of governors 25.

1831: patients 1,521, gratuitous visits 107; salary of surgeon or physician 40 pounds, dispensary rent 4 pounds 4s, medicine 44 pounds 15s 1d, other expenses 2 pounds 5s 8d, total expenditure 91 pounds 4s 9d; income: subscriptions 52 pounds 9s, county grant 52 pounds 9s, total 104 pounds 18s; number of governors 27.

1832: patients 2,113, gratuitous visits 114; salary of surgeon or physician 40 pounds, dispensary rent 4 pounds, medicine 60 pounds 4d; repairs: a house built by subscription, cost 50 pounds 6s; other expenses 2 pounds 6s 9d, total expenditure 156 pounds 13s 1d; income: subscriptions 62 pounds 2s 6d, county grant 60 pounds, total 122 pounds 2s 6d; number of governors 29.

1833: patients 1,539, gratuitous visits 106; salary of surgeon or physician 40 pounds; dispensary rent: none, a house having been built; medicine 34 pounds 6s 3d, other expenses 2 pounds 16s 8d, total expenditure 77 pounds 2s 11d; income: subscriptions 48 pounds 19s 6d, county grant 48 pounds 19s 6d, total 97 pounds 19s; number of governors 28.

1834: patients 1,820, gratuitous visits 139, vaccinations about 360, no midwife; salary of surgeon or physician 50 pounds, medicine 45 pounds, other expenses 3 pounds; total expenditure from 98 to 100 pounds; income: subscriptions 51 pounds 10s 6d, county grant 51 pounds 10s 6d, total 103 pounds 1s; number of governors 28.

1835, 1836, 1837: [blank].

Sunday Schools

[Table contains the following headings: situation, when established, patron, number of pupils subdivided by sex, remarks].

[Insert note: From Mr A. Neely's report, dated 14th October 1835].

Parish church, patron Revd S.G. Cary, 59 male and 44 female pupils, total 103.

Meeting house, patron Revd Carson, 52 male and 53 female pupils, total 105.

Catholic chapel, established 1829, patron Revd Mearan P.P., 22 male and 28 female pupils, total 50.

Lisdillon schoolhouse, established 1835, patron Revd Mearan P.P., 20 male and 19 female pupils, total 39.

Lisdillon schoolhouse, established 1827, patrons Mr Cary, Mr Carson, Mr Maughan, 24 male and 26 female pupils, total 50.

Ardmore, established 1815, 50 male and 78 female pupils, total 128; conducted by Messrs Smith and McCleland, visited by all the clergy of the parish.

Bellevue gate, patron Mr Maughan; 35 male and 25 female pupils, total 60; conducted by David Torrens.

Clondermot church, established 1824, 21 male and 27 female pupils, total 48; visited by Messrs Cary, Maughan and Carson.

Killymallaght, established 1824, 40 male and 44 female pupils, total 84; conducted by D. Michel.

Prehen, established 1818, patron Colonel Knox, 32 male and 40 female pupils, total 72; visited by Messrs Maughan and Carson.

Salem, established 1826, patron Revd A.G. Cary; 21 male and 34 female pupils, total 55.

Rosnagalliagh, established 1835, 14 male and 12 female pupils, total 26.

Gartan [Gortin], established 1833, 25 male and 15 female pupils, total 40; visited by Messrs Maughan and Carson.

Faughan bridge, Drumahoe, established 1831, 13 male and 23 female pupils, total 36; visited by all the clergymen.

Gorticross, established 1820, 30 male and 30 female pupils, total 60; visited by most of the clergymen.

Gortnessy, established 1832, patron Revd Maughan, 60 male and 49 female pupils, total 109.

Avish, established 1835; 20 male and 40 female pupils, total 60; visited [by] Mr Sweeney and others.

Sunday Schools

[Table contains the following headings: name, superintendent, number of teachers, number of scholars].

1. Ardmore (male), James Hanna, 5 teachers, 60 scholars.

2. Ardmore (female), Miss Smith, 7 teachers, 80 scholars.

3. Avish, A. Henry, 4 teachers, 50 scholars.

4. Bellevue, Thomas Allen, 4 teachers, 35 scholars.

5. Clondermot (new church), William Adams, 4 teachers, 40 scholars.

6. Clondermot (old church), Robert Hindman, 4 teachers, 36 scholars.

7. Faughan bridge, Miss Mills, 2 teachers, 24 scholars.

8. Gortnessy, William Lowry, 10 teachers, 100 scholars.

9. Gortycaw, Miss Mills, 3 teachers, 50 scholars.

10. Killymallaght, David Mitchell, 6 teachers, 70 scholars.

11. Lisdillon presbytery, William Burnside, 7 teachers, 63 scholars.

12. Prehen, Robert Dinsmore, 2 teachers, 28 scholars.

13. Presbyterian meeting house, James Adams, 9 teachers, 100 scholars.

14. Roman Catholic chapel (male), John Gill, 8 teachers, 47 scholars.

15. Roman Catholic chapel (female), Miss Walsh, 8 teachers, 80 pupils.

16. Rossnagalliagh, John Ward, 2 teachers, 24 scholars.

17. Salem, William Bond, 4 teachers, 60 scholars.

Constituency of Derry

[Table contains the following headings: year, number of householders, resident freemen, total].

1832: 429 householders, 203 resident freeman, total 632.

1833: 464 householders, 217 resident freemen, total 681.

1834: 485 householders, 218 resident freemen, total 703.

1835 (1st April): 504 householders, 220 resident freemen, total 724.

1836: 539 householders, 227 resident freemen, total 766.

1837: [blank].

1838 (day of the month of): [blank].

How many of the resident freemen reside in Clondermot? [Answer] 21 is all I have been able to make out properly; the numbers of freemen for 1836 I got from Mr Grig.

The [rota?] has made its appearance; of them I have got a pair.

Benevolence: Establishments for Instruction

[Table contains the following headings: name, object, when founded, management, funds from public and private sources, annual expense of management, number relieved, relief afforded].

8 schools wholly or partly supported by benevolence; object: the removal of ignorance; founded at sundry periods; funds: from public sources 57 pounds 6s 8d, from private sources 32 pounds; number relieved: 491 pupils receiving instruction.

Bequests; object: the removal of ignorance; founded 1721; management: executors to Colonel Mitchelburne's will; funds from private sources 4 pounds a year, being the interest on 67 pounds; number relieved: lapsed.

Establishments for the Indigent

3 money clubs; object: to create a loan fund, founded 1834 and '35; management: the contributors; funds from private sources: 3s a week from each member; house rent a ha'penny a week from each member; number relieved: 146 members; relief afforded, money: the certain advantage to the contributor of having, at the end of a period corresponding in weeks to the number of subscribers, the amount of his contributions, or the chance of having the use of this money from the commencement of the period.

2 temperance societies; object: to promote sobriety.

Poor Shop; object: to sell clothing to the poor at prime cost and receive the payments by instalments of 1d in the shilling; founded 1820; management: committee of ladies; funds from public sources: a loan of 30 pounds from the London Ladies' Society; private subscriptions 50 pounds 19s; number relieved: 1,641 articles sold in 1835.

Loan Fund; object: to aid the poor by small loans without interest, to be repaid by instalments; founded 1830; management: curate of the parish.

Bequest by Colonel Mitchelburne [insert marginal query: at one part it is said that the charity has lapsed, at another that it continues to be paid]; object: the relief of poverty; founded 1721; management: 16 [executors?]; income from private sources 86 pounds; expenses: lapsed; number relieved: 8 poor inhabitants; relief afforded: 3 pounds 4s a year.

Bequest by Colonel Mitchelburne; object: the relief of poverty; founded 1721; funds from private sources: interest on 35 pounds; expenses: lapsed; number relieved: 30 poor inhabitants; relief afforded: 1s a year to 30 poor people.

Bequest by Colonel Mitchelburne; object: the relief of poverty; founded 1721; income from private sources: interest on 140 pounds; expenses: lapsed; number relieved: 16 poor inhabitants; relief afforded: half a peck of meal to each weekly.

Bequest by Alderman George Tomkins; object: the relief of poverty; founded 1739; management: curate and churchwardens; funds from private sources: interest on 50 pounds at 6 per cent; expenses: lapsed; number relieved: 6 poor persons; relief afforded: 10s a year.

Bequest by Alderman Stanley; object: the relief of poverty; founded 1764; number relieved: 40 poor inhabitants.

Bequest by Joseph Miller; object: the relief of poverty; founded 1788; management: the executors; funds from private sources: interest on 100 pounds; number relieved: 12 or 24 poor housekeepers; relief afforded: interest on 100 pounds.

Bequest by Robert Miller; object: the relief of poverty; founded 1788; management: the executors; income from private sources: interest on 100 pounds; number relieved: 12 or 24 poor housekeepers; relief afforded: interest on 100 pounds.

Contingent charities; object: the relief of poverty; management: none; no special fund; number relieved: about 540 daily; relief afforded: various articles of food, old clothes given occasionally; money: from 2 pounds to 3 pounds a week.

Establishments for Relief of Mental and Bodily Diseases

Clondermot dispensary; object: to provide medical assistance for the poor residing within the parish; founded 1826; management 28 governors; funds from public sources: grand jury presentments, annual average for the last 7 years [blank], Irish Society 5 pounds a year, Grocers' Company 5 pounds 5s; from private sources: governors' subscriptions, annual average for 7 years [blank]; house rent: house built by the governors in 1832, cost 50 pounds 6s; salaries 50 pounds; number relieved: 1,690 annually on an average of 5 years; relief afforded: medicine and medical advice.

Faughanvale dispensary: see Templemore parish.

Public Schools

[Table contains the following headings: name, situation and description, when established, income and expenditure, physical, intellectual and moral education, number of pupils subdivided by age, sex and religion, name and religion of master

or mistress. Salaries 10s 6d per quarter. No physical instruction].

Altnagelvin, a large slated house, cost 100 pounds, established 1805; income; Dean of Derry 2 pounds, pupils 10 pounds, total 12 pounds; intellectual instruction: *Dublin Reading books, Murray's Spelling book* and *Manson's Dictionary*; moral instruction: visited weekly by the Revd Mr Cary, Authorised Version of Scripture; number of pupils: males, 18 under 10 years; females: 14 under 10 years; total number of pupils 32, 12 Established Church, 16 Presbyterians, 4 Roman Catholics; master Samuel McAlister, Established Church.

Ardmore, thatched house, cost 70 pounds, established 1819 [insert note: as the Beech Hill school]; income: Irish Society 10 pounds [insert marginal note: 50 in 1834], Goldsmiths' Company 15 pounds, benevolent individuals 14 pounds, pupils 13 pounds, total 52 pounds; intellectual instruction: books from Kildare Street Society; moral instruction: no regular visits from clergymen; number of pupils: males, 40 under 10 years, 9 from 10 to 15, total 49; females, 22 under 10 years, 32 from 10 to 15, 3 above 15, total 57; total number of pupils 106, 23 Established Church, 52 Presbyterians, 23 Roman Catholics, 8 other denominations; masters James Hanna, Presbyterian, M.A. Hamilton, Independent.

Ballyshasky, a small house, slated, cost 65 pounds, established 1829; income: National Board 15 pounds, pupils 8 pounds, total 23 pounds; intellectual instruction: *Dublin Reading books*; moral instruction: visited by Messrs Knox and White monthly, catechisms and Scripture extracts, Authorised Version; number of pupils: males, 36 under 10 years, 2 from 10 to 15, total 38; females, 40 under 10 years; total number of pupils 78, 1 Presbyterian, 77 Roman Catholics; master John Gill, Roman Catholic.

Cah, slated house, built by Kildare Place Society, cost 120 pounds, established 1826; income: benevolent individuals 8 pounds, pupils 8 pounds, total 16 pounds; intellectual instruction: books published by the Kildare Street Society; moral instruction: visited by the Revd J.D. Maughan, Authorised Version; number of pupils: males, 31 under 10 years, 12 from 10 to 15, total 43; females: 16 under 10 years, 8 from 10 to 15, total 24; total number of pupils 67, 11 Established Church, 44 Presbyterians, 11 Roman Catholics, 1 other denomination; master Henry Bond, Established Church.

Clooney, slated house, cost 80 pounds, established 1825; income: London Hibernian Society 8 pounds, ladies' committee 7 pounds, pupils 4 pounds, total 19 pounds; intellectual instruction: books provided by the London Hibernian Society; moral instruction: visited by the Revd J.D. Maughan, catechisms and Scriptures taught, Authorised Version; number of pupils: 20 under 10 years, 16 from 10 to 15, 2 above 15, total 38, all female, 14 Established Church, 13 Presbyterians, 8 Roman Catholics, 3 other denominations; mistress Sarah Simpson, Established Church.

Glebe, parish school, established 1738; income: Dean of Derry 2 pounds, pupils 7 pounds, 1 acre of ground and a house, total 9 pounds; intellectual instruction: children bring their own books; moral instruction: catechisms taught regularly; number of pupils: males, 7 under 10 years, 7 from 10 to 15, total 14; females, 6 under 10 years, 5 from 10 to 15, total 11; total number of pupils 25, 5 Established Church, 20 Presbyterians; master Robert Hinde, Established Church.

Gortin, established 1829; income: Mr Moore, county Antrim, 6 pounds, pupils 9 pounds, total 15 pounds; intellectual instruction: children bring their own books; moral instruction: catechisms taught regularly; number of pupils: males, 21 under 10 years, 2 from 10 to 15, total 23; females, 23 under 10 years, 3 from 10 to 15, total 26; total number of pupils 49, 40 Presbyterians, 9 other denominations; master Thomas Macklin, Covenanter.

Prehen, established 1818; income: Hibernian Society 4 pounds, pupils 8 pounds, total 12 pounds; intellectual instruction: *First and second spelling books*, Hibernian Society, *Dublin Reading books*; moral instruction: visited by the Revd Messrs Carey and Maughan, Old and New Testament read; number of pupils: males, 24 under 10 years, 27 from 10 to 15, total 51; females, 45 under 10 years, total number of pupils 96, 8 Established Church, 40 Presbyterians, 48 Roman Catholics; master Robert Dinsmore, Presbyterian.

[Totals] number of pupils: males, 177 under 10 years, 59 from 10 to 15, total 236; females, 186 under 10 years, 64 from 10 to 15, 5 above 15, total 255; total number of pupils 491, 73 Established Church, 226 Presbyterians, 171 Roman Catholics, 21 other denominations.

Private Schools

Classical school, Drumahoe, established 1829; income 130 pounds; expenditure on salaries: writing master 20 pounds; other expenses: stationery, fuel and candles 2 pounds; physical instruction: no regular system; intellectual instruction: grammar, arithmetic, algebra, *Euclid's Elements*, ancient and modern geography, history, books comprised in the entrance course of Trinity College, Dublin, and of the Belfast and Glasgow colleges;

moral instruction: the best elementary compilations for beginners, Protestants receive religious instruction; number of pupils: males, 5 under 10 years, 13 from 10 to 15, 16 above 15, total 34; females, 1 under 10 years; total number of pupils 35, 9 Established Church, 15 Presbyterians, 6 Roman Catholics, 5 other denominations; master Joseph Logue A.M., Established Church.

English Schools

Carn, a thatched cabin, cost 5 pounds, established 1830; income 17 pounds; physical instruction: none; intellectual instruction: pupils find their own books; moral instruction: children catechised by the master, Scripture taught in the usual way; number of pupils: males: 7 under 10 years, 8 from 10 to 15, 2 above 15, total 17; females, 5 under 10 years, 6 from 10 to 15, 3 above 15, total 14; total number of pupils 31, 4 Established Church, 12 Presbyterians, 8 Roman Catholics, 7 other denominations; master David Harpin, Presbyterian.

Curryfree, thatched cabin, cost 5 pounds, established 1832; income 2 pounds; physical instruction: none; intellectual instruction: pupils find their own books; moral instruction: catechism taught regularly; number of pupils: males, 7 under 10 years; females, 3 under 10 years; total number of pupils 10, 8 Presbyterians, 2 Roman Catholics; master John Barr, Covenanter.

Drumahoe, a small slated house, established 1825; income 1 pound; physical instruction: none; intellectual instruction: *Dublin Reading books*, geography etc.; moral instruction: Mr Radcliffe and the Revd Messrs Monteith and Carson visit, Authorised Version; number of pupils: males, 20 under 10 years; females, 25 under 10 years, 5 from 10 to 15, total 30; total number of pupils 50, 48 Presbyterians, 1 Roman Catholic, 1 other denomination; mistress Isabella Mills, Presbyterian.

Killymallaght, established 1823; income 15 pounds; physical instruction: none; intellectual instruction: children bring their own books; moral instruction: catechisms taught regularly, Scriptures read; number of pupils: males, 29 under 10 years, 6 from 10 to 15, total 35; females, 20 under 10 years, 4 from 10 to 15, 1 above 15, total 25; total number of pupils 60, 52 Presbyterians, 5 Roman Catholics, 3 other denominations; master David Mitchell, Presbyterian.

Lisdillon, established 1810; physical instruction: none; intellectual instruction: children bring their own books; moral instruction: catechisms taught every Saturday; number of pupils: males, 14 under 10 years, 3 from 10 to 15, 1 above 15, total 18; females, 17 under 10 years, 2 from 10 to 15, 3 above 15, total 22; total number of pupils 40, 4 Established Church, 6 Presbyterians, 28 Roman Catholics, 2 other denominations; master Thomas Donald, Roman Catholic.

Waterside, established 1832; physical instruction: none; intellectual instruction: children bring their own books; moral instruction: catechisms taught, Authorised and Douai Versions; number of pupils: males, 30 under 10 years, 20 from 10 to 15, total 50; females, 12 under 10 years, 7 from 10 to 15, 1 above 15, total 20; total number of pupils 70, 8 Established Church, 10 Presbyterians, 52 Roman Catholics; master James McNamee, Roman Catholic.

Waterside, established 1828; physical instruction: none; intellectual instruction: children bring their own books; moral instruction: catechisms of each persuasion taught, Authorised and Douai Versions; number of pupils: males, 5 under 10 years; females, 8 under 10 years, 7 from 10 to 15, total 15; total number of pupils 20, 4 Established Church, 11 Presbyterians, 2 Roman Catholics, 3 other denominations; mistress Rebecca Steele, Presbyterian.

Total number of pupils 316.

[Insert footnote: NB Add a paper of text, mentioning the hours of attendance in winter and summer, the locations and any information reporting the history or returns of each school which cannot be brought into this table].

School

Catholic chapel, established 1st March 1836; total number of pupils 75; mistress Miss Mary Jane Walsh [insert query: Welch?].

Dispensary Statistics, 1834

Table of Diseases

Report of the diseases treated at the dispensary with the results for one year ending in April 1834. [Table contains the following headings: name of disease, numbers treated, cured, relieved, incurable, died, under care, remarks as to how supported].

Pulmonic complaints including influenza: 322 treated, 236 cured, 42 relieved, 4 incurable, 6 died, 34 under care; supported in the usual manner by subscription.

Cutaneous disorders: 178 treated, 146 cured, 10 relieved, 22 under care.

Dyspeptic disorders: 170 treated, 127 cured, 24 relieved, 1 incurable, 2 died, 16 under care.

Injuries: 98 treated, 96 cured, 2 under care.

Fever: 68 treated, 62 cured, 4 died, 2 under care.

Diarrhoea and dysentery: 64 treated, 41 cured, 8 relieved, 3 died, 12 under care.

Diseases of the eye: 32 treated, 22 cured, 4 relieved, 6 under care.

Dropsy: 16 treated, 7 cured, 2 relieved, 3 died, 4 under care.

Cholera: 6 treated, 6 cured.

Diseases not referable to any of the above: 698 treated, 590 cured, 68 relieved, 4 incurable, 36 under care.

Total number: 1,652 treated, 1,333 cured, 158 relieved, 9 incurable, 18 died, 134 under care.

[Crossed out: Signed John Semple, [insert addition: surgeon].

Letter from Surgeon

[Insert addition:
  Sir,
  Since the establishment of the dispensaries some diseases [are much diminished?]: smallpox is scarcely seen, scrofula is much abated, fever is not so prevalent, in consequence of the cleanliness they are forced to adopt and the intimation afforded them that it is a contagious disease. Many others are much mitigated in severity by an early application for relief, and altogether I think the establishment of dispensaries is of the greatest use in alleviating human suffering amongst the poor. Yours most respectfully, John Semple, 17th December.

[To] Mr Ligar, Dungiven; forwarded to Lieutenant Larcom, 21st December 1834 [signed] R.K. Dawson, Lieutenant Royal Engineers].

Queries and Answers on Social Economy by Several Authors

Memoir Writing

Memoir Writing

Forwarded to Mr Ligar, 9th March 1835, [initialled] RKD; more information concerning this parish to be sent [signed] J.B. Williams, 18th May 1835.

Queries and Answers

In which Cumber are the O'Caireallians numerous as well as in Clondermot? [Answer] That part of Lower Cumber adjacent to Faughanvale.

Is the name of the substitute for milk used in some districts spelt thus: sowen shirings? [Answer] It is shire-ings.

What are the particulars of the murder of Miss Knox of Prehen by McNaghten; a short sketch would be interesting. What was McNaghten's Christian name? What was the locality of the murder? What was the date? [Answer] This I shall find out if I can. I know that it will be difficult, as it is a disagreeable subject to some families yet existing who are distant relations to this Mr McNaghten.

Extract from Lieutenant Lancey's report on Killygarvan in Donegal: "There are 2 tablets of the Knox family within the church, the oldest of which is (1774) is to the memory of Colonel Knox's father, who represented the county of Donegal for 27 years. At the head of the tablet is engraved 'Mariana filia obiit November 1761,' the unfortunate young lady who was shot by her lover McNaghten, for which he was tried, condemned and suffered at Strabane the utmost penalty of the law."

Was it in consequence of the death of Miss Knox by the hand of McNaghten that Colonel Knox left Prehen, or is some other Colonel Knox intended? [Answer] He only left it about a year ago on account of debts. [Insert note by T.A. Larcom: No, no, he only left the other day; debts I understand].

How far from Derry is Beech Hill (Connolly Skipton Esquire)? [Answer] Not a [illegible word] question; might have been measured on the map.

Cock Hall, Samuel Ewing, Mr or Esquire? [Answer] Mr.

Salem, Samuel Haslett, Mr or Esquire? [Answer] Esquire.

The Poor Shop of Altnagelvin was assisted by the "ladies of the London and Irish Society and afterwards by a subscription of 50 pounds 19s." Should this be "the Irish Society and afterwards by a subscription of 50 pounds 19s from the ladies of the neighbourhood?" [Answer] It should not be this. Or "the ladies of the neighbourhood and afterwards by a subscription of 50 pounds 19s from the Irish Society?" Or how else? [Answer] Nor this, because I did not ascertain who the individuals were who contributed to the amount of subscription. The London and Irish Society here spoken of is not identical with the Irish Society, but it is a society of ladies formed in London to give money by subscription to assist the poor in Ireland.

[Insert note by Dawson: This is not an answer to the question: it tells us only what is *not meant*, and does not state from what source the 50 pounds 19s came].

[Insert additional note: The Poor Shop of Altnagelvin was first established in 1822, at which time 30 pounds were lent by the "ladies of the London and Irish Society," upon the condition that 3 times that sum would be lent out yearly; in case it should not be the money was to be withdrawn. The accounts are sent annually to the society in London, and the condition having hitherto been fulfilled the sum has not been withdrawn. Owing to an insufficiency in the funds, which amounted only to those 30 pounds above mentioned, not much business was done, but in 1831 new life was given to the institution by an addition of 50 pounds 19s to the capital, which sum was raised by subscription in the neighbourhood. NB the proper name of this poor shop is the Clondermot Poor Shop, and not Miss Smyth's Poor Shop nor the Poor Shop of Altnagelvin].

The Christian name of Mr Hare the pastor, under whom in 1744 a schism arose in the Presbyterian congregation? [Answer] William. This is the same individual as that whose name is on the inscription on the north east gable, and on which the name is written "Hairs."

The Christian name of the Revd Mr Monteith, present minister of the old Presbyterian congregation? [Answer] William.

Names of the Roman Catholic curate or curates? [Answer] Only one curate, James McCarren.

As there is still much turf cut in Lisdillon, why are many obliged to go to other parishes for fuel, viz. to Lower Cumber or Donaghedy? [Answer] Because the supply from the Lisdillon turf is not equal to the demand. [Insert note by Dawson: Might it not be equal to the demand if more were cut?].

It is stated that the priest is paid thus: gentlemen 1 pound, farmers 10s, artisans 5s, cottiers and peasants 2s 6d. The fees of the priests are then stated: marriage, christening etc. It is then observed "the above are cheerfully paid, the stipends reluctantly, and in many cases not paid at all." Does the above mean the fees for marriage, christening etc. and the stipends the payments made by gentlemen, farmers etc., or is stipends to be referred to the Presbyterian clergy, whose stipends were mentioned just before the priest's emoluments? [Answer] The above means the fees for marriage, christening etc. The stipends mean the payments made by gentlemen, farmers etc. [Stipends] not to be referred to the Presbyterian clergy.

Do the parishioners resort promiscuously to the courts and sessions of Derry, Muff and Claudy, or are there 2 districts with a line of demarcation between them, one resorting to Derry, the other to Muff and Claudy? If so trace the line. [Answer]

They resort promiscuously. There is no exact line of demarcation.

Do the lessees of the Goldsmiths' Company possess and exercise the company's manorial rights. If so, where is the manor court? [Answer] The lessees of the Goldsmiths' Company possess but do not exercise the company's manorial rights. There is no manor court held.

Does the toll of the bridge prevent the inhabitants of Clondermot from resorting to the courts in Derry? [Answer] It does not.

See accompanying "Extract of Robert Miller's will" and query at bottom. [Answer] This extract was copied incorrectly; see accompanying correct extract.

In which of the Presbyterian meeting houses is the Poor Shop of Altnagelvin held and what description of goods is sold? [Answer] At that of the new Presbyterian congregation; male and female clothing with bedclothes.

What are the small weekly instalments of payment? [Answer] 1s or 1s 6d or 6d.

About 20 pounds were collected a few years ago to institute proceedings against the Warren family and recover Mitchelburne's property for the poor. What steps were taken and with what results? (John Bleakly heard of this from Mrs Brown and her son at the Waterside). [Answer] See Memoir of Clondermot in which it is fully related.

Queries and Answers on Ecclesiastical Administration

Queries and Answers

1836: the names and denominations of the parishes constituting each benefice or union? [Answer] Glendermot [insert addition: Faughanvale, deanery of Derry including Burt, Muff and Inch].

Whether with or without cure of souls? [Answer] A perpetual cure with spiritual duties annexed, erected within Glendermot parish, appropriated to the deanery of Derry.

And of any chapelry belonging thereto, and having a separate incumbent and whether subject to episcopal, or to what peculiar or exempt jurisdiction? [Answer] Subject to episcopal jurisdiction.

The extent of the respective parishes? [Answer] Length 7 miles, breadth 4 miles.

The reputed acreable contents, in statute measure, of each parish respectively, and in what county or counties each is locally situate? [Answer] 21,508 acres 1 rood 21 perches statute measure per Ordnance Survey; county Londonderry.

With an account of the general quality of the land in each? [Answer] The general quality of the land in this parish is reported to be of a good sort.

The population of the respective parishes, according to the census taken in 1831? [Answer] 10,315.

The names of the respective incumbents and the dates of their admission? [Answer] Anthony G. Cary, clerk, licensed in October 1811, perpetual curate.

With the names of the curates employed and for what parishes, and the amount of stipend or allowance paid to each and every curate? [Answer] No curate assistant employed.

Gross amounts of the annual income of the respective parishes and benefices on an average of 3 years ending with December 1831, or to the latest period to which the returns have been made? [Answer] 132 pounds 6s 7d ha'penny.

The sources from whence the said yearly incomes arise, specifying how much from tithes or tithe compositions and how much from glebe or any other source, with the acreable contents, profitable or not, of the glebe in statute measure, and its average value per acre; whether subject to any rent and whether let or in occupation of the incumbent? [Answer] From salary payable by the rector of the parish 69 pounds 4s 7d ha'penny, augmentation allowance payable by the Ecclesiastical Commissioners out of Boulter's fund 23 pounds 2s; 20 acres Cunningham, or 27 acres 2 roods 27 and a half perches statute measure of glebe, in incumbent's use, valued at 40s per Cunningham acre 40 pounds, [total] 132 pounds 6s 7d ha'penny.

The amount of any yearly payments or temporary charges, each under its proper title, made out of the gross incomes of the respective benefices, on an average of 3 years ending as before, excepting rates and taxes for the glebe houses and offices, repairs and curates' stipends; and, if only temporary, the time at which the same will terminate? [Answer] To glebe rent 23 pounds 5s 3d.

The net amounts of the annual incomes of the benefices respectively, after deducting such payments (except as aforesaid); and whether such incomes may be fairly considered as the average amounts of net income for the future or otherwise? [Answer] 109 pounds 1s 4d ha'penny.

The time and expense at which the respective glebe houses were built; from what funds; whether under the old or new acts? [Answer] Glendermot Glebe House is small and ill-built, and requires both repairs and enlargement.

With the amounts of the sums certified to have been paid by the present incumbent, as well as the amounts of those payable to them by their successors, or those remaining a charge on the benefice? [Answer] Incumbent was not chargeable with the payment of any sum to his predecessor; neither has he any demand against his successor on account of the house.

And whether the incumbent or his curate usually resides in the Glebe House; and if not, for what reason and where resident, with the name of the person by whom the Glebe House is occupied; or if there be no glebe house or none fit for residence, the amount of rent paid by the incumbent for a house or lodging for himself? [Answer] Incumbent is resident in the Glebe House. [Insert note: Wrong; the curate resides there and the incumbent in the deanery of Derry].

The number of churches and chapels in each benefice? [Answer] 1 church.

The accommodation which each is capable of affording? [Answer] Capable of accommodating 300 persons.

The duties performed in each, their distance from one another, if more than one? [Answer] Divine worship is performed twice on Sundays during two-thirds of the year and once during the remainder of the year, and on the festivals. The sacrament is administered once every 6 weeks.

When each was built, at what expense and from what funds? [Answer] Built about 50 years ago by parochial assessment, but at what cost is unknown.

How much of the cost of building remains charged on the benefice, and when the same will be paid off? [Answer] No charge on the parish in 1832, on account of this church.

The average annual amount of the sums assessed upon the respective benefices and vestries in the 3 years ending as aforesaid, distinguishing, as far as the same appears by the returns, the sums raised at the exclusive vestries from those raised at the open or general vestries. [Answer] Exclusive vestries: to parish clerk's salary 10 pounds, to sexton's salary 4 pounds, to com[munion?] elements 2 pounds 5s 4d, to repairs of roof 3 pounds 13s 4d, to repairs of steeple window 16s 8d, to painting church 6s 5d, to repairs of churchyard wall 10s, to chain for bell 2 pounds 2s, [total] 21 pounds 14s 2d.

General vestries: to care of foundlings 7 pounds 13s 3d ha'penny, to coffins for the poor 3 pounds 3s 4d, to repairs of schoolhouse 18s 10d ha'penny, to iron rails for schoolhouse 1 pound, to repairs of churchyard wall 1 pound 3s 4d, to graveyard implements 6s 5d, to act of parliament 2s 6d, to repairing lock 10d, to collector's fees 1 pound 6s 8d, [total] 15 pounds 15s 6d. NB the foregoing are the average amounts of the sums voted at vestries for the 3 years ending 1831.

The name of the person or lady to whom the advowson of each benefice belongs, or is reputed to belong? [Answer] The Dean of Derry.

If the benefice be not a rectory, the name of the person to whom the rectory is reputed to belong, its reputed value, how paid, and if from portions of tithes, distinguishing the amount payable to the rector from that payable to the vicar? [Answer] The benefice of Glendermot within which this cure has been established is a rectory.

Whether incumbents are, in right of their benefices, patrons of any and what ecclesiastical benefices, perpetual curacies or chapelries; and if so, the diocese in they are situated? [Answer] None.

The names or proper titles of every dignity, prebend or other ecclesiastical preferment or office whatever now held by any incumbent, and in what county and diocese situate, and whether with or without care of souls? [Answer] None.

Glendermot: annual value of land 11,480 pounds 5s; annual value of land exempt from tithe composition 471 pounds 8s; annual value of titheable land 11,008 pounds 17s; tithe 920 pounds 11s 8d; proportion of tithe to 1 pound in the value of titheable land 1s 8d.

Glendermot, 1834: amount of tithe 920 pounds 11s 8d; tithe owners Revd T.B. Gough; capacity of owner, rector.

Queries and Answers by Several Authors

Queries and Answers on Natural Features

Among the hills is mentioned Brown mountain; query, *the* B[rown] mountain? [Answer] Should be *the* B[rown] mountain.

"Another ridge similar in character but of less importance which extends into the county of Tyrone. Of this, the highest point at the southern extremity of the parish *is 496 feet*." Does this mean "the highest point *which is* at the" etc., that is, the highest point of the entire ridge (the Tyrone part of it included), or the highest point *in the parish of Clondermot*, which highest point is situated at the southern extremity etc., implying that there are still higher points in Tyrone? [Answer] There is a higher [point] in Tyrone; the highest point in the parish of Clondermot.

Queries and Answers on Productive Economy

In the list of occupations at the Waterside is mentioned "leather stores 1." Is not this the tannery (Mr Lindsay's), or distinct from it. Can any information be obtained respecting this tannery? [Answer] The leather store is distinct from the *tannery*, not Mr Lindsay's. The tannery belongs to Mr William McCarter, was [?] sunk or established upwards of a century ago (exact date cannot be ascertained). Mr McC[arter] keeps on an average 4 or 5 men, from 20 to 30 pounds per annum boarded out. Mr McC[arter] will not give the quantity of work done.

In ditto list leather stores are mentioned. Immediately after it is stated "2 merchants purchase corn at their own stores at the Waterside." Should not these 2 stores be specified on the list, or should they be rather called the corn market? What are the merchants' names? Is the corn all bought on commission for the Liverpool market? [Answer] These stores should be specified on the list and not called the corn market, as they are altogether private and no cranage or any other dues are charged; the merchants' names are Thomas Lindsay and Thomas White. Mr White buys all on his own account and sends it to Liverpool, London and Glasgow. Mr Lindsay buys all on commission for Glasgow market.

Queries and Answers on Modern Topography

New Buildings is said to contain 37 habitations and 75 inhabitants. Can the average be so small? [Answer] New Buildings contains 150 inhabitants.

Who lives at Culkeeragh now: Major Young lives at the opposite side of the river? [Answer] Major Young lives at Culkeeragh now. He formerly lived at Ballynagard, which place is at present for sale.

Is it not one and the same bleach green (the joint property of Messrs McClelland and Co.) that encroaches on the demesnes of Ardmore and Larchmount? [Answer] It is. [Insert note by Dawson: Query this; are there not 2 bleach greens, one belonging to Mr Smith [Smyth], the other to Mr McClelland?].

Are these expressions identical in meaning: "a mill has but 1 pair of wheels" and "a mill has but 1 hopper," for the term single-geared is applied in each case? [Answer] No such expression exists as "a mill has but 1 pair of wheels;" it was probably a mistake instead of "has but 1 pair of stones," which latter expression means single-geared. One water wheel and 1 pit wheel may work a double or a single-geared mill. The expression "a mill works but 1 hopper" is identical in meaning with "has

but one pair of stones" and also with "is single-geared."

The pit or main wheel: is wheel understood with pit (pit wheel) or is pit equivalent to the 2 words main and wheel? [Answer] Wheel is understood with pit. The 3 expressions "pit wheel," "main wheel" and "cog wheel" are identical in meaning.

Query and Answer on Natural Features

What is the height of Warbleshinny and should it not be reckoned among one of the most important elevations, as giving name to a large district? [Answer] The height of this important point has been given under the name of Clondermot hill, which name applies to the entire of the hill, while Warbleshinny is the name of only a part of it, namely the highest point.

Queries and Answers on Social Economy

A dispensary report has been furnished for the year ending in May 1834: can similar reports or even the totals be given for one or two years preceding? [Answer] See accompanying table.

What is the history of the dispensary, when built and opened, the costs, salaries etc. Is the district confined to the one parish. [Answer] The present dispensary house was built in 1832, at an expense of 50 pounds 6s. The district is confined to the parish of Clondermot.

Do children crossing the bridge to attend school in Derry pay toll? [Answer] Children crossing the bridge to attend school do pay toll.

One report speaks of Miss Smyth's Poor Shop opened in 1831. Another speaks of the Poor Shop of Altnagelvin, founded by a lady in 1822. Are there really 2 and if not, in what year was the Poor Shop instituted by Miss Smyth? [Answer] A mistake, it was instituted in 1822; there is only 1 poor shop; the Poor Shop instituted by Miss Smyth was instituted in 1822. See [elsewhere] for a more full account.

The curate is stated to have 100 pounds a year, but the items give more: from the dean 75 pounds, Board of First Fruits 26 pounds 6d, total 101 pounds 6d. What is the fact? [Answer] The curate receives from the dean 75 pounds, Board of First Fruits 25 pounds, total 100 pounds. The above sums are in Irish currency. That statement is wrong.

Queries and Answers on Modern Topography

Does the damming of the Faughan for mills etc. contribute to its inundations? [Answer] The damming of the Faughan does not contribute to its inundations; the cause of the increase in the height of the floods is the improvement in drains.

Is the Brae Face over the Waterside ever called the Quay Brae Face? [Answer] This place is never called the Brae Face, but it is sometimes called the Quay Brae Face, though rarely. Its common and usual name is the Brae Head.

What is the old inscription on the northern gable of Mr Monteith's old Presbyterian meeting house? [Answer] Inscription on the north east gable: "Rev. William Hairs, 1747;" inscription on the north west gable "1696."

What Clondermot magistrates are stipendiary, and what are not? [Answer] No Clondermot magistrates are stipendiary. The others are John Acheson Smyth of Ardmore and William Hamilton Ash of Ashbrook.

In what year was the money club started at Alexander McShane's in the Waterside? [Answer] April 5th 1834.

[Insert footnote: Alexander McShane is now dead. The money club continues to meet in his widow's house. (Additional information on the subject of this club): this club is not so beneficial to the community as might at first appear, for several reasons: first, the members [meet] in a public house and everyone takes a glass of whiskey; this is the custom, but many take more, drinking is thereby encouraged. Secondly, the manner of getting the prize, the money to be given on the day of meeting, is by a successful throw of dice, which custom would probably lead to gambling. Thirdly, it is not unusual to traffic with the prize, by the successful individual, if he should not want the money, immediately selling it with a large profit, often more than 1s in the pound, to one of those who were unsuccessful and who may require the money immediately, the 2 individuals concerned in the transaction exchanging their tickets].

Is not the church on the top of Clondermot hill? [Answer] The church is not on the top of Clondermot hill. (See answer to a previous query in which it is stated that Clondermot hill applies to the entire mountain including Warbleshinny). The church is on the brow of the steep eastern bank of the hill. [Insert note by Dawson: Not on the top, if the summit is meant by the word top, but it is on the top of the ridge and might in a general way be said to be on the top].

The gentry contribute sums for distribution twice a week at their different residences in rotation, and at the Waterside householders' dwellings in rotation. What is the average total sum distributed, and are equal portions distributed at the Waterside and throughout the rest of the parish? [Answer] The average total sum is not more than from 2 pounds to 3 pounds; not equal.

Are the mail coach roads that branch off from the Waterside repaired with limestone from Prehen or from what other quarter? [Answer] The mail coach roads that branch off from the Waterside are not repaired with limestone from the Prehen quarry. They are repaired for 2 or 3 miles from Derry with whinstone from a quarry at Drumahoe and one at Newtown Hamilton, which latter is the property of Sir Robert Ferguson. The stones are broken at the gaol.

In what year was the dispensary established, by whom, at what expense was it built, how is it supported, physician's salary? [Answer] The dispensary was established in 1826. See table referred to in a previous page for the answer to the other queries.

Was the George Tomkins to whom Colonel Mitchelburne left some property identical with Alderman Tomkins by whom 50 pounds was left to the poor? [Answer] Yes.

Can any further particulars be obtained respecting this bequest, such as its specific object, whether it has lapsed, and when and why, place and time of distribution etc.? [Answer] The 50 pounds bequeathed by George or Alderman Tomkins were raised by the curate and churchwardens of Clondermot and left (to interest as directed in the will) to Andrew Knox Esquire of Prehen, and the interest 3 pounds per annum (all being Irish currency) was regularly paid by Colonel Knox to the curate of the parish, until he became involved in difficulties, left the country and the interest could no more be procured. He has paid up to the month of June 1831, from which time to the present he owes each years's interest.

The object of this bequest was to give annually 10s each to 6 poor individuals of the Church of England not receiving any of Colonel Mitchelburne's charities. These sums were distributed on the 1st June of each year by the curate of Clondermot.

Obstructions to Improvement

The parish is much in want of a bridge, toll free, for communicating with Derry, the market for its agricultural produce. Indeed the tolls by which the county of Londonderry is debarred from free communication with its own capital were at one period so high as almost to amount to a prohibition to the entrance of either fuel or provisions from the opposite side of the Foyle (see the schedule of the tolls of Derry bridge in the parish of Templemore).

[Crossed out: The existence of the village of the Waterside is wholly attributable to the difficulty which has always prevailed of obtaining access to Londonderry and to the consequent necessity of elsewhere supplying the wants of the parishioners].

A ferryboat has been known to ply close to Derry for fares lower than the tolls. This interference with corporate authority was, however, suppressed. A ferry could be easily established between Prehen and the end of Bishop's Street, but this would probably share the fate of the former.

Local Government

The magistrates attend at Muff (see parish of Templemore) and under certain circumstances at Londonderry and Claudy. They are firm and respected by the people for their firmness and impartiality. There are no police as they are unnecessary. Illicit distillation became extinct about 40 years ago, owing to the increasing vigilance of the excise officers from Derry, by whom the parish is occasionally well searched.

Dispensaries

The health of the people has increased not only from the improvement of their worldly circumstances within the last 10 years but from the improvement in clothing effected by the benevolent exertions of the ladies of the Poor Shop. This institution is popularly believed to have been in many cases more beneficial than the dispensary, inasmuch as it has often checked disease by extending warmth and comfort. In the calamitous years of 1816 and 1817 many persons died of actual destitution and nearly as many by receiving too suddenly the nourishing broth distributed at the church. No case, however, of the kind has occurred since.

The famine of that period rose to such a degree that in the kitchens of the more fortunate parishioners, that is those who were not without the means of procuring potatoes, individuals were frequently seen to enter and lick that part of the table where the offal [insert alternative: remains] of the breakfast had lain, in the hope of finding perhaps some miserable crumb adhering to the wood! A violent calamitous fever was the consequence [insert alternative: followed this calamitous disease], which carried off many of the parishioners. The effects of this period were felt with equal severity over the whole county, but scenes of peculiar wretchedness appear to have

been of frequent occurrence in this parish. [Insert marginal note: This should be transferred to Poor].

Many individuals appear without noses, the effect in most cases of venereal complaints; many also are deeply pitted with smallpox. From the following table it would appear that the parishioners are subject to diseases of the skin, however [no further text].

Extracts from Working Papers by G. Downes and J. Stokes

MEMOIR WRITING

Queries and Answers

The original report says "about 5,000 barrels of beer are brewed annually at the brewery at Faughan bridge:" query? [Answer] That is wrong; the latter report is correct.

Captain Vicars mentions "12 old coins were discovered by a labourer while digging in the wood at Prehen in 1826. I attach etchings of them;" on which Captain Waters observes "not received." Can any information (with or without etchings) be obtained? [Answer] I have these etchings, [signed] T.A. Larcom.

In the report on Drumahoe parish Mr Stokes observes that "Presbyterians are divided into Covenanters, Arians and Seceders." To which division do the 2 clergymen of Altnagelvin belong? Does the above division belong to Drumahoe or is it applicable to all Presbyterians? [Answer] The 2 clergymen of Altnagelvin are Presbyterians. The divisions of Presbyterians, Covenanters, Arians and Seceders are more applicable to the parish of Drumahoe than to any other.

Is Mr Connolly Skipton's seat written Beechhill or Beech Hill? It is Beach Hill in the Ordnance map. [Answer] The Ordnance map is correct.

Christian names of Mr Hazlitt of Salem? [Answer] Samuel. Mr Ewing, Cock hall (or Cock Hall)? [Answer] Sam Ewing, Cock Hall. Charles Martin Esquire, Hollymount? [Answer] This is correct. William Henry Ash of Ashbrook? [Answer] William Hamilton Ash is the correct name.

Mr Stokes observes "there is still to be seen in the townland of Clooney an old road remarkable for a tradition which will be mentioned further on." The only tradition connected with Clooney is that of St Columbkille and the muzzled cocks. It contains no allusion to a road. Is the road supposed to be that by which the saint departed, or how is it connected with the tradition of Killsill?

[Answer] This old road led to the forest of Curragh Camon in Culkeeragh and is believed to have been the trace of the road which conveyed the timber to the first erection of Londonderry. For particulars of Curragh Camon, see [elsewhere].

[Crossed out: *Leech's* account of the Marquis of Stafford]? [Answer] Loch's.

Colonel Mitchelburne bequeathed but 86 pounds (according to the draft of his will) to pay 5 pounds 4s annually (3d weekly to each of 8 paupers). It would have required 86 pounds 13s 4d to pay this at 6 per cent, and more since the change of money. How was the surplus principal supplied? Do the corporation of Derry incur the trifling loss themselves? [Answer] I do not believe they do. I conceive that Colonel Mitchelburne made the mistake knowingly and on purpose, to exercise the charity of his executors.

The original report states that the Protestant curate receives 100 pounds a year late Irish currency, of which 75 pounds is paid by the dean, 26 pounds 6s by the First Fruits. Now, these sums make 101 pounds 6d instead of 100. Could Mr S. ascertain about this? [Answer] It would be safer merely to state that the Protestant curate receives 100 pounds a year? Particulars are dangerous? I will try to do so.

[Beginning of text obscured] so applied, except [illegible words] Poor Shop of Clondermot, which is called the Presbyterian vestry room? [Answer] I believe it is not [giving?], except to the poor.

Salmon fishery of the Faughan? [Answer] [Blank] Little Esquire.

McShane [of the] Waterside; query Alexander? [Answer] Yes.

Christian names of the Revd Messrs Carson, Presbyterian, Sweeny, Covenanter, Carron, Roman Catholic?

J. Smyth Junior (probably of Ardmore)? [Answer] Yes. Those who are respectable of that name spell their name Smyth; those not so, Smith. The family of Ardmore spell it in the former way.

Is Patrick Mehan (contributor to the poor fund) Mr or Esquire? [Answer] Mr.

Should Mrs Maughan be Revd J.D. Maughan? [Answer] It should be Mrs Maughan.

Where does Pitt Skipton live? Whether is he or Connolly the exemplary farmer, or both?

Should Mr McClellan (one of the exemplary farmers) be Carey McClellan Esquire? Is he the bleacher of Ardmore? [Answer] It should; he is the bleacher.

[Insert note by Downes: PS I regret giving Mr Stokes so much trouble about Christian names and other apparently insignificant matters, but feel bound to put such questions, from a conviction that it is impossible to be too minute in preparing a statistical work for publication; see additional queries etc. on the envelope].

Extracts from Queries and Answers by G. Downes and J. Stokes

Queries and Answers

Rivers: What does the mineral spring of Bogagh contain? [Answer] Bottle forwarded.

Public Buildings: is the following correct? 2 meeting houses in Altnagelvin, one Presbyterian, the other Covenanting? [Answer] Both Presbyterian. One Presbyterian in Drumahoe? [Answer] Covenanting; corrected, [signed] J. Stokes.

Where is the brewery of Faughan bridge, on the road between Derry and Dungiven, and in what parish is it? [Answer] At the bridge over the Faughan and 2 miles from Derry, in the townland of Drumahoe, parish of Clondermot; 1,000 barrels of beer brewed annually, belongs to Francis Horner.

Is the corn market of J. McCrea at the Waterside or where else? [Answer] Spell this name McCrea. Not at the Waterside: it is in the city of Londonderry. Mistake produced by misapprehension of Mr B's intro. All other particulars correct.

In the account of the money club at the Waterside should Donaghy be Donoughy? [Answer] It should be Donaghey. Mr Donovan would be a better judge. The name is a common one and no two persons spell it the same way.

Is C. McClellan correctly spelt? What is the name of C. McClellan's seat? Is it not Larchmount? [Answer] Spell the name McClellan; I have seen his visiting card. The name of Mr McClellan's place is Larchmount.

What is the Christian name of Alexander of Cah House? [Answer] John.

What is the Christian name of Mungan? [Answer] No such name in the parish; for Mungan read Maughan (John Dickinson).

One report gives Belvue, another Bellview, Revd Mr Maughan; which is correct? [Answer] It should be Bellevue.

Does Ashbrook belong to A. Ash or to W. Ashe? [Answer] Let Ashe be Ash. Ashbrook belongs to Mr H. Ash.

Does Beech Hill belong to P. Skipton or to C. Skipton. [Answer] Beech Hill belongs to Conolly Skipton Esquire.

Bleach greens: is the following enumeration of the parochial mills correct: 5 corn mills, 1 flour mill, 2 flax mills, 3 bleaching mills, 1 tuck mill? [Answer] Correct, except as to the bleaching mill; there is but 1 bleaching mill. Report in July, 1834; some alterations will always be going on. New mills probably are building.

The following passage occurs in the report: "the machinery (of Altnagelvin mill) is of the best description. In the common and poor mills it is all of wood and the corn kilns;" what should be added to complete the sentence? [Answer] Generally of stones and sticks (words interlined).

Poor: Lieutenant Vicars (under date October 1st 1831) mentions 9s 2d ha'penny paid to poor persons by bequest from Colonel Mickelburn. Is it still paid? [Answer] It is spelled Mitchelburne (in his will). I have obtained a copy of Mitchelburne's will and cannot find this bequest of 9s 2d ha'penny in it, from which I conclude that it was never either bequeathed or paid.

It is mentioned that in 1802 part of Mitchelburne's property was in the hands of Sir Robert Ferguson Baronet. The present Sir R.F. must have been then a boy. Was it another Sir R.F. or should it be Sir Andrew F., father to the present Sir R.F.? [Answer] Sir Andrew Ferguson. The present Sir R.F., however, offered to pay his share.

Contributions are "sent equally to the Waterside and Clondermot." What is here meant by Clondermot, being in contradistinction to the Waterside, which is a part of Clondermot when the latter is considered as a parish? [Answer] The word Clondermot is to be considered as the parish at large. The alms are distributed at all the gentlemen's places in rotation, in Waterside by the respectable householders in rotation.

Among the contributors to the Poor Shop are the following names correctly spelt? W.H. Ash, Carey McClellan, Revd Mr Carey, Patrick Mehan. [Answer] These are not contributors to the Poor Shop. If I remember right I returned them as contributors to the poor fund; all correctly spelt.

What are the Christian names of [crossed out: Boyle]? [Answer] Do not know; it is better to erase this name. [Insert query] Babington (Anthony or was it the late Revd Richard, or was it David)? [Answer] Anthony Babington. [Insert query] Blacker? [Answer] For Blacker read Lord De Blaquiere. This was a corruption of Thomas Fagan's. [Insert query] Bond? [Answer] William.

Why are the residences added to G. Hill (St Columb's) and to [blank] Bond (Clooney)? [Answer] For distinction.

Is not the Rea Esquire the late John Rea of St Columb's? [Answer] Yes.

Religion: is the Seceding congregation identi-

cal with the Methodist? [Answer] Not identical.

Are the Methodists Wesleyan Methodists? [Answer] They are; they have no place or building for a house of worship in the parish.

How many acres of glebe belong to the deanery? [Answer] Mr Lithgow, agent to the Marquis of Donegall, says that in Clondermot the terms churchland and glebe land are applied indifferently.

Habits of the People: the parishioners go to Donaghedy and Cumber for bog ground; which Cumber, Upper or Lower? [Answer] Lower Cumber.

Remarkable Events: was it actually in the parish that Miss Knox of Prehen was killed by McNaghten? Where is the exact locality of the killing, what was his Christian name and in what year did it happen? [Answer] I have no means of ascertaining the particulars exactly. If they *are* necessary, it would be as well to cancel the story altogether. It is, however, well known and familiar in the parish. [Insert note: Cancelled].

Queries and Answers on Productive Economy

Commercial: corn and barley for a distillery; what corn? Is it oats? [Answer] Oats.

Rural Productive Economy: are the titles of the exemplary agriculturalists (Esquire and Mr) properly distributed here. Supply the Christian name to the [blank] Esquires and to the 2 Hendersons, and examine the orthography of all.

[Blank] Alexander Esquire? [Answer] J. Alexander Esquire lives at Cah House; his name is John.

Mr Alexander? [Answer] Mr Alexander lives at Knockbrack and is a farmer; his name is in the list).

W.H. Ash Esquire, Mr Bond, Mr Burnside? Revd Cary? [Answer] Anthony. Lieutenant Carmalt, Revd Mr Carson, Mr Coghran, Mr Ewing, Mr Hannah, Mr Hattrick, Mr Hazlitt? Mr Henderson? [Answer] James. Mr Henderson, G. Hill Esquire, Mr Kirkpatrick, Mr Lithgow, Mr McCarter, Mr McClellan? Mr McClintock Esquire? [Answer] Samuel. Mr McCutchen, Revd J.D. Maughan, Mr Miller, Mr Morton, [blank] Reynolds, Mr Semple? [Blank] Skipton Esquire? [Answer] There are 2 Skiptons in the parish; one is called Pitt, the other Conolly. Conolly lives at Beech Hill. J.A. Smyth Esquire? [Blank] Stevenson Esquire? [Answer] Robert. Mr Tait, Mr Teadlie, Mr Thompson, Mr White, Mr Wills? [Answer] For Wills read Mills.

Are not some of the above clergymen officers? Query, Revd Mr Cary, Revd Mr Carson, Revd Mr Maughan, Captain Reynolds. Should Hannah be Hanna? [Answer] Hannah.

Are McClelland and Teadlie correctly spelt? [Answer] Teadlie is correctly spelt; for McClelland read McClellan.

Ascertain the correctness of the following statement and fill the blanks. The existing proprietors may be ranked in the following order: 1st Lady Ponsonby, Goldsmiths' proportion; 2nd Leslie Alexander Esquire, Crown freehold; 3rd Grocers' Company; 4th the Dean of Derry, deanery land; 5th W.H. Ashe Esquire, Crown freehold; 6th C. Skipton Esquire, Crown freehold; [crossed out: 7th Sir R. Ferguson]; 8th R. Young Esquire, Crown freehold? [Answer] Ponsonby and Alexander, Goldsmiths' proportion. They have a common agent, J.A. Smyth Esquire, Ardmore, and hold the estate conjointly. Sir R. Ferguson has property in Clooney, but he is only a middleman; his head proprietor is the bishop. For R. Young Esquire read Major Young.

Dunemanna turf is mentioned. Where and what is Dunemanna? Is it correctly spelt? [Answer] Dunemanna is a village in the parish of Donaghedy, county Tyrone and is adjacent to Upper Cumber. I do not know [how] to spell it correctly.

Why is there not enough turf cut in Lisdillon for the consumption of the parish? (Query based on a remark of Mr Dawson's). [Answer] Because, though abundant, there is not enough supplied to meet the demand.

Queries and Answers on Productive Economy

"These numbers (1,300 linen, 700 linen etc.) are apparently expressions of the quantity of thread in a given space." What is the real meaning? [Answer] "Apparently" should be scratched out. The real meaning is the former part of the query as it now stands. [Insert diagram showing the warp and weft of a piece of cloth].

"A spinning mill *near* Ardkill is in in contemplation." In what townland? [Answer] Townland of Ardkill.

The original report states: "Lime is procured from a quarry near Prehen and from the adjoining parish of Cumber, and sells at 6d a barrel." The additions state: "Lime is sold in the parish at the rate of 1s 4d per barrel of roche lime, or 8d the barrel of slack lime. No quarries are at present worked. It is chiefly procured from Lifford." Which of the above statements as to prices and the localities of the lime-working is applicable at present? [Answer] The latter is applicable at present, the former not applicable.

"In the valley of Warbleshinny in the neighbourhood of Disertowen:" should "and" be introduced after "in," or does the valley extend into other townlands besides that of Warbleshinny? [Answer] "And" should be introduced; it does [extend].

"Mr McClellan" (of Larchmount?) "spreads on his ground carpenter's chips?" [Answer] Yes, of Larchmount.

"The *seeding* and weeding of" onions, "expense of *sowing* and weeding:" which expression is to be preferred? [Answer] "Expense of sowing and weeding."

Queries addressed to Captain Portlock and Mr Petrie

MEMOIR WRITING

Rivers and Climate

[To Captain Portlock] Rivers: analysis of Bogagh spring?

Climate: what? The following notice was furnished long since: "the air of Clondermot is not considered so bracing as some of the other mountainous parishes. Throughout a considerable extent it is deteriorated by exhalations from the River Foyle. The seasons of the ripening of the various crops vary considerably in passing from the north eastern to the south eastern townlands. In some they ripen from 10 to 20 days sooner than in others. Harvest comes in July, August and the beginning of September. In a good soil, with an average season, the harvest is over by the 15th August, but in a bad and cold soil it lasts until the 10th October."

The air is not considered to be so bracing in this as in some of the other mountainous parishes. Excepting Clondermot hill, where cultivation has attained the height of 700 feet, the bog has not yet been reclaimed higher then about 600 feet. The crops at these elevations are seldom later than elsewhere and on the well sheltered and gradual slope of Slieve Kirk cultivation is continually extending upwards, without any impediment from difference of atmosphere.

Productive Economy: Suggestions

The reports of the Irish Society for 1827 to 1835 contain frequent allusions to the wretched state of Rossnagallagh farm, held by Mr Babington; has any improvement been effected?

The following passage occurs in the Report of the Deputation of the Irish Society in 1835: "We viewed the slob which had been reclaimed on the opposite side of the Foyle, [insert note by Downes: opposite is used in reference to Mr [?] McCrea's terrace, of which the deputation had just been speaking], by the bishop or his tenants, on an assumption that, from his possessing the lands of Cluney, he had a right to the slob; we are of opinion that this is a very important question to the society and that a case should be selected in order to determine this right by bringing an ejectment; and we further recommend that the part on which Mr Thomas White has erected saltworks would be the most eligible, as the possession could be easily proved to be much within the statute of limitations. We accordingly directed the general agent to confer with the law agents thereon."

The following passage occurs in J.C. Beresford's report on timber, dated 27th January 1803: "On the Goldsmiths' proportion, tenanted by Mr Ponsonby, there is no wood, except the demesne of Hamilton Ash Esquire, which is small but well planted; I should think the timber on it worth from 1,200 pounds to 1,400 pounds."

General Queries

[Mr Petrie] General Appearance and Scenery: what is to be said?

People: in a former draft <draught> of notices from the *Four masters* about Clondermot was an item (date 1132) respecting Dermot McEitieren. This is omitted in the latter draft: query, intentionally?

"1137, Connor O'Caireallain was killed by the inhabitants of Fermanagh." I have not found this in the *Annals of the four masters*. Is the date wrong, or the citation from some other annals?

[Crossed out: Was the allusion to the bard Carolan, given in the former schedule, intentionally omitted in the latter]? [Answer] Nil.

How is the following promise of "notices relating to some of their (i.e. the ancient inhabitants) successors in modern times" to be fulfilled, Colonel Mitchelburne included? Why was he buried in Clondermot churchyard instead of Enagh, which was his own desire?

Will there not be some notice in the ancient matter of 10 old coins found in 1826 at Prehen?

Is anything to be added to Habits of the People?

Queries and Answers

Enagh Castle

Regarding the inquiry about a castle near Enagh <Ainnach> loch, a few miles from Derry: St Columbcill being born in the county of Donegal,

and related to the house of Cineal Connel, was granted the district of Derry on Loch Foyle (*Loch Feabhail*); it is stated by different writers that he founded several religious houses about the middle of the sixth century, as the abbey of Londonderry, monastery of Glendermagh and monastery of Cil Sillach; this last was on the banks of Enagh loch.

A few years ago some remaining ruins were to be seen there, but not in such a state as to shew whether of a castle or monastery. There is a small wooded island in the lake, but I do not know if any remains of a building are on it. About 60 or 70 years ago a coat of mail of fine steel chain was found in the water, but I could not learn what had become of it.

A little way from this Lough Foyle is contracted into a deep and narrow channel, where the tide water rushes through with a rapid current; on this projecting point of land called Cul Mor (the great defence), commanding the approach to Derry, there was a castle now modernised into a dwelling house, and I do not know of any other castle around this place. Much might now be learned regarding this northern district of the kingdom if the *Leabhar a' Seachran* had not been burned at Dungiven.

Some old men in the neighbourhood of Dungiven were able to sing several old Irish poems of Ossian. *Laoigh Creagh na dTulaigh: Tulaigh creag na dTulach, a mbin da mullach re fiannuigh.*

Laoigh an Conluigh mac na Cuin: Air dteacht don mhorb on muir aisteacht, an curaidh croda conluigheach.

Oisin go mbruid na Lochlinne.

Orthographical Queries and Answers

1. "Mo doireggan, mo doireagan etc.:" where are these verses found? Whether in a manuscript or taken from the mouths of the people? [Answer] I have heard but 1 verse of this poem, taken from an old man singing. I will make an enquiry if more is to be got.

2. "The boat being driven into Loch Foyle, the saint sailed up the River Roe <Roa> until he came to the stop of Cabhan-an-Churadh:" from what authority is this passage taken? [Answer] The manuscript in the Stowe library agrees with the names of the places and states in the *Life of St Columb*, his sailing to Ireland, his vessel driven into Loch Foyle and, entering the River Roe, getting on to Cabhan-an-Churadh, near the beautiful hill of Drom Cead.

3. Is the name Cabhan-an-Churadh yet remembered in the country? [Answer] The name Cabhan-an-Churadh is known as on the River Roe, and

stated to be at Mual loch, the hill at the water, now the seat of a private gentleman near the great impediment on the River Roe.

4. Is this stop on the River Roe called Cabhan-an-Churadh now by the natives or from what authority is it stated that this stop is the Cabhan-an-Churadh of antiquity? [Answer] The name Cabhan-an-Churadh is not general. The stop is in the townland of Limavady, Lia-ma-madhm, the great breach of the waters through the massive schistos[e] rocks and it ends at Cabhan-an-Churadh by Mual loch.

5. Where has it been found that St Columbcill was scoffed at by a boy? Is it from written authority or from a tradition among the natives? [Answer] The story is among the old natives, and as far as Keating can be depended on, saying he heard it with some little differing particulars about the 2 cranes.

6. How is it known that Ceade is the Drom Ceat of antiquity? Whether is it a conjecture or is it pointed out by the natives as the place where the assembly was held? [Answer] Keating, O'Brien, the Stowe manuscript and other manuscripts notice the great assembly of the nobles, of St Columb being driven into the River Roe, and the stop is at the plain leading to the hill of Ceade.

7. How is it known that cabhan means "a plain?" [Answer] By looking into O'Brien or any Irish dictionary. The plain mentioned here may be 2 miles to where the drom begins and 1 mile to the summit of the hill.

At this day it might be thought very ridiculous to speak of a small vessel sailing up the River Roe; however, there can be no doubt that some ages ago the great plains of Moy Roe were covered with the sea water. By digging only 18 inches down the water appears, but of a quality unfit for use; also decayed shells are turned up with the clay, and sinking a few miles inland, at 10 feet deep in looking to procure good water, the shells appeared intermixed with the rich loam turned out. From this it may be certain the River Roe was navigable for small vessels, and at Newtownlimavady a deep pool in the river is to this day called the Boat Hole. Half a mile above this the rocky stop begins and never could have admitted a boat. [Signed] A.O.

Queries and Answers by Lieutenants T. Larcom and E. Vicars

Queries and Answers on Townlands

The townland called by us Glenkeen is on the Down Survey map Clonkeine; is there a glen in the townland or is it a plain? [Answer] Glenkeen is the only way I can find this townland is called in the neighbourhood; the boundaries joining the Faughan both pass in a glen.

The townland Gobnascale is on Down Survey called Gortniskall; would this orthography be objectionable? [Answer] This townland is almost invariably called Gobnascale. I have consulted the oldest and most respectable people, and can learn no other. Gob is "a point of land running into low ground," scail "a shady plain" (maybe "wood"); formerly there was a wood here. Gort is "a field for the public to meet in," nastal "a spear" (may have been "a place to exercise in"). I cannot find that such a use was ever made of it, and it is very unfit for the purpose, the ground being very steep.

Kittybane ought to be Keddybane ("white hillock"). Would the change be objectionable? It is Kedebayne in the Charter of Derry, so it would therefore not be too violent perhaps. [Answer] Either Kittybane or Keddybane is a dreadful corruption of the original; ceidin is "a small round hill," ban "fair or uncultivated;" the first is the method of writing it here. [Insert footnote: Captain Waters, Royal Engineers].

Is Rosnagalliagh so invariably pronounced liquid, as to make the omission of the "i" objectionable? [Signed] Thomas Larcom, Lieutenant Royal Engineers, 20th June 1831. [Answer] There is no objection to omit the "i" in Rosnagalliagh; ros is "rocky," na gallagh "stormy" (a place much exposed). [Signed] Edward Vicars, Lieutenant Royal Engineers, 28th June 1831.

Notes by Larcom

In Irish the letter "o" has the sound of "o" in "mothu;" would it be objectionable to spell Gobnascale Gubnascale?

[Kittybane]: Keady is the nearest, and we have a hill and a parish so spelled without question.

[Rosnagalliagh]: Is it so invariably pronounced Galliagh (liquid), as to make the omission objectionable? If it is mostly pronounced liquid there is no reason for omitting it; the best of all as to correctness would be Rosnagally.

Statistical Tables of Race and Religion

Social Economy

Race Tables

[Table contains the following headings: name of townland, numbers of English, Irish and Scotch subdivided by religion, number of families and children, value of houses and land per acre].

Altnagelvin. English: 17 Established Church, 43 Presbyterians, 12 Roman Catholics, total 72, 13 families, 43 children; Irish: 17 Established Church, 18 Presbyterians, 66 Roman Catholics, total 101, 22 families, 60 children; Scotch: 21 Established Church, 60 Presbyterians, 1 Roman Catholic, 10 other Dissenters, total 92, 15 families, 66 children. [Insert addition: Value of houses per acre 1s 4.2d, value of land per acre 14s 2d].

Ardkill. English: 4 Presbyterians, total 4, 1 family, 2 children; Irish: 18 Presbyterians, 144 Roman Catholics, total 162, 29 families, 105 children; Scotch: 38 Presbyterians, total 38, 6 families, 21 children. [Insert addition: Value of houses per acre 9.9d, value of land per acre 5s 2.88d].

Ardlough. English: 13 Established Church, 6 Presbyterians, 5 Roman Catholics, 1 other Dissenter, total 25, 4 families, 15 children; Irish: 6 Established Church, 1 Presbyterian, 29 Roman Catholics, 2 other Dissenters, total 38, 9 families, 22 children; Scotch: 18 Established Church, 32 Presbyterians, 7 other Dissenters, total 57, 10 families, 37 children. [Insert addition: Value of houses per acre 1s 2.11d, value of land per acre 12s 11.9d].

Ardmore. English: 19 Established Church, 11 Presbyterians, 5 Roman Catholics, 5 other Dissenters, total 40, 8 families, 26 children; Irish: 2 Established Church, 15 Presbyterians, 160 Roman Catholics, total 177, 30 families, 119 children; Scotch: 12 Established Church, 50 Presbyterians, 20 Roman Catholics, 5 other Dissenters, total 87, 13 families, 51 children. [Insert addition: Value of houses per acre 3s 2.2d, value of land per acre 8s 3.89d].

Ardnabrocky. English: 6 Established Church, 8 Presbyterians, total 14, 3 families, 7 children; Irish: 27 Presbyterians, 20 Roman Catholics, total 47, 9 families, 28 children; Scotch: 33 Established Church, 65 Presbyterians, 2 Roman Catholics, total 100, 12 families, 69 children. [Insert addition: Value of houses per acre 2s 5.9d, value of land per acre 15s 7.17d].

Avish. English: 5 Presbyterians, total 5, 1 family, 3 children; Irish: 4 Presbyterians, 2 Roman Catholics, total 6, 2 families, 6 children; Scotch: 5 Established Church, 38 Presbyterians, 6 other Dissenters, total 49, 7 families, 26 children. [Insert addition: Value of land per acre 9s 4d].

Ballyoan. English: 12 Presbyterians, 4 Roman Catholics, 6 other Dissenters, total 22, 4 families, 14 children; Irish: 54 Roman Catholics, total 54, 10 families, 40 children; Scotch: 12 Established Church, 54 Presbyterians, 15 other Dissenters, total 81, 12 families, 50 children. [Insert addition: Value of houses per acre 4.4d, value of land per acre 15s 10.5d].

Ballyore. English: 13 Established Church, 7 Presbyterians, total 20, 5 families, 12 children; Irish: 17 Presbyterians, 35 Roman Catholics, total 52, 11 families, 33 children; Scotch: 3 Established Church, 42 Presbyterians, 4 Roman Catholics, 2 other Dissenters, total 51, 14 families, 26 children. [Insert addition: Value of houses per acre 7.8d, value of land per acre 17s 0.8d].

Ballyshasky. English: 7 Established Church, 16 Presbyterians, 18 Roman Catholics, total 41, 7 families, 20 children; Irish: 13 Presbyterians, 87 Roman Catholics, 1 other Dissenter, total 101, 21 families, 62 children; Scotch: 3 Presbyterians, 5 Roman Catholics, total 8, 2 families, 5 children. [Insert addition: Value of houses per acre 2s 9.7d, value of land per acre 14s 1.5d].

Bogagh. English: 7 Presbyterians, 8 other Dissenters, total 15, 3 families, 9 children; Irish: 16 Presbyterians, 4 Roman Catholics, total 20, 3 families, 15 children; Scotch: 34 Presbyterians, 2 other Dissenters, total 36, 7 families, 22 children. [Insert addition: Value of land per acre 13s 3.4d].

Bolies. Irish: 6 Established Church, 90 Roman Catholics, total 96, 18 families, 55 children; Scotch: 3 Roman Catholics, total 3, 1 family, 2 children. [Insert addition: Value of land per acre 17s 4.5d].

Brick-kilns. Irish: 24 Roman Catholics, total 24, 4 families, 16 children; Scotch: 6 Established Church, 5 Presbyterians, 6 other Dissenters, total 17, 3 families, 10 children. [Insert addition: Value of houses per acre 4d, value of land per acre 12s 9.[?3]d].

Cah. English: 11 Established Church, 19 Presbyterians, total 30, 5 families, 16 children; Irish: 9 other Dissenters, total 9, 1 family, 7 children; Scotch: 19 Presbyterians, 12 other Dissenters, total 31, 5 families, 18 children. [Insert addition: Value of houses per acre 3s 4d, value of land per acre 17s 8.6d].

Carn. English: 11 Presbyterians, total 11, 3 families, 5 children; Irish: 3 Presbyterians, 19 Roman Catholics, total 22, 4 families, 16 children; Scotch: 67 Presbyterians, 4 Roman Catholics, total 71, 14 families, 38 children. [Insert addition: Value of houses per acre 1s 4.4d, value of land per acre 13s 10.3d].

Carnafarn. English: 9 Presbyterians, total 9, 1 family, 7 children; Irish: 77 Roman Catholics, total 77, 13 families, 43 children; Scotch: 39 Presbyterians, 3 other Dissenters, total 42, 7 families, 35 children. [Insert addition: Value of land per acre 5s 5.3d].

Carrakeel. English: 22 Presbyterians, 5 Roman Catholics, total 27, 4 families, 17 children; Irish: 18 Roman Catholics, total 18, 3 families, 12 children; Scotch: 4 Roman Catholics, total 4, 1 family, 2 children. [Insert addition: Value of houses per acre 5.9d, value of land per acre 6s 10.1d].

Clampernow. Scotch: 18 Presbyterians, 1 other Dissenter, total 19, 3 families, 9 children. [Insert addition: Value of houses per acre 8.8d, value of land per acre 14s 5.7d].

Cloghore. English: 25 Presbyterians, total 25, 4 families, 15 children; Irish: 25 Roman Catholics, total 25, 5 families, 15 children; Scotch: 40 Presbyterians, 5 other Dissenters, total 45, 7 families, 28 children. [Insert addition: Value of houses per acre 4.8d, value of land per acre 13s 9d].

Clondermot. English: 5 Established Church, 4 Presbyterians, 1 Roman Catholic, total 10, 2 families, 5 children; Irish: 1 Established Church, 10 Presbyterians, 3 Roman Catholics, total 14, 4 families, 5 children; Scotch: 16 Established Church, 24 Presbyterians, 1 Roman Catholic, total 41, 4 families, 32 children. [Insert marginal note: Glebe in population return]. [Insert addition: Value of houses per acre 1s 1.2d, value of land per acre 11s 3.7d].

Clooney. English: 104 Established Church, 87 Presbyterians, 27 Roman Catholics, 28 other Dissenters, total 246, 43 families, 141 children; Irish: 4 Established Church, 9 Presbyterians, 323 Roman Catholics, 3 other Dissenters, total 380, 65 families, 222 children; Scotch: 75 Established Church, 155 Presbyterians, 23 Roman Catholics, 75 other Dissenters, total 328, 51 families, 220 children. [Insert addition: Value of houses per acre 24s 7.4d, value of land per acre 1 pound 2s 4.9d].

Corrody. English: 8 Established Church, 8 Presbyterians, 10 Roman Catholics, total 26, 11 families, 16 children; Irish: 3 Established Church, 55 Roman Catholics, total 58, 11 families, 38 children; Scotch: 9 Established Church, 22 Presbyterians, 2 Roman Catholics, total 33, 9 families, 18 children. [Insert addition: Value of land per acre 9s 6.6d].

Craigtown. English: 8 Presbyterians, total 8, 2 families, 4 children; Irish: 48 Presbyterians, 7 Roman Catholics, total 55, 11 families, 39 children; Scotch: 35 Presbyterians, 26 other Dissenters, total 61, 10 families, 31 children. [Insert addition: Value of land per acre 9s 6.8d].

Creevedonnel. English: 6 Established Church, 11 Presbyterians, total 17, 4 families, 6 children; Irish: 4 Presbyterians, 38 Roman Catholics, total 42, 9 families, 26 children; Scotch: 48 Presbyterians, 5 Roman Catholics, 1 other Dissenter, total

54, 11 families, 34 children. [Insert addition: Value of land per acre 4s 1.3d].

Cromkill. Irish: 36 Presbyterians, total 36, 6 families, 21 children; Scotch: 10 Presbyterians, total 10, 2 families, 6 children. [Insert addition: Value of land per acre 11s 10.3d].

Culkeeragh. English: 9 Established Church, 27 Presbyterians, 12 Roman Catholics, 4 other Dissenters, total 52, 8 families, 31 children; Irish: 20 Presbyterians, 12 Roman Catholics, total 32, 6 families, 16 children; Scotch: 27 Presbyterians, 3 Roman Catholics, total 30, 5 families, 15 children. [Insert addition: Value of houses per acre 4d, value of land per acre 12s 2d].

Curryfree. English: 48 Presbyterians, 10 other Dissenters, total 58, 10 families, 38 children; Irish: 31 Established Church, 25 Presbyterians, 39 Roman Catholics, total 95, 13 families, 29 children; Scotch: 4 Established Church, 46 Presbyterians, 7 other Dissenters, total 57, 17 families, 59 children. [Insert addition: Value of land per acre 4s 10.7d].

Currynierin. English: 11 Established Church, 2 Roman Catholics, total 13, 2 families, 1 child; Irish: 6 Roman Catholics, total 6, 1 family, 4 children; Scotch: 6 Presbyterians, 12 other Dissenters, total 18, 2 families, 13 children. [Insert addition: Value of houses per acre 3s 9.9d, value of land per acre 13s 7.4d].

Disertowen. Irish: 13 Presbyterians, 18 Roman Catholics, 14 other Dissenters, total 45, 7 families, 31 children; Scotch: 1 Established Church, 32 Presbyterians, 3 Roman Catholics, 11 other Dissenters, total 47, 8 families, 29 children. [Insert addition: Value of land per acre 12s 8.4d].

Drumagore. English: 17 Presbyterians, 18 Roman Catholics, 6 other Dissenters, total 31, 6 families, 14 children; Scotch: 35 Presbyterians, 3 Roman Catholics, 9 other Dissenters, total 47, 12 families, 27 children. [Insert addition: Value of houses per acre 3.3d, value of land per acre 13s 5.4d].

Dunhugh. English: 22 Presbyterians, total 22, 4 families, 14 children; Irish: 25 Roman Catholics, total 25, 4 families, 17 children; Scotch: 13 Established Church, 34 Presbyterians, total 47, 9 families, 30 children.

Drumconan. English: 17 Presbyterians, 2 other Dissenters, total 19, 5 families, 10 children; Irish: 4 Presbyterians, 23 Roman Catholics, total 27, 7 families, 15 children; Scotch: 9 Established Church, 47 Presbyterians, 4 Roman Catholics, 14 other Dissenters, total 74, 14 families, 43 children.

Drumahoe. English: 18 Established Church, 54 Presbyterians, 18 Roman Catholics, total 90,

16 families, 50 children; Irish: 19 Established Church, 27 Presbyterians, 95 Roman Catholics, total 141, 27 families, 94 children; Scotch: 27 Established Church, 85 Presbyterians, 8 Roman Catholics, 7 other Dissenters, total 127, 27 families, 86 children.

Edenreaghbeg. English: 2 Established Church, 7 Presbyterians, 3 Roman Catholics, 5 other Dissenters, total 17, 4 families, 9 children; Irish: 1 Presbyterian, 27 Roman Catholics, total 28, 9 families, 13 children; Scotch: 55 Presbyterians, total 55, 12 families, 35 children.

Edenreaghmore. English: 13 Presbyterians, 11 Roman Catholics, total 24, 5 families, 15 children; Irish: 15 Presbyterians, 52 Roman Catholics, total 67, 17 families, 35 children; Scotch: 30 Presbyterians, 6 Roman Catholics, total 36, 8 families, 21 children.

Enagh. English: 1 other Dissenter, total 1, 1 family; Irish: 9 Presbyterians, 20 Roman Catholics, total 29, 6 families, 16 children; Scotch: 32 Presbyterians, total 32, 5 families, 19 children.

Fincarn. English: 9 Established Church, 23 Presbyterians, total 32, 5 families, 21 children; Irish: 14 Established Church, 10 Presbyterians, 40 Roman Catholics, total 64, 11 families, 41 children; Scotch: 5 Established Church, 26 Presbyterians, 6 Roman Catholics, 3 other Dissenters, total 40, 7 families, 3 children.

Glenderowen. Irish: 4 Presbyterians, 7 Roman Catholics, total 11, 2 families, 7 children; Scotch: 11 Presbyterians, 11 Roman Catholics, total 22, 2 families, 18 children.

Glenkeen. English: 9 Established Church, 7 Presbyterians, 10 Roman Catholics, 10 other Dissenters, total 36, 8 families, 20 children; Irish: 12 Established Church, 1 Presbyterian, 179 Roman Catholics, 11 other Dissenters, total 203, 39 families, 139 children; Scotch: 15 Established Church, 26 Presbyterians, 12 Roman Catholics, total 53, 12 families, 3 children.

[Subtotals] English: 267 Established Church, 538 Presbyterians, 151 Roman Catholics, 86 other Dissenters, total 1,062, 195 families, 596 children; Irish: 156 Established Church, 368 Presbyterians, 1,823 Roman Catholics, 40 other Dissenters, total 2,387, 449 families, 1,462 children; Scotch: 284 Established Church, 1,390 Presbyterians, 130 Roman Catholics, 239 other Dissenters, total 2,043, 366 families, 1,257 children.

Gobnascale. English: 14 Established Church, 15 Presbyterians, 8 Roman Catholics, 10 other Dissenters, total 47, 10 families, 28 children; Irish: 3 Presbyterians, 45 Roman Catholics, 1 other Dissenter, total 49, 9 families, 32 children;

Scotch: 1 Established Church, 51 Presbyterians, total 52, 10 families, 24 children.

Gortica. English: 51 Presbyterians, 3 other Dissenters, total 54, 10 families, 35 children; Irish: 5 Presbyterians, 26 Roman Catholics, 5 other Dissenters, total 36, 9 families, 20 children; Scotch: 1 Established Church, 63 Presbyterians, 13 other Dissenters, total 77, 15 families, 49 children.

Gorticross. English: 13 Presbyterians, 2 Roman Catholics, total 15, 2 families, 9 children; Irish: 5 Presbyterians, 20 Roman Catholics, 8 other Dissenters, total 33, 6 families, 20 children; Scotch: 9 Established Church, 94 Presbyterians, 34 other Dissenters, total 137, 23 families, 67 children.

Gortgranagh. English: 24 Presbyterians, 1 other Dissenter, total 25, 3 families, 19 children; Irish: 4 Presbyterians, 49 Roman Catholics, total 53, 11 families, 35 children; Scotch: 67 Presbyterians, total 67, 10 families, 41 children.

Gortin. English: 11 Presbyterians, total 11, 2 families, 7 children; Irish: 15 Presbyterians, 6 Roman Catholics, 15 other Dissenters, total 36, 6 families, 24 children; Scotch: 21 Presbyterians, 3 Roman Catholics, 29 other Dissenters, total 53, 7 families, 35 children.

Gortinure. English: 10 Established Church, 3 Roman Catholics, total 13, 2 families, 9 children; Irish: 10 Presbyterians, 9 Roman Catholics, total 19, 3 families, 13 children; Scotch: 27 Presbyterians, total 27, 4 families, 19 children.

Gortnessy. English: 7 Established Church, 79 Presbyterians, 5 other Dissenters, total 91, 18 families, 64 children; Irish: 6 Established Church, 26 Presbyterians, 17 Roman Catholics, 2 other Dissenters, total 51, 12 families, 26 children; Scotch: 12 Established Church, 149 Presbyterians, 3 Roman Catholics, 26 other Dissenters, total 190, 34 families, 109 children.

Gortree. English: 28 Presbyterians, total 28, 5 families, 16 children; Irish: 15 Roman Catholics, 11 other Dissenters, total 26, 6 families, 14 children; Scotch: 76 Presbyterians, 2 other Dissenters, total 78, 14 families, 44 children.

Gransha. Irish: 17 Roman Catholics, total 17, 3 families, 11 children; Scotch: 6 Presbyterians, 6 Roman Catholics, total 12, 2 families, 7 children.

Kilfinnan. English: 10 Established Church, 6 Presbyterians, 9 Roman Catholics, total 25, 4 families, 16 children; Irish: 5 Presbyterians, 97 Roman Catholics, total 102, 19 families, 65 children; Scotch: 3 Established Church, 42 Presbyterians, 4 Roman Catholics, 16 other Dissenters, total 65, 12 families, 35 children.

Killymallaght. English: 10 Established Church, 25 Presbyterians, 4 other Dissenters, total 39, 9 families, 21 children; Irish: 25 Presbyterians, 11 other Dissenters, total 36, 7 families, 22 children; Scotch: 73 Presbyterians, 19 other Dissenters, total 92, 17 families, 44 children.

Kittybane. English: 14 Established Church, 18 Presbyterians, 1 other Dissenter, total 33, 7 families, 18 children; Irish: 2 Established Church, 13 Presbyterians, 11 Roman Catholics, 1 other Dissenter, total 27, 8 families, 13 children; Scotch: 7 Established Church, 19 Presbyterians, total 26, 5 families, 18 children.

Knockbrack. English: 9 Established Church, 7 Presbyterians, total 16, 2 families, 14 children; Irish: 1 Presbyterian, 72 Roman Catholics, 7 other Dissenters, total 80, 15 families, 55 children; Scotch: 58 Presbyterians, 3 Roman Catholics, 12 other Dissenters, total 73, 12 families, 29 children.

Lisaghmore. English: 6 Presbyterians, total 6, 1 family, 4 children; Irish: 44 Roman Catholics, total 44, 9 families, 29 children; Scotch: 5 Established Church, 64 Presbyterians, 6 Roman Catholics, 9 other Dissenters, total 84, 13 families, 55 children.

Lisahawley. Irish: 13 Roman Catholics, total 13, 3 families, 6 children; Scotch: 25 Presbyterians, 3 other Dissenters, total 28, 5 families, 18 children.

Lisdillon. English: 28 Established Church, 56 Presbyterians, 5 Roman Catholics, 11 other Dissenters, total 100, 20 families, 63 children; Irish: 8 Established Church, 18 Presbyterians, 208 Roman Catholics, 27 other Dissenters, total 261, 45 families, 173 children; Scotch: 50 Presbyterians, 30 Roman Catholics, 18 other Dissenters, total 98, 19 families, 54 children.

Lisglass. English: 10 Presbyterians, 7 other Dissenters, total 17, 2 families, 13 children; Irish: 4 Presbyterians, 87 Roman Catholics, total 91, 17 families, 57 children; Scotch: 6 Presbyterians, 22 other Dissenters, total 28, 5 families, 16 children.

Lismacarol. English: 7 Established Church, 69 Presbyterians, 9 other Dissenters, total 85, 15 families, 55 children; Irish: 1 Established Church, 15 Presbyterians, 133 Roman Catholics, total 149, 26 families, 99 children; Scotch: 24 Established Church, 78 Presbyterians, 11 Roman Catholics, 4 other Dissenters, total 117, 20 families, 69 children.

Lisnagelvin. English: 22 Presbyterians, 5 Roman Catholics, total 27, 4 families, 17 children; Irish: 18 Roman Catholics, total 18, 2 families, 12 children; Scotch: 1 Presbyterian, 4 Roman Catholics, total 5, 2 families, 2 children, [insert marginal note: Drumafife, Curraughean].

Lisneal. English: 5 Presbyterians, 6 other Dissenters, total 11, 2 families, 7 children; Irish: 7 Presbyterians, 7 Roman Catholics, total 14, 3 families, 8 children; Scotch: 3 Established Church,

37 Presbyterians, total 40, 9 families, 22 children.

Magheracanon. Irish: 6 Presbyterians, total 6, 2 families, 4 children; Scotch: 33 Presbyterians, 2 other Dissenters, total 35, 6 families, 21 children.

Managhbeg. English: 6 Presbyterians, total 6, 1 family, 4 children; Irish: 11 Roman Catholics, total 11, 3 families, 5 children; Scotch: 17 Presbyterians, 7 other Dissenters, total 24, 5 families, 16 children.

Managhmore. English: 10 Presbyterians, total 10, 2 families, 6 children; Irish: 8 Roman Catholics, total 8, 1 family, 6 children; Scotch: 46 Presbyterians, 16 other Dissenters, total 62, 10 families, 42 children.

Maydown. English: 4 Presbyterians, 4 other Dissenters, total 8, 2 families, 5 children; Irish: 8 Roman Catholics, total 8, 3 families, 2 children; Scotch: 30 Presbyterians, total 30, 4 families, 20 children.

Prehen. English: 5 Established Church, 4 Roman Catholics, 4 other Dissenters, total 13, 3 families, 7 children; Irish: 5 Presbyterians, 32 Roman Catholics, total 37, 7 families, 23 children; Scotch: 10 Established Church, 25 Presbyterians, 11 Roman Catholics, 3 other Dissenters, total 49, 6 families, 26 children.

Primity. English: 10 Established Church, 36 Presbyterians, total 46, 8 families, 29 children; Irish: 44 Roman Catholics, total 44, 9 families, 27 children; Scotch: 4 Established Church, 29 Presbyterians, 12 Roman Catholics, 8 other Dissenters, total 53, 9 families, 34 children.

Rossnagalliagh. English: 15 Established Church, 7 Presbyterians, 15 Roman Catholics, total 37, 8 families, 24 children; Irish: 2 Established Church, 21 Presbyterians, 61 Roman Catholics, 1 other Dissenter, total 85, 17 families, 48 children; Scotch: 3 Established Church, 9 Presbyterians, 5 Roman Catholics, 20 other Dissenters, total 37, 8 families, 23 children.

Stradreaghbeg. Irish: 7 Roman Catholics, total 7, 1 family, 6 children; Scotch: 3 Roman Catholics, 9 other Dissenters, total 12, 2 families, 7 children.

Stradreaghmore. English: 3 Presbyterians, 14 Roman Catholics, 4 other Dissenters, total 21, 5 families, 13 children; Irish: 10 Presbyterians, 60 Roman Catholics, total 70, 13 families, 42 children; Scotch: 3 Presbyterians, 6 Roman Catholics, 4 other Dissenters, total 13, 4 families, 8 children.

Tagharina. English: 10 Presbyterians, 2 other Dissenters, total 12, 3 families, 5 children; Scotch: 2 Presbyterians, 3 Roman Catholics, 14 other Dissenters, total 19, 4 families, 2 children.

Tamnymore. English: 16 Established Church, 7 Presbyterians, 18 Roman Catholics, total 41, 9 families, 26 children; Irish: 6 Established Church,

87 Roman Catholics, total 93, 16 families, 58 children; Scotch: 12 Presbyterians, 3 Roman Catholics, total 15, 3 families, 10 children.

Templetown. English: 1 Established Church, 15 other Dissenters, total 16, 3 families, 9 children; Irish: 6 Roman Catholics, 3 other Dissenters, total 9, 3 families, 3 children; Scotch: 9 Presbyterians, total 9, 1 family, 5 children.

Tirbracken. English: 16 Presbyterians, total 16, 3 families, 10 children; Irish: 2 Established Church, 2 Presbyterians, 8 Roman Catholics, total 12, 3 families, 6 children; Scotch: 17 Presbyterians, 1 Roman Catholic, 1 other Dissenter, total 19, 3 families, 11 children.

Tirkeeveny. English: 24 Presbyterians, total 24, 4 families, 16 children; Irish: 3 Presbyterians, 8 Roman Catholics, 12 other Dissenters, total 23, 5 families, 15 children; Scotch: 7 Established Church, 36 Presbyterians, 19 other Dissenters, total 62, 13 families, 37 children.

Tully Lower. English: 3 Established Church, 30 Presbyterians, total 33, 8 families, 17 children; Irish: 8 Established Church, 11 Presbyterians, 4 Roman Catholics, total 23, 5 families, 14 children; Scotch: 53 Presbyterians, total 53, 8 families, 37 children.

Tully Upper. English: 8 Presbyterians, 16 other Dissenters, total 24, 5 families, 13 children; Irish: 20 Presbyterians, total 20, 3 families, 14 children; Scotch: 14 Presbyterians, 1 other Dissenter, total 15, 3 families, 10 children.

Tullyally Lower. English: 20 Presbyterians, total 20, 3 families, 12 children; Irish: 5 Established Church, 10 Presbyterians, 16 Roman Catholics, total 31, 6 families, 19 children; Scotch: 43 Presbyterians, 2 Roman Catholics, 5 other Dissenters, total 50, 9 families, 27 children.

Tullyally Upper. English: 9 Presbyterians, total 9, 1 family, 7 children; Irish: 12 Roman Catholics, total 12, 2 families, 8 children; Scotch: 22 Presbyterians, total 22, 5 families, 10 children.

Warbleshinny. English: 9 Roman Catholics, total 9, 1 family, 7 children; Irish: 4 Established Church, 59 Roman Catholics, total 63, 16 families, 34 children; Scotch: 24 Presbyterians, 25 Roman Catholics, total 49, 8 families, 4 children.

[Totals] English: 426 Established Church, 1,193 Presbyterians, 243 Roman Catholics, 188 other Dissenters, total 2,050, 382 families, 1,221 children; Irish: 200 Established Church, 612 Presbyterians, 3,148 Roman Catholics, 144 other Dissenters, total 4,104, 783 families, 2,530 children; Scotch: 373 Established Church, 2,821 Presbyterians, 271 Roman Catholics, 555 other Dissenters, total 4,020, 715 families, 2,364 children.

Townland Statistics by Several Authors

NATURAL STATE

Extent of Townlands

Altnagelvin, 292 acres 2 roods 31 perches; Ardlough, 168 acres 1 rood 10 perches; Ardmore, 502 acres 2 roods 18 perches; Ardnabrocky, 256 acres 1 rood 19 perches.

Ballyoan, 299 acres 6 perches; Ballyore, 123 acres 1 roods 34 perches; Ballyshasky, 306 acres 2 roods 30 perches; Bogagh, 168 acres 1 rood 24 perches; Bolies, 154 acres 2 roods 32 perches; Brickkilns, 176 acres 3 roods 12 perches.

Cah, 277 acres 3 roods 26 perches; Carn, 214 acres 34 perches; Carnafarn, 342 acres 38 perches; Carrakeel, 383 acres 2 roods 8 perches; Clampernow, 96 acres 2 roods 8 perches; Cloghore, 182 acres 2 roods 19 perches; Clondermot, 301 acres 2 roods 31 perches; Clooney, 615 acres 3 roods 12 perches; Corrody, 192 acres 2 roods 24 perches; Craigtown, 244 acres 1 roods 36 perches; Creevedonnel, 353 acres 32 perches; Cromkill, 108 acres 3 roods; Culkeeragh, 555 acres 1 rood 39 perches; Curryfree, 622 acres 12 perches; Currynierin, 188 acres 3 roods 10 perches.

Disertowen, 193 acres 2 roods 6 perches; Drumagore, 218 acres 1 rood 5 perches; Drumahoe, 286 acres 1 rood 1 perch; Drumconan, 157 acres 1 rood 10 perches; Dunhugh, 138 acres 2 roods 35 perches.

Enagh, 184 acres 2 roods 33 perches; Fincarn, 273 acres 9 perches.

Glenderowen, 132 acres 1 rood 28 perches; Glenkeen, 369 acres 3 roods 30 perches; Gobnascale, 179 acres 2 roods 22 perches; Gortica, 264 acres 1 rood 6 perches; Gorticross, 470 acres 18 perches; Gortgranagh, 349 acres 1 rood; Gortin, 244 acres 2 roods 13 perches; Gortinure, 179 acres 3 roods 25 perches; Gortree, 328 acres 2 roods 33 perches; Gransha, 299 acres 23 perches.

Kilfinnan, 287 acres 29 perches; Killymallaght, 571 acres 2 roods 23 perches; Kittybane, 210 acres 2 roods 14 perches.

Lisaghmore, 295 acres 2 roods 7 perches; Lisahawley, 142 acres 1 rood 9 perches; Lisdillon, 1,590 acres 3 roods 26 perches; Lisglass, 554 acres 1 rood 18 perches; Lismacarol, 516 acres 3 roods 18 perches; Lisnagelvin, 36 acres 3 roods 27 perches; Lisneal, 153 acres 1 rood 32 perches.

Magheracanon, 115 acres 2 roods 22 perches; Managhbeg, 121 acres 3 roods 13 perches; Managhmore, 105 acres 3 roods 31 perches; Maydown, 167 acres 7 perches.

Prehen, 222 acres 35 perches; Primity, 189 acres 2 roods 15 perches; Rosnagalliagh, 201 acres 1 rood 3 perches; Stradreaghbeg, 57 acres 2 roods 30 perches; Stradreaghmore, 130 acres 2 roods 4 perches.

Tagharina, 120 acres 3 roods 9 perches; Tamnymore, 254 acres 3 roods 11 perches; Templetown, 184 acres 2 roods 25 perches; Tirbracken, 300 acres 6 roods 17 perches; Tirkeeveny, 224 acres 10 perches; Tully Lower, 195 acres 9 perches; Tully Upper, 161 acres 2 roods 17 perches; Tullyalley Lower, 238 acres 2 roods 27 perches; Tullyally Upper, 126 acres 3 roods 8 perches; Warbleshinny, 218 acres 2 roods 31 perches.

Townlands not within the liberties: map 14, Avish, 144 acres 1 rood 8 perches; Gortnafry, 723 acres 3 roods 22 perches; Edenreaghmore, 270 acres 28 perches; Edenreaghbeg 217 acres 4 perches.

Townlands in liberties 71, townlands not in liberties 4, [total] 75; [insert query: is this the number in the parish?].

Extent of municipal jurisdiction in Clondermot: Lisdillon, Glenkeen, Lismacarol, Gortica, Tirbracken, Managhmore, Managhbeg, Gortree, Gorticross, Carn, Ballyoan, Stradreaghbeg, Maydown, Carrakeel, Culkeeragh, Lisahawley, [total area] 5,888 acres 5 perches; add to the townlands in [parish?], 5,888 acres 5 perches plus 12,944 acres 1 rood 30 perches, [total] 18,832 acres 1 rood 35 perches.

Sheet 21 has 18; 22 has 5; 14 has 18; 13 has 1; 20 has 29.

Productive Economy Tables by Captain J.E. Portlock

PRODUCTIVE ECONOMY

Distribution of Land

[Table contains the following headings: name of townland, proprietor, chief tenure, acreage, aspect, ground levels, surface, soil, subsoil, proportions of land, supply of water, size of farms, manures used and distance from centre of townland, communications, markets].

1, Altnagelvin, proprietors Ponsonby and Alexander; 292 acres; aspect: north easterly, exposed to north easterly and easterly wind, sheltered from south westerly wind; ground levels: highest 310 feet, lowest Faughan, average 200 feet; surface: undulating, smooth; soil: moor, loam; subsoil: blue clay and till; land: pasture 19.4%, meadow 0.6%,

arable 80%; water supply: Faughan river, 2 brooks, 1 lake; farms: 7 under 10 acres, 8 under 20 acres, 2 under 50 acres; manures: farmyard dung 1 mile, bog, shells half a mile, lime, seaweed; communications: Faughan river, road from Derry to Claudy; markets: Derry, 1 mile.

2, Ardkill, proprietor Captain [crossed out: Skipton] Hagin, tenure 60 years and 3 lives; 565 acres 3 roods 23 perches; aspect: north easterly, exposed to northerly wind, sheltered from southerly wind; ground levels: highest 1,049 feet, lowest 96 feet, average 300 feet; surface: smooth, undulating, rough; soil: light clay, sand, moor; subsoil: red and blue till; land: bog waste 50%, pasture 9%, arable 41%; water supply: Faughan river, 2 brooks, 12 springs; farms: 12 under 10 acres, 2 under 50 acres, 2 above 50 acres; manures: farmyard dung, bog up to 1 mile, lime 4 miles; communications: Derry to Dungiven through Oaks; markets: Derry, 3 and a half miles.

3, Ardlough, proprietor church, tenure 21 years; 168 acres 1 rood 10 perches; aspect: easterly, exposed to easterly wind, sheltered from westerly wind; ground levels: highest 276 feet, lowest 61 feet, average 200 feet; surface: smooth, hilly, sloping; soil: loam, some moory; subsoil: blue and red till; land: bog waste 1.2%, pasture 12.5%, meadow 0.3%, arable 86%; water supply: Faughan river; farms: 4 under 50 acres; manures: farmyard dung, bog up to 1 mile, shells 2 miles, lime 6 miles; communications: Faughan, Derry to Dungiven; markets: Derry, 5 miles.

4, Ardmore, proprietors Grocers and Captain Skipton, tenure 31 years; 502 acres 2 roods 18 perches; aspect: north easterly, exposed to north easterly wind, sheltered from south westerly wind; ground levels: highest 900 feet, lowest Faughan, average 400 feet; surface: smooth, undulating, rocky; soil: light clay, heavy clay; subsoil: blue till; land: bog waste 40%, pasture 20%, meadow 1%, arable 39%; water supply: Faughan river, 2 brooks, 10 springs; farms: 1 under 10 acres, 3 under 20 acres, 5 under 50 acres, 1 above 50 acres; manures: farmyard dung, bog, shells 3 miles, lime 5 miles; communications: Faughan, Derry to Dungiven road through Oaks; markets: Derry, 3 and a half miles.

5, Ardnabrocky, proprietor Dean of Derry, tenure 21 years; 256 acres 1 rood 19 perches; aspect: south easterly, exposed to southerly wind, sheltered from north westerly wind; ground levels: highest 276 feet, lowest Faughan, average 150 feet; surface: smooth, undulating; soil: light clay; subsoil: red and white till; land: bog waste 2.3%, pasture 14.2%, meadow 2.3%, arable 81.2; water supply: Faughan river, 1 brook, 6 springs; farms: 1 under 20 acres, 6 under 50 acres, 1 above 50 acres; manures: farmyard dung, bog, lime 6 miles; communications: Faughan, coach road Derry to Dungiven; markets: Derry, 1 and a half miles.

6, Avish, proprietor Grocers, 144 acres 1 rood 8 perches; aspect: westerly, exposed to westerly wind, sheltered from easterly wind; ground levels: highest 558 feet, lowest 251 feet, average 400 feet; surface: undulating, below rocky; soil clay; subsoil rock; land: bog waste 10%, pasture 16.6%, arable 78.3%; water supply: 1 brook, 4 springs; farms: 1 under 10 acres, 2 under 20 acres, 4 under 50 acres; manures: farmyard dung, bog up to half a mile, shells 2 miles; communications: Drumahoe to Muff; markets: Derry, 4 miles.

7, Ballyoan, proprietor bishop, 299 acres [crossed out: 184 acres 2 roods 25 perches]; aspect: north westerly; ground levels: highest 186 feet, lowest 18 feet, average 100 feet; surface: ridgy, rocky; soil: light clay; subsoil: gravel; land: pasture 1.6%, arable 98.3%; water supply: Faughan river, 3 springs; farms: 1 under 10 acres, 3 under 20 acres, 3 under 50 acres; manures: farmyard dung, bog 1 mile, shells 2 and a half miles; communications: coach road, Derry to Newtownlimavady and conversely; markets: Derry, 2 and a quarter miles.

8, Ballyore, proprietors Ponsonby and Alexander, 123 acres 1 rood 34 perches; aspect: south westerly, exposed to southerly and westerly wind, sheltered from easterly and northerly wind; surface: smooth and undulating; soil: light clay; subsoil: gravel, blue clay; land: pasture 14.2%, arable 85.7%; water supply: Foyle river, 1 brook; farms: 1 under 10 acres, 4 under 20 acres, 1 under 50 acres; manures: farmyard dung, bog; communications: Foyle, road to Strabane with branch; markets: Derry, 3 and a quarter miles.

9, Ballyshasky, proprietor Captain Skipton, tenure 25 years; 306 acres 2 roods 30 perches; aspect: northerly, exposed to northerly wind, sheltered from south easterly wind; ground levels: lowest 160 feet; surface: smooth, undulating; soil: light clay, clay; subsoil: yellow till; land: bog waste 33%, pasture 20%, meadow 3.3%, arable 66.6%; water supply: Faughan river, 1 brook, 5 springs; farms: 4 under 10 acres, 2 under 20 acres, 3 under 50 acres, 1 above 50 acres; manures: farmyard dung up to 1 mile, bog 1 mile; lime 5 miles; communications: Faughan, Derry to Dungiven road; markets: Derry, 2 and a half miles.

10, Bogagh, proprietors Ponsonby and Alexander, no lease; 168 acres 1 rood 24 perches; surface: smooth and undulating; soil: clay; subsoil: blue and white clay; land: pasture 25%,

meadow 2%, arable 74.8%; water supply: 1 brook; farms: 4 under 10 acres, 4 under 20 acres, 1 above 50 acres; manures: farmyard dung, bog two-thirds of a mile, shells 2 miles; communications: Derry to Strabane road; markets: Derry, 4 miles.

11, Bolies, proprietor Colonel Knox, 154 acres 2 roods 32 perches; aspect: south westerly, exposed to westerly wind, sheltered from easterly wind; ground levels: highest 360 feet, lowest 16 feet, average 150 feet; surface: smooth, undulating, steep; soil: light clay, clay; subsoil: till, rock; land: pasture 8.3%, arable 91.6%; water supply: Foyle river, 3 brooks; farms: 10 under 10 acres; manures: farmyard dung, bog; communications: Foyle, Derry to Strabane, 2 roads; markets: Derry, 1 mile.

12, Brickkilns, proprietor Colonel Knox, 176 acres 3 roods 12 perches; aspect: south westerly, exposed to westerly and northerly wind, sheltered from easterly and southerly wind; ground levels: highest 340 feet, lowest Foyle, average 150 feet; surface: smooth, undulating but rough; soil: light clay; subsoil: till, rock; land: bog waste 12.5%, pasture 9%, arable 78%; water supply: Foyle river, 1 brook; farms: 3 under 10 acres, 1 under 20 acres; manures: farmyard dung, bog; communications: Foyle, Derry to Strabane, 2 roads; markets: Derry, 1 and a quarter miles.

13, Cah, proprietors church and L.J. Alexander, tenure 21 years; 277 acres 3 roods 26 perches; aspect: northerly, exposed to northerly wind, sheltered from southerly wind; ground levels: highest 177 feet, lowest Foyle, average 100 feet; surface: smooth, undulating; soil: clay, sand; subsoil: red till; land: pasture 11.1%, meadow 2.1%, arable 83.3%, water 2.1%; water supply: Foyle river, 1 brook, 8 springs; farms: 4 under 10 acres, 7 under 20 acres, 3 under 50 acres; manures: farmyard dung 1 and a half miles, bog 1 mile; communications: Foyle, Derry to Newtown, good; markets: Derry, 1 and a half miles.

14, Carn, proprietor church, tenure 21 years; 214 acres 34 perches; aspect: easterly, exposed to easterly and north easterly wind, sheltered from westerly wind; ground levels: highest 290 feet, lowest 21 feet, average 150 feet; surface: smooth, hilly, sloping; soil: light loam; subsoil: blue and red till; land: bog waste 1.8%, pasture 10%, arable 80%, water 2.8%; water supply: Faughan river, 4 springs; farms: 3 under 10 acres, 3 under 20 acres, 3 under 50 acres; manures: farmyard dung, bog up to 1 mile, shells 2 miles, lime 7 miles; communications: Faughan, branch road; markets: Derry, 2 miles.

15, Carnafarn, proprietors Ponsonby and Alexander, tenure 71 years and 3 lives; 622 acres 12 perches [insert alternative: 362 acres 38 perches];

aspect: north westerly, exposed to north westerly wind, sheltered from south easterly wind; ground levels: highest 900 feet, lowest 100 feet, average 500 feet; surface: smooth, rocky, mountain; soil: moor, light clay; subsoil: white till, rock; land: bog waste 33.3%, pasture 16.6%, arable 50%; water supply: 2 brooks; farms: 1 under 10 acres, 9 under 20 acres, 3 under 50 acres; manures: bog up to half a mile, lime 4 miles; communications: Dunnamanagh road; markets: Derry, 4 miles.

16, Carrakeel, proprietor Grocers, 555 acres 1 rood 39 perches; aspect: north easterly, exposed to easterly wind; ground levels: highest 52 feet, lowest 10 feet, average 25 feet; surface: smooth, level; soil: dark gravelly loam; subsoil: gravel; land: bog waste 16.6%, pasture 9%, meadow 4%, arable 66.6%; water supply: Faughan river, 1 lake, 1 spring; farm size, 1 under 20 acres, 2 under 50 acres, 2 above 50 acres; manures: farmyard dung, bog up to half a mile, shells up to 2 miles; communications: coach road, Derry to Newtown; markets: Derry, 4 and a half miles.

17, Clampernow, proprietors Ponsonby and Alexander, tenure 71 years and 3 lives; 96 acres 2 roods 8 perches; surface: smooth and undulating; soil: light clay; subsoil: red till; land: pasture 16.6%, arable 83.3%; water supply: Foyle river, 1 brook; farms: 2 under 50 acres; manures: farmyard dung, bog up to half a mile, shells 4 and a half miles, lime 4 and a half miles; communications: Foyle, road from Derry to Strabane; markets: Derry, 4 and a half miles.

18, Cloghore, proprietors Ponsonby and Alexander, tenure 71 years and 3 lives; 182 acres 2 roods 19 perches; aspect: northerly, exposed to north easterly and westerly wind, sheltered from southerly wind; ground levels: highest 298 feet, lowest 108 feet, average 190 feet; surface: smooth, sloping; soil: light clay, clay; subsoil: blue till; land: bog waste 11.1%, pasture 33.3%, arable 50%; water supply: 1 brook; farms: 5 under 20 acres, 3 under 50 acres; manures: farmyard dung, bog, lime 5 miles; communications: Derry to Strabane, branch road; markets: Derry, 3 miles.

19, Clondermot, proprietor Ash, 301 acres 2 roods 31 perches; aspect: easterly, exposed to easterly and southerly wind, sheltered from north westerly wind; ground levels: highest 726 feet, lowest 70 feet, average 300 feet; surface: smooth, undulating, rocky; soil: light clay, clay; subsoil: till, rock; land: bog waste 12.5%, pasture 14.2%, arable 80%; water supply: 1 brook; farms: 11 under 50 acres, 1 above 50 acres; manures: farmyard dung, bog; communications: Derry to Strabane, branch road; markets: Derry, 2 miles.

20, Clooney, proprietor Charles Ferguson Lecky, tenure 21 years; 615 acres 3 roods 12 perches; aspect: westerly, exposed to north westerly wind, sheltered from easterly wind; ground levels: highest 241 feet, lowest Foyle, average 100 feet; surface: smooth, undulating; soil: clay, gravel; subsoil: red till; land: pasture 14.2%, meadow 7.6%, arable 22.2%; water supply: Foyle river, 2 brooks, 6 springs; farms: 23 under 10 acres, 4 under 20 acres, 7 under 50 acres, 2 above 50 acres; manures: farmyard dung 1 mile, 1s 6d per ton in Derry; communications: Foyle, Derry to Newtown; markets: Derry, 1 mile.

21, Corrody, proprietor Colonel Knox, 192 acres 2 roods 24 perches; aspect: westerly, exposed to westerly and northerly wind, sheltered from easterly wind; ground levels: highest 620 feet, lowest 350 feet, average 480 feet; surface: smooth on side, rocky; soil: light clay; subsoil: yellow and blue till; land: bog waste 16.6%, pasture 10%, arable 62.5%; farms: 4 under 10 acres, 6 under 20 acres; manures: farmyard dung, bog; communications: Derry to Lisaghmore, branch road; markets: Derry, 1 mile.

22, Craigtown, proprietors Ponsonby and Alexander, 244 acres 1 rood 36 perches; aspect: easterly, exposed to northerly and easterly wind, sheltered from southerly wind; ground levels: highest 496 feet, lowest 139, average 250; surface: smooth, rough, stony; soil: light clay; subsoil: red till; land: bog waste 10%, pasture 12.5%, arable 75%; water supply: 1 brook; farms: 5 under 20 acres, 5 under 50 acres; manures: farmyard dung, bog; communications: Derry to Strabane; markets: Derry, 4 miles.

23, Creevedonnel, proprietors Ponsonby and Alexander, tenure 71 years and 3 lives; 353 acres 32 roods; aspect: north westerly, exposed to northerly and westerly wind, sheltered from south easterly wind; ground levels: highest 900 feet, lowest 100 feet, average 500 feet; surface: smooth lower, rocky upper; soil: moor, light clay; subsoil: white till, rock; land: bog waste 50%, pasture 12.5%, arable 34.7%; water supply: 3 brooks; farms: 7 under 10 acres, 2 under 20 acres, 2 above 50 acres; manures: farmyard dung up to half a mile, bog up to half a mile; communications: Dunnamanagh road; markets: Derry, 4 miles.

24, Cromkill: [blank].

25, Culkeeragh, proprietor Grocers, 551 acres 1 rood 39 perches; aspect: north easterly, exposed to northerly wind; ground levels: highest 142 feet, lowest Foyle, average 100 feet; surface: smooth, undulating; soil: clay; subsoil: clay; land: bog waste 7.1%, pasture 12.5%, meadow 0.9%, arable 79.5%; water supply: Foyle and Faughan rivers, 3 springs; farms: 12 under 20 acres; manures: farmyard dung up to 4 miles, bog up to half a mile, shells up to 2 miles; communications: Foyle and Faughan rivers, and 2 roads; markets: Derry, 4 to 4 and a half miles.

26, Curryfree, proprietors Ponsonby and Alexander, 622 acres 12 perches; aspect: north westerly, exposed to northerly and westerly wind, sheltered from south easterly wind; ground levels: highest 973 feet, lowest 140 feet, average 350 feet; surface: smooth, rough, rocky, mountain; soil: moor, light clay; subsoil: red till, rock; land: bog waste 50%, pasture 7.1%, arable 42.8%; water supply: 2 brooks; farms: 8 under 10 acres, 5 under 50 acres, 1 above 50 acres; manures: farmyard dung, bog up to half a mile; communications: 1 road, good; markets: Derry, 5 miles.

27, Currynierin, proprietors Grocers and W. Ash, no lease; [189?] acres 3 roods 20 perches; aspect: north easterly, exposed to north easterly wind, sheltered from southerly wind; ground levels: highest 250 feet, lowest Faughan; surface: smooth, undulating; soil: light loam, gravel; subsoil: red and blue till; land: bog waste 2%, pasture 5%, meadow 5%, arable 88%; water supply: Faughan river, 6 springs; farms: 2 under 20 acres, 1 above 50 acres; manures: farmyard dung, bog, lime 5 miles; communications: Faughan, Derry to Dungiven road; markets: Derry, 2 miles.

28, Disertowen, proprietors Ponsonby and Alexander, tenure 71 years and 3 lives; 195 acres 2 roods 6 perches; aspect: south easterly, exposed to north easterly and southerly wind, sheltered from westerly and north westerly wind; ground levels: highest 383 feet, lowest 140, average 240; surface: smooth, sloping; soil: light clay; subsoil: red and blue till; land: bog waste 3.3%, pastures 33.3%, arable 57.1%; water supply: 1 brook; farms: 2 under 20 acres, 3 under 50 acres; manures: farmyard, bog; communications: Derry to Strabane, branch road; markets: Derry, 5 miles.

29, Drumagore, proprietors Ponsonby and Alexander, tenure 71 years and 3 lives; 218 acres 1 rood 3 perches; ground levels: average 220 feet; surface: smooth, undulating, level; soil: light clay; subsoil: red till; land: bog waste 5%, pasture 12.5%, meadow 0.3%, arable 75%; water supply: 2 brooks; farms: 4 under 10 acres, 4 under 20 acres, 4 under 50 acres; manures: farmyard dung, bog two-thirds of a mile; communications: Derry to Strabane, main road; markets: Derry, 4 miles.

30, Drumahoe, proprietors Ponsonby and Alexander, tenure 71 years and 3 lives; 286 acres 1 rood 1 perch; aspect: south westerly, exposed to

westerly wind, sheltered from north easterly wind; ground levels: highest 256 feet, lowest Faughan; surface: smooth, undulating; soil: loam; subsoil: gravel, rock; land: bog waste 3.3%, pasture 20%, arable 66.6%; water supply: 2 brooks, 4 springs; farms: 9 under 10 acres, 4 under 20 acres, 2 under 50 acres; manures: farmyard dung, bog 2 miles; communications: Derry to Belfast, coach road; markets: Derry, 2 and a half miles.

31, Drumconan, proprietors Ponsonby and Alexander, tenure 71 years and 3 lives; 157 acres 1 rood 10 perches; aspect: south easterly, exposed to westerly and northerly wind, sheltered from easterly wind; ground levels: average 120 feet; surface: smooth, sloping; soil: light clay, clay; subsoil: gravelly rock; land: pasture 16%, arable 82.3%; water supply: 2 brooks; farms: 5 under 10 acres, 4 under 20 acres, 1 under 50 acres; manures: farmyard dung, bog; communications: Derry to Strabane, branch road; markets: Derry, 3 and a half miles.

32, Dunhugh, proprietors Ponsonby and Alexander, tenure 71 years and 3 lives; 138 acres 2 roods 35 perches; aspect: westerly, exposed to south westerly and northerly wind, sheltered from easterly wind; ground levels: highest 340, lowest Foyle, average 200 feet; surface: undulating, rocky, rough; soil: clay; subsoil: till, rock; land: bog waste 12.5%, pasture 25%, arable 62.5%; water supply: Foyle river; farms: 3 under 10 acres, 4 under 20 acres; manures: farmyard dung, bog; communications: Foyle, Derry to Strabane, 2 roads; markets: Derry, 2 and a half miles.

33, Edenreagh-beg: [blank].

34, Edenreagh-more: [blank].

35, Enagh, proprietor bishop, 184 acres 2 roods 33 perches; aspect: westerly, exposed to southerly and westerly wind; ground levels: highest 146 feet, lowest Foyle, average 70 feet; surface: smooth, undulating; soil: loam and gravel; subsoil: gravel and clay; land: bog waste 5%, pasture 15%, arable 80%; water supply: Foyle river, 1 lake; farms: 4 under 20 acres, 1 above 50 acres; manures: farmyard dung 2 and a half miles, bog half a mile; communications: Foyle, on public road; markets; Derry, 2 and a half miles.

36, Fincarn, proprietors Ponsonby and Alexander, 273 acres; aspect: westerly, exposed to all winds, sheltered from none; ground levels: highest 276 feet, lowest 61 feet, average 150 feet; surface: smooth and undulating; soil: clay; subsoil: rock; land: bog waste 7.7%, pasture 14.2%, meadow 1%, arable 78.5%; water supply: Faughan river, 1 brook, 8 springs; farms: 1 under 10 acres, 6 under 50 acres; manures: farmyard dung, bog 1 mile, shells 3 miles; communications: Faughan bridge to Muff road; markets: Derry, 3 miles.

37, Glenderowen, proprietors Ponsonby and Alexander, tenure 71 years and 3 lives; 132 acres 1 rood 28 perches; aspect: southerly, exposed to south westerly wind, sheltered from northerly wind; ground levels: highest 726 feet, lowest 108 feet, average 400 feet; surface: smooth, undulating, rough and rocky; soil: light clay; subsoil: till rock; land: bog waste 11.1%, pasture 20%, arable 66.6%; water supply: 1 brook; farms: 1 under 20 acres, 2 under 50 acres; manures: farmyard dung, bog; communications: Derry to Strabane, branch road; markets: Derry, 2 and a half miles.

38, Glenkeen, proprietor Captain Skipton, tenure 21 years; 396 acres 3 roods 30 perches; aspect: north easterly, exposed to northerly wind, sheltered from southerly and south easterly wind; ground levels: highest 689 feet, lowest 90 feet, average 300 feet; surface: smooth and undulating; soil: moor, light clay; subsoil: blue till, gravel; land: bog waste 7.6%, pasture 14.2%, arable 77.7%; water supply: Faughan river, 3 brooks, 7 springs; farms: 2 under 10 acres, 3 under 20 acres, 8 under 50 acres; manures: farmyard dung, bog, shells 3 miles, lime 4 miles; communications: Derry to Dungiven road; markets: Derry, 3 miles.

39, Gobnascale, proprietors Moore and Boyle, tenure 31 years and 3 lives; 179 acres 2 roods 22 perches; aspect: north westerly, exposed to northerly wind, sheltered from south easterly wind; ground levels: highest 493 feet, lowest Foyle, average 200 feet; surface: smooth, stony, rocky; soil: moor, light clay; subsoil: white till; land: bog waste 2%, pasture 16%, arable 82%; water supply: Foyle river, 3 springs; farms: 4 under 10 acres, 4 under 20 acres, 2 under 50 acres; manures: farmyard dung, bog half a mile; communications: Foyle, Derry to Claudy, Derry to Strabane; markets: Derry, half a mile.

40, Gortica: [blank].

41, Gorticross, proprietor Grocers, 470 acres 18 perches; aspect: westerly, exposed to westerly wind, sheltered from easterly wind; ground levels: highest 471 feet, lowest Faughan, average 200 feet; surface: undulating, rocky at top; soil: clay; subsoil: rock; land: pasture 20%, meadow 3.3%, arable 76.6%; water supply: Faughan river, 2 brooks, 3 springs; farms: 6 under 50 acres, 3 above 50 acres; manures: farmyard dung, bog 1 mile, shells 2 miles; communications: Faughan, Drumahoe to Muff road; markets: Derry, 3 and a half miles.

42, Gortgranagh, proprietors Grocers and G. Hoey, tenure 31 years and 3 lives; 349 acres 1 rood; aspect: westerly, exposed to south westerly wind, sheltered from easterly wind; ground levels: highest 986 feet, lowest 74 feet, average 300 feet; surface: smooth, undulating, rough; soil: light clay, moor; subsoil: till, red and blue rock; land: bog waste 25%, pasture 12.5%, meadow 1%, arable 61.5%; water supply: 2 brooks, 3 springs; farms: 2 under 20 acres, 4 under 50 acres, 1 above 50 acres; manures: farmyard dung up to half a mile, bog up to half a mile, lime 4 miles; communications: Derry to Strabane road, bad order; markets: Derry, 3 and a half miles.

43, Gortin, proprietors Moore, Boyle and Stevenson, tenure 21 years; 244 acres 2 roods 12 perches; aspect: westerly, flat; ground levels: highest 110 feet, lowest 73 feet, average 80 feet; surface: smooth, undulating, stony; soil: clay; subsoil: red and blue clay; land: bog waste 25%, pasture 25%, meadow 4.1%, arable 41.6%; water supply: 2 brooks; farms: 1 above 50 acres; manures: farmyard dung, bog, shells half a mile; communications: Derry to Strabane; markets: Derry, 3 and a half miles.

44, Gortinure, proprietor [blank] Ash, 179 acres 3 roods 25 perches; aspect: southerly, exposed to southerly and westerly wind, sheltered from northerly wind; ground levels: highest 620 feet, lowest 108 feet, average 200 feet; surface: smooth, undulating, rough, rocky; soil: light clay; subsoil: till, rock; land: bog waste 11.1%, pasture 11.1%, arable land 77.7%; water supply: 1 brook; farms: 1 under 20 acres, 1 under 50 acres, 1 above 50 acres; manures: farmyard dung, bog; communications: Derry to Strabane, branch road; markets: Derry, 3 miles.

45, Gortnessy: [blank].

46, Gortree, proprietor Grocers, 328 acres 2 roods 33 perches; aspect: westerly, exposed to westerly wind, sheltered from easterly wind; ground levels: highest 303 feet, lowest 40, average 300 feet; surface: smooth, rocky, hilly; soil: gravel, loam, clay; subsoil: rock, till; land: bog waste 6.2%, pasture 16.6%, meadow 0.6%, arable 75%; water supply: Faughan river, 3 brooks, 2 springs; farms: 3 under 20 acres, 2 under 50 acres, 1 above 50 acres; manures: farmyard dung, bog up to half a mile, shells 2 and a half miles; communications: Faughan, road to Muff; markets: Derry, 3 miles.

47, Gransha, proprietor Fishmongers, 299 acres 23 perches; aspect: westerly, exposed to northerly and westerly wind, sheltered from southerly and easterly wind; ground levels: highest 122 feet, lowest bay, average 50 feet; surface: smooth, undulating, flat, ridge; soil: gravel, light clay; subsoil: gravel, blue clay; land: pasture 14.2%, meadow 8%, arable 77.8%; water supply: Foyle,

1 brook, 1 lake; farms: 1 above 50 acres; manures: farmyard dung 2 miles, bog 1 and a half miles, shells 1 mile, lime 9 miles; communications: Derry, Newtownlimavady road, car road; markets: Derry, 2 miles.

48, Kilfinnan, proprietor Dean [of Derry], tenure 21 years; 287 acres 29 perches; aspect: exposed to all winds; ground levels: highest 277 feet, lowest 160 feet, average 250 feet; surface: smooth, rough; soil: light clay, clay; subsoil: red till, yellow clay; land: bog waste 20%, pasture 20%, arable 60%; water supply: 12 springs; farms: 1 under 20 acres, 5 under 50 acres, 1 above 50 acres; manures: farmyard dung up to 1 and a half miles, bog up to 1 mile, shells 1 and a half miles, lime 6 miles; communications: Derry to Dungiven, branch road; markets: Derry, 1 and a half miles.

49, Killymallaght, proprietors Moore and Boyle, no lease; 571 acres 2 roods 23 perches; aspect: north westerly, exposed to northerly and westerly wind, sheltered from southerly wind; ground levels: highest 803 feet, lowest 151 feet, average 350 feet; surface: undulating, smooth, rough; soil: clay, moor; subsoil: till, rock; water supply: 4 brooks; manures: farmyard dung, bog up to half a mile, lime 5 miles; communications: mountain road to Strabane; markets: Derry, 5 miles.

50, Kittybane, proprietors Ponsonby and Alexander, tenure 71 years and 3 lives; 210 acres 2 roods 14 perches; aspect: north westerly, exposed to south westerly and northerly wind, sheltered from easterly wind; ground levels: highest 701 feet, lowest Foyle, average 250 feet; surface: undulating, smooth, rough and rocky; soil: light clay; subsoil: till and rock; land: bog waste 20%, pasture 15%, arable 65%; water supply: Foyle river, 1 brook; farms: 4 under 20 acres, 4 under 50 acres; manures: farmyard dung and bog; communications: Foyle, Derry to Strabane, 2 roads; markets: Derry, 2 miles.

51, Knockbrack, proprietor Lord De Blacquiere, tenure 31 years; 488 acres 2 roods 7 perches; aspect: north easterly, exposed to northerly and north easterly wind, sheltered from south westerly wind; ground levels: highest 1,006 feet, lowest 115 feet, average 400 feet; surface: smooth, undulating, rough, mountain; soil: light clay, moor, gravel; subsoil: yellow till, gravel; land: bog waste 50%, pasture 10%, meadow 1.6%, arable 38.4%; water supply: Faughan river, 2 brooks, 8 springs; farms: 4 under 10 acres, 7 under 50 acres, 1 above 50 acres; manures: farmyard dung, bog half a mile, lime 4 and a half miles; communications: Derry to Dungiven road; markets: Derry, 5 miles.

52, Lisaghmore, proprietors Ponsonby and Alexander, 295 acres 2 roods 7 perches; aspect: east-

erly, exposed to easterly wind, sheltered from westerly wind; ground levels: highest 493, lowest 60 feet, average 300 feet; surface: smooth, undulating, sloping; soil: light clay; subsoil: clay and white rock; land: bog waste 2.5%, pasture 20%, meadow 2.5%, arable 57%; water supply: 3 brooks; farms: 3 under 20 acres, 3 under 50 acres, 1 above 50 acres; manures: farmyard dung, bog; communications: 1 road, 1 by-road; markets: Derry, 1 mile.

53, Lisahawley, proprietor bishop, 142 acres 1 rood 9 perches; aspect: north westerly, exposed to northerly and westerly wind, sheltered from south easterly wind; ground levels: highest 100 feet, lowest Foyle, average 50 feet; surface: smooth, undulating; soil: light clay: subsoil: gravelly clay; land: bog waste 10%, pasture 16.6%, meadow 1.4%, arable 72%; water supply: Foyle, 1 spring; farms: 3 under 50 acres; manures: farmyard dung, bog up to half a mile, shells up to half a mile; communications: Foyle, no internal roads; markets: Derry, 4 miles.

54, Lisdillon, proprietors Bond and Lynn, tenure 21 years and 3 lives; 1,590 acres 3 roods 26 perches; aspect: north easterly, exposed to northerly wind, sheltered from southerly wind; ground levels: highest 1,209 feet, lowest 178 feet, average 600 feet; surface: smooth, undulating, rough, mountain; soil: light clay, clay, moor; subsoil: blue clay, till; land: bog waste 60%, pasture 7.6%, meadow 1%, arable 30.7%; water supply: 3 brooks, 20 springs; farms: 45 under 10 acres, 1 under 20 acres, 3 under 50 acres; manures: farmyard dung, bog up to half a mile, lime 3 miles; communications: 2 mountain roads, Derry, Dungiven; markets: Derry, 3 and a half miles.

55, Lisglass, proprietors Grocers and G. May, tenure 31 years and 3 lives; 554 acres 1 rood 18 perches; aspect: westerly, exposed to westerly and northerly wind, sheltered from easterly and southerly wind; ground levels: highest 986 feet, lowest 80 feet, average 500 feet; surface: smooth, undulating, rough, rocky, mountain; soil: light clay, clay, moor; subsoil: red and blue till, rock; land: bog waste 60%, pasture 10%, arable 30%; water supply: 9 brooks; farms: 6 under 20 acres, 8 under 50 acres; manures: farmyard dung up to half a mile, bog up to half a mile; communications: by-road, bad; markets: Derry, 4 miles.

56, Lismacarol, proprietors Ponsonby and Alexander, tenure 71 years and 3 lives; 516 acres 3 roods 18 perches; aspect: westerly, exposed to westerly wind, sheltered from easterly wind; ground levels: highest 306 feet, lowest 167 feet, average 300 feet; surface: smooth, undulating; soil: light clay, gravel; subsoil: red and blue till, gravel; land: bog waste 1.9%, pasture 14.2%, arable 83.9%; water supply: Faughan, 1 brook, 4 springs; farms: 2 under 10 acres, 7 under 20 acres, 9 under 50 acres; manures: farmyard dung, bog half a mile, shells 3 miles, lime 5 and a half miles; communications: Faughan, from Derry to Dungiven through Oaks; markets: Derry, 4 miles.

57, Lisnagelvin: [blank].

58, Lisneal, proprietor churchlands, tenure 21 years; 153 acres 32 roods; aspect: southerly, exposed to southerly and northerly wind, sheltered from westerly wind; ground levels: highest 287 feet, lowest 70 feet, average 178 feet; surface: smooth, hilly, sloping; soil: light, loam; subsoil: blue and red till; land: pasture 16.6%, arable 83.3%; water supply: Faughan river, 1 brook, 5 springs; farms: 2 under 50 acres, 1 above 50; manures: farmyard dung, bog 1 mile, shells 2 miles, lime 6 miles; communications: Faughan, Derry to Newtownlimavady or Dungiven; markets: Derry, 2 miles.

59, Magheracanon, proprietors Ponsonby and Alexander, tenure 71 years and 3 lives; 115 acres 2 roods 32 perches; aspect: southerly, exposed to southerly wind, sheltered from north easterly wind; ground levels: highest 300 feet, lowest 200 feet, average 220 feet; surface: smooth, undulating; soil: light clay; subsoil: till, rock; land: bog waste 2.5%, pasture 16.6%, arable 80.9%; water supply: 1 brook, 1 mill; farms: 3 under 50 acres; manures: farmyard dung, bog; communications: Derry to Strabane, 2 or 3 internal branches; markets: Derry, 3 and a half miles.

60, Managh-beg, proprietor Grocers, 121 acres 3 roods 13 perches; aspect: south westerly, exposed to southerly and westerly wind, sheltered from northerly and easterly wind; ground levels: highest 515 feet, lowest 80 feet, average 300 feet; surface: smooth, undulating; soil: clay; subsoil: rock; land: bog waste 5%, pasture 14.2%, arable 78.5%; water supply: 1 brook: farms: 2 under 20 acres, 1 above 50 acres; manures: farmyard dung, bog up to half a mile, shells 3 miles; communications: from Faughan bridge to Muff; markets: Derry, 3 miles.

61, Managh-more, proprietor Grocers, 105 acres 3 roods 31 perches; aspect: southerly, exposed to southerly wind, sheltered from northerly wind; ground levels: highest 423 feet, lowest 200 feet, average 200; surface: smooth, undulating; soil: clay; subsoil: rock; land: bog waste 2.8%, pasture 7.6%, meadow 0.2%, arable 88.4%; water supply: 1 brook; farms: 2 under 20 acres, 1 under 50 acres; manures: farmyard dung, bog up to half a mile, shells 3 miles; communications: internal branch roads; markets: Derry, 3 miles.

62, Maydown, proprietor Grocers, 167 acres 7 perches; aspect: flat, exposed to southerly and easterly winds; ground levels: highest 60, lowest 20, average 40 feet; surface: level; soil: gravelly, loam; subsoil: gravel; land: bog waste 12.5%, pasture 16.6%, meadow 6.2%, arable 62.5%; water supply: Faughan river, 1 lake; farms: 1 over 50 acres; manures: farmyard dung, bog half a mile, shells 2 miles, lime 8 miles; communications: Faughan, Derry to Newtownlimavady, branch to Muff; markets: Derry, 4 miles.

63, Prehen, proprietor Colonel Knox, 222 acres 35 perches; aspect: westerly, exposed to south westerly and northerly wind, sheltered from easterly wind; ground levels: highest 353 feet, lowest 16 feet, average 200 feet; surface: smooth, undulating; soil: clay; subsoil: till; land: bog waste 25%, pasture 25%, meadow 14.2%, arable 35.7%; water supply: Foyle, 1 brook; farms: 4 under 10 acres, 2 under 20 acres; manures: farmyard dung; communications: Derry to Strabane, upper and lower; markets: Derry, 2 miles.

64, Primity, proprietors Ponsonby and Alexander, tenure 71 years and 3 lives; 189 acres 2 roods; aspect: southerly, exposed to southerly and westerly wind, sheltered from north easterly wind; ground levels: highest 300 feet, lowest Foyle, average 100 feet; surface: smooth, undulating; soil: light clay; subsoil: till and rock; land: bog waste 5%, pasture 14.2%, arable 80.8%; water supply: 2 brooks, 1 mill-pond; farms: 9 under 10 acres, 3 under 20 acres, 1 under 50 acres; manures: farmyard dung, bog; communications: Foyle, Derry to Strabane; markets: Derry, 2 and a half miles.

65, Rossnagalliagh, proprietor Goldsmiths, tenure 31 years; 201 acres 1 rood 3 perches; surface: smooth, undulating; soil: light loam; subsoil: blue and white clay; land: bog waste 4%, pasture 20%, arable 76%; water supply: 2 brooks, 2 springs; farms: 7 under 10 acres, 8 under 20 acres, 2 under 50 acres; manures: farmyard dung, bog 1 mile; communications: Foyle, Derry to Strabane and Dublin; markets: Derry, 4 miles.

66, Stradreagh-beg, proprietor Grocers, 57 acres 2 roods 30 perches; aspect: northerly, exposed to all winds; surface: smooth, undulating; soil: gravelly clay; subsoil: gravel; water supply: Faughan river, 1 lake; farms: 1 under 50 acres, 1 above 50 acres; manures: farmyard dung, bog up to half a mile, shells 1 mile; communications: Faughan, Derry to Newtownlimavady; markets: Derry, 2 miles.

67, Stradreagh-more, proprietor [blank] Smyth, 130 acres 2 roods 4 perches; aspect: northerly, exposed to all winds; surface: smooth, undulating; soil: light clay; subsoil: gravel; land: bog waste 5%, pasture 5%, arable 75%; water supply: 2 lakes; farm size: 5 under 50 acres; manures: farmyard dung, bog up to half a mile, shells 1 and a quarter miles; communications: Derry to Newtownlimavady; markets: Derry, 2 and a quarter miles.

68, Tagharina, proprietors Ponsonby and Alexander, tenure 71 years and 3 lives; 120 acres 3 roods 9 perches; aspect: northerly; ground levels: highest 265 feet, lowest 73 feet, average 120 feet; surface: smooth, undulating; soil: light clay; subsoil: red till; land: bog waste 2.5%, pasture 20%, arable 75%; water supply: 1 brook; farms: 1 under 10 acres, 3 under 50 acres; manures: farmyard dung, bog two-thirds of a mile; communications: Derry to Strabane, inland; markets: Derry, 4 miles.

69, Tamnymore, proprietors Skipton, Brown and Irvine, tenure 31 years; 254 acres 3 roods 11 perches; aspect: north westerly, exposed to northerly wind, sheltered from easterly and southerly wind; ground levels: highest 498 feet, lowest 16 feet, average 300 feet; surface: smooth, undulating, steep, rough at top; soil: clay; subsoil: gravel and rock; land: bog waste 5.8%, pasture 7.1%, arable 85.7%; water supply: Foyle, 2 brooks; farms: 17 under 10 acres, 4 under 20 acres; manures: farmyard dung, bog; communications: Derry to Strabane, upper and lower; markets: Derry, half a mile.

70, Templetown, proprietor bishop, 184 acres 7 roods 25 perches; aspect: north westerly; ground levels: highest 53 feet, lowest Enagh Lough, average 30 to 40 feet; surface: ridgy, undulating; soil: light clay; subsoil: gravel; land: bog waste 11.1%, pasture 16.6%, arable 60%, water 20%; water supply: 2 lakes; farms: 2 under 20 acres, 2 under 50 acres; manures: farmyard dung, bog, shells 1 mile, lime 8 miles; communications: Derry to Newtownlimavady, branch; markets: Derry, 2 and a half miles.

71, Tirbracken: [blank].

72, Tirkeeveny, proprietors Ponsonby and Alexander, tenure 71 years and 3 lives; 227 acres 10 perches; aspect: westerly, exposed to westerly wind, sheltered from easterly wind; ground levels: highest 735 feet, lowest 139 feet, average 350 feet; surface: undulating, smooth below, rough above; soil: light clay; subsoil: red till, rock; land: bog waste 25%, pasture 10%, arable 65%; water supply: 1 brook; farms: 4 under 10 acres, 6 under 2 acres, 2 under 50 acres; manures: farmyard dung, bog 10 miles; communications: mountain road towards Strabane; markets: Derry, 5 miles.

73, Tully Lower, proprietors Ponsonby and Alexander, tenure 71 years and 3 lives; 195 acres 9 perches; surface: smooth and undulating; soil: light clay; subsoil: red till; land: bog waste 5%,

pasture 25%, meadow 0.2%, arable 69.8%; water supply: Foyle river, 1 brook; farms: 1 under 10 acres, 7 under 20 acres, 2 under 50 acres; manures: farmyard dung, bog up to half a mile, shells 4 and a quarter miles, lime 4 and a quarter miles; communications: Foyle, Derry to Strabane and Dublin; markets: Derry, 4 and a quarter miles.

74, Tully Upper, proprietors Ponsonby and Alexander, tenure 71 years and 3 lives; 161 acres 2 roods 17 perches; aspect: westerly, exposed to westerly and northerly wind, sheltered from south easterly wind; ground levels: highest 300 feet; surface: smooth and undulating; soil: light clay; subsoil: red till; land: bog waste 5%, pasture 16.6%, arable 38.3%; water supply: 1 brook; farms: 3 under 10 acres, 1 under 20 acres, 3 under 50 acres; manures: farmyard dung, bog three-quarters of a mile, shells 1 mile; communications: Derry to Strabane and Dublin; markets: Derry, 4 and a half miles.

75, Tullyally Lower, proprietor Lord De Blacquiere, tenure 31 years and 3 lives; 238 acres 2 roods 27 perches; aspect: north westerly, exposed to northerly and south westerly wind, sheltered from easterly wind; surface: smooth, sloping, undulating; soil: light loam, gravel, 12 to 13 feet deep; subsoil: red and blue till; land: bog waste 4.1%, pasture 25%, meadow 10%, arable 22.3%; water supply: Faughan river, 2 brooks; farms: 2 under 20 acres, 3 under 50 acres, 1 over 50 acres; manures: farmyard dung, bog; communications: Derry to Dungiven through Oaks, branch to Strabane; markets: Derry, 1 mile.

76, Tullyally Upper, proprietor Lord De Blacquiere, tenure 31 years and 3 lives; 126 acres 3 roods 8 perches; aspect: westerly by northerly, exposed to northerly and south westerly wind, sheltered from easterly wind; ground levels: highest 310 feet, lowest 70 feet, average 200 feet; surface: smooth, undulating, sloping strongly; soil: light clay, gravel; subsoil: red and blue till, gravel; land: bog waste 10%, pasture 16.6%, meadow 3.1%, arable 70.3%; water supply: 1 brook, 1 spring; farms: 1 over 50 acres; manures: farmyard dung; communications: Derry to Dungiven, branch of, good; markets: Derry, 2 and a half miles.

77, Warbleshinny, proprietors Ponsonby and Alexander, tenure 71 years and 3 lives; 218 acres 2 roods 31 perches; aspect: south easterly, exposed to southerly and easterly, and south westerly wind, sheltered from northerly and westerly wind; ground levels: highest 726 feet, lowest 80 feet, average 200 feet; surface: smooth and undulating, rough, rocky; soil: light clay, clay; subsoil: till, rock; land: bog waste 14.2%, pasture 20%, meadow 1.3%, arable 60%; water supply: 1 lake; farms: 4 under 10 acres, 1 under 20 acres, 2 under 50 acres, 1 above 50 acres; manures: farmyard dung, bog; communications: Derry to Strabane through Glenderowen [?]; markets: Derry, 2 and a quarter miles.

Cultivation, its Mode and Results

[Table contains the following headings: name of townland, depth of soil, quantity, in proportions, of manures per acre, rotation of crops, quantity of seed and produce per acre, woods, livestock].

1, Altnagelvin, soil: depth from 6 to 10 inches; manures, quantity per acre: farmyard dung 1,200, bog 1,200, shells 180, compost 2,400; rotation of crops: 1st rotation, oats, flax, oats, pasture; 2nd rotation, potatoes, wheat, oats, pasture; wheat: 3 and a half bushels seed, 35 bushels produce; 6 bushels seed, 50 bushels produce; oats: 6 bushels seed, 40 bushels produce; [seed blank], 64 bushels produce; potatoes: 32 bushels seed, 280 bushels produce; [seed blank], 560 bushels produce; flax: 21 and four-fifth gallons seed, 4 lbs produce; 3 and a half gallons seed, 6 lbs produce; [insert marginal note: hay, 2 and a half to 3 tons]; woods: plantations 339 [acres?], alder, larch, Scotch, 1810 to 1820; livestock: 18 horses, 24 cattle, 2 sheep, 3 hogs, 149 poultry.

2, Ardkill, soil: depth from 6 to 18 inches; rotation of crops: oats, flax, potatoes, wheat, clover soil, pasture; wheat: 3 and a half bushels seed, 50 bushels produce; [seed blank], 60 bushels produce; oats: 4 and a half bushels seed, 40 bushels produce; 6 bushels seed, 64 bushels produce; potatoes: 26 bushels seed, 300 bushels produce; 32 bushels seed, 500 bushels produce; flax: 3 gallons seed, 5 lbs produce; 3 and a half gallons seed, 6 lbs produce; livestock: 26 horses, 72 cattle, 2 sheep, 9 hogs, 300 poultry.

3, Ardlough, soil: depth from 6 to 12 inches; rotation of crops: oats, flax, oats, potatoes, wheat, clover soil, pasture; wheat: 3 and a half bushels seed, 35 bushels produce; 4 bushels seed, 50 bushels produce; oats: 5 and one-third bushels seed, 32 bushels produce; 6 and a half bushels seed, 64 bushels produce; potatoes: 24 bushels seed, 200 bushels produce; 30 bushels seed, 300 bushels produce; livestock: 9 horses, 28 cattle, 12 sheep, 7 hogs, 136 poultry.

4, Ardmore, soil: depth from 3 to 16 inches; manures, quantity per acre: farmyard 800, bog 1,600, shells 180, lime 100, kelp 120; rotation of crops: oats, flax, oats, potatoes, oats, barley, pasture; [insert marginal query: 6th, order of crops?];

barley: 3 and three-quarter bushels seed, 42 bushels produce; [seed blank], 54 bushels produce; oats: 4 and a half bushels seed, 32 bushels produce; 6 and a half bushels seed, 64 bushels produce; potatoes: 30 bushels seed, 300 bushels produce; 32 bushels seed, 360 bushels produce; flax: 3 gallons seed, 4 lbs produce; 3 and a half gallons seed, 6 lbs produce; livestock: 33 horses, 1 ass, 110 cattle, 213 sheep, 3 goats, 19 hogs, 195 poultry.

5, Ardnabrocky, soil: depth from 8 to 18 inches; manures, quantity per acre: farmyard 800, bog 1,600, lime 100; rotation of crops: oats, flax, potatoes, wheat, hay, pasture; wheat: 3 and a half bushels seed, 40 bushels produce; [seed blank], 50 bushels produce; oats: 6 bushels seed, 48 bushels produce; 6 and a half bushels seed, 64 bushels produce; potatoes: 30 bushels seed, 300 bushels produce; 32 bushels seed, 480 bushels produce; flax: 3 gallons seed, 5 lbs produce; 3 and half gallons seed, 6 and a half lbs produce; [insert note: hay, 2 and a half to 3 tons]; livestock: 18 horses, 62 cattle, 19 sheep, 7 hogs, 79 poultry.

6, Avish, soil: depth from 8 to 16 inches; manures, quantity per acre: farmyard 800, bog, 1,600, compost 2,400; rotation of crops: potatoes, oats, flax, oats; oats: 6 and a half bushels seed, 32 bushels produce; 8 bushels seed, 56 bushels produce; potatoes: 26 bushels seed, 240 bushels produce; 30 bushels seed, 380 bushels produce; flax: 2 and two-third gallons seed, 4 lbs produce; 3 and a half gallons seed, 5 lbs produce; woods: a few trees; livestock: 8 horses, 22 cattle, 1 goat, 133 poultry.

7, Ballyoan, soil: depth 12 inches; manures, quantity per acre: farmyard 800, bog 1,600; rotation of crops: oats, potatoes, wheat, flax, oats, pasture; wheat: 4 bushels seed, 25 bushels produce; [seed blank], 50 bushels produce; oats: 6 and a half bushels seed, 30 bushels produce; 8 bushels seed, 56 bushels produce; potatoes: 30 bushels seed, 240 bushels produce; 32 bushels seed, 360 bushels produce; flax: 2 and two-third gallons seed, 3 lbs produce; 3 and a half gallons seed, 5 lbs produce; woods: a few trees; livestock: 25 horses, 27 cattle, 6 hogs, 153 poultry.

8, Ballyore, soil: depth from 6 to 12 inches; manures, quantity per acre: farmyard 800, bog 1,600, compost 2,400; rotation of crops: oats, flax, oats, potatoes, wheat, pasture; wheat: 3 and three-quarter bushels seed, 35 bushels produce; [seed blank], 50 bushels produce; oats: 7 bushels seed, 50 bushels produce; [seed blank], 56 bushels produce; potatoes: 32 bushels seed, 240 bushels produce; [seed blank], 360 bushels produce; flax: 2 and three-twelfth gallons seed, 5 lbs produce; 3 and a half gallons seed, 6 lbs produce;

woods: some trees; livestock: 10 horses, 3 asses, 11 cattle, 5 sheep, 1 hog, 99 poultry.

9, Ballyshasky, soil: depth from 8 to 14 inches; manures, quantity per acre: farmyard 800, bog 1,600, lime 60 to 80; rotation of crops: oats, flax, oats, potatoes, oats, pasture, pasture, pasture; oats: 6 bushels seed, 40 bushels produce; 7 and one-third bushels seed, 64 bushels produce; potatoes: 25 bushels seed, 230 bushels produce; 30 bushels seed, 240 bushels produce; flax: 3 gallons seed, 4 lbs produce; 3 and a half gallons seed, 6 lbs produce; woods: beech, ash, elm, some 100 and some 7 years; livestock: 16 horses, 46 cattle, 6 sheep, 1 hog, 112 poultry.

10, Bogagh, soil: depth from 6 to 15 inches; manures, quantity per acre: farmyard 800, bog 1,600, shells 240, compost 2,400; rotation of crops: oats, flax, potatoes, oats, oats, pasture; oats: 6 bushels seed, 40 bushels produce; [seed blank], 72 bushels produce; potatoes: 30 bushels seed, 280 bushels produce; [seed blank], 350 bushels produce; flax: 3 gallons seed, 4 lbs produce; 3 and a half gallons seed, 5 lbs produce; woods: a few trees, sycamore and alder; livestock: 11 horses, 36 cattle, 8 sheep, 3 hogs, 130 poultry.

11, Bolies, soil: depth from 6 to 12 inches; manures, quantity per acre: farmyard 800, bog 1,600, compost 2,400; rotation of crops: potatoes, oats, oats, potatoes; oats: 7 and a half bushels seed, 32 bushels produce; [seed blank], 48 bushels produce; potatoes: 26 bushels seed, 240 bushels produce; 30 bushels seed, 380 bushels produce; flax: 2 and four-fifth gallons seed, 4 lbs produce; 3 and a half gallons seed, 5 lbs produce; no woods, nor plantation; livestock: 10 horses, 1 ass, 19 cattle, 2 goats, 94 poultry.

12, Brickkilns, soil: depth from 8 to 10 inches; manures, quantity per acre: farmyard 800, bog 1,600, compost 2,400; rotation of crops: oats, flax, potatoes, oats, clover soil, pasture; oats: 6 and a half bushels seed, 32 bushels produce; 7 and a half bushels seed, 48 bushels produce; potatoes: 26 bushels seed, 240 bushels produce; 30 bushels seed, 380 bushels produce; flax: 2 and four-fifth gallons seed, 4 lbs produce; 3 and a half gallons seed, 5 lbs produce; woods: some old beech; livestock: 7 horses, 20 cattle, 1 hog, 36 poultry.

13, Cah, soil: depth from 16 to 20 inches; manures, quantity per acre: farmyard 1,000; rotation of crops: oats, flax, oats, potatoes, wheat, clover soil, pasture; wheat: 3 and a half bushels seed, 45 bushels produce; 4 bushels seed, 50 bushels produce; oats: 5 and one-third bushels seed, 40 bushels produce; 6 and a half bushels seed, 60 bushels produce; potatoes: 30 bushels

seed, 280 bushels produce; 32 bushels seed, 400 bushels produce; flax: 2 and one-third gallons seed, 5 and a half lbs produce; 3 and a half gallons seed, 6 lbs produce; woods: plantation and forest trees; livestock: 15 horses, 1 ass, 33 cattle, 6 sheep, 1 goat, 10 hogs, 181 poultry.

14, Carn, soil: depth from 6 to 10 inches; rotation of crops: oats, flax, oats, potatoes, wheat, clover soil, pasture; wheat: 3 bushels seed, 40 bushels produce; 3 and a half bushels seed, 50 bushels produce; oats: 5 and one-third bushels seed, 32 bushels produce; 6 and a half bushels seed, 56 bushels produce; potatoes: 30 bushels seed, 300 bushels produce; 36 bushels seed, 380 bushels produce; flax: 3 gallons seed, 4 lbs produce; 3 and a half gallons seed, 6 and a half lbs produce; woods: a few trees; livestock: 6 horses, 16 cattle, 1 goat, 2 hogs, 68 poultry.

15, Carnafarn, soil: depth from 6 to 12 inches; manures, quantity per acre: farmyard 800, bog 1,600, lime 80; rotation of crops: oats, flax, oats, potatoes, oats, flax, pasture; oats: 6 and a half bushels seed, 32 bushels produce; 8 bushels seed, 56 bushels produce; potatoes: 28 bushels seed, 280 bushels produce; 32 bushels seed, 420 bushels produce; flax: 2 and four-fifth gallons seed, 3 and a half gallons seed; woods: a few trees; livestock: 16 horses, 44 cattle, 7 sheep, 2 goats, 174 poultry.

16, Carrakeel, soil: depth from 3 to 8 inches; manures, quantity per acre: farmyard 800, bog 1,600, shells 300; rotation of crops: barley, potatoes, flax, wheat, oats, clover soil, pasture; wheat: 3 and a half bushels seed, 30 bushels produce; [seed blank], 50 bushels produce; oats: 6 bushels seed, 36 bushels produce; 6 and a half bushels seed, 48 bushels produce; potatoes: 30 bushels seed, 280 bushels produce; 32 bushels seed, 400 bushels produce; flax: 2 and four-fifth gallons seed, 3 lbs produce; 3 and a half gallons seed, 6 lbs produce; woods: plantation, 4 or 5 years; livestock: 15 horses, 32 cattle, 34 sheep, 6 hogs, 198 poultry.

17, Clampernow, soil: depth from 7 to 11 inches; manures, quantity per acre: farmyard 1,200, bog 1,200, compost 2,400; rotation of crops: oats, flax, oats, potatoes, oats, clover soil; wheat: 3 and a half bushels seed, 40 bushels produce; [seed blank], 50 bushels produce; oats: 5 and a half bushels seed, 48 bushels produce; 6 and a half bushels seed, 64 bushels produce; potatoes: 28 bushels seed, 260 bushels produce; 32 bushels seed, 560 bushels produce; flax: 2 and one-fifth gallons seed, 4 lbs produce; 3 and a half gallons seed, 6 lbs produce; woods: a few oak, ash and alder, about 40 years; livestock: 5 horses, 20 cattle, 6 hogs, 65 poultry.

18, Cloghore, soil: depth from 3 or 9 to 12 inches; manures, quantity per acre: farmyard 800, bog 1,600, lime 100; rotation of crops: oats, flax, potatoes, barley, pasture; wheat: 4 bushels seed, 35 bushels produce; [seed blank], 45 bushels produce; oats: 6 bushels seed, 32 bushels produce; 6 and a half bushels seed, 60 bushels produce; potatoes: 28 bushels seed, 200 bushels produce; 30 bushels seed, 350 bushels produce; flax: 2 and four-fifth gallons seed, 4 lbs produce; 3 and a half gallons seed, 6 lbs produce; woods: a few trees; livestock: 16 horses, 36 cattle, 10 sheep, 3 goats, 2 hogs, 134 poultry.

19, Clondermot, soil: depth from 3 or 9 to 14 inches; manures, quantity per acre: farmyard 800, bog 1,600, compost 2,400; rotation of crops: oats, flax, oats, potatoes, wheat, clover soil; wheat: 3 and a half bushels seed, 30 bushels produce; [seed blank], 50 bushels produce; oats: 6 bushels seed, 32 bushels produce; 8 bushels seed, 56 bushels produce; potatoes: 28 bushels seed, 240 bushels produce; 32 bushels seed, 380 bushels produce; woods: larch, alder, fir, 1815; livestock: 13 horses, 53 cattle, 8 sheep, 2 hogs, 217 poultry.

20, Clooney, soil: depth from 9 to 14 inches; manures, quantity per acre: farmyard 1,000, bog 1,600; rotation of crops: oats, potatoes, barley or wheat, clover seed, pasture; wheat: 3 and a half bushels seed, 45 bushels produce; 4 bushels seed, 55 bushels produce; barley: 4 bushels seed, 48 bushels produce; [seed blank], 60 bushels produce; oats: 5 bushels seed, 36 bushels produce; 7 and a half bushels seed, 60 bushels produce; potatoes: 28 bushels seed, 280 bushels produce; 30 bushels seed, 400 bushels produce; flax: 2 and four-fifth gallons seed, 4 lbs produce; 3 and a half gallons seed, 6 lbs produce; woods: plantations of various kinds; livestock: 41 horses, 1 ass, 96 cattle, 68 sheep, 2 goats, 22 hogs, 276 poultry.

21, Corrody, soil: depth from 6 to 10 inches; manures, quantity per acre: farmyard 800, bog 1,600; rotation of crops: potatoes, oats, flax, oats or pasture; oats: 6 bushels seed, 32 bushels produce; 7 and a half bushels seed, 48 bushels produce; potatoes: 30 bushels seed, 240 bushels produce; [seed blank], 300 bushels produce; flax: 3 gallons seed, 4 lbs produce; 3 and a half gallons seed, 5 lbs produce; woods: a few trees; livestock: 11 horses, 16 cattle, 41 poultry.

22, Craigtown, soil: depth from 10 to 16 inches; manures, quantity per acre: farmyard 800, bog 1,600, compost 2,400; rotation of crops: oats, flax, oats, oats, potatoes, oats, clover soil, pasture; oats: 7 and one-third bushels seed, 48 bushels produce; [seed blank], 70 bushels produce;

potatoes: 24 bushels seed, 240 bushels produce; 28 bushels seed, 350 bushels produce; flax: 3 gallons seed, 4 lbs produce; 3 and a half gallons seed, 5 lbs produce; woods: a few trees; livestock: 13 horses, 26 cattle, 2 sheep, 2 goats, 75 poultry.

23, Creevedonnel, soil: depth from 9 to 12 inches; manures, quantity per acre: farmyard 800, bog 1,600; rotation of crops: oats, flax, oats, potatoes, oats, pasture; oats: 6 bushels seed, 32 bushels produce; 8 bushels seed, 48 bushels produce; potatoes: 28 bushels seed, 280 bushels produce; 32 bushels seed, 42 bushels produce [insert marginal query: see potatoes, one figure omitted?]; flax: 2 and four-fifth gallons seed, 4 lbs produce; 3 and a half gallons seed, 5 lbs produce; livestock: 11 horses, 36 cattle, 52 sheep, 237 poultry.

24, Cromkill, soil: depth from 8 to 12 inches; rotation of crops: oats, flax, oats, potatoes, oats, pasture; oats: 6 bushels seed, 30 bushels produce; 7 bushels seed, 56 bushels produce; potatoes: 28 bushels seed, 300 bushels produce; 32 bushels seed, 360 bushels produce; flax: 2 and four-fifth gallons seed, 5 lbs produce; 3 and a half gallons seed, 6 lbs produce; livestock: 8 horses, 25 cattle, 4 sheep, 3 goats, 5 hogs, 62 poultry.

25, Culkeeragh, soil: depth from 6 to 12 inches; manures, quantity per acre: farmyard 800, bog 1,600, shells 480; rotation of crops: potatoes, wheat, oats, pasture; wheat: 3 and a half bushels seed, 30 bushels produce; [seed blank], 50 bushels produce; oats: 6 bushels seed, 36 bushels produce; 6 and a half bushels seed, 54 bushels produce; potatoes: 30 bushels seed, 280 bushels produce; 32 bushels seed, 400 bushels produce; flax: 2 and three-fifth gallons seed, 3 lbs produce; 3 and a half gallons seed, 6 lbs produce; livestock: 17 horses, 4 asses, 63 cattle, 42 sheep, 11 hogs, 161 poultry.

26, Curryfree, soil: depth from 6 to 8 inches; manures, quantity per acre: farmyard 800, bog 1,600, lime 80; rotation of crops: oats, flax, oats, potatoes, oats, pasture; oats: 6 bushels seed, 32 bushels produce; 8 bushels seed, 48 bushels produce; potatoes: 28 bushels seed, 280 bushels produce; 32 bushels seed, 420 bushels produce; flax: 2 and four-fifth gallons seed, 4 lbs produce; 3 and a half gallons seed, 5 lbs produce; livestock: 14 horses, 52 cattle, 41 sheep, 4 goats, 6 hogs, 192 poultry.

27, Currynierin, soil: depth from 5 to 12 inches; manures, quantity per acre: farmyard 800, bog 1,600, lime 150; rotation of crops: oats, flax, oats, potatoes, wheat, clover soil, pasture; wheat: 3 bushels seed, 40 bushels produce; 3 and a half bushels seed, 50 bushels produce; oats: 5 and a half bushels seed, 40 bushels produce; 6 and a half bushels seed, 64 bushels produce; potatoes: 30 bushels seed, 280 bushels produce; 32 bushels seed, 340 bushels produce; flax: 3 gallons seed, 4 lbs produce; 3 and a half gallons seed, 6 lbs produce; livestock: 4 horses, 18 cattle, 2 sheep, 3 hogs, 75 poultry.

28, Disertowen, soil: depth from 4 or 10 to 15 inches; manures, quantity per acre: farmyard 800, bog 1,600; rotation of crops: oats, flax, potatoes, oats, pasture; oats: 6 bushels seed, 32 bushels produce; 7 and a half bushels seed, 64 bushels produce; potatoes: 28 bushels seed, 200 bushels produce; 30 bushels seed, 350 bushels produce; flax: 2 and one-fifth gallons seed, 4 lbs produce; 3 and a half gallons seed, 6 lbs produce; livestock: 13 horses, 41 cattle, 12 sheep, 135 poultry.

29, Drumagore, soil: depth from 8 to 12 inches; manures, quantity per acre: farmyard 800, bog 1,600, compost 2,400; rotation of crops: oats, flax, potatoes, oats, oats, pasture; oats: 5 and a half bushels seed, 48 bushels produce; 6 and a half bushels seed, 64 bushels produce; potatoes: 30 bushels seed, 280 bushels produce; [seed blank], 350 bushels produce; flax: 3 gallons seed, 4 lbs produce; 3 and a half gallons seed, 5 lbs produce; livestock: 11 horses, 24 cattle, 2 sheep, 2 goats, 2 hogs, 66 poultry.

30, Drumahoe, soil: depth from 3 to 9 inches; manures, quantity per acre: farmyard 800, bog 1,600; rotation of crops: oats, wheat or flax, oats, potatoes; oats: 6 and a half bushels seed, 30 bushels produce; 7 bushels seed, 54 bushels produce; potatoes: 30 bushels seed, 240 bushels produce; 32 bushels seed, 360 bushels produce; flax: 2 and four-fifth gallons seed, 3 lbs produce; 3 and a half gallons seed, 5 lbs produce; livestock: 19 horses, 29 cattle, 1 sheep, 1 goat, 4 hogs, 275 poultry.

31, Drumconan, soil: depth from 3 to 9 or 12 inches; manures, quantity per acre: farmyard 800, bog 1,600; rotation of crops: oats, potatoes, oats, flax, oats, pasture; oats: 6 bushels seed, 32 bushels produce; 6 and a half bushels seed, 60 bushels produce; potatoes: 28 bushels seed, 200 bushels produce; 30 bushels seed, 350 bushels produce; flax: 2 and four-fifth gallons seed, 4 lbs produce; 3 and a half gallons seed, 6 lbs produce; [insert marginal note: peas 10 stones, 120 stones [produce]; livestock: 6 horses, 14 cattle, 5 sheep, 78 poultry.

32, Dunhugh, soil: depth from 4 to 8 inches; manures, quantity per acre: farmyard 800, bog 1,600, compost 2,400; rotation of crops: 1st rotation, potatoes, oats, flax, clover soil; 2nd rotation, oats, potatoes, oats, pasture; oats: 6 and a half bushels seed, 24 bushels produce; 7 and a half

bushels seed, 48 bushels produce; potatoes: 26 bushels seed, 200 bushels produce; 30 bushels seed, 300 bushels produce; flax: 2 and three-quarter gallons seed, 3 lbs produce; 3 and a half gallons seed, 4 lbs produce; livestock: 8 horses, 28 cattle, 6 sheep, 2 goats, 2 hogs, 142 poultry.

33, Edenreagh-beg, soil: depth from 8 to 16 inches; rotation of crops: oats, flax, oats, potatoes, oats, flax, oats, pasture; oats: 6 bushels seed, 30 bushels produce; 6 and a half bushels seed, 60 bushels produce; potatoes: 30 bushels seed, 300 bushels produce; 36 bushels seed, 340 bushels produce; flax: 3 gallons seed, 4 lbs produce; 3 and a half gallons seed, 6 lbs produce; livestock: 10 horses, 24 cattle, 5 sheep, 3 hogs, 136 poultry.

34, Edenreagh-more, soil: depth from 7 to 14 inches; rotation of crops: oats, potatoes, oats, flax, oats, pasture; oats: 5 bushels seed, 30 bushels produce; 6 and a half bushels seed, 64 bushels produce; potatoes: 30 bushels seed, 300 bushels produce; 36 bushels seed, 320 bushels produce; flax: 2 and four-fifth gallons seed, 4 lbs produce; 3 and a half gallons seed, 6 lbs produce; livestock: 11 horses, 25 cattle, 182 poultry.

35, Enagh, soil: depth from 4 to 8 inches; manures, quantity per acre: farmyard 1,600, bog 800, shells 300; rotation of crops: potatoes, wheat, oats or flax, pasture; wheat: 3 and three-quarters bushels seed, 25 bushels produce; [seed blank], 50 bushels produce; oats: 6 bushels seed, 42 bushels produce; [seed blank], 60 bushels produce; potatoes: 30 bushels seed, 300 bushels produce; 32 bushels seed, 420 bushels produce; flax: 2 and four-fifth gallons seed, 3 lbs produce; 3 and a half gallons seed, 5 lbs produce; livestock, 10 horses, 20 cattle, 1 sheep, 1 goat, 6 hogs, 114 poultry.

36, Fincarn, soil: depth from 6 to 8 inches; manures, quantity per acre: farmyard 800, bog 1,600; rotation of crops: oats, flax, oats, potatoes; oats: 6 and a half bushels seed, 30 bushels produce; 7 bushels seed, 56 bushels produce; potatoes: 30 bushels seed, 240 bushels produce; 32 bushels seed, 360 bushels produce; flax: 2 and four-fifth gallons seed, 3 lbs produce; 3 and a half gallons seed, 5 lbs produce; livestock: 13 horses, 4 asses, 39 cattle, 7 sheep, 13 hogs, 204 poultry.

37, Glenderowen, soil: depth from 6 to 12 inches; manures, quantity per acre: farmyard 800, bog 1,600, compost 2,400; rotation of crops: oats, flax, oats, potatoes, wheat, flax, pasture; wheat: 3 and a half bushels seed, 30 bushels produce; [seed blank], 50 bushels produce; oats: 6 bushels seed, 32 bushels produce; 8 bushels seed, 56 bushels produce; potatoes: 28 bushels seed, 240 bushels produce; 32 bushels seed, 380 bushels produce;

livestock: 5 horses, 23 cattle, 18 sheep, 2 hogs, 64 poultry.

38, Glenkeen, soil: depth from 6 to 18 inches; rotation of crops: 1st rotation, oats, potatoes or flax, wheat, oats, clover soil, pasture; 2nd rotation, oats, potatoes, wheat, flax, hay, pasture; wheat: 3 and a half bushels seed, 50 bushels produce; [seed blank], 60 bushels produce; oats: 5 bushels seed, 40 bushels produce; 6 bushels seed, 64 bushels produce; potatoes: 24 bushels seed, 300 bushels produce; 34 bushels seed, 500 bushels produce; flax: 3 gallons seed, 5 lbs produce; 3 and a half gallons seed, 6 lbs produce; livestock: 13 horses, 4 asses, 44 cattle, 4 hogs, 267 poultry.

39, Gobnascale, soil: depth from 6 to 14 inches; manures, quantity per acre: farmyard 800, bog 1,600; rotation of crops: potatoes, oats, flax, pasture; oats: 6 bushels seed, 32 bushels produce; 8 bushels seed, 56 bushels produce; potatoes: 30 bushels seed, 200 bushels produce; 32 bushels seed, 250 bushels produce; flax: 2 and four-fifth gallons seed, 4 lbs produce; 3 and a half gallons seed, 5 lbs produce; livestock: 11 horses, 2 asses, 30 cattle, 11 sheep, 7 hogs.

40, Gortica: [blank]; [insert query: Gortree?].

41, Gorticross, soil: depth from 4 to 5 inches; manures, quantity per acre: farmyard 800, bog 1,600; rotation of crops: potatoes, oats, flax, oats; oats: 6 and a half bushels seed, 30 bushels produce; 8 bushels seed, 50 bushels produce; potatoes: 30 bushels seed, 240 bushels produce; 32 bushels seed, 360 bushels produce; flax: 2 and four-fifth gallons seed, 3 lbs produce; 3 and a half gallons seed, 5 lbs produce; livestock: 26 horses, 112 cattle, 77 sheep, 3 goats, 14 hogs, 529 poultry.

42, Gortgranagh, soil: depth from 10 to 12 inches; manures, quantity per acre: farmyard 800, bog 1,600, compost 2,400; rotation of crops: oats, potatoes or flax, oats, oats, pasture; oats: 3 bushels seed, 40 bushels produce; 3 and half bushels seed, 56 bushels produce; potatoes: 24 bushels seed, 300 bushels produce; [seed blank], 360 bushels produce; flax: 3 and a half gallons seed, 5 lbs produce; 4 gallons seed, 6 lbs produce; livestock: 16 horses, 42 cattle, 18 sheep, 4 hogs, 221 poultry.

43, Gortin, soil: depth from 12 to 20 inches; manures, quantity per acre: farmyard 800, bog 1,600, shells 240, compost 2,400; rotation of crops: oats, barley, potatoes, wheat, potatoes, flax, clover soil; wheat: 5 bushels seed, 45 bushels produce; [seed blank], 50 bushels produce; barley: 3 and a half bushels seed, 48 bushels produce; [seed blank], 60 bushels produce; oats: 6 bushels seed, 56 bushels produce; 7 and a half bushels seed, 80 bushels produce; potatoes: 28

bushels seed, 280 bushels produce; 32 bushels seed, 350 bushels produce; flax: 3 gallons seed, 4 lbs produce; 3 and a half gallons seed, 5 lbs produce; livestock: 6 horses, 34 cattle, 11 hogs.

44, Gortinure, soil: depth from 4 to 12 inches; manures, quantity per acre: farmyard 800, bog 1,600, compost 2,400; rotation of crops: 1st rotation, oats, flax, clover soil, pasture; 2nd rotation, potatoes, wheat, flax, clover soil, pasture; wheat: 3 and a half bushels seed, 30 bushels produce; [seed blank], 45 bushels produce; oats: 6 and a half bushels seed, 32 bushels produce; [seed blank], 56 bushels produce; potatoes: 28 bushels seed, 240 bushels produce; 32 bushels seed, 380 bushels produce; flax: 2 and eight-tenth gallons seed, 5 lbs produce; 3 and a half gallons seed, 6 lbs produce; livestock: 5 horses, 18 cattle, 3 hogs, 65 poultry.

45, Gortnessy, soil: depth 14 inches; rotation of crops: potatoes, oats, flax, oats, clover soil, pasture; oats: 6 bushels seed, 32 bushels produce; 6 and a half bushels seed, 56 bushels produce; potatoes: 30 bushels seed, 340 bushels produce; 36 bushels seed, 360 bushels produce; flax: 3 gallons seed, 4 lbs produce; 3 and a half gallons seed, 6 lbs produce; livestock: 47 horses, 122 cattle, 47 sheep, 5 hogs, 238 poultry.

46, Gortree: [blank]; [insert query: Gortica, query Gortin?].

47, Gransha, soil: depth from 4 to 8 inches; manures, quantity per acre: farmyard 800, bog 1,800, lime 180; rotation of crops: 1st rotation, potatoes, wheat, oats, clover soil or pasture; 2nd rotation, oats, potatoes, wheat, pasture; wheat: 3 and a half bushels seed, 30 bushels produce; [seed blank], 50 bushels produce; oats: 5 and seven-eighth bushels seed, 42 bushels produce; [seed blank], 60 bushels produce; potatoes: 26 bushels seed, 360 bushels produce; 32 bushels seed, 480 bushels produce; livestock: 8 horses, 20 cattle, 70 sheep, 1 hog.

48, Kilfinnan, soil: depth from 6 or 9 to 18 inches; manures, quantity per acre: farmyard 800, bog 1,600, shells 360, lime 100; rotation of crops: oats, flax, oats, potatoes, wheat, clover soil, pasture; wheat: 3 and a half bushels seed, 35 bushels produce; [seed blank], 60 bushels produce; oats: 5 and a half bushels seed, 32 bushels produce; 6 and a half bushels seed, 72 bushels produce; potatoes: 24 bushels seed, 300 bushels produce; 32 bushels seed, 480 bushels produce; flax: 3 gallons seed, 4 lbs produce; 3 and a half gallons seed, 6 lbs produce; livestock: 16 horses, 43 cattle, 8 sheep, 7 hogs, 220 poultry.

49, Killymallaght, soil: depth from 9 to 15 inches; manures, quantity per acre: farmyard 800, bog 1,600, compost 2,400; rotation of crops: oats, flax, oats, oats, potatoes, oats, clover soil, pasture; oats: 6 bushels seed, 38 bushels produce; [seed blank], 64 bushels produce; potatoes: 24 bushels seed, 240 bushels produce; 30 bushels seed, 350 bushels produce; flax: 2 and one-third gallons seed, 4 and a half lbs produce; 3 and a half gallons seed, 5 and a half lbs produce; livestock: 19 horses, 54 cattle, 4 sheep, 3 goats, 186 poultry.

50, Kittybane, soil: depth from 4 to 10 inches; manures, quantity per acre: farmyard 800, bog 1,600, compost 2,400; rotation of crops: potatoes, oats, flax, pasture; oats: 6 and a half bushels seed, 24 bushels produce; 8 bushels seed, 40 bushels produce; potatoes: 32 bushels seed, 240 bushels produce; [seed blank], 300 bushels produce; flax: 2 and four-fifth gallons seed, 4 lbs produce; 3 and a half gallons seed, 5 lbs produce; livestock: 11 horses, 26 cattle, 84 poultry.

51, Knockbrack, soil: depth from 4 to 15 inches; manures, quantity per acre: farmyard 800, bog 1,600, shells 150; rotation of crops: oats, flax, potatoes, wheat, clover soil, pasture; wheat: 3 and one-third bushels seed, 40 bushels produce; 3 and a half bushels seed, 50 bushels produce; oats: 6 bushels seed, 40 bushels produce; 7 and a half bushels seed, 72 bushels produce; potatoes: 24 bushels seed, 240 bushels produce; 32 bushels seed, 300 bushels produce; flax: 3 gallons seed, 4 and a half lbs produce; 3 and a half gallons seed, 5 and a half lbs produce; [insert marginal note: half an acre of [turnips?]; livestock: 16 horses, 80 cattle, 1 goat, 5 hogs, 352 poultry.

52, Lisaghmore, soil: depth from 8 to 12 inches; manures, quantity per acre: farmyard 1,200, bog 1,200, compost 2,400; rotation of crops: potatoes, oats, flax, oats, potatoes or clover soil, oats, hay; oats: 6 bushels seed, 32 bushels produce; 7 and one-third bushels seed, 56 bushels produce; potatoes: 30 bushels seed, 280 bushels produce; [seed blank], 560 bushels produce; flax: 2 and four-fifth gallons seed, 4 lbs produce; 3 and a half gallons seed, 6 lbs produce; [insert marginal note: hay 2 and a half to 3 tons]; livestock: 17 horses, 49 cattle, 8 sheep, 1 hog, 245 poultry.

53, Lisahawley, soil: depth from 3 to 8 inches; manures, quantity per acre: farmyard 800, bog 1,600, compost 1,688; rotation of crops: potatoes, wheat, oats, pasture; wheat: 3 bushels seed, 25 bushels produce; 3 and a half bushels seed, 40 bushels produce; oats: 6 and a quarter bushels seed, 42 bushels produce; [seed blank], 60 bushels produce; potatoes: 30 bushels seed, 280 bushels produce; 32 bushels seed, 400 bushels produce; flax: 2 and four-fifth gallons seed, 3 lbs

produce; 3 and a half gallons seed, 5 lbs produce; livestock: 7 horses, 12 cattle, 37 poultry.

54, Lisdillon, soil: depth from 4 to 18 inches; manures, quantity per acre: farmyard 800, bog 1,600, lime 100; rotation of crops: 1st rotation, oats, flax, potatoes, wheat or oats, pasture; 2nd rotation, oats, flax, potatoes, clover soil or pasture; wheat: 3 and a half bushels seed, 45 bushels produce; [seed blank], 60 bushels produce; oats: 6 bushels seed, 32 bushels produce; 6 and a half bushels seed, 64 bushels produce; potatoes: 24 bushels seed, 300 bushels produce; 32 bushels seed, 500 bushels produce; flax: 2 and two-fifth gallons seed, 5 lbs produce; 3 gallons seed, 6 lbs produce; livestock: 58 horses, 1 ass, 148 cattle, 45 sheep, 2 hogs, 637 poultry.

55, Lisglass, soil: depth from 6 to 10 inches; manures, quantity per acre: farmyard 1,800, bog 1,600, compost 2,400; oats, flax, oats, potatoes, oats, pasture; oats: 3 bushels seed, 40 bushels produce; 3 and a half bushels seed, 56 bushels produce; potatoes: 24 bushels seed, 300 bushels produce; 30 bushels seed, 360 bushels produce; flax: 3 gallons seed, 5 lbs produce; 3 and a half gallons seed, 6 lbs produce; [insert marginal query: potatoes?]; livestock: 23 horses, 80 cattle, 77 sheep, 5 hogs, 221 poultry.

56, Lismacarol, soil: depth from 6 to 16 inches; manures, quantity per acre: farmyard 800, bog 1,600, shells 100, lime 150; rotation of crops: 1st rotation, oats, flax, potatoes, wheat, clover soil, pasture; 2nd rotation, oats, flax, potatoes, barley, clover soil, pasture; wheat: 3 and a half bushels seed, 35 bushels produce; [seed blank], 45 bushels produce; barley: 3 and a half bushels seed, 48 bushels produce; [seed blank], 66 bushels produce; oats: 6 bushels seed, 40 bushels produce; 6 and a half bushels seed, 56 bushels produce; potatoes: 28 bushels seed, 300 bushels produce; 32 bushels seed, 360 bushels produce; flax: 3 gallons seed, 4 and a half lbs produce; 3 and a half gallons seed, 6 lbs produce; [insert marginal note: turnips 4 acres]; livestock: 34 horses, 83 cattle, 17 sheep, 10 hogs, 337 poultry.

57, Lisnagelvin, soil: depth from 9 to 18 inches; rotation of crops: oats, flax, potatoes, wheat, clover soil, pasture; wheat: 3 and a half bushels seed, 40 bushels produce; [seed blank], 45 bushels produce; oats: 6 bushels seed, 36 bushels produce; 6 and a half bushels seed, 64 bushels produce; potatoes: 26 bushels seed, 300 bushels produce; 32 bushels seed, 400 bushels produce; flax: 2 and four-fifth gallons seed, 5 lbs produce; 3 gallons seed, 6 lbs produce; livestock: 5 horses, 13 cattle, 13 sheep, 4 hogs, 87 poultry.

58, Lisneal, soil: depth from 5 to 12 inches; rotation of crops: oats, flax, oats, potatoes, wheat, clover soil, pasture; wheat: 3 bushels seed, 40 bushels produce; 3 and a half bushels seed, 58 bushels produce; oats: 5 bushels seed, 40 bushels produce; 7 bushels seed, 60 bushels produce; potatoes: 30 bushels seed, 340 bushels produce; 36 bushels seed, 360 bushels produce; flax: 3 gallons seed, 4 lbs produce; 3 and a half gallons seed, 6 lbs produce; livestock: 7 horses, 1 ass, 16 cattle, 18 sheep, 3 hogs, 85 poultry.

59, Magheracanon, soil: depth from 4 to 12 inches; manures, quantity per acre: farmyard 800, bog 1,600, compost 2,400; rotation of crops: oats, potatoes, oats, flax, oats, pasture; oats: 6 bushels seed, 32 bushels produce; 6 and a half bushels seed, 48 bushels produce; potatoes: 30 bushels seed, 240 bushels produce; 32 bushels seed, 380 bushels produce; flax: 2 and three-tenth gallons seed, 5 lbs produce; 3 and a half gallons seed, 6 lbs produce; livestock: 5 horses, 14 cattle, 19 poultry.

60, Managhbeg, soil: depth from 3 to 8 inches; manures, quantity per acre: farmyard 800, bog 1,600; rotation of crops: potatoes, oats, flax, oats; oats: 6 and a half bushels seed, 30 bushels produce; 8 bushels seed, 50 bushels produce; potatoes: 30 bushels seed, 240 bushels produce; 32 bushels seed, 360 bushels produce; flax: 2 and four-fifth gallons seed, 3 lbs produce; 3 and a half gallons seed, 5 lbs produce; livestock: 6 horses, 22 cattle, 54 poultry.

61, Managhmore, soil: depth from 2 to 9 inches; manures, quantity per acre: farmyard 800, bog 1,600; rotation of crops: potatoes, oats, flax, oats; oats: 6 and a half bushels seed, 30 bushels produce; 8 bushels seed, 50 bushels produce; potatoes: 30 bushels seed, 240 bushels produce; 32 bushels seed, 360 bushels produce; flax: 2 and four-fifth gallons seed, 3 lbs produce; 3 and a half gallons seed, 5 lbs produce; livestock: 12 horses, 28 cattle, 5 sheep, 1 hog, 50 poultry.

62, Maydown, soil: depth from 3 to 8 inches; manures, quantity per acre: farmyard 800, bog 1,600, shells 360, lime 240; rotation of crops: 1st rotation, potatoes, wheat, hay, pasture, oats or clover soil, potatoes; 2nd rotation, oats, flax, potatoes, wheat, pasture; wheat: 4 and a half bushels seed, 30 bushels produce; [seed blank], 50 bushels produce; oats: 7 and a half bushels seed, 30 bushels produce; [seed blank], 56 bushels produce; potatoes: 28 bushels seed, 280 bushels produce; 34 bushels seed, 420 bushels produce; flax: 2 and four-fifth gallons seed, 3 lbs produce; 3 and a half gallons seed, 5 lbs produce; livestock: 8 horses, 30 cattle, 3 hogs, 55 poultry.

63, Prehen, soil: depth from 8 to 10 inches; manures, quantity per acre: farmyard 800, bog 1,600, compost 2,400; rotation of crops: potatoes, barley, oats, clover soil; barley: 3 and a half bushels seed, 48 bushels produce; [seed blank], 60 bushels produce; oats: 6 and a half bushels seed, 32 bushels produce; 7 and a half bushels seed, 48 bushels produce; potatoes: 26 bushels seed, 240 bushels produce; 38 bushels seed, 380 bushels produce; flax: 2 and four-fifth gallons seed, 4 lbs produce; 3 and a half gallons seed, 5 lbs produce; livestock: 1 horse, 2 cattle, 7 poultry.

64, Primity, soil: depth from 8 to 12 inches; manures, quantity per acre: farmyard 800, bog 1,600, compost 2,400; rotation of crops: oats, flax, oats, potatoes, oats, pasture; oats: 6 bushels seed, 24 bushels produce; 8 bushels seed, 42 bushels produce; potatoes: 32 bushels seed, 240 bushels produce; [seed blank], 300 bushels produce; flax: 2 and four-fifth gallons seed, 4 lbs produce; 3 and a half gallons seed, 5 lbs produce; livestock: 10 horses, 20 cattle, 184 poultry.

65, Rossnagalliagh, soil: depth from 8 to 12 inches; manures, quantity per acre: farmyard 1,200, bog 1,200, compost 2,400; rotation of crops: oats, flax, oats, potatoes, oats, clover soil; oats: 6 bushels seed, 48 bushels produce; [seed blank], 60 bushels produce; potatoes: 28 bushels seed, 260 bushels produce; 32 bushels seed, 560 bushels produce; flax: 2 and four-fifth gallons seed, 4 lbs produce; 3 and a half gallons seed, 6 lbs produce; [insert marginal note: hay, 2 and a half tons to 3 tons]; livestock: 14 horses, 36 cattle, 3 goats, 207 poultry.

66, Stradreagh-beg, soil: depth from 3 to 8 inches; manures, quantity per acre: farmyard 800, bog 1,600; rotation of crops: oats, potatoes, wheat, flax, oats, pasture; wheat: 4 bushels seed, 25 bushels produce; [seed blank], 40 bushels produce; oats: 6 and a half bushels seed, 30 bushels produce; 8 bushels seed, 50 bushels produce; potatoes: 30 bushels seed, 240 bushels produce; 32 bushels seed, 360 bushels produce; flax: 2 and four-fifth gallons seed, 3 lbs produce; 3 and a half gallons seed, 5 lbs produce; livestock: 6 horses, 20 cattle, 1 goat, 1 hog, 100 poultry.

67, Stradreagh-more, soil: depth from 3 to 8 inches; manures, quantity per acre: farmyard 800, bog 1,600; rotation of crops: oats, potatoes, wheat, flax, oats, pasture; wheat: 4 bushels seed, 25 bushels produce; [seed blank], 40 bushels produce; oats: 6 and a half bushels seed, 30 bushels produce; 8 bushels seed, 56 bushels produce; potatoes: 30 bushels seed, 240 bushels produce; 32 bushels seed, 360 bushels produce; flax: 2 and four-fifth gallons seed, 3 lbs produce; 3 and a half gallons seed, 5 lbs produce; livestock: 6 horses, 20 cattle, 1 goat, 1 hog, 100 poultry.

68, Tagharina, soil: depth from 8 to 12 inches; manures, quantity per acre: farmyard 800, bog 1,600, compost 2,400; rotation of crops: oats, flax, potatoes, oats, oats, pasture; oats: 5 and one-fifth bushels seed, 48 bushels produce; 6 and a half bushels seed, 64 bushels produce; potatoes: 30 bushels seed, 280 bushels produce; [seed blank], 350 bushels produce; flax: 3 gallons seed, 4 lbs produce; 3 and a half gallons seed, 5 lbs produce; livestock: 8 horses, 13 cattle, 2 hogs, 64 poultry.

69, Tamnymore, soil: depth from 6 to 12 inches; manures, quantity per acre: farmyard 800, bog 1,600, compost 2,400; rotation of crops: potatoes, oats, flax, clover soil; oats: 6 and a half bushels seed, 40 bushels produce; [seed blank], 56 bushels produce; potatoes: 26 bushels seed, 240 bushels produce; 32 bushels seed, 380 bushels produce; flax: 2 and four-fifth gallons seed, 4 lbs produce; 3 and a half gallons seed, 5 lbs produce; livestock: 16 horses, 38 cattle, 2 sheep, 135 poultry.

70, Templetown, soil: depth from 4 to 8 inches; manures, quantity per acre: farmyard 800, bog 1,600; rotation of crops: potatoes, wheat or oats, flax, pasture; oats: 6 and a half bushels seed, 30 bushels produce; 7 and a half bushels seed, 56 bushels produce; potatoes: 28 bushels seed, 280 bushels produce; 30 bushels seed, 420 bushels produce; flax: 2 and four-fifth gallons seed, 3 lbs produce; 3 and a half gallons seed, 5 lbs produce; livestock: 6 horses, 26 cattle, 1 goat, 3 hogs, 35 poultry.

71, Tirbracken, soil: depth from 6 to 12 inches; rotation of crops: potatoes, oats, flax, oats, pasture; oats: 5 and one-third bushels seed, 30 bushels produce; 7 and one-third bushels seed, 64 bushels produce; potatoes: 24 bushels seed, 300 bushels produce; 26 bushels seed, 350 bushels produce; flax: 3 gallons seed, 4 lbs produce; 3 and a half gallons seed, 5 lbs produce; livestock: 10 horses, 26 cattle, 4 sheep, 2 hogs, 32 poultry.

72, Tirkeeveny, soil: depth from 5 to 12 inches; manures, quantity per acre: farmyard 800, bog 1,600, compost 2,400; rotation of crops: oats, flax, oats, oats, potatoes, oats, clover soil, pasture; oats: 7 and one-third bushels seed, 48 bushels produce; [seed blank], 70 bushels produce; potatoes: 24 bushels seed, 240 bushels produce; 30 bushels seed, 350 bushels produce; flax: 3 gallons seed, 4 lbs produce; 3 and a half gallons seed, 5 lbs produce; livestock: 11 horses, 22 cattle, 1 hog, 108 poultry.

73, Tully Lower, soil: depth from 10 to 14 inches; manures, quantity per acre: farmyard 1,200, bog 1,200, shells 75, lime 80, compost 2,400; rotation of crops: oats, flax, oats, potatoes, wheat, clover soil, oats, potatoes, wheat, clover soil; wheat: 3 and a half bushels seed, 40 bushels produce; [seed blank], 50 bushels produce; oats: 5 and one-third bushels seed, 48 bushels produce; 6 and a half bushels seed, 64 bushels produce; potatoes: 30 bushels seed, 260 bushels produce; [seed blank], 500 bushels produce; flax: 3 and one-fifth gallons seed, [produce blank]; 4 gallons seed, from 6 to 6 and a half lbs produce; [insert marginal query: potatoes?]; livestock: 18 horses, 45 cattle, 8 hogs, 223 poultry.

74, Tully Upper, soil: depth from 8 to 10 inches; manures, quantity per acre: farmyard 600, bog 1,800, shells 240, compost 2,400; rotation of crops: oats, flax, potatoes, oats, oats, pasture; oats: 5 bushels seed, 45 bushels produce; 8 bushels seed, 48 bushels produce; potatoes: 30 bushels seed, 280 bushels produce; [seed blank], 350 bushels produce; flax: 3 gallons seed, 4 lbs produce; 3 and a half gallons seed, 5 lbs produce; livestock: 9 horses, 27 cattle, 14 sheep, 1 goat, 3 hogs, 112 poultry.

75, Tullyally Lower, soil: depth from 12 to 15 inches; rotation of crops: potatoes, oats, flax, oats, pasture; wheat: 3 and a half bushels seed, 35 bushels produce; 4 bushels seed, 50 bushels produce; oats: 4 bushels seed, 42 bushels produce; 6 and a half bushels seed, 54 bushels produce; potatoes: 24 bushels seed, 240 bushels produce; 30 bushels seed, 360 bushels produce; flax: 3 gallons seed, 5 lbs produce; 3 and a half gallons seed, 6 lbs produce; livestock: 21 horses, 73 cattle, 40 sheep, 8 hogs, 277 poultry.

76, Tullyally Upper, soil: depth from 4 or 8 to 15 inches; manures, quantity per acre: farmyard 2,400; rotation of crops: potatoes, oats, flax, wheat, oats, clover soil, pasture; wheat: 3 and a half bushels seed, 45 bushels produce; 4 bushels seed, 50 bushels produce; oats: 6 bushels seed, 56 bushels produce; 7 and a half bushels seed, 72 bushels produce; potatoes: 24 bushels seed, 300 bushels produce; 30 bushels seed, 380 bushels produce; flax: 3 gallons seed, 5 lbs produce; 3 and a half gallons seed, 6 lbs produce; livestock: 5 horses, 24 cattle, 9 sheep, 1 hog, 49 poultry.

77, Warbleshinny, soil: depth from 8 to 12 inches; manures, quantity per acre: farmyard 800, bog 1,600, compost 2,400; rotation of crops: 1st rotation, oats, flax, oats, pasture; 2nd rotation, oats, flax, potatoes, wheat, pasture; wheat: 3 and a half bushels seed, 30 bushels produce; [seed blank], 50 bushels produce; oats: 6 bushels seed, 32 bushels produce; 8 bushels seed, 56 bushels produce; potatoes: 28 bushels seed, 240 bushels produce; 32 bushels seed, 380 bushels produce; livestock: 11 horses, 53 cattle, 18 sheep, 5 goats, 1 hog, 168 poultry.

Application of Power

[Table contains the following headings: name of townland, number of farms, simple labour in farming and quarrying, simple auxiliary power, compound auxiliary power in grain and flax mills].

1, Altnagelvin, 17 farms, 39 working farmers and family, 7 male and 8 female domestic servants, 3 male farming servants, 46 male and 6 female occasional labourers, total 18,465 working days; auxiliary power: 13 ploughs, 16 harrows, 17 carts, 18 horses, 30 spinning wheels; compound power: grain mill, overshot wheel, diameter 18 feet; grain ground: barley 28,800 cwt, worked for 9 months, 2 attendants, including miller.

2, Ardkill, 16 farms, 60 working farmers and family, 9 male and 2 female domestic servants, 6 male farming servants, 35 male and 3 female occasional labourers, total 24,840 working days; 1 building quarry, not in use; auxiliary power: 11 ploughs, 21 harrows, 1 hoe, 2 wheel cars, 24 carts, 26 horses, 34 spinning wheels; compound power: grain mill, undershot wheel, diameter 12 feet, grain ground: oatmeal 7,920 cwt; worked for 11 months, full-time, 2 attendants, including miller.

3, Ardlough, 4 farms, 7 working farmers and family, 5 male and 2 female domestic servants, 2 male farming servants, 31 male and 4 female occasional labourers, total 5,864 working days; auxiliary power: 3 ploughs, 6 harrows, 28 wheel cars, 7 carts, 9 horses, 24 spinning wheels; compound power: grain mill, undershot wheel, diameter 12 feet; grain ground: oatmeal 1,400 cwt, maximum 1,600 cwt, worked for 3 months, time possible 4 months, 3 attendants, including miller; flax mill, undershot wheel, diameter 12 feet; quantity: raw 1,440 cwt, maximum 1,600 cwt, worked 10 months, attendants 4 males, 2 females.

4, Ardmore [insert marginal note: none], 10 farms, 22 working farmers and family, 12 male and 9 female domestic servants, 16 male farming servants, 103 male and 25 female occasional labourers, total 21,489 working days; 2 building quarries, not in use; auxiliary power: 14 ploughs, 23 harrows, 1 hoe, 5 wheel cars, 21 carts, 33 horses, 50 spinning wheels.

5, Ardnabrocky, 8 farms, 14 working farmers and family, 9 male and 4 female domestic servants, 2 male farming servants, 45 male and 6 female occasional labourers, total 10,260 working days; auxiliary power: 6 ploughs, 11 harrows, 2 hoes, 11 carts, 18 horses, 16 spinning wheels.

6, Avish, 6 farms, 17 working farmers and family, 5 male domestic servants, 21 male and 9 female occasional labourers, total 6,886 working days; auxiliary power: 5 ploughs, 8 harrows, 1 wheel car, 7 carts, 8 horses, 21 spinning wheels.

7, Ballyoan, 7 farms, 10 working farmers and family, 11 male and 4 female domestic servants, 1 male farming servant, 41 male and 11 female occasional labourers, total 8,967 working days; 1 building quarry, not in use; auxiliary power: 8 ploughs, 16 harrows, 1 hoe, 3 wheel cars, 14 carts, 25 horses, 20 spinning wheels.

8, Ballyore, 6 farms, 15 working farmers and family, 3 male and 1 female domestic servant, 1 male farming servant, 20 male and 1 female occasional labourer, total 6,682 working days; auxiliary power: 6 ploughs, 9 harrows, 1 wheel car, 6 carts, 10 horses, 20 spinning wheels.

9, Ballyshasky, 10 farms, 31 working farmers and family, 7 male and 7 female domestic servants, 2 male farming servants, 50 male and 16 female occasional labourers, total 16,152 working days; auxiliary power: 7 ploughs, 9 harrows, 1 wheel car, 12 carts, 16 horses, 15 spinning wheels; compound power: flax mill, undershot wheel, diameter 17 feet; quantity: raw 360 cwt, maximum 90 cwt; worked 5 months, full-time, 5 male and 2 female attendants.

10, Bogagh, 9 farms, 31 working farmers and family, 4 male and 3 female domestic servants, 16 male occasional labourers, total 12,034 working days; auxiliary power: 8 ploughs, 10 harrows, 9 carts, 11 horses, 17 spinning wheels.

11, Bolies, 10 farms, 21 working farmers and family, 1 female domestic servant, 1 male farming servant, 11 male occasional labourers, total 7,299 working days; auxiliary power: 6 ploughs, 10 harrows, 3 slide cars, 1 wheel car, 5 carts, 10 horses, 22 spinning wheels.

12, Brickkilns, 4 farms, 28 working farmers and family, 2 male and 1 female domestic servant, 12 male occasional labourers, total 9,703 working days; 1 building quarry, 3 men, 939 days labour, [for] flags; auxiliary power: 5 ploughs, 8 harrows, 1 slide car, 1 wheel car, 6 carts, 7 horses, 10 spinning wheels.

13, Cah, 14 farms, 10 working farmers and family, 7 male and 5 female domestic servants, 2 male farming servants, 39 male and 2 female occasional labourers, total 20,777 working days; 1 building quarry, 800 days labour; auxiliary power: 8 ploughs, 12 harrows, 2 slide cars, 1 wheel car, 12 carts, 15 horses, 24 spinning wheels.

14, Carn, 9 farms, 9 working farmers and family, 2 male and 1 female domestic servant, 1 male farming servant, 13 male occasional labourers, total 4,279 working days, auxiliary power: 3 ploughs, 7 harrows, 1 hoe, 3 slide cars, 5 carts, 6 horses, 5 spinning wheels.

15, Carnafarn, 13 farms, 45 working farmers and family, 6 male domestic servants, 26 male and 3 female occasional labourers, total 16,332 working days; auxiliary power: 9 ploughs, 12 harrows, 2 slide cars, 2 wheel cars, 16 carts, 16 horses, 31 spinning wheels.

16, Carrakeel, 5 farms, 8 working farmers and family, 3 male and 4 female domestic servants, 8 male farming servants, 50 male and 11 female occasional labourers, total 8,766 working days; auxiliary power: 8 ploughs, 11 harrows, 2 hoes, 12 carts, 15 horses, 12 spinning wheels.

17, Clampernow, 2 farms, 6 working farmers and family, 4 male and 2 female domestic servants, 1 male farming servant, 17 male and 3 female occasional labourers, total 4,361 working days; 1 road and lime quarry, not in use; auxiliary power: 2 ploughs, 4 harrows, 1 slide car, 4 carts, 5 horses, 3 spinning wheels.

18, Cloghore, 8 farms, 28 working farmers and family, 4 male and 2 female domestic servants, 20 male and 3 female occasional labourers, total 11,642 working days; 1 building quarry, not in use; auxiliary power: 8 ploughs, 10 harrows, 1 slide car, 2 wheel cars, 5 carts, 16 horses, 20 spinning wheels.

19, Clondermot, 12 farms, 17 working farmers and family, 3 male and 2 female domestic servants, 3 male farming servants, 66 male occasional labourers, total 9,891 working days; 1 road quarry, 312 days labour, [for] roads; auxiliary power: 8 ploughs, 14 harrows, 2 hoes, 4 slide cars, 3 wheel cars, 11 carts, 13 horses, 20 spinning wheels.

20, Clooney, 36 farms, 29 working farmers and family, 14 male and 24 female domestic servants, 14 male farming servants, 91 male and 30 female occasional labourers, total 27,757 working days; 2 building quarries, not in use; auxiliary power: 18 ploughs, 28 harrows, 5 hoes, 1 wheel car, 32 carts, 41 horses, 60 spinning wheels.

21, Corrody, 10 farms, 24 working farmers and family, 6 male occasional labourers, total 8,320 working days; auxiliary power: 8 ploughs, 10 harrows, 1 slide car, 2 wheel cars, 8 carts, 11 horses, 26 spinning wheels.

22, Craigtown, 10 farms, 23 working farmers and family, 6 male and 1 female domestic servant, 19 male occasional labourers, total 9,894 working days; auxiliary power: 11 ploughs, 14 har-

rows, 9 slide cars, 7 wheel cars, 4 carts, 13 horses, 24 spinning wheels.

23, Creevedonnel, 11 farms, 53 working farmers and family, 1 male and 1 female domestic servant, 19 male occasional labourers, total 17,791 working days; auxiliary power: 10 ploughs, 18 harrows, 3 slide cars, 10 carts, 11 horses, 30 spinning wheels.

24, Cromkill, 5 farms, 13 working farmers and family, 2 male and 2 female domestic servants, 24 male and 3 female occasional labourers, total 5,897 working days; auxiliary power: 4 ploughs, 8 harrows, 1 hoe, 5 slide cars, 1 wheel car, 6 carts, 8 horses, 15 spinning wheels.

25, Culkeeragh, 12 farms, 9 working farmers and family, 6 male and 7 female domestic servants, 3 male farming servants, 36 male and 9 female occasional labourers, total 9,057 working days; 2 building quarries, not in use; auxiliary power: 8 ploughs, 12 harrows, 1 hoe, 2 slide cars, 4 wheel cars, 11 carts, 17 horses, 20 spinning wheels.

26, Curryfree, 14 farms, 46 working farmers and family, 15 male and 3 female occasional labourers, total 14,930 working days; 1 lime quarry, not in use; auxiliary power: 8 ploughs, 13 harrows, 3 slide cars, 11 carts, 14 horses, 34 spinning wheels.

27, Currynierin, 3 farms, 12 working farmers and family, 1 male domestic servant, 6 male and 4 female occasional labourers, total 4,115 working days; auxiliary power: 2 ploughs, 5 harrows, 1 hoe, 5 carts, 4 horses, 3 spinning wheels.

28, Disertowen, 5 farms, 14 working farmers and family, 6 male and 6 female farming servants, 14 male and 9 female occasional labourers, total 8,999 working days; auxiliary power: 5 ploughs, 8 harrows, 6 slide cars, 8 carts, 13 horses, 20 spinning wheels.

29, Drumagore, 11 farms, 22 working farmers and family, 4 male and 2 female domestic servants, 14 male and 5 female occasional labourers, total 9,112 working days; auxiliary power: 6 ploughs, 9 harrows, 8 slide cars, 5 wheel cars, 4 carts, 11 horses, 15 spinning wheels.

30, Drumahoe, 15 farms, 27 working farmers and family, 2 male and 1 female domestic servant, 1 male farming servant, 40 male and 11 female occasional labourers, total 10,500 working days; 1 road quarry, 1 lime quarry, 3,756 days labour; auxiliary power: 9 ploughs, 15 harrows, 2 wheel cars, 13 carts, 19 horses, 38 spinning wheels; [insert marginal note: 12 men daily, 1 quarry]; compound power: grain mill, diameter of wheel 16 feet, grain ground: oatmeal 6,540 cwt, 100 barrels of wheat,

300 barrels of barley; worked 6 months, time possible 11 months, 3 attendants, including miller; flax mill, undershot wheel, diameter 18 feet; quantity: raw 1,824 cwt, tow 456 cwt, maximum 1,144 cwt; worked 4 months, 11 months possible, 9 male and 1 female attendant.

31, Drumconan, 10 farms, 22 working farmers and family, 1 female domestic servant, 4 male occasional labourers, total 7,235 working days; 1 building quarry, not in use; auxiliary power: 5 ploughs, 5 harrows, 5 slide cars, 3 carts, 6 horses, 24 spinning wheels; compound power: flax mill, undershot wheel, diameter 12 feet; quantity: raw 320 cwt, tow 80 cwt; worked 5 and a half months, 4 male and 1 female attendant.

32, Dunhugh, 7 farms, 19 working farmers and family, 3 male and 1 female domestic servant, 11 male occasional labourers, total 7,359 working days; 3 building quarries, not in use; auxiliary power: 4 ploughs, 6 harrows, 3 wheel cars, 3 carts, 8 horses, 18 spinning wheels.

33, Edenreagh-beg, 11 farms, 27 working farmers and family, 3 male and 3 female domestic servants, 34 male and 7 female occasional labourers, total 10,029 working days; auxiliary power: 7 ploughs, 9 harrows, 5 wheel cars, 3 carts, 10 horses, 30 spinning wheels.

34, Edenreagh-more, 10 farms, 36 working farmers and family, 3 male and 1 female domestic servant, 39 male and 12 female occasional labourers, total 12,819 working days; auxiliary power: 9 ploughs, 13 harrows, 1 slide car, 9 wheel cars, 2 carts, 11 horses, 25 spinning wheels.

35, Enagh [insert marginal note: some queries?], 5 farms, 8 working farmers and family, 5 male and 3 female domestic servants, 19 male and 4 female occasional labourers, total 5,735 working days; auxiliary power: 5 ploughs, 9 harrows, 2 wheel cars, 6 carts, 10 horses, 17 spinning wheels.

36, Fincarn, 7 farms, 21 working farmers and family, 5 male and 5 female domestic servants, 2 male farming servants, 26 male and 5 female occasional labourers, total 10,434 working days; auxiliary power: 7 ploughs, 13 harrows, 1 wheel car, 9 carts, 13 horses, 27 spinning wheels.

37, Glenderowen, 3 farms, 18 working farmers and family, 1 male and 1 female domestic servant, 5 male occasional labourers, total 5,919 working days; 1 lime quarry, not in use; auxiliary power: 3 ploughs, 4 harrows, 3 slide cars, 2 wheel cars, 4 carts, 5 horses, 19 spinning wheels.

38, Glenkeen, 13 farms, 39 working farmers and family, 8 male and 4 female domestic servants, 4 male farming servants, 48 male occasional

labourers, total 18,084 working days; 1 building quarry, [for] slates; [insert marginal note: 1 quarry, not in use]; auxiliary power: 13 ploughs, 16 harrows, 2 hoes, 6 slide cars, 14 carts, 13 horses, 35 threshing machines.

39, Gobnascale, 10 farms, 29 working farmers and family, 3 male and 5 female domestic servants, 1 male farming servant, 45 male and 4 female occasional labourers, total 12,419 working days; auxiliary power: 8 ploughs, 11 harrows, 10 carts, 11 horses, 32 spinning wheels.

40, Gortica, 8 farms, 28 working farmers and family, 4 male and 2 female domestic servants, 5 male farming servants, 9 male and 9 female occasional labourers, total 9,617 working days; auxiliary power: 6 ploughs, 9 harrows, 3 wheel cars, 13 carts, 14 horses, 34 spinning wheels.

41, Gorticross, 9 farms, 22 working farmers and family, 19 male and 8 female domestic servants, 82 male and 2 female occasional labourers, total 15,789 working days; 1 building quarry, 2,191 days labour, [for] roofing; [insert marginal note: 1 slate quarry, 7 men only]; auxiliary power: 10 ploughs, 20 harrows, 2 slide cars, 4 wheel cars, 17 carts, 26 horses, 40 spinning wheels.

42, Gortgranagh, 8 farms, 26 working farmers and family, 5 male and 4 female domestic servants, 23 male and 22 female occasional labourers, total 11,741 working days; auxiliary power: 7 ploughs, 14 harrows, 4 slide cars, 2 wheel cars, 11 carts, 16 horses, 22 spinning wheels.

43, Gortin, 1 farm, 3 working farmers and family, 2 male and 1 female domestic servant, 1 male farming servant, 16 male and 4 female occasional labourers, total 2,476 working days; auxiliary power: 1 plough, 2 harrows, 6 carts, 6 horses, 32 spinning wheels.

44, Gortinure, 3 farms, 11 working farmers and family, 2 male and 2 female domestic servants, 8 male and 2 female occasional labourers, total 5,005 working days; auxiliary power: 3 ploughs, 4 harrows, 1 hoe, 1 slide car, 4 carts, 5 horses, 10 spinning wheels.

45, Gortnessy, 20 farms, 73 working farmers and family, 17 male and 6 female domestic servants, 138 male and 43 female occasional labourers, total 31,978 working days; auxiliary power: 17 ploughs, 32 harrows, 1 hoe, 12 wheel cars, 16 carts, 47 horses, 90 spinning wheels.

46, Gortree, 6 farms, 14 working farmers and family, 5 male and 2 female domestic servants, 2 male farming servants, 39 male and 3 female occasional labourers, total 5,043 working days; auxiliary power: 6 ploughs, 10 harrows, 2 slide cars, 3 wheel cars, 5 carts, 13 horses, 25 spinning wheels.

47, Gransha, [insert marginal note: 1, 4 days occasionally] 1 farm, 1 male and 3 female domestic servants, 8 male and 3 female farming servants, 33 male and 3 female occasional labourers, total 6,667 working days; auxiliary power: 3 ploughs, 4 harrows, 1 hoe, 4 carts, 8 horses.

48, Kilfinnan, 7 farms, 6 working farmers and family, 12 male and 8 female domestic servants, 46 male and 28 occasional female labourers, total 9,186 working days; auxiliary power: 6 ploughs, 12 harrows, 1 hoe, 1 wheel car, 12 carts, 16 horses, 40 spinning wheels.

49, Killymallaght, 14 farms, 26 working farmers and family, 9 male and 4 female domestic servants, 4 male farming servants, 52 male and 2 female occasional labourers, total 14,623 working days; 1 building quarry, 3 men; [insert marginal note: 1 quarry, opened for building a schoolhouse]; auxiliary power: 12 ploughs, 20 harrows, 6 slide cars, 4 wheel cars, 10 carts, 19 horses, 34 spinning wheels.

50, Kittybane, 8 farms, 18 working farmers and family, 5 male and 3 female domestic servants, 13 male occasional labourers, total 8,258 working days; 1 building quarry, not in use; auxiliary power: 8 ploughs, 10 harrows, 5 wheel cars, 6 carts, 11 horses, 14 spinning wheels.

51, Knockbrack, 12 farms, 33 working farmers and family, 10 male and 6 female domestic servants, 1 male farming servant, 56 male and 11 female occasional labourers, total 17,805 working days; 1 building quarry, not in use; auxiliary power: 9 ploughs, 17 harrows, 1 hoe, 5 slide cars, 13 carts, 16 horses, 45 spinning wheels.

52, Lisaghmore, 7 farms, 27 working farmers and family, 6 male and 2 female domestic servants, 2 male farming servants, 42 male and 2 female occasional labourers, total 12,063 working days; 1 road quarry, not in use; auxiliary power: 8 ploughs, 15 harrows, 3 wheel cars, 13 carts, 17 horses, 30 spinning wheels.

53, Lisahawley, 3 farms, 3 working farmers and family, 3 male and 1 female domestic servant, 12 male occasional labourers, total 2,428 working days; 1 building quarry, not in use; auxiliary power: 3 ploughs, 6 harrows, 2 wheel cars, 3 carts, 7 horses, 7 spinning wheels.

54, Lisdillon, 49 farms, 139 working farmers and family, 8 male and 8 female domestic servants, 2 male farming servants, 94 male and 6 female occasional labourers, total 50,660 working days; auxiliary power: 40 ploughs, 56 harrows, 26 slide cars, 2 wheel cars, 45 carts, 58 horses, 110 spinning wheels; compound power: flax mill, overshot wheel, diameter 18 feet; quantity: raw, 10,192 cwt, tow 2,548 cwt, maximum

4,382 cwt; worked 7 months, 12 months possible; 4 male and 3 female attendants.

55, Lisglass, 14 farms, 48 working farmers and family, 8 male and 5 female domestic servants, 1 male and 1 female farming servant, 23 male and 17 female occasional labourers, total 20,046 working days; auxiliary power: 12 ploughs, 12 harrows, 9 slide cars, 7 wheel cars, 11 carts, 23 horses, 31 spinning wheels.

56, Lismacarol [insert marginal note: none], 18 farms, 59 working farmers and family, 8 male and 7 female domestic servants, 1 male farming servant, 65 male and 20 female occasional labourers, total 24,706 working days; 1 building quarry, not in use; auxiliary power: 15 ploughs, 22 harrows, 4 wheel cars, 25 carts, 34 horses, 52 spinning wheels; compound power: grain mill, overshot wheel, diameter 14 feet; grain ground: oatmeal 1,920 cwt, maximum 2,880 cwt, time worked 4 months, time possible 6 months, 2 attendants, including miller; flax mill, overshot wheel, diameter 12 feet, quantity: raw 816 cwt, tow 204 cwt, maximum 312 cwt; worked 4 months, 6 months possible, 4 male and 2 female attendants.

57, Lisnagelvin, 1 farm, 3 male and 2 female domestic servants, 3 male farming servants, 10 male and 4 female occasional labourers, total 3,332 working days; auxiliary power: 2 ploughs, 3 harrows, 1 hoe, 10 wheel cars, 6 carts, 5 horses, 2 spinning wheels.

58, Lisneal [insert marginal note: none], 3 farms, 5 working farmers and family, 6 male and 4 female domestic servants, 15 male and 2 female occasional labourers, total 5,017 working days; 1 road quarry, 1 building quarry, not in use; auxiliary power: 3 ploughs, 6 harrows, 1 slide car, 3 wheel cars, 4 carts, 7 horses, 25 spinning wheels.

59, Magheracanon, 3 farms, 8 working farmers and family, 5 male and 1 female domestic servant, 1 male farming servant, 10 male and 2 female occasional labourers, total 4,801 working days; auxiliary power: 3 ploughs, 5 harrows, 2 slide cars, 3 carts, 5 horses, 8 spinning wheels.

60, Managhbeg, 3 farms, 14 working farmers and family, 2 male and 1 female domestic servant, 7 male and 4 female occasional labourers, total 5,515 working days; auxiliary power: 3 ploughs, 4 harrows, 2 wheel cars, 2 carts, 6 horses, 9 spinning wheels.

61, Managhmore, 8 farms, 41 working farmers and family, 3 female domestic servants, 5 male and 4 female occasional labourers, total 13,777 working days; auxiliary power: 8 ploughs, 10 harrows, 1 slide car, 6 wheel cars, 3 carts, 12 horses, 21 spinning wheels.

62, Maydown, 1 farm, 2 working farmers and family, 3 male and 1 female domestic servant, 2 male farming servants, 12 male and 2 female occasional labourers, total 3,110 working days; auxiliary power: 3 ploughs, 6 harrows, 1 hoe, 1 wheel car, 4 carts, 8 horses, 7 spinning wheels.

63, Prehen, [insert marginal note: kind?], 6 farms, 1 male and 3 female domestic servants; 1 road quarry, 1 lime quarry, 3 building quarries; auxiliary power: 1 plough, 2 harrows, 1 hoe, 2 carts, 1 horse.

64, Primity, 13 farms, 23 working farmers and family, 1 male and 1 female domestic servant, 1 male farming servant, 14 male and 2 female occasional labourers, total 8,556 working days; 1 lime quarry, not in use; auxiliary power: 8 ploughs, 11 harrows, 1 slide car, 2 wheel cars, 9 carts, 10 horses, 30 spinning wheels; compound power: grain mill, undershot wheel, diameter 12 feet 8 inches; grain ground: oatmeal 140 barrels; worked 6 months, full-time, 2 attendants, including miller.

65, Rossnagalliagh, 12 farms, 59 working farmers and family, 2 male domestic servants, 39 male and 4 female occasional labourers, total 19,949 working days; 1 lime quarry, not in use; auxiliary power: 13 ploughs, 15 harrows, 3 slide cars, 13 carts, 14 horses, 37 spinning wheels.

66 and 67, Stradreaghbeg, 1 farm, and Stradreaghmore, 5 farms, 5 working farmers and family, 1 male and 1 female domestic servant, 1 male farming servant, 23 male and 4 female occasional labourers, total 11,255 working days; auxiliary power: 4 ploughs, 6 harrows, 1 wheel car, 4 carts, 6 horses, 20 spinning wheels.

68, Tagharina, 4 farms, 9 working farmers and family, 4 male and 1 female domestic servant, 19 male and 12 female occasional labourers, total 9,670 working days; auxiliary power: 3 ploughs, 5 harrows, 3 slide cars, 3 wheel cars, 3 carts, 8 horses, 5 spinning wheels.

69, Tamnymore, 16 farms, 35 working farmers and family, 3 male and 4 female domestic servants, 22 male and 3 female occasional labourers, total 13,526 working days; auxiliary power: 14 ploughs, 18 harrows, 2 slide cars, 1 wheel car, 16 carts, 14 horses, 28 spinning wheels.

70, Templetown, 4 farms, 6 working farmers and family, 3 male and 3 female domestic servants, 13 male occasional labourers, total 3,912 working days; auxiliary power: 4 ploughs, 7 harrows, 4 wheel cars, 2 carts, 6 horses, 11 spinning wheels.

71, Tirbracken, 3 farms, 10 working farmers and family, 3 male and 1 female domestic servant, 2 male farming servants, 31 male and 8 female occasional labourers, total 5,668 working days; auxiliary power: 4 ploughs, 9 harrows, 5 carts, 10 horses, 18 spinning wheels.

72, Tirkeeveny, 12 farms, 23 working farmers and family, 2 male domestic servants, 23 male occasional labourers, total 8,311 working days; auxiliary power: 7 ploughs, 11 harrows, 6 slide cars, 4 wheel cars, 5 carts, 11 horses, 20 spinning wheels.

73, Tully Lower, 10 farms, 36 working farmers and family, 7 male and 2 female domestic servants, 1 male farming servant, 40 male and 15 female occasional labourers, total 15,607 working days; auxiliary power: 9 ploughs, 13 harrows, 4 slide cars, 1 wheel car, 9 carts, 18 horses, 30 spinning wheels.

74, Tully Upper, 7 farms, 34 working farmers and family, 1 male domestic servant, 2 male farming servants, 24 male and 4 female occasional labourers, total 11,[remaining figures blank] working days; auxiliary power: 5 ploughs, 8 harrows, 1 slide car, 7 carts, 9 horses, 24 spinning wheels.

75, Tullyally Upper, 2 working farmers and family, 5 male and 2 female domestic servants, 24 male and 10 female occasional labourers, total 3,405 working days; auxiliary power: 2 ploughs, 4 harrows, 1 slide car, 3 carts, 5 horses, 2 spinning wheels.

76, Tullyally Lower [insert marginal note: none], 11 working farmers and family, 16 male and 14 female domestic servants, 9 male farming servants, 73 male and 15 female occasional labourers, total 1,565 working days; 1 building quarry, not in use; auxiliary power: 8 ploughs, 16 harrows, 1 hoe, 3 slide cars, 16 carts, 21 horses, 30 spinning wheels; compound power: flax mill, overshot wheel, diameter 17 feet 4 inches; quantity: new mill has not commenced working yet.

77, Warbleshinny, 8 farms, 34 working farmers and family, 2 male domestic servants, 29 male and 5 female occasional labourers, total 11,862 working days; 1 lime quarry, not in use: auxiliary power: 8 ploughs, 11 harrows, 4 slide cars, 3 wheel cars, 9 carts, 11 horses, 30 spinning wheels.